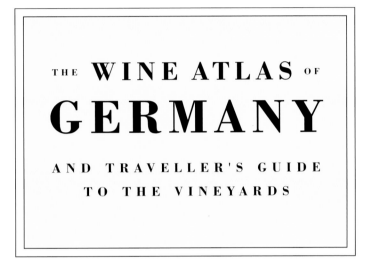

THE **WINE ATLAS** OF
GERMANY
AND TRAVELLER'S GUIDE
TO THE VINEYARDS

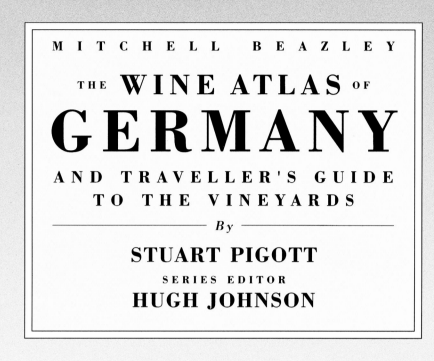

MITCHELL BEAZLEY

THE WINE ATLAS OF
GERMANY

AND TRAVELLER'S GUIDE
TO THE VINEYARDS

By

STUART PIGOTT

SERIES EDITOR

HUGH JOHNSON

The Wine Atlas of Germany
edited and designed by
Mitchell Beazley International Limited
part of Reed Books Limited
Michelin House, 81 Fulham Road,
London SW3 6RB
and Auckland, Melbourne, Singapore
and Toronto

First published in 1995
Copyright © Mitchell Beazley
International Limited 1995
Text copyright © Stuart Pigott 1995
Maps copyright © Mitchell Beazley
International Limited 1995
All rights reserved

A CIP catalogue record for this book is
available from the British Library

ISBN 1 85732 625 3

Senior Editor: Diane Pengelly
Senior Art Editor: Paul Drayson
Cartographic Editor: Zoë Goodwin
Photography: Armin Faber
Index: Marie Lorimer
Gazetteer: Sally Chorley
Production: Juliette Butler
Executive Editor: Anne Ryland
Art Director: Jacqui Small
Cartography: Lovell Johns Limited,
Map Creation Limited

Typeset in Century Old Style and Gill Sans

Origination by Mandarin Offset, Singapore
Produced by Mandarin Offset
Printed in Hong Kong

Contents

Foreword

A shimmering straw-gold glass, broad-hipped and brimming, is the happy emblem of German wine-country. It expresses the unique welcome waiting for visitors to this most dramatically beautiful of all the landscapes of the vine. There is a garden seat in summer, a fireside seat in winter, and the grower's wine in its generous pokal, open, cool, aromatic, crisp or rich, but above all accessible, shared, festive.

Does this picture contrast with another image of Germany – of straight-backed waiters fingering elegant tapered bottles whose intricate labels hark back to monkish manuscripts? It does, and the contrast points us to a paradox: the wines of Germany are the easiest on earth to enjoy. They are also the hardest to understand.

Germany has no system of appellations as guidance to the style, quality or even the grape variety of its wines. Within her broadly-drawn regions she has only a bewildering list of vineyard and village names, which by a peculiar official logic may or may not mean what they seem to mean. Such a famous name as Johannisberg, for example, or Piesport, may mean the simple commune or a vast area of largely indifferent land around it.

Imposed on this looking-glass geography is the only classification Germany officially accepts: quality measured by 'must-weight' – or the ripeness of the grapes at vintage time. It has been Germany's official policy, since the passing of the new Wine Law of 1971, that all grape varieties in all vineyards rank equal; that only higher sugar-content can qualify them for higher ranking.

It is sad to have to say it, but this denial of reality has gradually reduced the standing of German wine in the eyes of the world over the past 20 years from the most prestigious of all white wines to a cut-price commodity. It has made the bulk of the export wine from the country with Europe's highest standard of living into Europe's cheapest plonk.

Needless to say the owners of Germany's finest vineyards are the same proud farmer-artist as you will find in France. Needless to say they are frustrated to desperation by the politics that thwart their legitimate aspirations; the laws that set dismally low minimum standards in contempt of both producer and consumer.

By banding together in self-policing organisations, of which the VDP and Charta are the two most prominent, Germany's best wine-growers have asserted their true standing. But their message is not simple to put across. The law still allows simple sugary wines from early-ripening grapes in mediocre fields to claim equal ranking with the best.
What is lacking, above all, is a ranking of vineyard by the actual or potential quality of their wine when planted with the appropriate grapes. In Bordeaux the First and second Growths produce the best wines year after year. In Burgundy the Grands and Premiers Crus are palpably distinct. The consumer is guided; the grower properly rewarded and the whole complex business of choosing wine made (relatively) simple.

To identify the best vineyards and to explain what makes them stand out, to describe the individuality of their wines and to name the growers who make them best is the purpose of this atlas. It goes further in each of these directions than any other book so far published. Its classification of vineyards is necessarily provisional; it should lead to debate which in turn will lead to future revisions. But its main purpose is to lead you, the reader, to the places and people that represent the great traditions of German wine and are re-interpreting them for the next millennium.

The Mosel Valley's spectacular Piesporter Goldtröpfchen vineyard, whose succulent Rieslings are some of the greatest white wines in the world.

Introduction

It could have been a German Riesling that James Joyce was thinking of when he wrote 'white wine is electricity', since no other white wines can match the breathtaking vibrancy and aromatic intensity of the best German examples. Light, crisp and refreshing yet full of character and personality, they are perfectly in tune with contemporary taste.

This unique style is the result of a combination of factors: Germany's cool climate and stony soils, the grape varieties cultivated and a winemaking tradition that has developed separately from those of neighbouring countries for many centuries. Vintners outside Germany have attempted to imitate the country's wines but none has yet matched the elegance and complexity of its top-class examples. Northern Italy, South Africa, New York State, California, Washington State, Ontario, British Columbia, South Australia and New Zealand have all made some excellent wines in the German mould, but only rarely have these possessed the miraculous combination of intensity and subtlety that make the greatest German Rieslings the most expensive and highly sought-after white wines in the world.

Compared to the 12–14 degrees of alcohol typical in French, Italian and New World whites, the finest German wines can have as few as seven degrees and rarely have more than 12. Even when they match the alcoholic content of their foreign counterparts, they taste lighter and cleaner. It is their other elements that make them electrifying. The best examples are all perfume, fruit, elegance and delicacy without a trace of the heaviness and heat that high alcohol so often imparts to wine.

Although wine styles are influenced by changes in fashion, top-class German Rieslings have enjoyed the highest international reputation since the beginning of the 19th century. Their zenith was during the last decades of the 19th and first years of the 20th century. A glance at the list of any leading wine merchant or restaurant of the period reveals that German white wines were then the most expensive in the world, their prices exceeding even those of the finest red Bordeaux. This position was steadily eroded during the late 1960s, the 1970s and early 1980s, mainly as a result of over-commercialisation. Recently, however, there has been a dramatic revival of interest in German Riesling, principally due to the achievements of a new generation of winemakers who are determined to rebuild the reputation of these once-celebrated wines.

Today's great German Rieslings, no less than those of the past, have enormous ageing potential. As charming and seductive as they are in their youth, their full glory reveals itself only with age. A century ago this was well understood and mature German wines of up to 50 years old sold for record prices. But modern commercial pressures have contrived to give many wine-drinkers the erroneous impression that only top-class reds can improve with age and that all whites must be drunk young. While this is true for simple-quality whites wherever they come from, it is not true of German Rieslings. At some point between the five and 50 years of age favoured by the Victorians they reach an elegant harmony, depth and subtlety unsurpassed in the white wine world.

German Rieslings are extraordinarily diverse, ranging from feather-light to imposing and powerful, from bone dry to lusciously sweet; yet they represent only one aspect of the country's wine. The Pinot family of grapes: Weissburgunder (Pinot Blanc), Grauburgunder (Pinot Gris), Spätburgunder (Pinot Noir), Chardonnay, Auxerrois and Schwarzriesling (Pinot Meunier) are all cultivated, many of them widely and with great success. Weissburgunder and Grauburgunder yield some of the best dry white wines made from these varieties anywhere in the world.

During the last decade there has also been an astonishing rise in the standard of the country's red winemaking. The thin, pale red wines lacking body, fruit and character that used to be typical could not be taken seriously outside Germany. But a group of pioneer winemakers has begun attracting international attention with rich, silky and powerful Spätburgunder reds. The other red grape that shows signs of great potential is Lemberger. In its homeland, Württemberg, it seems to give the best results when blended with other red grapes. Given plenty of new oak it can achieve a deeply coloured, firm red wine with more grip than Spätburgunder.

One factor contributing to the demise of German wines' image during recent decades is the increasing acreage planted with non-traditional grape varieties, or *Neuzuchtungen*. These plantings date largely from the 1960s and 1970s when there was a fashion in Germany for spicy, sweet wines. The crudest of these varieties, grapes such as Siegerrebe, Ortega and Optima, ripen every year in sites too cold for any of the traditional vine varieties.

The German Wine Law of 1971 created a situation where these bland, sugary wines were put on an equal footing with the finest Rieslings from the best and most famous vineyard sites. Although no legal remedy is in sight, quality-conscious producers have turned their backs on the *Neuzuchtungen* with two important exceptions: Scheurebe and Rieslaner. In the hands of a committed winemaker both these varieties can produce wines with a Riesling-like harmony and great intensity of aroma and flavour. The traditional aromatic grape varieties, Muskateller and Traminer, can both give remarkable wines with intense aromas that are far nobler than those of most *Neuzuchtungen*.

Muskateller may well have been brought to Germany by the Romans, who established the first vineyards around 100AD. The scale of Roman viticulture is apparent from the remains of wine press houses, many of which have been excavated in the Mosel Valley. Towards the end of the Roman Empire's period of ascendancy, around 300AD, the Romans planted many of the top sites of the Mosel-Saar-Ruwer, creating a distinctive vineyard landscape of steeply sloping valleys that impresses visitors to this day. The remarkable Rieslings of this region, including some of the finest wines in Germany, would not exist were it not for these vineyards. But the indigenous people also had an important contribution to make: it was from them that the Romans learned to construct wooden barrels, which from then on became the conventional vessel for making and storing wine in Germany, France and Italy.

Much of the wine produced by the Romans would be unrecognisable as wine to modern tastes, since it was flavoured with herbs and spices and often sweetened with honey. Modern German wine-making has its roots in the monastic wine production of the Middle Ages. The oldest written records of viticulture in many regions date from this period: the first surviving records from the Rheingau, for example, were made in 779AD.

A propitious combination of the noble Riesling vine, stony soil and a steep-sided, south-facing river valley site is responsible for most of Germany's great wines.

8

The Rheingau became Germany's most important wine-growing area following the establishment of the Johannisberg monastery by Benedictine monks in around 1100 and Kloster Eberbach in 1136. The monks not only established some of the region's best vineyards but also made numerous advances in vineyard cultivation and cellar technology. They built up considerable markets for their products, Kloster Eberbach becoming the world's largest producer during the 13th century.

Tradition has it that the reason why wooden barrels are round in the Mosel-Saar-Ruwer and oval in the Rhine regions stems from the difference in form between the round Roman arch and the the narrow, pointed Gothic arch. It certainly seems logical that these differing barrel forms should be linked to the twin sources of contemporary German wine culture.

While the vineyards and winemaking techniques responsible for the best German wines have their origins in the distant past, German wine in a recognisable form was developed much more recently. Its history is inseparable from that of the Riesling vine which was first recorded in Rüsselsheim close to Hochheim at the eastern extremity of the Rheingau in 1435, then in Trier in the Mosel-Saar-Ruwer in 1465 and Worms in Rheinhessen in 1490. During that period Riesling was always planted with other varieties in *Gemischte Satz* or mixed plantings. In 1720 the first recorded Riesling monoculture was established at Schloss Johannisberg in the Rheingau, just as the bottling of high-quality wines was becoming a regular practice in Germany.

It was rapidly discovered that while most wines lost their liveliness and charm after bottling, Rieslings retained their character, or even improved it, with maturation in the bottle. By the end of the 18th century Riesling was regarded as the noble grape variety in the Rhine regions and the Mosel-Saar-Ruwer. The Prince-Bishop of Trier, Clemens Wenzeslaus, commanded in his decree of 1787 that inferior grape varieties in all the church's vineyards be systematically replaced with the superior Riesling.

By this time the next critical step in establishing Germany's modern wine culture had already been taken. In 1775, the messenger bearing the Bishop of Fulda's order for the monks of Johannisberg to begin harvesting the monastery vineyards was delayed. As a result, the grapes that were eventually picked were over-ripe and 'rotten'. However the 'rot' was *Botrytis cinerea* or noble rot. This imparted to the resulting wine a character which all who tasted found astonishing.

During the succeeding years Schloss Johannisberg and several other clerical and aristocratic estates on the Rhine began perfecting the techniques of late and selective harvesting. The rich, naturally sweet wines that resulted were to establish Germany's international reputation as the world's premier white wine-producing nation. Even in Parisian restaurants the best Rhine wines pushed all French white wines into second place during the first decades of the 19th century.

By this time the different quality levels of bottled wines were being marked by the use of coloured wax seals; this was the beginning of the Prädikat system under which German wines are still categorised by law.

A combination of exactly the same elements – Riesling vines grown in top sites, late and selective harvesting and the retention of natural sweetness in the finished wine – is still responsible for Germany's greatest whites. Vineyard and cellar technology have developed enormously in the last 200 years but it is remarkable how closely the best contemporary winemakers stick to the methods painstakingly developed by the Rhine regions' great monastic and aristocratic estates during the late 18th and early 19th centuries.

Sadly, uncompromising commitment to quality is not universal among German winemakers. Over-zealous commercialisation was one blow dealt to German wine's reputation, the other was the spread of industrialised winemaking methods which resulted in neutral, characterless wines. Some of the most famous estates in the country fell victim to this tendency during the 1970s and 1980s. Ignoring the fundamental maxim that wine quality comes from the vineyard, directors and winemakers were seduced by the idea that modern technology and chemistry could somehow solve every one of their problems.

In the last decade, however, the industry has been undergoing both a renaissance and a revolution. As a result, the names of the influential winemakers in most of Germany's 13 wine-growing regions have changed. Many of these rising stars were virtually unheard of ten years ago, but they are now responsible for some of the finest wines in Germany.

The diversity of style and character among the country's best wines is staggering. More than anywhere else in the world this diversity is the result of geological and microclimatic factors which, I hope, the text and specially commissioned maps in this atlas will help bring to life.

This book (alongside perhaps a bottle or two from some of the wine producers described in it) should lead any wine-lover to a fuller understanding some of the world's most remarkable and rewarding wines.

The precious harvest at Schloss Johannisberg, the Rhine's most famous estate and birthplace of Germany's modern wine culture. The vineyards, spread uninterrupted on the ideally sloping skirts of the castle hill, are planted entirely with Riesling.

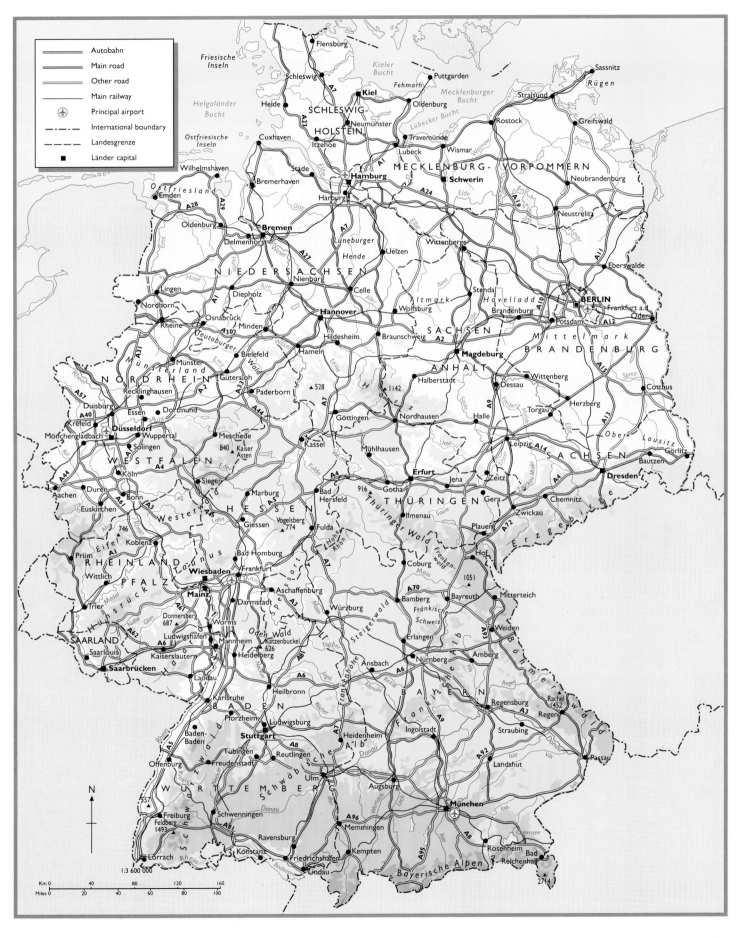

Vineyard Classification

Differing grape varieties, climates, vineyard exposures and soil types all have their part to play in the extraordinary range of wines produced from Germany's 105,000 hectares of vineyard.

It is ironic that, though there is this rich diversity in style and quality, the official classification system in Germany is singularly unhelpful to consumer and quality-conscious producer alike. Whatever the weaknesses of French, Spanish or Italian wine laws, based on the matching of particular grape varieties with specific vineyards, they ensure that labels give clear guidance as to the wine's style and at least a rough idea of its quality.

Conversely, although many of the Grosslagen or Bereiche names appearing on German labels can read like top vineyard designations, they actually allude to collective vineyard sites and broad areas embracing many wine towns and villages whose individual products may be of wildly disparate quality. In this way, the huge commercial success of Grosslage wines such as Piesporter Michelsberg and Niersteiner Gutes Domtal, for example, has completely undermined the standing of wines from truly great vineyard sites such as the Piesporter Goldtröpfchen and Niersteiner Pettenthal.The Prädikat system, classifying Germany's better quality wines (see right) is also an unreliable indicator. A

Here in Württemberg, no less than in the Mosel-Saar-Ruwer or the Rheingau, it is the well-exposed, steep vineyards that give the best wines.

Kabinett wine, nominally the most humble of the four subdivisions, can easily be superior to a Trockenbeerenauslese (supposedly the most exalted category) if the former is made from noble grapes and the latter from an inferior variety. The system takes account only of the grapes' sugar-content at harvest time, ignoring such other critical elements as the acids, aromatic substances and minerals absorbed by the ripening fruit.

During the last decade, interest in an effective classification of Germany's top vineyards has grown in direct proportion to the frustration engendered by the 1971 German Wine Law.

In this atlas, the vineyard classification bands launched in the fourth edition of Hugh Johnson's *World Atlas of Wine* have been refined and, with advice and assistance from many authorities includng leading members of the Verband Deutscher Prädikatsweingüter (VDP), the German association of quality-wine producers, extended nationwide.

These quality levels have been researched independently of the German government, and as yet are not legally recognised. Individuals and organisations from each of the 13 regions were involved in their development, and their contributions are reflected in different approaches to vineyard classification. The Rheingau, for example, has since 1994 had its own official classification: *Erstes Gewächs* (literally 'first growths') and all vineyards in that chapter (see pages 94–119) that have the potential to yield superior

quality wines regularly are accordingly plotted and keyed on the maps as 'first-class' vineyards. In the Mosel-Saar-Ruwer, however, only those vineyards that are currently producing superior wines are identified as first class, so excellent vineyards such as the Paulinshofberg of Kesten and the Batterieberg of Enkirch do not appear in that category. All such anomalies are fully explained in the accompanying text.

The future of fine German wine surely depends on classifications such as these gaining wide acceptance. Until they do, however, this atlas at least will enable the interested wine-drinker to identify at a glance the finest sites, to understand why they make the finest wines and to unravel the perplexing, sometimes infuriating but always fascinating enigma that is German wine.

IN THIS ATLAS

The chapters in this atlas correspond with the Germany's 13 wine-growing areas. Where it is helpful, regions have been sub-divided and mapped in separate sections. The best and most interesting of the nation's wines are described alongside detailed maps of the vineyards where they are grown, illustrating why one wine can have completely different characteristics from another, even if the two are grown in neighbouring sites.

Portraits of each of the winegrowing areas are followed by a selection of 'benchmark wines', typical examples of the region's best produce, and concise details of the region's best and most prominent producers. Travel information in each chapter gives a colourful summary of local places of interest and lists hotels, restaurants and useful addresses.

From the pruning in winter through to the autumn harvest, the conscientious vintner has work to do among the vines every day of the year.

GERMAN WINE LAW

While the French classify their wine according to where it is grown, under German wine law the land is neutral and the quality of each vintage decided according to the degree of sugar (measured in degrees Oechsle) the crushed grapes contain.

The vineyard classifications in this atlas as yet have no official status. Germany's legal classification system consists of the four basic grades of wine quality listed below.

Deutscher Tafelwein
Ordinary table wine, which accounts for only a very small proportion of the nation's product, need attain only five percent natural alcohol (around 44° Oechsle) and must be made from approved grape varieties. A region or subregion may be named on the label, but not a village or vineyard. If a grape variety is specified, that variety must account for at least 85 percent of the grapes used in the wine.

If the Tafelwein is not 'Deutscher' it is usually a blend of wines from other EC countries.

Landwein
Introduced in 1982 as the approximate equivalent to a French Vin de Pays, this category is slightly more exacting. Landwein must come from one of 15 designated regions and contain half a degree of natural alcohol more than Tafelwein. It must have no more than 18 grams per litre of residual sugar, which makes it trocken or halbtrocken.

Qualitätswein bestimmter Anbaugebiete
QbA wine must come from one of the 13 wine-growing regions, be made only from permitted grape varieties, attain a certain must-weight and carry an official quality test number. If at least 85 percent of the grapes are grown in one vineyard, the label may carry the vineyard name. It may also specify a Grosslage or Bereich name or the name of a village.

Qualitätswein mit Prädikat (QmP)
Wine in this top category may not be chaptalised, a rule peculiar to Germany, but the precise vineyard and degree of ripeness may be specified on the label. The grapes must be of a certain variety, from a particular area and be quality tested. The natural must should attain a certain minimum weight and the label must carry the quality test number (AP Nr).

QmP is subdivided into five categories according to the grapes' ripeness. The minimum must-weights listed in each category below vary slightly depending on area and grape variety.

	Minimim must-weight (° Oechsle)	Potential alcohol (% by volume)
Kabinett	about 70	8.8
Spätlese	about 80	10
Auslese	about 90	12
Beerenauslese	about 120	16.4 *
Trockenbeerenauslese	about 150	19 *

* These wines are always sweet because yeast cannot ferment sugar at this degree of alcohol.

Grape Varieties

RIESLING/KLINGELBERGER 22,801 hectares

The first step towards understanding the wines of Germany, or of any other wine-producing nation, is to identify the characteristics of its most important grape varieties. Riesling, also known as Klingelberger in the Ortenau area of Baden, is not only the noblest variety in Germany, it is one of the finest of all white wine grapes.

A quarter of a century ago this was a widely accepted fact. In 1968 no one was surprised when Michael Broadbent MW wrote in his in his book *Wine Tasting* that Riesling was the finest of all white wine grapes and that 'it scales the greatest heights in Germany, in the Rheingau and Moselle districts in particular...'. The international trend during the 1980s towards the Chardonnay grape and its wines, combined with problems associated with Riesling's image during that period, have shifted popular opinion away from Riesling. Today Michael Broadbent's statement will probably surprise most readers, just as the contemporary fixation with Chardonnay would have surprised the wine drinkers of 25 years ago.

Anyone fortunate enough to have drunk great German Riesling will find the popular ignorance of the wine hard to understand. Usually a delicate straw colour, often with shimmers of green or gold, it look as charming and elegant as it smells and tastes. Perhaps the most common mistake made by inexperienced wine-drinkers is to pay too little attention to the wine's aroma or bouquet. Great German Rieslings have the most subtle perfume of all white wines – to ignore this is to miss fully half the pleasure they have to give. Although peach is the classic aroma of the ripe grape, a great Riesling wine has other aromas that range across countless

Riesling, Germany's model noble grape, at its earliest stage of development. Over 40 successful crosses have been produced from the variety in the last century, but only Riesling grapes manage to retain their acidity throughout the long growing season right up to their traditionally late harvest.

fruits, flowers, herbs and spices. Woven into this aromatic tapestry are less easily defined mineral notes from the soil where the grapes ripened. Such a bouquet is as fascinating as it is seductive.

In the mouth great German Rieslings give an impression of lightness, almost of weightlessness, however intense their flavour. Unlike many other great wines, they are never overbearing and therefore do not tire the palate. This has a great deal to do with the grapes' high natural acidity. While acidity can make simple-quality wines taste too tart, in better-quality examples it is lively and refreshing without any trace of sharpness. Just as a ray of light striking a diamond makes each of it facets flash a different colour, so the acidity of these wines 'illuminates' their flavours, making them scintillate as they flow across the palate. This mouthwatering interplay of fruit and acidity can be found in all good examples, but at the highest quality level it is merely the carrier which conveys waves of flavour to the taste buds. Long after the wine has been swallowed an intense and piquant aftertaste remains.

No other wine can give quite this experience. It has driven collectors to pursue the greatest German Rieslings with such fervour that prices for the most sought-after wines have reached dizzy heights. Their unique qualities may be known only to a number of wine-drinkers, but few who have tasted the best can be unmoved.

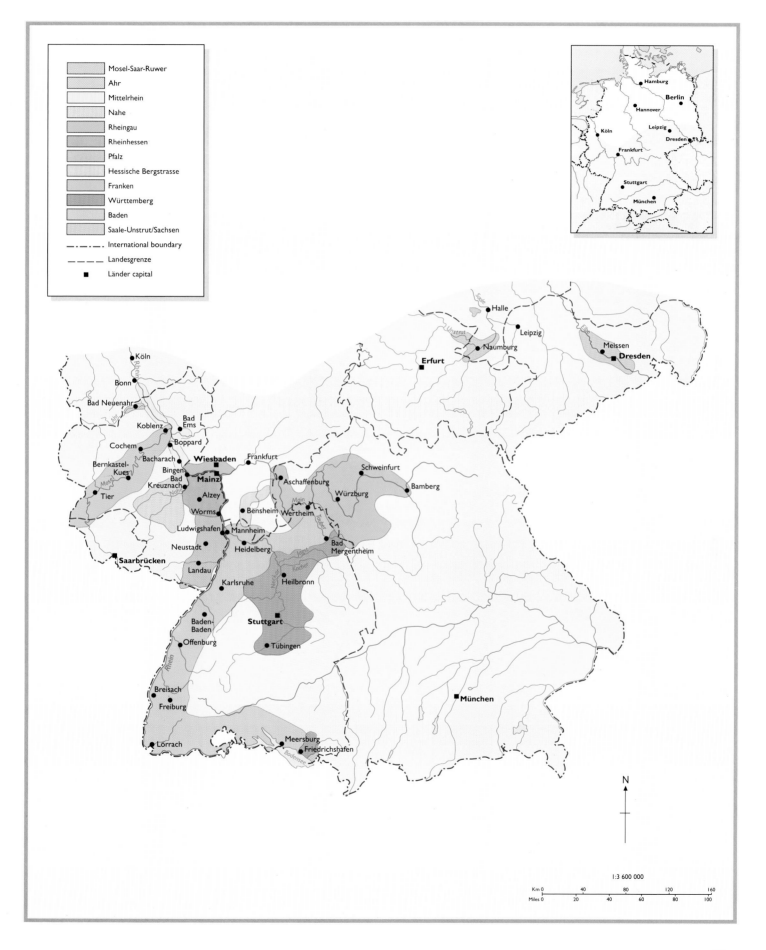

Mosel-Saar-Ruwer
Ahr
Mittelrhein
Nahe
Rheingau
Rheinhessen
Pfalz
Hessische Bergstrasse
Franken
Württemberg
Baden
Saale-Unstrut/Sachsen
International boundary
Landesgrenze
Länder capital

1:3 600 000

Km 0   40   80   120   160
Miles 0   20   40   60   80   100

Unfortunately, when most wine-drinkers think of Germany it is the cheap generic wines – Liebfraumilch, Piesporter Michelsberg, Niersteiner Gutes Domtal and so on – that come to mind: wines which have almost nothing in common with the nation's finest Rieslings.

However well they are made, simple-quality German wines possess neither the elegance nor the individuality of fine Rieslings. At their best they are reasonably fruity and well balanced. The finest Rieslings have another dimension of aromas and flavours in addition to these qualities: character that comes from the vineyard

Riesling is a transparent wine whose bouquet and taste precisely reflect the climate and soil conditions of the site where the grapes ripened. In this respect it is the opposite of Chardonnay; a wine whose character is largely the result of the winemaking techniques used in the cellar, rather than of the grapes' natural flavour. Simply put, most Chardonnays are 'made' wines, while the finest Rieslings are 'grown'.

The stylistic diversity of German Riesling can be seen as another factor placing the variety above all others, or it can simply seem frustrating and confusing. The diversity results from the fact that Riesling is one of the latest-ripening varieties.

By picking at different times and separating the grapes at different stages of ripeness, styles of wine ranging from the most delicate to the extremely powerful can be produced from a single vineyard. Furthermore, all but the very richest of these can either be fermented to dryness or vinified with a certain amount of sweetness. The palate of possible styles thus extends from feather-light, bone-dry wines to some of the most intense and luscious dessert wines in the world.

During the 1980s German vintners 'discovered' the matching of food and wine in a big way. Although some of them pursued it with almost fanatical seriousness, they succeeded at least in opening the eyes of many chefs and part of the wine-drinking public to Riesling's gastronomic possibilities. Just as the old rule that red wine should be drunk with meat and white wine with fish excludes dozens of delicious combinations, so the common prejudice that

The labour-intensive business of selecting shrivelled botrytized berries to make Trockenbeerenauslese requires patience and a keen eye.

only dry white wines can be drunk with savoury dishes ignores many wonderful matches. There is no better wine for smoked salmon than a Mosel-Saar-Ruwer Riesling Kabinett, for example. Riesling Spätlese from the Pfalz could have been made for roast duck and Rheingau Auslese for roast venison. A century ago the best Rieslings were regularly drunk with food, as numerous cookery books and menu cards from the period attest.

When devising food and wine partnerships it is worth remembering that mature wines tend to harmonise better with food than young ones. For many dry Rieslings this presents a problem, since as very young wines they possess a rather aggressive acidity which makes them difficult to match. By the time this has softened to the point where they are harmonious, the wines' freshness is often fading. Only the best examples can accompany food from their earliest youth and still have the potential to age for five years, or often more.

Rieslings vinified with some natural sweetness are a different matter. They begin to show their best at between five and 25 years of age, depending on their provenance and quality. A well made Riesling QbA or Kabinett should live at least ten years if well stored, while top-class Riesling Spätlese and Auslese can retain their charm for 20 years or more. This is the age at which Riesling BA, TBA and Eiswein are just approaching their best form.

As a general rule the wines from the northerly regions take longer to develop and have a greater ageing potential than those from further south. Whether young or mature, they are wonderful before, during or after a meal, drunk by themselves or simply as a stimulant to conversation and conviviality.

With so many facets to its character, Riesling is a fascinating white variety. In Germany, as in no other wine-growing region, every side of its personality finds full expression.

WEISSBURGUNDER (Pinot Blanc) 1,552 hectares

This relative of Pinot Noir has been grown in Germany since at least the 16th century but has only recently become an important variety. The acreage it covers has increased by one third during the last five years. This can be attributed to the ease with which harmonious dry white wines can be made from it: the best of these being among the few great Pinot Blancs produced anywhere in the world. However, the variety's real strength is in the large quantities of pleasant, modestly priced dry white wine it yields, particularly in Rheinhessen, the Pfalz and Baden.

Weissburgunder has a number of characteristics that predestine it for German vineyards. In Germany it gives wines with more body, less acidity and a more pronounced fruitiness than Chardonnay. These attributes make it well suited to traditional German winemaking which emphasises fruit and crispness. Perhaps this is why German vintners have only recently begun to experiment with fermenting and maturing these wines in new-oak barrels: Weissburgunders from good vineyard sites have enough character of their own without the additional flavour of wood.

A typical German Weissburgunder has about 11.5 degrees of alcohol, is crisp yet supple and has ripe apple- or pear-like fruit. It makes an excellent companion to all manner of lighter foods. More serious examples are much more powerful, with 13–15 degrees of alcohol, rich peach-like fruit and notes of caramel and melted butter. New oak adds vanilla and nut aromas.

Top producers: Hermann Dönnhof (Nahe), Freiherr Heyl zu Herrnsheim, Schales (Rheinhessen), Bergdolt, Müller-Catoir, Ökonomierat Rebholz (Pfalz), Rudolf Fürst (Franken), Bercher, Dr Heger, Reichsgraf & Marquis zu Hoensbroech, Karl Heinz Johner (Baden)

Grauburgunder ('grey Burgundy'), sometimes labelled Ruländer, is one of Germany's most important varieties for dry white wines.

GRAUBURGUNDER/RULÄNDER

(Pinot Gris) 2,525 hectares

Most of this grape variety's wines have undergone not only a change of name in Germany during the last decade, but also a stylistic transformation. Old-style Ruländer was a golden-amber, sweet, alcoholic white wine that was frequently plump, cloying and bitter. At its best it was rich and honeyed, but such examples were few and far between. The new-style Grauburgunder, a drier, fruitier, more elegant wine, is therefore a welcome arrival. However, while good Grauburgunders are not difficult to find, top-class examples are rare.

In spite of the image of lightness promoted for Grauburgunder, its alcoholic content is usually around 12–13 degrees. There are few successful examples with less alcohol than this. The typical flavours are melon, honey and butter, though the best wines can have intense exotic fruit, smoke and mineral aromas. A typical Grauburgunder is medium-bodied with discreet fruit and is soft but clean and refreshing. These are excellent wines to enjoy with food. Top-class examples are rich and powerful with an impression of sweetness from the high alcoholic content, without being either fat or over-blown. Experts agree that the variety is ideally suited to new-oak ageing, but while some interesting wines have been produced in this style, nothing as good as the top traditionally vinified Grauburgunders has so far emerged.

Top producers: Schlossgut Diel (Nahe), Müller-Catoir, Ökonomierat Rebholz (Pfalz), Johann Ruck (Franken), Drautz-Able (Württemberg) Bercher, Dr Heger, Karl Heinz Johner, Salwey, Rudolf Stigler (Baden)

SPÄTBURGUNDER (Pinot Noir) 6,812 hectares

Ten years ago the idea that Germany could produce Pinot Noir reds comparable with wines from Burgundy's Côte d'Or would have seemed laughable. However, the climatic conditions in Baden and the Pfalz are warm enough in good vintages to ripen Pinot Noir grapes fully. The problems of the past were associated with the winemaking, Germany's red wine tradition having been all but lost. Since a handful of pioneers began to attack this problem a decade ago enormous strides have been made but this progress has yet to be communicated to a large majority of Spätburgunder producers, so an average German example is still rather pale, with only a modest amount of cherry- or raspberry-like fruit and little tannin. The best Spätburgunders do not lack colour, body or tannins, however, being powerful and firm. They have intense black cherry- and blackberry-like fruit, with pronounced smoke and vanilla notes from the small new-oak barrels in which they are matured.

Germany has a great tradition for making high-class dry Spätburgunder rosés. These can be among the best in the world (those from Salwey and Wolff Metternich in Baden, for example) but in wines from many estates and co-operatives quality has declined because all the good grapes are now used for red wine production. One exciting development is the introduction of champagne-style sparkling wines made from this grape and vinified white. The best of these (from Bernhard Huber and WG Königschaffhausen in Baden, for example) compare favourably with many 'Blanc de Noirs' champagnes.

Top producers: Meyer-Näkel (Ahr), August Kesseler (Rheingau), Knipser, Koehler-Ruprecht, Ökonomierat Rebholz (Pfalz), Rudolf Fürst (Franken), Bercher, Dr Heger, Bernhard Huber, Karl Heinz Johner (Baden)

SILVANER 7,642 hectares

Traditionally Silvaner was the second most widely cultivated grape in Germany after Riesling, occupying most of the second-class vineyards along the Rhine. However, during the last 30 years it has lost a great deal of ground to Müller-Thurgau and Kerner. Silvaner's popular image is limited by the fact that, outside Germany, it produces few if any high-class wines. A great deal of it is used in cheap generic wines where its character is lost and almost all the good-quality varietal Silvaners are drunk within Germany, which leaves it with no recognisable international profile.

Although the grape can give wonderful dry and sweet wines, average examples certainly deserve the euphemistic description 'rustic'. With a slightly coarse apple-like fruit, some earthy flavours and a distinctly tart character, it is no more than a dry thirst-quencher during warm weather. The best dry Silvaners marry this earthiness to rich, ripe fruit-like flavours, most prominently yellow plum, aromatic apple (such as Cox's Orange Pippin) and melon. Rich and substantial, with hints of spice and minerals, these are serious wines that have as much character as the best German Weissburgunders and Grauburgunders.

Silvaner wines are marvellous companions for food since they have enough power to cope with strong flavours. Among traditional German grape varieties Silvaner is second only to Riesling for dessert wines from botrytized grapes. Its wines may lack some of the finesse and sophistication of Riesling Auslese, BA and TBA, but they have an excellent harmony and age for ten to 25 years, depending on their quality.

Top producers: Geil, Heyl zu Herrnsheim, Georg Albrecht Schneider (Rheinhessen), Martin Goebel, Juliusspital, Johann Ruck, Egon Schäffer, Robert Schmitt, Schmitt's Kinder, Hans Wirsching (Franken)

In Franken, the usually humble Silvaner can give sophisticated dry whites.

RIESLING'S CLOSE RELATIVES

SCHEUREBE 3,738 hectares

Given the strong trend back to traditional grape varieties in Germany it is astonishing how much excitement the wines of this *Neuzuchtung* have generated recently. The reason for this is the exceptional quality of the best dry and dessert Scheurebe wines. Georg Scheu crossed Silvaner and Riesling to produce the grape in 1916. Its potential was recognised when, planted in top vineyards at the Annaberg estate of Kallstadt/Pfalz, it produced a string of great Scheurebe dessert wines from 1945. 'Scheu' of this kind has an opulent exotic fruit character, richness, spice and a Riesling-like elegance. When excessive botrytis is avoided and the wine vinified dry, the classic blackcurrant and grapefruit aromas of the variety are pronounced. Young dry Scheurebes are more appealing than comparable Rieslings because they have more body and are less tart. The disadvantage of Scheurebe is that, planted in poor vineyards or picked unripe, it gives sharp wines with an unpleasant cattiness.

Top producers: H&R Lingenfelder, Müller-Catoir (Pfalz), Hans Wirsching (Franken), Andreas Laible, Wolff Metternich (Baden)

RIESLANER 58 hectares

Considering the tiny area planted with this Silvaner x Riesling cross which was first produced in 1921, the number of outstanding wines produced from it is remarkable. Nicknamed 'Super Riesling', it yields wines with all the characteristics of fine Rieslings but raised to a higher level of intensity. This creates problems for the winemaker, since Rieslaner's acidity can be rapier-like, and as a dry wine it can sustain 15 degrees of alcohol or more. However, when alcohol and acidity are tamed the result is a wine with an explosive fruitiness and a dazzling brilliance. This balancing act

Scheurebe BA and TBA are among the world's greatest dessert wines.

succeeds most frequently in dessert Rieslaners, though it is sometimes achieved in dry examples. Good Rieslaner has not only a Riesling-like harmony, it also has Riesling-like aromas – apricot and passion fruit being the most common – and Riesling-like ageing potential. The difficulty of cultivating this fickle vine and the fact that, like Scheurebe, it requires vineyard land good enough for Riesling, limit its potential for more widespread cultivation.

Top producers: Müller-Catoir (Pfalz), Rudolf Fürst, Martin Goebel, Juliusspital, Schmitt's Kinder (Franken)

HUXELREBE 1,499 hectares

While wine-drinkers in Germany and abroad have begun to realise how exceptional the wines of the Scheurebe and Rieslaner grapes can be, Huxelrebe remains virtually unknown. This is unfortunate because it too can yield dessert wines of the highest quality. Another result of Georg Scheu's work, in this case a crossing of Gutedel and Courtillier Musqué in 1927, Huxelrebe has a split personality. A relatively undemanding vine to grow it can easily give huge yields but if the crop is cut back severely wines with considerable power and vigour result. They tend to have an intense grapefruit and spice character somewhat reminiscent of Muscat. This is clearest in Huxelrebe wines made from botrytized grapes which are rich and refreshing, lush and clean. Their sweetness is balanced by a tart acidity that gives the best examples a Riesling-like raciness.

Top producers: Geil, Schales (Rheinhessen), Kurt Darting, Koehler-Ruprecht (Pfalz), Johann Ruck (Franken)

KERNER 7,747 hectares

Kerner is a Riesling x Trollinger cross made by the Weinsberg research station in Württemberg. Considering that it has been cultivated in Germany for only a quarter of a century its success has been enormous. It is now the fourth most widely cultivated variety in the country. The reasons for this have more to do with the vine's flexibility regarding soil and climate, its resistance to disease and the ease with which the grape ripens than simply the character of its wines. Nevertheless, Kerner frequently gives pleasant, fruity wines with plenty of substance and a good balance of fruit and acidity. What the wines usually lack, however, is elegance and individuality. Only in its native Württemberg does Kerner give wines that approach the depth and subtlety of fine Riesling. When Kerner is successful it is a supple, juicy wine with a pineapple and citrus or 'jelly beans' character. Not capable of long ageing, it is best drunk fresh and young.

Top producers: Geil (Rheinhessen), Jürgen Ellwanger, WG Flein, Karl Haidle (Württemberg), Jan Ulrich (Sachsen)

AROMATIC VARIETIES

(GELBER) MUSKATELLER
(Muscat Blanc à Petits Grains) 71 hectares

In spite of the tiny area planted with Muskateller and the erratic quality of the wines it yields, the unique nature and quality of the finest examples makes it the most noble aromatic grape variety in Germany. Already known to the Ancient Greeks, its recorded history in Germany goes back to the 12th century, fully 300 years before that of Riesling. It remains an extremely difficult vine to cultivate and is therefore grown only by vintners with a personal enthusiasm for the variety. What makes the struggle to harvest healthy, ripe Muskateller grapes worthwhile is the intense yet delicately perfumed grapey aromas of the resulting wine. Muskateller

The fickle Muskateller (right) yields Germany's finest aromatic dry whites.

is unique among the noble aromatic grapes in giving wines with a mineral character from the soil. This is often allied to a piercing acidity that wins the wines as many friends as it does enemies. Muskateller gives excellent dry and dessert wines.

Top producers: Koehler-Ruprecht, Müller-Catoir, Ökonomierat Rebholz (Pfalz), Juliusspital (Franken), Bercher (Baden)

GEWÜRZTRAMINER AND TRAMINER 789 hectares

The favourite and best-known grape variety of Alsace used to be just as highly regarded in Germany, but changes in fashion combined with a lack of interest on the part of German vintners have left Gewürztraminer's popularity floundering. The principal problems are that it is difficult to match with food and that its wines are usually too heavy to be consumed in any quantity by themselves. The best German Gewürztraminers are quite different from the lush, perfumed, soft wines the variety gives in Alsace. They are fruitier, more delicate and elegant. Although they have 12–13 degrees of alcohol this is not obvious and, while the acidity is low, the wines still manage to be lively and clean. The most typical aromas are of Turkish Delight and rosewater. As dessert wines they gain intense exotic fruit notes and have more in common with their Alsatian cousins. Although they can age well, German Gewürztraminers are usually best drunk young.

Top producers: Fritz Becker, Müller-Catoir, Ökonomierat Rebholz (Pfalz), Martin Goebel (Franken), Andreas Laible (Baden)

MÜLLER-THURGAU/RIVANER 24,405 hectares

Although this grape variety is responsible for the greater part of Germany's generic wine production it is capable of giving high-quality wines in addition to the thin 'sugar-water' typical of the cheapest examples. First produced in 1882, Müller-Thurgau is the oldest cultivated cross in the world, a product of Riesling x Silvaner. It was originally introduced as a Riesling-like grape that would ripen in vineyards too cool for its noble parent.

The most elegant Gewürztraminers are made in the Ortenau.

The sweet earthiness of Lemberger wines is balanced by its relatively high acidity.

Unfortunately, clonal selection in recent decades has turned it into a mass-producer. A number of vintners have attempted to make something more serious out of the grape, however, and there are now some attractive fruity wines being made without the spurious spiciness and blandness typical of the variety. Some of these new Müller-Thurgaus are given new-oak ageing, others benefit from lower yields and the selection of riper grapes. In order to distance these wines from the mass-produced Müller-Thurgaus they are often sold under the synonym Rivaner.

Top producers: Dr Loosen (Mosel-Saar-Ruwer), Juliusspital, Hans Wirsching (Franken), Karl Heinz Johner, Markgräflich Badis'ches (Baden)

BACCHUS 3,509 hectares

Although named after the god of wine this widely cultivated *Neuzuchtung* is something of a mixed blessing. Well made Bacchus can be appealingly spicy and juicy but poor examples are often exaggeratedly aromatic, broad and flabby. Although Bacchus seems to do best in Franken and around Lake Constance in Baden and to be most problematic in the Mosel-Saar-Ruwer and Nahe, the real key to producing satisfying wines with this variety lies with the winemaker. He or she must select grapes picked early enough to be rot-free, but which also have a healthy acidity. Attempts to make late-harvested dessert wines from Bacchus almost always end in failure, while light, fruity wines can often be successful. In these cases Bacchus can have some of the charm and grace of a good Riesling Kabinett.

Top producers: Schales (Rheinhessen), Juliusspital, Hans Wirsching (Franken), Markgräflich Badis'ches (Baden), Klaus Zimmerling (Sachsen)

SERIOUS RED VARIETIES

LEMBERGER/LIMBERGER 849 hectares

Either as a varietal wine or as the backbone of a blended wine, Lemberger is responsible for most of the high-quality red wines produced in Württemberg today. This is because of the comparative ease with which the variety gives deeply coloured, full-bodied reds full of blackberry- and plum-like fruit and ample tannins. It also has the advantage of taking equally well to traditional wine-making in large neutral barrels and to maturation in small new-oak casks. The wines lack some sophistication, which is prompting winemakers to experiment with blends of Lemberger and the red grapes of the Pinot family with a view to giving the wine a more complex aroma and more elegance. The first results are encouraging, suggesting that with low yields and two years' ageing in new oak these Lemberger-Pinot blends can make red wines as impressive as Germany's best Spätburgunder reds.

Top producers: Graf Adelmann, Dautel, Drautz-Able, Fürst zu Hohenlohe-Öhringen, Staatliche Lehr-und Versuchsansalt Weinsberg (Württemberg)

SCHWARZRIESLING/MÜLLERREBE
(Pinot Meunier) 2,096 hectares

Schwarzriesling is the confusing name for the grape variety that forms the base of the blend in most cheaper non-vintage champagnes. In Germany, as in Champagne, the grape enjoys the reputation of being the smaller, more rustic sister of Spätburgunder (Pinot Noir). Its red wines are paler, lighter and tarter than Spätburgunders, and lack their silkiness. Nevertheless, good Schwarzriesling has plenty of fresh cherry-like fruit. Almost 90 percent of the Schwarzriesling in Germany is grown in Württemberg, where it is used increasingly in blends with red varieties such as Lemberger and Dornfelder. These varieties become less chunky and considerably fruitier when mixed with Schwarzriesling but because Spätburgunder red wines sell more readily and at better prices than Schwarzriesling ever will, the variety is unlikely to gain in popularity.

Top producers: Dautel, Drautz-Able, Fürst zu Hohenlohe-Öhringen, Graf von Neipperg, Staatliche Lehr-und Versuchsansalt Weinsberg (Württemberg)

DORNFELDER 1,625 hectares

Dornfelder is the most interesting red *Neuzuchtung* in Germany. Not only is it a generous yielder and easy to cultivate, but unlike the traditional mass-production red grapes it yields wines with plenty of colour, fruit, body and tannin. German vintners, particularly in the Pfalz where almost half the Dornfelder vineyards are planted, have been quick to spot its advantages. Its acreage there has quadrupled in less than ten years. The result is the production of large volumes of 'real' red wine at modest prices. Most Dornfelders are well made country wines but the best examples are considerably more serious. They have a combination of berry-like fruit, a supple texture and enough body to compare well with Cru Beaujolais. The first successful experiments with new-oak ageing have recently been made in the Pfalz and in Württemberg.

Top producers: Bergdolt, Knipser, H&R Lingenfelder (Pfalz), Dautel, Drautz-Able (Württemberg)

FRÜHBURGUNDER/CLEVNER 37 hectares

Frühburgunder, or Clevner as it is called in Württemberg, is a close relative of Spätburgunder and it shares a good part of that variety's nobility. As its name, 'early burgundy', implies, Frühburgunder is an earlier-ripening mutation of Pinot Noir and gives full-bodied, rich, silky wines. Given good conditions during the harvest and timely picking, these wines can also have a deep colour and a seductive fruitiness. If picked too late the grapes rot and the result is a poor colour and raisiny character. Although Frühburgunder wines typically mature quickly, with low yields it is possible to produce more serious, long-lived examples. The effort involved in caring for this vine during the growing season and harvest prevent it from being planted more widely.

Top producers: Kreuzberg, Meyer-Näkel (Ahr), Rudolf Fürst (Franken), Graf Adelmann, Staatliche Lehr-und Versuchsansalt, Weinsberg (Württemberg)

TRADITIONAL MASS-PRODUCING VARIETIES

ELBLING 1,163 hectares

The most notable thing about this variety is its long history, set against which the wines themselves look very plain. Elbling was brought to Germany by the Romans, who planted it in the Mosel Valley around 300AD. Only during the 18th century did Riesling begin to gain the upper hand in the region, pushing Elbling back until by the middle of the 20th century the latter had been reduced to an enclave in the Ober Mosel Valley between the city of Trier and the French border. On the limestone soil here it gives light, dry white wines that are tart and simple in flavour. It is an extremely generous yielder and only when this tendency is kept in check by vigorous pruning can refreshing rather than sour wines result. Much Elbling is turned into sparkling wine or Sekt, to which it is well suited. Given the simple quality of both its still and sparkling wines, Elbling enjoys a remarkably good image in Germany.

GUTEDEL (Chasselas) 1,360 hectares

Although the French monarch François I is thought to have introduced this variety to western Europe it would be hard to make a case for its nobility. Almost all Germany's Gutedel grows in the Markgräflerland area of Baden, where it yields light, rather neutral dry white wines that tend to be soft but clean. A generous yielder and easy to grow, there is much to be said for the variety as a source of country wine for everyday drinking. The best producers claim that with lower yields and conscientious winemaking it gains a more nutty character and can age for ten years or more, but it is hard to see that the extra effort is worthwhile.

The generous Trollinger, work-horse of Württemberg's wine industry.

(BLAUER) PORTUGIESER 4,419 hectares

The red wine boom in Germany resulted in high prices for all mass-produced red wines, making the cultivation of this generous-yielding red an attractive proposition. Unfortunately almost all the Portugieser produced is of extremely simple quality, very pale red or pink in colour with little fruit, body or character. It would be a good thirst-quencher on hot summer days were it not for the fact that it is generally over-priced. This mass-producing vine takes on a completely different personality, however, when the vines are fully mature or the yield is deliberately reduced. In such rare instances Portugieser can give deep-coloured, rich, velvety reds with as much depth as good Spätburgunder. Although they are not suitable for long ageing, such wines will keep for a good five years.

TROLLINGER (Vernatsch) 2,495 hectares

Not only is it impossible to imagine Württemberg's wine industry without Trollinger, it is hard to imagine Swabia without Trollinger. The Swabian's thirst for this wine is the only reason it is produced in any quantity. There is nothing special about its pale, thin, rather tart red wines. Unlike Portugieser, it does not respond well when its natural vigour is held in check: controlled yields give wines with more body and fruit, but even these are unremarkable. For those with reasons for drinking wine other than local patriotism, the red wines of the Dornfelder grape are preferable. They offer more fruit and character in this low-price category.

Vineyard Sites: Climate and Soil

The flavour of peaches, strawberries or any soft fruit ripened in a cool northern climate is palpably different from that of fruit grown close to the Mediterranean. Compared to the simply sweet taste of Mediterranean-grown fruits and berries the taste of those which have struggled to ripen in more temperate climates is more intense, vibrant and refreshing. 'Cool-climate viticulture' is the term for wine production that capitalises on this effect to make wines with exceptional elegance and aromatic intensity. Centuries before this phrase became a buzz word on the west coast of the United States or a marketing slogan in New Zealand, German vintners were producing magnificent wines of this kind. Their success can be measured by the unparalleled international standing of German Riesling during the 19th century and the first half of the 20th.

Just as an older oyster tastes better than a younger one because it has had longer to absorb flavours from the flora and fauna in the sea water around it, so wine tastes better the longer the grapes have remained on the vine to absorb minerals from the soil and

A combination of warm sunny days and cool nights gives Mosel-Saar-Ruwer Rieslings their aromatic intensity and subtlety.

develop the aromas of fully ripened fruits. In Germany there are usually around 120 days between the flowering of the Riesling vine and the development of fully ripe grapes. Many of the greatest wines, however, result from late-picked grapes which have spent up to 150 days on the vine. This gives them a longer ripening period than any other white wine grape. Combined with the vine's unique sensitivity to its soil, this makes German Rieslings the most individual white wines on the globe. Others may be more imposing or dramatic, but none possesses comparable aromatic subtlety. The image of a wine expert being presented 'blind' with a glass of wine and being able to identify the vineyard from which it came is a cliché but there are those who can do precisely this, so distinct are the personalities of the best German Rieslings.

This is why a wine atlas is important when studying the wines of Germany. With an understanding of which conditions make a vineyard site well suited to the Riesling vine it becomes clear from a glance at the maps where the best wines of a particular region grow. With further study it is possible to understand why the wines of one village smell and taste different from those of its neighbour. Often these differences are the result of differing vine-

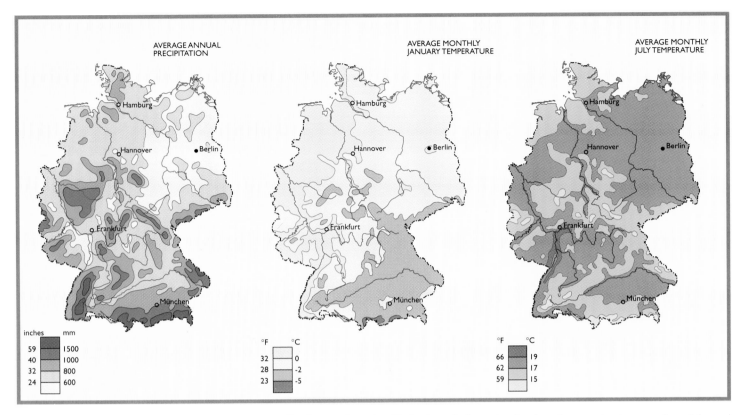

AVERAGE ANNUAL
PRECIPITATION

AVERAGE MONTHLY
JANUARY TEMPERATURE

AVERAGE MONTHLY
JULY TEMPERATURE

inches	mm
59	1500
40	1000
32	800
24	600

°F	°C
32	0
28	-2
23	-5

°F	°C
66	19
62	17
59	15

yard exposure to sun and wind or of differing soils; factors best understood with the aid of a good map.

The influence of soil on the character and quality of wine has been well documented in France, but in Germany wine scientists have concentrated their energies upon the influence of microclimatic factors – the light intensity, air temperature, wind speed, rainfall and frost danger, for example. The soil's influence on German wines is afforded scant attention compared to the meticulous study devoted to the microclimates' role.

In a flat vineyard landscape each plot of land receives the same amount of sunshine and rainfall and is blown by the same winds. Microclimate comes into play when hills and valleys create slopes with differing exposures. The river valleys in which most of Germany's best vineyards are sited include some of the most extreme vineyard landscapes in the world. Only parts of the Rhône Valley in France, the Danube Valley in Austria and the Douro Valley in Portugal possess vineyards as steeply sloping as the most precipitous vineyards on the Rhine, Nahe, Mosel, Saar and Ruwer. These *Weinberge* or wine mountains not only present a dramatic picture for the eye, but also result in dramatically differing microclimates.

A steep, south-facing inclination receives 50 percent more solar radiation than a comparable north-facing slope, making it warmer as well as brighter. Should it be protected by surrounding hills, situated in the bend of a twisting river valley for example, then it will be sheltered from cold winds. Instead of the air being swept away before it has warmed properly, the air temperature will continue to rise through the day. If this site also has a stony soil, the stones will absorb the warmth of the air during the day and radiate it back at night. A stony soil will also warm more rapidly after the cold of winter because of the pockets of air trapped around the stones. Heavy loam or clay soils are denser; it takes longer for the warmth of spring to penetrate to the vines' roots. So on stony ground, vines can start their spring growth earlier, flower earlier and thus extend their ripening season. A vineyard situated on the bank of a river will also benefit from the river's action as a heat reservoir and from sunlight reflected from the water's surface.

The best combination of these physical characteristics adds up to ideal conditions for the Riesling vine in a northerly climate. Similar conditions can be found in such famous German vineyards as the Brauneberger Juffer-Sonnenuhr, Wehlener Sonnenuhr and Erdener Prälat in the Mittel Mosel Valley, the Niederhauser Hermannshöhle in the Upper Nahe Valley, the Bacharacher Hahn in the Mittelrhein, the Rüdesheimer Berg Schlossberg and Berg Rottland in the Rheingau, the Nackenheimer Rothenberg and Niersteiner Pettenthal on the Rheinfront and the Würzburger Stein on the river Main in Franken.

In warmer more southerly climates, similarly blessed vineyards are responsible for the great Syrah red wines of Côte Rôtie and Hermitage in the Rhône Valley of France, the magnificent dry Riesling and Grüner Veltliner white wines of the Wachau in Austria and Vintage Port in the Douro Valley. In these regions the wines from less favoured locations may lack the richness and sophistication of their famous cousins, but they share their basic character and style. In Germany's cool climate the difference in quality between Rieslings from the top vineyard sites and those from unfavourable locations is more dramatic. Wines from the former can possess a miraculous combination of richness and refinement while those from the latter can taste raw, fruitless and sour.

The exact effect of any particular microclimate is difficult to pin down: the concept operates on many levels. A south-facing vineyard may have more sun than its east-facing neighbour, but one corner of that vineyard will be sunnier and warmer than the others. Some rows will have more sun than others and within each row, one side of the vine will be better exposed. Even within a single bunch, the grapes facing the sun will turn gold while the rest of the bunch stays green. These differences in exposure are reflected in the differing sweetness and flavour of the grapes. Not surprisingly, the golden berries from the sunny side of the bunch will taste sweeter and be more juicy than the green ones from the shady side.

23

Roots of the Riesling vine push many metres down through the soil into the bedrock. The slate stone typical of the Mosel-Saar-Ruwer gives the region's wines their strong mineral character.

The winemaker sorts the fruit at harvest to separate grapes of differing ripeness levels. This process requires skill, patience and a keen eye. It is also labour-intensive and therefore expensive. The selective harvesting of individual berries affected by noble rot, the fungus which causes grapes to shrivel and concentrates their juice, is yet more demanding. Even a master of this technique such as Egon Müller of the Egon Müller-Scharzhof estate of Wiltingen on the Saar insists that, however well practised the pickers, he needs to supervise the selection process personally. Harvests can be so stringent that they yield as little as one litre of wine per picker per day – but the resulting Riesling BA and TBA dessert wines are matchless.

Some wine scientists maintain that the vineyard soil does not directly influence the character of the wine, but the evidence of experienced palates proves the contrary. Wilhelm Haag of Weingut Fritz Haag in Brauneberg on the Mosel tells the story of how one spring he broke up a small redundant stone wall in one of his best vineyards. It was made of the slate stone typical in the region and Haag scattered the debris throughout the plot. Top-class Mosel Rieslings frequently have a mineral smell and taste which experts refer to as 'slatey'. Haag insists that he has never experienced such

Early morning fog, which encourages the development of Botrytis cinerea *or noble rot, is a typical feature of the region's climate.*

slatey wines as those made with grapes from this vineyard the following harvest.

The fruit aromas of young Rieslings are no less influenced by the soil. It is not, for example, mere chance that the wines of the Kaseler Nies'chen on the Ruwer, the Piesporter Goldtröpfchen and the Graacher Domprobst in the Mittel Mosel all have a characteristic smell of blackcurrants. The deep slate soil, rich in finely weathered material common to these widely separate locations, gives their wines a strong family resemblance. In the same way the deep marl-clay of the top vineyard sites of Hochheim in the Rheingau – the Domdechaney and Hölle – is responsible for the tell-tale earth, citrus peel and apricot character of these wines. The grapefruit and exotic fruit aromas of Rieslings from vineyards with sandy soils in the Pfalz are unmistakable. Wines with such an expressive character from the vineyard were rare in Germany during the 1970s and early 1980s due to the creeping industrialisation of winemaking methods, but a new generation of winemakers is committed to making wines with the characteristic aromas and flavours of their

vineyards. The resulting trend towards wines with authentic regional character is gaining momentum each year.

On a more basic level the structure of the soil determines much of the resulting wine's character. Light, stony soils, those composed of slate, sand and granite, tend to give wines that develop quickly and even when young show a subtle floral bouquet. They taste fine and elegant however rich they are, but can lack some muscle and power. In contrast, deep, heavy soils composed of clay or marl yield wines that develop more slowly but gain more intense, even opulent, aromas as they age. Firm and angular in less favoured years, in great vintages the wines from this kind of soil have lots of power and depth but can be heavy or clumsy. Sour soils, such as those typical in the Mosel-Saar-Ruwer, tend to give wines with a pointed acidity that can be aggressive when the wines are young. Alkaline soils, such as the limestone typical of Franken, soften the impression that the wines' acidity makes. These characteristics are most pronounced in Germany's Rieslings, but wines from other grape varieties also show them to a lesser degree.

To illustrate the importance of all these factors it is worth comparing Rieslings of a single vintage from different vineyard sites of one of the top German estates. The wines from the Dr Loosen estate of Bernkastel in the Mittel Mosel are perfect for such a comparison, since Ernst Loosen is fascinated by the the special aromas and flavours given by each vineyard to its particular wines. With holdings in five top sites – the Erdener Treppchen and Prälat, Ürziger Würzgarten, Wehlener Sonnenuhr and Graacher Himmelreich – the contrasts between Loosen's Rieslings from a single vintage can be dramatic.

The most extreme contrast is between the wines from the Wehlener Sonnenuhr and the Ürziger Würzgarten. The shallow, stony grey slate soil of the Sonnenuhr gives its wines a filigree peachy-floral bouquet with delicate slatey notes. The epitome of elegance on the palate, it could hardly be more subtle. The racy acidity makes the fruit seem to dance on the tongue and gives the wine an extremely clean aftertaste. Wines from the red sandstone soil of the Ürziger Würzgarten are much bigger and more powerful. Intense exotic fruit, herbal and mineral aromas pour from the glass while the brain is inundated with signals from the tastebuds. The aftertaste is a cascade of fruit and minerals: the ultimate in depth and complexity that Riesling can achieve.

Which of Riesling's many qualities appeals to an individual is a matter of personal taste. The extraordinary diversity of German wines means that there is surely something to please every palate.

Mosel-Saar-Ruwer

In the dramatic and picturesque landscape of the Mosel-Saar-Ruwer, vines cling to the precipitous slopes of narrow, winding valleys cut deep into the stark hilly upland of the Eifel to the north and the undulating Hunsrück to the south. Without these valleys no wine of any consequence could be produced here, the climates of the Eifel and Hunsrück being too inclement for noble grapes to ripen without some protection from the elements. But, sheltered from cold and wind on sunny slopes in the valleys of the Mosel and its tributaries the Saar and Ruwer, the Riesling gives wines of remarkable aromatic intensity and sublime grace.

The finest Mosel-Saar-Ruwer wines have an exceptional depth and harmony and a unique character. Although the region is the biggest exporter of estate-bottled German wines and has a loyal domestic following, the magnificence these wines can achieve is still not widely appreciated. This may be because the Mosel-Saar-Ruwer's international success has been primarily with its crisp, delicate Riesling Kabinett wines. These are the best naturally light – that is, low-alcohol – wines in the world, with an extraordinary amount of fruit, character, and elegance for only 7–9 degrees of alcohol. However, it is with the richer but no more alcoholic Riesling Spätlese, Auslese and higher quality Prädikat wines that the region stakes its claim to greatness.

Both the strength and the potential weakness of Mosel-Saar-Ruwer wines is in their lightness; at their best they possess the ultimate vinous delicacy: at their worst they are simply thin. Should the vintner force his vines to carry a heavy crop or fail to apply the necessary care in the cellar, the resulting wine will lack fruit and character, tasting sweet-sour.

Grape varieties such as Müller-Thurgau and Kerner are planted in vineyards too cold for Riesling and cultivated for maximum yield. The wines they produce tend also to be thin, but taste soft and bland. The legal designations under which these wines are sold, for example the Grosslagen 'Piesporter Michelsberg', 'Bernkasteler Kurfürstlay' and 'Ürziger Schwarzlay' and regional designations such as 'Bereich Bernkastel' are seriously misleading. Almost none of the wine sold under these designations originates from the villages named, and almost all of it deserves to be

Just downriver of the Mittel Mosel the terraced Bremmer Calmot, one of the world's steepest vineyards, faces southeast and enjoy river reflection.

described as 'sugar-water'. Unfortunately, German Wine Law does nothing to discourage such deceptive nomenclature.

Thankfully, an increasing number of Mosel-Saar-Ruwer vintners are striving to produce the highest possible quality wine instead of ever-larger quantities of indifferent stuff. A decade ago the region could boast only a handful of 'star' producers making top-class Rieslings. Now the number of Mosel-Saar-Ruwer wines that marry delicacy and elegance with depth and character has dramatically increased. Indeed the quality revolution has been such that the Mosel-Saar-Ruwer is now the leading quality wine producer among Germany's 13 regions.

As impressive as the wines from southern Germany can be, they remain relatively similar in style to the white wines produced in neighbouring Alsace and Austria. In the Mosel-Saar-Ruwer, however, at the northwestern extremity of Germany's vineyard, a style of wine is made that is distinct from any other. The combination of low alcohol, mouthwatering acidity and natural sweetness from the grape is indigenous to northern Germany and finds its clearest expression in the wines of the Mosel-Saar-Ruwer. The local vintners' claim that their Rieslings represent 'the ultimate German wine' is not without some justification.

It is hardly surprising that these Rieslings smell and taste distinctive. The extremely long growing season in this cool climate results in wines that are light-bodied but exceptionally rich in aroma. The popular image of Mosel-Saar-Ruwer Riesling is one of light 'flowery' wines, a characterisation that suggests something appealing but rather superficial. Certainly they frequently possess a floral character: elderflower, honeysuckle, rose and lavender being the most common notes, but this is only a small part of their wide spectrum of aromas.

As in all high-quality table wines, the fruit character is strongest in a young Mosel-Saar-Ruwer Riesling. Green-fruit aromas and flavours such as gooseberry and sharp, crisp apples usually result from poor vintages or the harvesting of unripe grapes. Fine Mosel-Saar-Ruwer Rieslings can smell and taste of apple, quince, pear, peach, apricot, mango, pineapple, passion fruit, lemon, orange, grapefruit, redcurrant, blackcurrant, strawberry or blackberry depending upon the vineyard site, the vintage and the

Many of the Mosel's vines are still trained in the Roman manner. Each is secured to its own pole and two canes pulled downward from the trunk to form a heart shape.

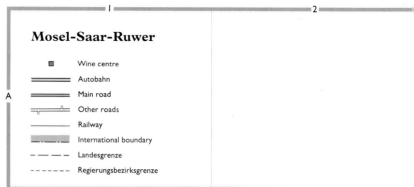

Mosel-Saar-Ruwer

- ■ Wine centre
- Autobahn
- Main road
- Other roads
- Railway
- International boundary
- Landesgrenze
- Regierungsbezirksgrenze

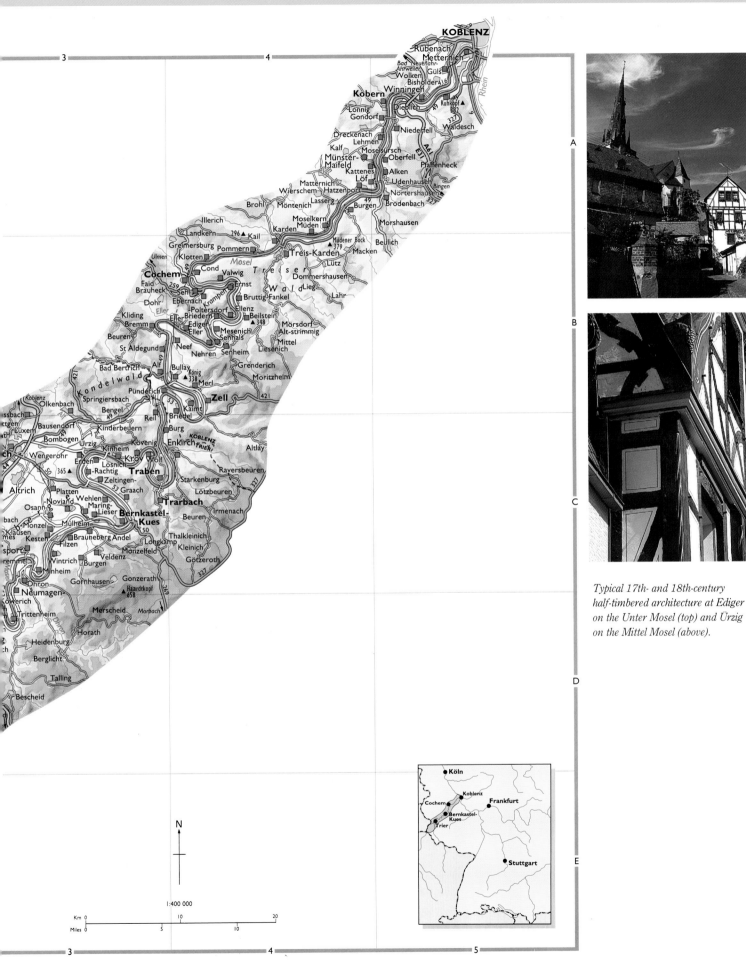

Typical 17th- and 18th-century half-timbered architecture at Ediger on the Unter Mosel (top) and Ürzig on the Mittel Mosel (above).

ripeness of the grapes at harvest. If the wine is of high quality, this fruit character will be pronounced: in the greatest Mosel-Saar-Ruwer Rieslings it can achieve an almost supernatural intensity.

The herb and spice notes can be almost as dramatic as their fruit character, spanning the entire range from parsley and dill to aniseed and allspice. Many of these come directly from the soil and are closely allied to the pronounced mineral character of so many fine examples. This is something far more easily demonstrated than described, since there is no familiar aroma quite comparable to the 'slatey' character of fine Mosel-Saar-Ruwer Rieslings. It comes directly from the region's typical grey slate soils. Free-draining through the stones, water-retentive where it crumbles to a clay-like consistency, this soil is ideally suited to the Riesling vine.

Riesling also grows on slate soils in the Upper or Ober Nahe Valley, at Nierstein and Nackenheim in Rheinhessen, in a few isolated vineyards in the Pfalz and Alsace and in the Wachau of Austria, but these are all different types of slate and result in wines with their own distinct style. The subtle, indefinable mineral quality of a great Mosel-Saar-Ruwer Riesling is quite unique.

A different combination of these aromas can be found in each wine and as it ages its bouquet and flavour undergo several transformations. A simple-quality example is best drunk during the first two years after bottling since it lacks the structure for longer ageing. The fruit character of a top-class Riesling from the region is at its most expressive during its first few years in the bottle: the initial phase of its development. After this youthful exuberance there follows a period of several years during which the wine will be rather unforthcoming and lacking in charm; a phenomenon which affects many great wines. Between seven and ten years of age the wine gains the subtle mellowness of maturity and comes to its peak. While young Mosel-Saar-Ruwer Rieslings seem to express a tense balance between sweetness and acidity, mature wines have a marvellous harmony which is neither completely dry nor sweet, neither acidic nor soft.

In this phase of the wine's development, which lasts between ten and 30 years, the mineral and spice or herbal characteristics are at their strongest. These are intertwined with the special aromas and flavours of bottle age: butter, caramel or waxy notes. When the wine finally starts to taste old after several decades in the bottle, it gains a mushroom character or smells like a forest floor after rain. This intense smell and taste of maturity is referred to by connoisseurs as *Firn* or, when it adds something to the wine rather than dominating it, *Edelfirn* (noble *Firn*).

Dry Mosel-Saar-Ruwer Rieslings go through these transformations much more quickly than the region's classic wines. There are some well made dry wines in the region but few attempts to produce top-class examples have been successful. Fewer than half-a-dozen producers regularly make such wines and only the Maximin Grünhaus estate in the Ruwer Valley has an impressive track record for this style going back more than a decade. The problem is that high-class dry whites require a certain amount of body and an acidity that is supple without being soft. Few of the region's dry wines exceed 11 degrees of alcohol and even fewer match this alcohol level with acidity that is harmonious in the absence of sweetness. It is difficult to find exciting Riesling Trocken wines here but the success rate of Halbtrocken (just off-dry) wines is far higher. The merest touch of sweetness seems to bring the fruit to life.

The real strength of the region's top vintners is at the opposite end of the scale: dessert wines made from selectively harvested

The Laurentiuslay site of Leiwen and the Felsenberg site of Trittenheim, which is owned by the Milz estate. Both are first class vineyards.

botrytized grapes. Here they are simply the best – not only in Germany, but in the world. The acidity that makes top-class dry wines so difficult to make here gives these wines an unmatched brilliance, highlighting every nuance of fruit and spice.

Production of these wines is on a small scale. Annual production of Riesling Auslese is frequently limited to a single 1,000-litre *Fuder* barrel; BA and TBA wines to one or two hundred bottles. The number of producers is fortunately large enough to make wine in this category an affordable rarity. A bottle of top-quality Auslese from a famous estate such as Egon Müller-Scharzhof in the Saar Valley may be too expensive for most occasions, but high-quality examples from less famous producers are some of the few bargains available in Europe's classic wine regions.

In the Ober Mosel Valley, between the Saar's confluence with the Mosel close to Konz and the border with France, Elbling replaces Riesling as the principal grape variety. Brought to the region by the Romans, Elbling survived to become the dominant variety during the Middle Ages. But the wines it yields are simple and its poor frost-resistance used to mean that on average one harvest in three was lost. (This latter weakness is less of a problem to modern winemakers as the variety's frost-resistance has been improved by clonal selection.) Although Riesling was grown in the region in *Gemischte Satz* (mixed plantings) from at least the 15th century, its greater frost-resistance and the vastly superior quality of its wines were not clearly recognised until the 18th century.

The Catholic Church, as the largest vineyard owner until the Napoleonic sequestration of its assets in 1802, actively promoted the switch to Riesling vines. In 1787 Clemens Wenzeslaus, the

The training of vines on wires is a recent innovation on the Mosel. Wires glisten like spiders' webs in the spring sunshine.

Prince-Bishop of Trier, issued an edict ordering the replacement of inferior vine varieties with superior ones in the Mosel-Saar-Ruwer, which meant up-rooting Elbling and replacing it with Riesling. By the time of the Napoleonic classification of the region's wine villages in 1804, Riesling dominated plantings in most of the top sites. The wine's international success resulted in a wave of Riesling plantings which continued into the early years of the 20th century. The Ober Mosel was the only part of the region that remained unaffected.

Ober Mosel Elbling wines, which at their best are no more than fresh dry country wines, were generally regarded as inferior, but in recent years local vintners have done a remarkable job of promoting them. They have focused on dry QbA wines and promoted them as unpretentious wines to drink with food or pleasant thirst-quenchers in warm weather.

The secularisation of Church assets (including large areas of vineyard) during the first years of the 19th century and the period of Prussian rule which followed from 1815 were important to the development of the region's Riesling wine production. Many leading estates, such as Egon Müller-Scharzhof, Maximin Grünhaus and Joh Jos Prüm, came into existence in their present form through the secularisation. The Prussian administration undertook the world's first official vineyard classification in the region between 1816 and 1832, publishing the results in map form, the *Saar und Mosel Weinbau-Karte*, in 1868. The precision of this classification could hardly be improved upon now – even using modern technology.

During the second half of the 19th century and the first decades of the 20th, Prussia was the principal market for Mosel Rieslings and the English-speaking world the second. Demand for Mosel-Saar-Ruwer wines was great and prices were high. The many

The precipitous Ürziger Würzgarten, one of the Mittel Mosel's great first-class sites. Red sandstone and slate soils give the wine strawberry and exotic fruit aromas as well as a fascinating spiciness.

magnificent Art Nouveau houses to be found in Bernkastel-Kues, Traben-Trarbach, Ürzig and Wehlen are evidence of the region's economic success during the period.

The vineyard sites that were the most highly prized during that period are to a large extent still considered the best. Wines from the only village in the first category of the Napoleonic classification, Brauneberg, are now among the most highly sought-after and expensive wines in the Mosel-Saar-Ruwer.

Other top sites such as the Wehlener Sonnenuhr and Erdener Prälat have gained in standing during this century mostly because of the efforts of individual vintners. The Saarburger Rausch site is different. Its reputation has had less time to establish itself because much of it was first planted during the early 1900s. It is typical of plantations founded in the region around that time when uncultivated or forested slopes with good southerly exposure were sought out, cleared and planted with Riesling.

More recent plantings, however, were established with quite different goals in mind. The international success of Mosel-Saar-Ruwer Rieslings prompted the region's farmers during the 1960s to begin planting whatever land they had at their disposal with inferior, early-ripening varieties. Orchards, fields and meadows were turned over to the mass-production of generic wine.

Looking at the vineyard maps of the Mosel-Saar-Ruwer it is easy to see which are the top Riesling sites that were planted in Roman times and which are the newer mass-production sites. On the banks of the river facing south, southeast or southwest where the contour lines are packed closely together there are steeply sloping vineyards with slate soils that produce unique Riesling wines. Only a few hundred metres away on the opposite bank are flat vineyards on heavy alluvial soils which yield large volumes of characterless wine that could equally be made in Eastern Europe, South America or almost any other temperate country.

The falling demand for generic Mosel wines stands in marked contrast to the steadily growing interest in the region's fine

Rieslings; a development which promises eventually to undermine the ill-advised plantings of recent decades. Since the price of mass-produced wine fell dramatically at the beginning of the 1990s, the vineyards producing it have slowly been falling out of cultivation. Although it is certainly possible to produce drinkable, reasonably fruity wines from Müller-Thurgau or Kerner in the Mosel-Saar-Ruwer, such wines can never possess the depth and individuality of Rieslings from top sites.

The differences between the wines of the sub-regions of the Saar Valley, the Ruwer Valley, the Mittel Mosel and the Unter Mosel are clear enough for any interested wine-drinker to identify. With practice it is possible to pinpoint the village or even the vineyard site from which the wine originates. There are few places in the world where wines as distinctive and expressive as these are still being produced. In a wine world dominated by standardisation, the Mosel-Saar Ruwer is a haven of individuality.

Saar

Saar Rieslings represent one extreme of the Mosel-Saar-Ruwer's range of styles, having the lightest body and most pronounced acidity. This acidity makes them lean and 'steely' in lesser vintages, but gives them an astonishing brilliance and vigour in top years. Saar wines also have the most discrete aromas: apple, citrus and white peach are the typical fruit notes, often accompanied by subtle mineral notes from the slate soil.

It is often supposed that this character is due to the Saar's northerly situation, though the region actually lies further south than both the Mittel Mosel and the Rheingau. The real explanation for their 'northerly' character is quite different. Compare the map of the Saar's vineyards (right) with those of the Mittel Mosel (pages 42–3) and the contrast is apparent. While the Mittel Mosel Valley twists and turns around the river's numerous loops, there is only one extreme change of course in the Saar, between Konz and Serrig. There are also many more valleys running adjacent to the Saar than there are to the Mittel Mosel and many of the Saar's top sites are found in these 'side' valleys. While the Mosel Valley frequently rises steeply straight from the river bank, this is rarely the case on the Saar. These factors combine to leave the Saar's vineyards less protected than those of the Mittel Mosel and this greater exposure is responsible for the wines' pronounced acidity or 'steeliness'.

Large areas of flat land in the Mosel Valley were planted during recent decades but the vineyard area of the Saar expanded only modestly, since good quality wine can be produced only from vines planted on sunny slopes. Vineyards still alternate with orchards, meadows and forests, creating one of the most appealing wine landscapes in Germany. While it can be raw and inhospitable here in January, the weather frequently harsher than in the Mosel Valley, it would be hard not to succumb to the region's rural charm during the spring or summer months.

Mittel Mosel Rieslings can seem positively extrovert compared with the more classical style of those from the Saar. Even Ruwer wines, which have a similar piercing acidity, are considerably more aromatic. So far no satisfactory scientific explanation has been proffered to account for this, but the general opinion among local vintners is that the cause is the soil, which is stonier here than in either the Mittel Mosel or the Ruwer.

It seems logical when describing the Saar and its wines to begin with the Rieslings from the great Scharzhofberg vineyard, since these are the region's most elegant wines. At their ravishing best they are exceptionally refined and have a perfect balance of peach-like fruit and racy acidity. The Scharzhofberger Auslese and higher-quality Prädikat wines from the renowned Egon Müller-Scharzhof estate are legendary. To taste one of these honeyed elixirs is to know what perfection can be achieved in the Saar

The first-class Serriger Würtzberg vineyard in the Saar Valley.

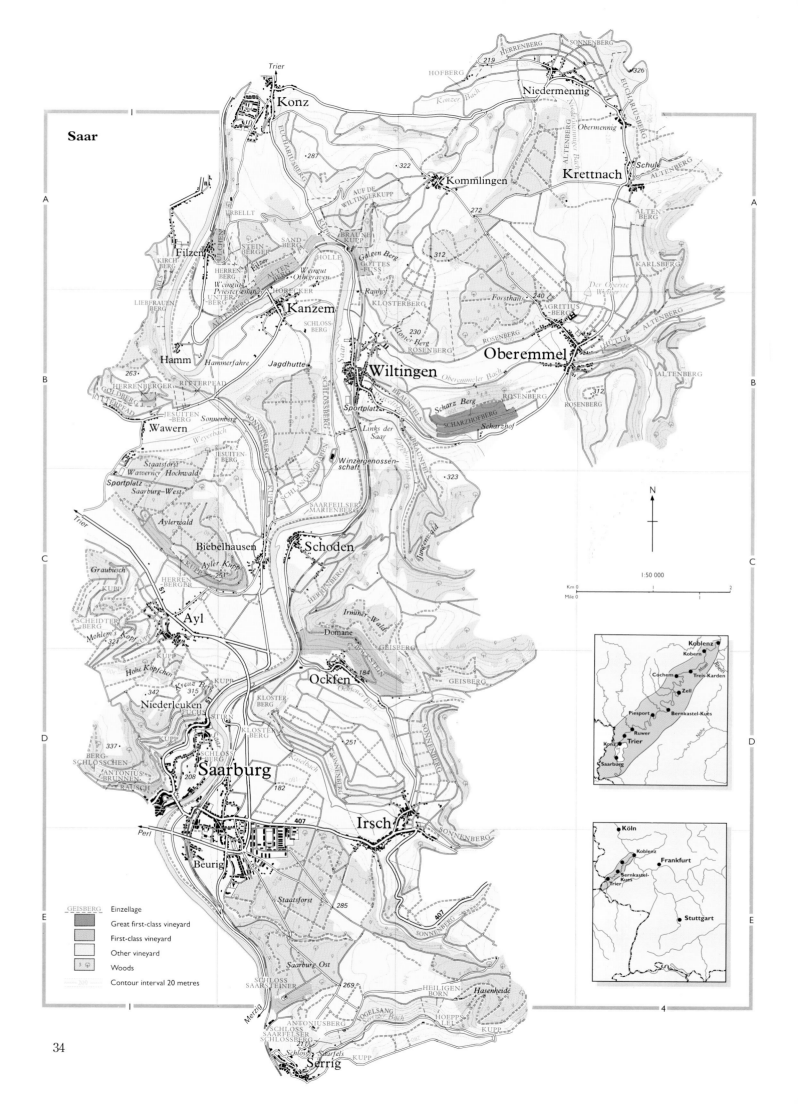

Saar

Konz

Trier

Filzen

KIRCH-BERG

HERREN-BERG

Weingut Priesterseminar UNTER-BERG

LIEBFRAUEN-BERG

ALTENBERG

Kanzem

HÖRECKER

SCHLOSS-BERG

Hamm

Hammerfahre

Jagdhutte

HERRENBERGER

RITTERPEAD

263

GOLDBERG

RITTERPEAD

JESUITEN-BERG

Wawern

Sonnenberg

SONNENBERG

Weyerbach

Staatsforst

Wawerner Hochwald

JESUITENBERG

Sportplatz

Saarburg-West

Aylerwald

Biebelhausen

Graubusch

KUPP

KUPP

Ayler Kupp

251

HERRENBERGER

Schoden

HERRENBERG

Ayl

SCHEIDTER-BERG

Mohlem's Kopf

321

KUPP

KUPP

Hohe Kopfchen

Kreuz Berg

342

315

KUPP

Niederleuken

FUCHS

51

Irmuner-Wald

Domane

GEISBERG

Ockfen

BOCKSTEIN

184

GEISBERG

KLOSTER-BERG

Ockfener Bach

251

BERG-SCHLOSSCHEN

337

Saarburg

KLOSTER-BERG

Kuselbach

SONNENBERG

SCHLOSS-BERG

208

ANTONIUS-BRUNNEN

RAUSCH

182

407

Irsch

SONNENBERG

Beurig

Perl

Staatsforst

285

407

SONNENBERG

Saarburg Ost

SCHLOSS SAARSTEINER

269

HEILIGEN-BORN

Hasenheide

HOEPPS-LEI

Merzig

VOGELSANG

ANTONIUSBERG

SCHLOSS SAARFELSER SCHLOSSBERG

211

Schloss Saarfels

KUPP

Serrig

Herrenberg

SONNENBERG

HERRENBERG

219

HOFBERG

Niedermennig

Obermennig

EUCHARIUSBERG

326

ALTENBERG

Obermennig

Schule

Krettnach

ALTENBERG

272

KARLSBERG

312

ALTEN BERG

EUCHARIUSBERG

287

322

AUF DE WILTINGERKUPP

KUPP

BRAUNE KUPP

Galgen Berg

GOTTES-FUSS

Rauhof

KLOSTERBERG

240

Forsthau

Der Oberste Weiher

AGRITIUS-BERG

240

HÜTTE

Oberemmel

ALTENBERG

230

Kloster Berg

ROSENBERG

ROSENBERG

ROSENBERG

312

SAND-BERG

STEIN-BERGER

HÖLLE

Filzer

ALTEN-BERG

Weingut Othegraven

SCHLOSS-BERG

Kommlingen

Wiltingen

Sportplatz

BRAUNFELS

Links der Saar

Winzergenossen-schaft

SCHLANGENGRABEN

SAARFEILSER MARIENBERG

323

Scharz Berg

SCHARZHOFBERG

Scharshof

Jungenwald

Saar

Obermennnler Bach

1:50 000

N

Km 0   1   2

Mile 0   1

GEISBERG   Einzellage

Great first-class vineyard

First-class vineyard

Other vineyard

Woods

Contour interval 20 metres

34

Valley. Even Château d'Yquem, the first wine of Sauternes, can seem unremarkable alongside of one of Egon Müller's greatest wines; at the Trier auctions of the Grosser Ring (the Mosel-Saar-Ruwer section of the VDP wine estates' association) the Müller's wines have frequently fetched comparable prices.

The Scharzhof itself nestles at the foot of the Scharzhofberg's wall of vines. Perhaps the most imposing mansion-house in the entire region, it was bought by the Müller family in 1797 when the estate was secularised. Sitting in the magnificent library, inhaling aromas of leather-bound books and wood panelling and sipping one of the Müller's great old wines, it is easy to imagine that the last two centuries have been no more than a dream.

The Scharzhofberg has more to its name than Egon Müller. The Reichsgraf von Kesselstatt and von Hövel estates have frequently made impressive wines from this site during recent years. Both also make excellent wines from the neighbouring Oberemmel vineyards. Von Hövel's top wines usually come from the estate's wholly-owned Hütte site and Kesselstatt's best Oberemmelers come from the Agritiusberg vineyard. Oberemmel Rieslings are more delicate and floral than the more noble Scharzhofberg wines. Neighbouring Krettnach and Niedermennig can producing similar wines, but it is hard to find good examples.

The simplest way to reach the vineyards of the Saar is to drive from Trier via Konz, at which point the valley's most dramatic landscape suddenly wheels into view. The River Saar makes only one loop, between Kanzem and Wiltingen, during its course from Konz to Serrig. The steep slopes rising from its right bank here create a patchwork of excellent vineyard sites that lie in a bowl-like formation. Vines are better protected from cold winds here than anywhere else on the Saar.

The most famous site is the Wiltinger braune Kupp which is wholly owned by the Le Gallais estate. Le Gallais wines are made in the same cellars as Egon Müllers' Scharzhofbergers, but coming from the deeper, loamier soil of the Wiltinger braune Kupp they have a very different style: richer, broader and often a little earthy.

Oberemmel vineyards in the Saar Valley follow a typical pattern, monopolising the favourably exposed hillsides below the forest and leaving the flat land for agricultural crops.

The Wiltinger Kupp and Kanzemer Altenberg once enjoyed the highest international standing, but wines are now rarely made that fully realise either site's great potential. Looking at their precipitous slopes drenched in evening sunshine it is not hard to imagine what these vineyards could yield. Older examples from estates such as Bischöfliche Priesterseminar and von Othegraven attest their real calibre.

Other good wines from this area are the succulent, slightly exotic wines made by Reichsgraf von Kesselstatt from the little-known Wiltinger Gottesfuss site. The new Jordan & Jordan estate in Wiltingen (previously van Volxem) which also has holdings in the Scharzhofberg and Ockfener Bockstein is beginning to offer Kesselstatt serious competition. Wiltingen's large old houses are evidence that a century and more ago considerable profits were made from viticulture here.

Filzen, just downstream from Kanzem, does not make the richest or most complex wines of the Saar Valley but its Rieslings can be racy, fine and elegant. Here Piedmont is the leading producer. Nearby Wawern, on the left bank of the river, was one of the Saar's most famous wine villages a century ago. Until the early 1960s the Wawerner Herrenberg wines from the Lintz family's estate enjoyed an excellent reputation. This site is now wholly owned by the Dr Fischer estate in Ockfen and in recent years has given the estate's best wines. Part of the Wiltinger Braunfels vineyard adjoins the Scharzhofberg here and in top vintages can give impressive wines with a distinctive, almost pungent earthy note.

The beautiful old town of Saarburg brings many visitors to the area. At its heart lies a cascade or *Rausch* of white water surrounded by well-preserved half-timbered houses. Atop the Schlossberg the Burg, or medieval keep, from which the town derives its name now houses a fine restaurant. Set back slightly from the river are the town's best vineyards: the Kupp and Antoniusbrunnen and the first-class Saarburger Rausch.

The Saarburger Rausch deserves special attention, since two of the region's best winemakers both make classic Saar wines from the vines clinging to its steep slopes. Although the Zilliken and Dr Heinz Wagner estates use similar winemaking methods, their owners' contrasting personalities give their wines striking stylistic differences. Wines from the Rausch are intensely mineral in

character, with a distinct citrus element in addition to the peach-like fruit typical of Saar Rieslings. Hanno Zilliken's are always steely and tightly wound when young, opening very gradually as they develop, while Heinz Wagner's are rounder and juicier with plenty of spice.

Architecturally, both estates have plenty to offer. The Zilliken family live in a typical suburban house, beneath which lies a three-storey vaulted cellar dating from the 1920s. The lowest level is nine metres below ground and among the barrels some impressive stalagmites and stalactites climb and fall. The family's original home, the house which once stood above their present cellar, was destroyed along with much of Saarburg during the last months of World War II.

Across the river next to the railway station stands the Wagner family's imposing 19th-century mansion. The Wagners used to be important sparkling wine producers. Below their park-like garden lie gallery after gallery of cellars. The modest number of wine barrels needed today almost looks lost in this vast cavern dating from more expansive times.

Ockfener Bockstein's magnificent amphitheatre of vines, with forest above and the village of Ockfen nestling at its foot, is one of the most beautiful sights on the Saar. The town's renown as a source of fine Rieslings is rather recent, dating back no more than 40 years, while the wines of the Ockfener Bockstein have long enjoyed an excellent reputation. During the 1980s, however, there were few exciting Ockfen wines. Currently the Dr Wagner and Zilliken estates are the best sources and competition among estates to make good wines is beginning to show positive results. In good years Bockstein wines, some of the Saar's most appealing, combine rich fruit with creaminess and a crisp but not aggressive acidity.

Ayl is an unspectacular village which would be easy to overlook on the way to or from Trier if it did not have an excellent vineyard site, the Ayler Kupp, and a first-class hotel and restaurant, or Weinhaus, by the same name. The Kupp site was greatly expanded when the 1971 Wine Law was introduced. In fact only the slope to the north of Ayl, below the hill called Ayler Kupp, deserves the good name. The wines from the true Ayler Kupp possess the classic Saar acidity, combining raciness with a floral character and crisp, juicy fruit aromas. Where better to sample these delights than Weinhaus Ayler Kupp, also home of the Peter Lauer estate, where the standard of cooking matches the excellent wines?

The vineyards of Serrig are only about a century old but are among the best in the valley. The leading producer is the Ebert family's Schloss Saarstein estate. Situated on a hilltop with magnificent views over the valley, the estate is best reached by driving from Saarburg through the beautiful Saarburg East Forest. The estate is unique on the Saar in that all its vineyards lie immediately around the estate house, as they often do in Bordeaux. The Ebert's wholly-owned Serriger Schloss Saarstein site gives Rieslings with a pronounced blackcurrant aroma reminiscent of Ruwer wines, but their sleek raciness is unmistakably Saar.

Potentially the (confusingly named) Serriger Schloss Saarfelser Schlossberg, Vogelsang, Würtzberg and Herrenberg sites can all yield wines of similar quality. Schloss Saarstein's most serious competition is the Bert Simon estate situated just south of Serrig. At their best the wines from his wholly-owned Würtzberg and Herrenberg sites have rich fruit and plenty of mineral character. Sadly, the Mosel-Saar-Ruwer State Domain, which harvested the Saar's first Trockenbeerenauslese from the slopes of the Serriger Vogelsang in 1921, is no longer the force it once was. After losing its way during the 1980s many of its vineyards have been sold off.

By the turn of the century it is likely that only its holdings in Avelsbach in the Ruwer will remain.

The best view of this stretch of the river is from the tiny, ancient chapel above Kastel-Staadt. A century ago the Saar's vineyards extended south along the river all the way to Saarbrücken and some, particularly those of Kleinplittersdorf, were highly regarded. But now they come to an abrupt end just south of Serrig and in their place beautiful countryside stretches out, rolling alongside the great Saar Loop close to Mettlach.

Left: The vineyards of Serrig on the Saar were planted only about a century ago, but in spite of their relative youth those of Schloss Saarstein produce some of the area's finest wines.

Below: Stalactites bristle from the ceiling in the ancient cellar of Weingut Zilliken in Saarburg. Fully nine metres below ground, the temperature and humidity are stable all year round.

BENCHMARK WINES

Saarburger Rausch Riesling Spätlese
Weingut Forstmeister Geltz Zilliken, Saarburg
Vineyard site: Saarburger Rausch
Site area: 10 hectares, 5 hectares Forstmeister Geltz Zilliken
Exposure: south to east
Inclination: very steep
Soil: weathered grey slate and diabase
Description: Classic Saar Rieslings made for long ageing. Firm and steely, these are neither flatterers nor charmers, the discreet peach- and lemon-like fruit dominated by an intense mineral character. In spite of considerable natural sweetness they have an almost dry balance due to the palate-cleansing acidity. The long finish tastes like an essence of slate.
Best vintages: '94, '93, '91, '90, '89, '85, '83, '79, '76, '75, '71
Best drunk: Best after ten years in the bottle, they can also show well during the first three years after the vintage. Bizarre as it may sound, they make excellent partners for spicy dishes.

Scharzhofberger Riesling Auslese 'Gold Cap'
Weingut Egon Müller-Scharzhof, Wiltingen
Vineyard site: Scharzhofberg (an *Ortsteil* of Wiltingen)
Site area: 27 hectares, 8 hectares Egon Müller-Scharzhof
Exposure: south to southeast
Inclination: very steep
Soil: weathered grey slate, stony top-soil, deep sub-soil
Description: These, the richest Auslese wines of the region, are among the world's finest dessert wines. They possess a wonderful honey, caramel and dried-fruits character, the bouquet opulent yet delicate. Very powerful and succulent on the palate but perfectly balanced, they have a seductively silky texture in spite of their pronounced acidity. Perfection – but at a price.
Best vintages: '94, '93, '91, '90, '89, '88, '83, '76, '75, '71
Best drunk: These are marvellous wines to drink with mild blue cheese such as forme d'Ambert and Bresse Bleu or with liver pâté. However, they give their best when they are the centre of attention.

Ruwer

Although only a few hills and the city of Trier separate the Ruwer and Saar Valleys, the difference between the two areas' wines is startling. Ruwer wines can have as much acidity as Saar wines but they marry it with a more expressive fruit and pronounced earthy, herbal and floral aromas. Like Saar wines they can be aggressively acidic in poor vintages, but in years with hot summers such as '89, '83 and '76 the wines from the Ruwer's meagre 280 hectares of vineyard (a figure which is slowly declining) shine no less brightly than those of the Saar.

With rolling hillsides, woodlands and the narrow Ruwer stream winding through meadows, the valley could hardly be more picturesque. Only the imposing steep south- and southwest-facing slopes of the best vineyards give the scene a sterner aspect. The best Ruwer wines are at once charming and sublime, perfectly reflecting the two sides of this landscape. They are delightful and refreshing enough to drink without any thought, yet subtle and serious enough to merit the closest scrutiny.

The most important of the Ruwer's top sites, the Abtsberg of Maximin Grünhaus, is in the sole ownership of the von Schubert family, along with the neighbouring Herrenberg and Bruderberg sites. They all benefit from the barrier to cold northerly winds provided by the Grüneberg and all lie on steep to precipitous slopes with south or southeasterly exposure. The Abtsberg and Bruderberg have grey slate soils, while the Herrenberg is mainly red slate, which tends to give its wines more aroma. The sites' names originate in the estate's monastic past and allude to their simple classification system: the wines from the Abtsberg were

The Kaseler Nies'chen, one of the Ruwer Valley's first-class vineyards.

reserved for the Abbot, those from the Herrenberg were for the monks and the uninitiated brothers drank the wines from the far less-well situated Bruderberg. The brothers apparently enjoyed large quantities of the stuff notwithstanding its inferior origins: there was an outcry when at one point the daily ration was reduced to two litres per day!

The recorded history of the Grünhaus estate dates from February 6, 966, when the Holy Roman Emperor Otto I presented the house and vineyards to the Benedictine monastery of St Maximin in Trier. But the oldest part of the Grünhaus cellar is Roman, suggesting that the vineyards were planted many centuries earlier. A subterranean Roman aqueduct runs all the way from the estate to Trier. Although it has never been restored it is still passable through its entire length.

Maximin Grünhaus was secularised during the Napoleonic occupation, passing into the von Schubert family's ownership in 1882. The renovations and additions made shortly thereafter turned the estate into the valley's most prominent landmark. With its battlements and great old trees, it looks like a fairy-tale image of a Gothic German castle.

Maximin Grünhaus Rieslings are refined and aromatically complex wines in which summer flower and ripe berry aromas mingle with freshly chopped herb and mineral notes. Even professional tasters are amazed at how many decades these wines retain their vivid balance of fruit and acidity. Many consider them among the greatest white wines in the world. Their combination of extravagance and delicacy is reflected in the estate's unmistakable Art Nouveau label, which has remained virtually unchanged since 1904. It has adorned some legendary wines, including the 1921 Trockenbeerenauslese, the first wine of this style ever produced on the Ruwer. The US Board of Alcohol, Tobacco and Firearms tried to ban the pink colouring of the cherubs on the grounds that it made the label pornographic: fortunately common sense prevailed and the attempt was not successful.

Across the valley from Grünhaus lies the Ruwer's other great estate, the Tyrell family's Karthäuserhof. It too has monastic origins, having been owned by the Carthusian Order from 1335 until 1803. The tower of Karthäuserhof, which once had a moat, dates from the early part of this period. The estate buildings are rather less grand than those of Grünhaus but their secluded location has a timeless charm. Like Grünhaus, the estate is sole owner of a perfectly situated vineyard, the Eitelsbacher Karthäuserhofberg. Its wines carry only a narrow-neck label of the kind common a century ago but rarely seen now.

The style of wine however is very different from that at Grünhaus. In their youth the Karthäuserhofbergers have a vivacious fruit character which often includes intense grapefruit and blackcurrant notes together with mouthwatering acidity. Wines from earlier vintages such as '64 and '59 are legendary for their sublime marriage of richness and elegance. Those from the neighbouring Eitelsbacher Marienholz cannot match these but they can be fresh, typical Ruwer wines and make an ideal introduction to the area. Bischöfliche Weingüter is the most important producer.

Only a kilometre upstream from Eitelsbach lies the Karlsmühle. Now a hotel, restaurant and wine estate, it was originally a Roman mill used for cutting imported Italian marble for Trier's important buildings. The Roman poet Ausonius described the mill in his poem *Mosella* written in 371.

Karlsmühle wines are perhaps the most vivid and extrovert fruity of all Ruwer Rieslings. The estate is also sole owner of the Lorenzhöfer Felslay and Mäuerchen but many of its best wines come from the nearby Kaseler Kehrnagel and Kaseler Nies'chen,

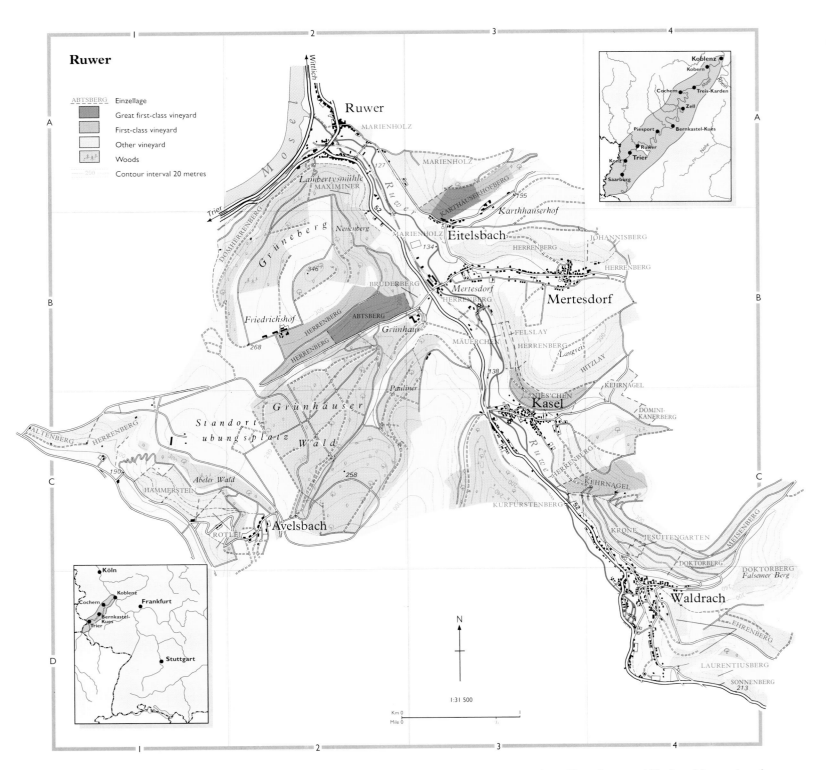

Ruwer

ABTSBERG Einzellage

Great first-class vineyard

First-class vineyard

Other vineyard

Woods

200 Contour interval 20 metres

1:31 500

Km 0

Mile 0

N

both of which have fine reputations. Kasel deserves to be better known, not only because of these wines, but also because it is the valley's most appealing village. Although Trier commuters account for much of the area's population, its rural character has not been lost.

Kasel's wines have the crispness and delicacy typical of the area's wines but they also have intense fruit and complex aromas. Kaseler Nies'cheners are richer and more earthy than the leaner, stonier Kaseler Kehrnagelers, but both have tell-tale black or red berry notes with ripe peach-like fruit. Sometimes they can literally smell like Peach Melba. These, together with the wines from Maximin Grünhaus and Karthäuserhof are the longest-living

Ruwer wines. Reichsgraf von Kesselstatt and Karlsmühle regularly make first-class wines; Bischöfliche Weingüter and the village's tiny co-operative are also good sources.

Waldrach is the last village in the valley producing high-quality wines. The Ruwer generally needs a good year to give exciting wines but Waldrach needs a great vintage to come into its own. Here it is cooler and more exposed to wind than on the slopes closer to the Mosel, giving wines that are lighter, sleeker and more floral than those of Kasel. They can be delightful and refreshing in a good vintage but hard and sour if the summer is cool and wet. A few isolated vineyards can be found high up the valley, even as far as Sommerau, but no wines of any consequence are produced here.

In years with hot summers, fine light Rieslings can be produced from the vineyards of Waldrach high in the Ruwer Valley.

The wines of Avelsbach on the other side of the Grünhäuser Wald are capable of greater things. An Avelsbach Riesling from a top vintage can make one of Mosel-Saar-Ruwer's most alluring marriages between ripeness and delicacy. The important producers are the region's State Domain and the Bischöfliche Weingüter, both based in Trier, but in recent years neither has made wines that fully realise the site's potential.

The Ruwer Valley's vineyard area is shrinking and may eventually cover fewer than 250 hectares, but the vineyards falling out of cultivation are those in the least-favoured locations where commercial wine production is marginal at best. When good vineyards come onto the market they quickly find a buyer. With Maximin Grünhaus, Karthäuserhof, Karlsmühle and Reichsgraf von Kesselstatt the Ruwer has four top producers who promote its wines very effectively. The recently formed Ruwer Riesling Association is also encouraging less well-known vintners in the area to strive towards better quality wine, all of which makes the Ruwer's winemaking future look positive indeed.

BENCHMARK WINES

Kaseler Nies'chen Riesling Spätlese
Weingut Reichsgraf von Kesselstatt, Trier
Vineyard site: Kaseler Nies'chen
Site area: 14.5 hectares, 3.5 hectares Reichsgraf von Kesselstatt
Exposure: south
Inclination: very steep
Soil: deep grey slate with plenty of finely weathered material
Description: White wine can hardly be more fruity and juicy than this. A cascade of peach- and summer berry-like fruit pours across the palate, its sheer intensity pushing the wine's sweetness into the background. The acidity makes these wines extremely fresh and clean, reining it in tightly to give a crisp, almost dry aftertaste.
Best vintages: '94, '93, '92, '90, '89, '88, '86, '83
Best drunk: Hard to resist for their youthful exuberance, they also age well. As young wines they are best drunk alone or with light snacks. With some bottle-age they are perfect with roast pork or chicken.

Maximin Grünhauser Abtsberg Riesling Spätlese
C von Schubert'sche Gutsverwaltung, Grünhaus
Vineyard site: Maximin Grünhaus Abtsberg
Site area: 13 hectares; wholly owned by the von Schubert family
Exposure: south-southeast
Inclination: very steep
Soil: weathered grey slate; very stony
Description: The epitome of good German Riesling. Intensely aromatic with peach, berry, floral and slatey notes, yet extremely elegant: filigree. The scintillating interplay of juicy fruit and mineral acidity on the palate ends in a dazzling crescendo of flavours.
Best vintages: '94, '93, '92, '90, '89, '88, '86, '85, '83, '79, '76 '75, '71
Best drunk: Drier than most Mosel-Saar-Ruwer Spätlese these are consequently more flexible partners with food. Even as younger wines they can be drunk with all manner of fish and lighter meat dishes. Best within the first three years after the vintage or from eight years of age.

Mittel Mosel

The Mosel snakes its way between Schweich, just downstream from Trier, and Koblenz in a narrow, tightly twisting valley. Far more densely planted than the Rhine Gorge, this is one of the world's most spectacular vineyard landscapes. Vines line the valley along almost its entire course. Seventeen hundred years of continuous vineyard cultivation have woven natural and cultivated landscape into a seamless whole.

To appreciate how this remarkable vista influences the region's wines the Mosel Valley should be seen in late summer or autumn. At this time of year most days begin with the valley submerged in dense fog, above which is brilliant sunshine. The thick white blanket fills the valley like piped cream in a cake, but it slowly dissipates during the morning until the last wisps of cloud hanging in the valley visibly shrink, then vanish. In the vineyards the temperature rises rapidly. By mid-morning, the upper side of the slate on the ground is hot to the touch while the underside is still coated with dew. By the time the sun disappears at the end of the day the slate stones have absorbed enough warmth to radiate it back during the cool of the evening.

This oscillation between warmth and coolness, high humidity and intense sunlight has a decisive influence on the ripening of the grapes and on the development of botrytis, or noble rot. In such conditions barely ripe green grapes that are still firm and tart quickly turn golden and sweet, then gain the purple-brown hue of botrytis and start to shrivel, concentrating their juice. It is from such botrytized grapes that all the greatest Mosel Rieslings are made. However, the weather here is unpredictable and vintners who wait to take advantage of such conditions take a considerable risk. Should heavy rain suddenly arrive then everything can be lost within a couple of days.

Making great Mosel Riesling from these steep vineyards is always a gamble. The risks are worth taking only in the best sites, where the grapes can take advantage of every ray of sunshine and are well protected from cold and wind. Thankfully the Mosel Valley has a large number of steep, south-facing vineyards that enjoy just such conditions.

Moving down the valley from Trier towards Koblenz, the first of these are the Schweicher Annaberg and the Longuicher Maximiner-Herrenberg, which can best be seen from the Autobahn bridge crossing the Mosel at Schweich or from the right bank of the Mosel at Longuich. Their slate soil has a reddish tinge which, together with the sites' excellent southwesterly exposure, gives the wines a smell of summer fruits, richness and perfect balance. Schmitt-Wagner is the leading producer for Maximiner-Herrenberg Rieslings and O Werner & Sohn the best source of Annaberg

Goldtröpfchen, the most famous of all the vineyards within the steep, south-facing amphitheatre of vineyards surrounding Piesport.

Middle Mosel:South

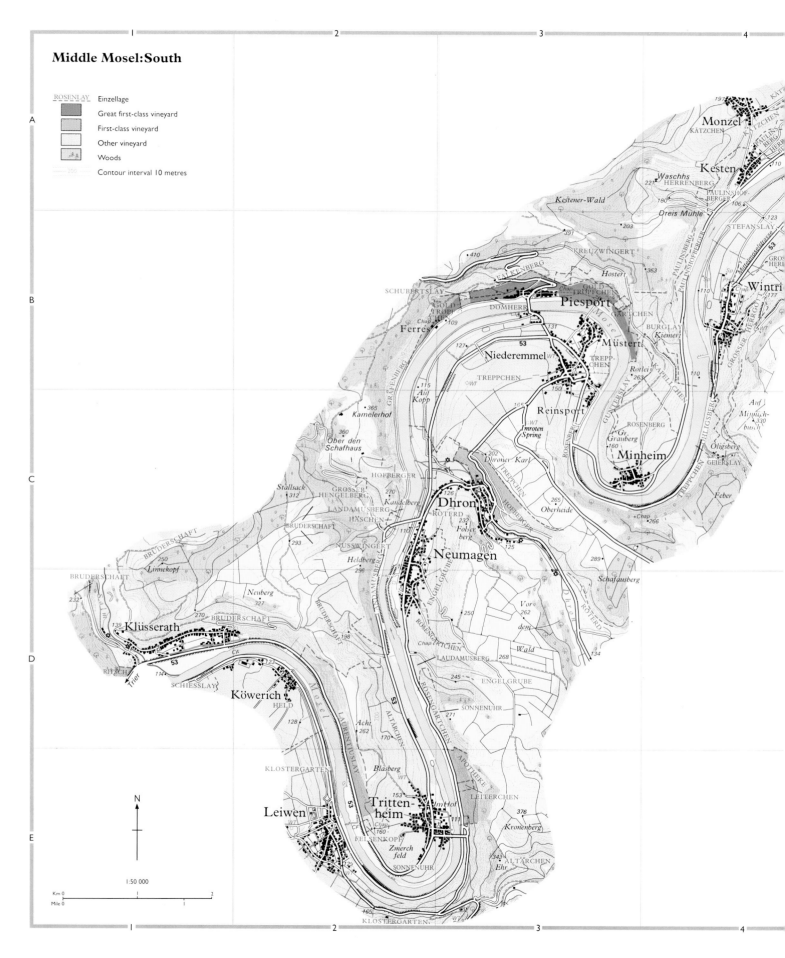

ROSENLAY Einzellage

Great first-class vineyard

First-class vineyard

Other vineyard

Woods

Contour interval 10 metres

N

1:50 000

Km 0   2
Mile 0   1

wines, although the area is actually better known for Longuich's 'Auf der Festung' restaurant.

Few of the region's famous or important wine estates own vineyards between Schweich and Trittenheim so there are many unknown names by this lovely stretch of river. The Mehringer Blattenberg, Pölicher Held and Detzemer Maximiner Klosterlay can all yield good, crisp, lighter-style Rieslings while the narrow terraces of the Thörnicher Ritsch have the potential to produce intense, racy wines of considerable subtlety. A handful of younger vintners are now beginning to build reputations for these wines. Georg Lenhardt is the rising star of Mehring wines, Carl Loewen the new champion of Pölich and Detzem wines and the Sankt Urbanshof estate the first to recognise the enormous potential of the Thörnicher Ritsch.

These villages and their wines deserve to be better known. It is no accident, however, that the neighbouring wines from the 50-kilometre stretch between Leiwen and Ürzig are the best-known in the world. Here vines cling to every sunny slope for up to 200 metres above the river and they produce more high-class Riesling than anywhere in Germany. A decade ago Leiwen would not have been included among this elite, since the town was best known for mass-produced wines. Through a combination of ambition, hard work and self-criticism however a handful of Leiwen's young vintners, including Carl Loewen, Gerhard Grans of Grans-Fassian and Nic Weiss of Sankt Urbanshoft, have built reputations for elegant, refined Rieslings from the excellent Leiwener Laurentiuslay site.

Only ten years ago the vintners of neighbouring Trittenheim might have laughed about Leiwen, but now they are well aware of the tough competition it offers. Trittenheim sits on a tongue of flat land within one of the Mosel's most dramatic loops. From here there is a magnificent view that extends upstream to Thörnich and downstream to Neumagen. Trittenheim wines, particularly those from the Apotheke and Leiterchen sites (the latter is wholly owned by the Milz estate) are more substantial than those from Leiwen and potentially finer. Unfortunately, there is currently no reliable

Sun dials of all shapes and sizes scattered among the vines were used as timekeepers by vineyard workers before watches became commonplace.

This Roman wine press, recently excavated from the great first-class Goldtröpfchen site, has been restored and reconstructed to working order.

source. The village's first estate is Milz-Laurentiushof, but Ernst Clüsserath should also be taken seriously.

The truly great vineyards begin at Piesport. The Piesporter Goldtröpfchen's enormous amphitheatre of vines was also described by the Roman poet Ausonius in his poem *Mosella* in 371. Walking down into the valley today through the expanse of the Goldtröpfchen, the ravishing views presented at each of the river's many turns have changed little since Ausonius wondered at them over 16 centuries ago.

A Roman wine press was recently discovered at the western edge of Piesport in the middle of the best part of the Goldtröpfchen. It is now beautifully restored and every year during the first weekend of October local vintners recreate a Roman wine harvest and pressing. Calculations made by Dr Gilles of the Landesmuseum in Trier suggest that the Romans cultivated fully 50 hectares of vines here in the fourth century AD.

Piesporter Goldtröpfchen Rieslings are among the most powerful Mosel-Saar-Ruwer wines. With their intense aromas of blackcurrant, citrus and peach they have an almost baroque personality. Their body, richness and firm structure come from deep slate soil that does not suffer from drought even in the hottest summers. In vintages like '94, '89, '83 and '76, there are few other Mittel Mosel wines that can compete. Piesporters can also be very long-living wines, the best Auslese from '71 still showing magnificently in the mid-1990s.

The international success of the Reinhold Haart estate, whose wines marry opulent fruit with racy elegance, has done much to encourage other vintners to strive for better quality. The neighbouring Kurt Hain, Lehnert-Veit, Reuscher-Haart and Weller-Lehnert estates are close on his heels. Piesporters from Reichsgraf von Kesselstatt of Trier, which come from both the Goldtröpfchen and Domherr sites, are among the most impressive wines in their extensive portfolio. This is one of the Mosel wine villages where the vintners are aware that the future lies in improving quality, and that this is best achieved through friendly competition.

Piesport is worth a visit not just for its excellent wines but also for its idyllic character. It may not have Bernkastel's picturesque half-timbered houses, but neither is it overwhelmed by bus-loads of day-trippers. Its fine 18th-century buildings are testament to the high standing of the village's wines during that period. Even then, however, its good name was being used to sell mediocre wines from neighbouring villages. Now the 1971 Wine Law has created the Piesporter Michelsberg Grosslage (collective site), which enables wines from neighbouring villages such as Minheim and Rivenich, made from inferior grape varieties in poor vineyards, to be sold as Piesporter. It is nothing short of a scandal that Piesport is better known internationally for these poor wines than for the noble Goldtröpfchen Rieslings. Thankfully, the village's vintners are determined to change this regrettable situation.

Nearby Dhron can also produce Rieslings full of fruit and charm, but most of these are best drunk in their youth since they lack the structure to age. Only those from the best part of the Hofberg, the slope directly behind the village, come close to matching well-made Goldtröpfchens. Similar potential exists in Wintrich, from whose Ohligsberg site the von Schorlemer estate made legendary wines during the 1930s, 1940s and 1950s. Since the Reinhold Haart estate bought into this site in 1991 its reputation has been gaining ground: it is good to see a forgotten top site being rediscovered.

The Brauneberger Juffer and Juffer-Sonnenuhr sites cover the entire face of one of the valley's most dramatic hillsides. Until well into this century its wines enjoyed the best reputation and sold for the highest prices in the region. In 1836 Cyrus Redding wrote in *A History and Description of Modern Wines* that the Brauneberg wines were 'the most celebrated' in the Mosel-Saar-Ruwer.

The Brauneberg could not have achieved this position were it not for a special combination of factors. It differs significantly from the valley's other top sites in that behind most of them lie expanses of forested hilly plateau from which water flows, irrigating the vineyards deep underground. The Brauneberg is an isolated hill with no significant underground water sources. The soil here dries out more quickly than in other top Mosel vineyards, giving the Brauneberg an enormous advantage in vintages with wet summers. Years such as '85 and '79 are great vintages here, but not elsewhere in the region, and generally average vintages such as '87 and '81 are far better than average in the Brauneberg.

In the Fritz Haag and Max Ferd Richter estates the Brauneberg has two champions producing wines worthy of its glorious history and special reputation. Rich and substantial with a subtle earthiness, the Richter wines are traditional Brauneberg Rieslings. The concentrated, exceptionally elegant wines from Fritz Haag combine typical Brauneberg power with a sleekness and clarity that puts them among the very finest Mosel Rieslings. The estate's top Auslese and higher quality Prädikat wines continue to command some of the highest prices of all Mosel-Saar-Ruwer wines. Brauneberg wines from Willi Haag, Paulinshof, Dr Pauly-Bergweiler and Wwe Dr H Thanisch are also worth seeking out.

Strangely, the many generations of commercial success enjoyed by the Brauneberg's are hardly evident in the village's architecture. Almost more impressive than the village itself is the Roman wine press that was recently excavated at the foot of the Brauneberg in the middle of the Juffer-Sonnenuhr site. From the top of the Brauneberg there are magnificent views of the surrounding country. The nearby Veldenz Valley is one of the most idyllic corners of the region, its hills and meadows ignored by many tourists. Veldenz's vineyards also deserve to be better known since in hot summers they can give brilliant wines reminiscent of good Saar examples. The best are the Veldenzer Elisenberg wines made by Max Ferd Richter. Their gooseberry and blackcurrant bouquet and piquant acidity makes them most distinctive.

The village of Kesten is one of the most attractive in this part of the valley and its wines ought to offer Brauneberg more serious competition. The Kestener Paulinshofberg has almost as much top-quality Riesling potential as its more famous neighbour. Currently Kees-Kieren and Paulinshof make the best examples. Lieser used to enjoy a better reputation largely because it was home to the von Schorlemer estate which made some of the region's best wines between the 1940s and 1960s. The massive grey slate mansion of Schloss Lieser, where the family lived, is still the village's most prominent landmark. Thankfully several vintners (not least in the recently revived Schloss Lieser estate) are now working hard to realise the potential of the excellent Lieserer Niederberg-Helden site. Both Kesten's and Lieser's wines bear a family resemblance to those of Brauneberg.

The eight-kilometre wall of vines stretching from the bridge at Bernkastel to the village of Zeltingen is the longest continuous stretch of vineyard in Europe. Whether light or rich the Rieslings from here are always expressive and delicate. Those from Bernkastel's lesser vineyards tend towards leanness and the steeliness of Saar wines, but a top-class example from the alte Badstube am Doctorberg, Graben or Lay sites is a different matter. These stony south- and southwest-facing slopes can give wines with great breed and elegance. The best producers are Lauerburg, Dr Loosen, Joh Jos Prüm and Wwe Dr H Thanisch.

The wines of the world-famous Bernkasteler Doctor are among the most expensive Rieslings in Germany. Taste a great old example from Wegeler-Deinhard or Wwe Dr H Thanisch and it is easy to understand why, but the high prices of modern examples are more difficult to justify. Bernkasteler Doctor wines have written some of the most glorious chapters in the history of Mosel wine. In 1921 the Mosel Valley's first Riesling Trockenbeerenauslese was produced from the Bernkasteler Doctor by the Thanisch estate. This wine and its successors from the '37 and '38 vintages became the legends upon which the 'Doctor cult' was founded. In fact there are at least half a dozen other vineyard sites in the Mosel Valley – the Erdener Prälat, for example, the Brauneberger Juffer-Sonnenuhr or the Piesporter Goldtröpfchen – capable of yielding extraordinary wines such as these TBAs.

Bernkastel should be high on the list of any visitor to the region – in spite of the tourists and kitsch that sometimes threaten to overwhelm it. The old town on the right bank of the river is packed with interesting buildings, perhaps the best being the magnificent half-timbered houses surrounding the marketplace and the baroque St Michael fountain. This scene has not changed significantly since the Middle Ages, though most of the town dates from after the Thirty Years' War (1618–48) during which it was badly damaged.

The 17th-century buildings dominating Old Bernkastel are worth close examination: the beams of many are carved with proverbs, homespun philosophy and quotations from the Bible. The narrow, leaning *Spitzhäuschen*, or pointed house, just off the market square, has no such carvings but must be the most frequently photographed building in this part of Germany. Few venture in to discover that it is now a wine bar.

Elsewhere in Bernkastel's restaurants and bars good wine is not easy to find. The same applies to the town's wine festival, which takes place during the first weekend in September each year. This is the biggest wine festival in the region, but could not be described as a celebration of good quality local produce. The *Strassenfeste*, or street festivals, of villages such as Old Kues, Pünderich and Ürzig are far more authentic and interesting than this boozy melée.

Only the church tower and Bernkastel's ruined Burg Landshut

Trittenheim sits in the centre of a dramatic horse-shoe bend, its steep vineyards giving elegant, racy wines.

One of Bernkastel's many fine 17th-century half-timbered houses, with flags bearing the town's coat-of-arms.

Middle Mosel:North

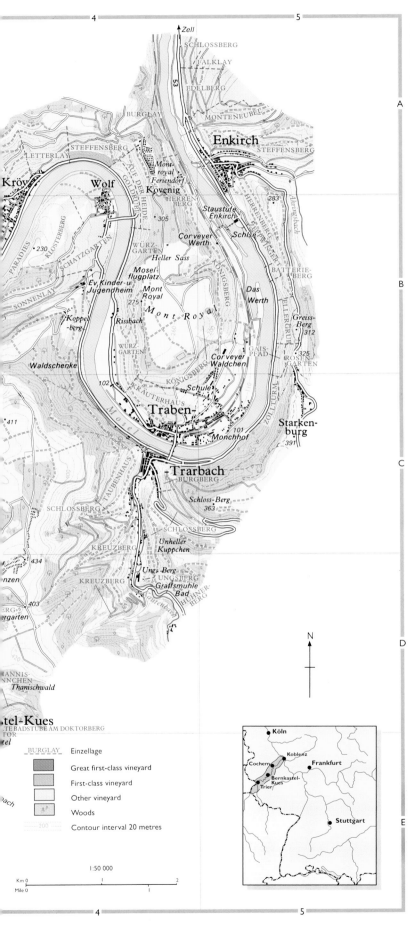

castle survive from the Middle Ages. The most impressive medieval buildings lie on the opposite bank in Kues. Directly across the bridge lies the St Nikolaus hospital, founded in the late 15th century by the philosopher and theologian Nikolaus Cusanus. The beautifully preserved house where Cusanus was born lies a short distance away on the bank of the Mosel.

In spite of these riches many would contend that the Art Nouveau buildings represent Bernkastel-Kues' architectural highpoint. Wonderful discoveries can be made at almost every corner of the town's narrow streets. Both the former railway stations are fine examples, as are several hotels, such as Hotel Drei Könige and Hotel Kardinalsberg (both in Kues) and wine estates such as Wwe Dr H Thanisch (Saarallee, Kues) and Dr Pauly-Bergweiler (Gestade, Bernkastel).

Graach by contrast has only a couple of grand houses. Winemaking is and always has been its first industry and its wines deserve to be taken very seriously. Set back somewhat from the river, even its most precipitous vineyards have deep soil. This makes its wines fuller and firmer than those of Bernkastel. Not necessarily the most charming of Mosel wines in their youth, they have tremendous ageing potential – particularly the wines from the village's top site, the Graacher Domprobst. Domprobst wines from the Willi Schaefer estate are classic Graacher Rieslings with pronounced blackcurrant and citrus notes. Kees-Kieren, Max Ferd Richter, Selbach-Oster and Dr Weins-Prüm make Domprobst wines that often come close to matching those from Willi Schaefer.

Just outside the village lies the Josephshof, a complex of fine old buildings which was once the jewel in Graach's crown. Sadly, it is now in desperate need of renovation. Nevertheless the owners, the Reichsgraf von Kesselstatt estate of Trier, continue to make some impressively big, firm and rich wines from their wholly-owned Josephshof site. The Graacher Himmelreich is an extremely large site, parts of which are excellent, others only moderately good. The finest Himmelreich wines come from the Dr Loosen and Joh Jos Prüm estates and are comparable with Domprobst's best.

For wine-lovers around the world the Wehlener Sonnenuhr name is synonymous with great Rieslings. In top vintages the site yields the richest, silkiest, most seductive wines on the Mosel. The fame of these Rieslings is inextricably linked with that of the Joh Jos Prüm estate whose late-harvest Auslese and higher quality Prädikat wines are perhaps the most elegant dessert wines in the world. These are some of the most widely collected of all German wines and one of them – the '90 Riesling Trockenbeerenauslese – broke the world record in 1994 for the most expensive young white wine by selling for DM 1575,50 per bottle.

Joh Jos Prüm occupies one of a row of magnificent houses lining the Uferallee on the river bank at Wehlen. These houses and the suspension bridge give Wehlen a uniquely aristocratic appearance among Mosel wine villages. The sun dial that gave the vineyard its name is set among rocks high in the precipitous slope of the Wehlener Sonnenuhr. It was constructed by Jadocus Prüm in 1842 and has become one of the area's best known landmarks.

The Wehlener Sonnenuhr gives wines that are easy to appreciate even in their youth. Excepting the very slow-developing wines from Joh Jos Prüm, Wehlener Sonnenuhrs are charmers virtually from the moment they are in the bottle. A top-class example should possess a combination of pure peach-like fruit and a haunting scent of honeysuckle and be rich yet refined. At their glorious best the wines manage an astonishing balancing act between depth and concentration of flavour on the one hand and tremendous subtlety and delicacy on the other. Recent vintages producing such wines were the '90 and '88, both of which were sensational.

Fine Wehlener Sonnenuhr wines are also regularly made by Heribert Kerpen, Dr Loosen, SA Prüm, Christoffel-Prüm, Willi Schaefer, Selbach-Oster and Dr Weins-Prüm. The number of good producers here is a product of the fierce quality competition among the Prüm family's various branches and other ambitious vintners. This rivalry dates back to the 1920s when Wehlen wines enjoyed a good reputation, but even then it was nothing like the fame or popularity they enjoy today. Joh Jos Prüm and Wehlen began their present ascendancy during the late 1940s and early 1950s.

The Zeltinger Sonnenuhr site by contrast has only one real champion: Selbach-Oster. A single estate, alone in its league, has less opportunity to publicise the quality of its wines and as a result this site does not enjoy such prestige as its competitively marketed neighbour. The wines tend to be a little more powerful and earthy than those of Wehlen, and to develop more slowly. Certainly the site's potential is no less than that of the Wehlener Sonnenuhr, and with its many small cliffs and ruined castle the Zeltinger Sonnenuhr is every bit as impressive to the eye as its more famous neighbour. Joh Jos Prüm is also a very good source for these wines.

Although rather lighter, the wines from the slopes of the Zeltinger Schlossberg behind the town's church can also have an impressive mineral piquancy in years with hot summers. The smaller part of the Zeltinger Himmelreich, situated directly above the Sonnenuhr site, also has the potential to give classic Mosel Rieslings up to Spätlese quality, but sadly it shares the site name with a larger area of flat, heavy-soiled vineyards. Across the Mosel in a small side valley lies the Wehlener Klosterberg, which in good vintages can give appealing, crisp, blackcurrant-scented wines.

The distance between Zeltingen and Ürzig is a mere two-and-a-half kilometres as the crow flies, yet the contrast between their vineyards' appearance and their wines' style is enormous. The loop of the Mosel, the massive red slate cliffs which form the border between the top vineyards of Ürzig and Erden and Ürzig's red sandstone soil make this one of the most spectacular corners of the Mosel Valley. Spectacular also describes the wines of Erden and Ürzig, which have long divided even expert opinion. For some they are among the best German Rieslings while for others they are too atypical to be counted among the Mosel-Saar-Ruwer's greatest wines.

An extremely warm microclimate gives these wines remarkable richness and power for Mosel Rieslings and the special soil results in unique aromas. Strawberry, banana, spice and earth notes are typical for Ürziger Würzgarten wines, while those from the Erdener Treppchen are herbal, creamy and mineral. The greatest wines of all are the concentrated, seductively tropical wines from the Erdener Prälat, a narrow strip of vines with perfect south-westerly exposure nestling between the cliffs and the river bank.

Since the late 1980s Bernkastel's Dr Loosen estate has been producing sensational wines, some of the greatest German Rieslings, from these three sites. No wines have such intense character from the soil as these masterpieces. Their quality has much to do with the old, ungrafted vines planted in most of the estate's vineyards. Grafted vines with American root stock were introduced after the Phylloxera mite virtually destroyed European vineyards during the late 19th and early 20th centuries. American root stock is immune to the Phylloxera mite, but in the eyes of many top Mosel vintners grafted vines cannot not give such high-quality fruit as ungrafted ones. Only a few soil types, such as Mosel slate, are so inhospitable to Phylloxera that ungrafted vines can still be cultivated. Other important producers of Ürzig and Erden wines are Joh Jos Christoffel, Merkelbach, Dr F Weins-Prüm, Christoffel Prüm and Meulenhof.

The first-class Erdener Prälat vineyard (above and right), the furthest downstream of the Mosel's truly great vineyards, enjoys the warmest microclimate in the Mosel-Saar-Ruwer. Its ancient ungrafted vines give rich, opulent wines.

Further downstream there are a number of good vineyard sites but few vintners who can translate this into wines of any special quality. The Kinheimer Hubertuslay, Kröver Steffensberg, Wolfer Goldgrube, Enkircher Zeppwingert and Batterieberg are all marvellous vineyards looking for champions.

This section of the valley is home to many of the region's organic wine producers. They are remarkable and frequently eccentric characters to whom an entire book could easily be devoted. Among them, Clemens Busch of Pünderich is particularly worthy of mention since his wines are as full of character as he is. These intensely mineral and spicy Rieslings are among the best dry wines in the region. At Pünderich the river makes its tightest loop: looking down from the vantage point of Marienburg Castle, the Mosel can be seen sweeping by on both sides.

Wine-lovers around the world tend to assume that Mittel Mosel wines are all light, crisp and flowery. In fact the diversity of soils and varying exposure of the area's top sites results in an exceptionally wide range of wines. This, combined with the dedication to quality of the region's best winemakers, makes it without question one of the great wine-producing regions of the world.

BENCHMARK WINES

Brauneberger Juffer-Sonnenuhr Riesling Kabinett
Weingut Fritz Haag, Brauneberg
Vineyard site: Brauneberger Juffer-Sonnenuhr
Site area: 10.5 hectares, 2 hectares Fritz Haag
Exposure: southeast
Inclination: very steep
Soil: weathered grey slate, stony top-soil, deep sub-soil
Description: Fritz Haag's Brauneberg Kabinetts have exceptional depth and character but, with about eight degrees of alcohol, no more body than other Mosel-Saar-Ruwer wines of this style. Vibrant white peach, vanilla and mineral aromas, together with a mouthwatering racy acidity, make them some of the most intense 'light' wines in the world.
Best vintages: '93, '91, '90, '88, '87, '86, '85, '83, '81, '79
Best drunk: Although they can live 15 to 20 years, Fritz Haag's Kabinett wines can also give enormous pleasure in their youth, especially when partnered by smoked salmon or ham.

Piesporter Goldtröpfchen Riesling Spätlese
Weingut Reinhold Haart, Piesport
Vineyard site: Piesporter Goldtröpfchen
Site area: 65 hectares, 3 hectares Reinhold Haart
Exposure: southeast, south and southwest
Inclination: very steep
Soil: deep, weathered grey slate, plenty of clay-like material
Description: Explosively fruity, brimming with blackcurrant, citrus and peach, Reinhold Haart's Goldtröpfchens are proof that Piesport's top wines are among the Mosel-Saar-Ruwer's finest. In spite of their exuberance and intensity they are not lush or over-blown but refined and perfectly poised.
Best vintages: '94, '93, '91, '90, '89, '88, '83, '76, '75, '71
Best drunk: Reinhold Haart's wines are less inclined to have a 'closed' or 'dumb' phase between youth and maturity than most Mosel-Saar-Ruwer wines. These Spätlese are delicious drunk at two or three years of age but can also mature for more than 20 years without losing any of their charm.

Tending the vertiginous slopes of the best vineyards is arduous and labour-intensive work which must be done entirely by hand. It can also but can be dangerous: hand rails, ropes and pulleys are not provided!

Ürziger Würzgarten Riesling Auslese
Weingut Dr Loosen, Bernkastel

Vineyard site: Ürziger Würzgarten
Site area: 55, 2 hectares Dr Loosen
Exposure: south to southeast
Inclination: moderately to very steep
Soil: red sandstone; some red slate in the top-soil
Description: Not all Mosel Rieslings are light and flowery. Dr Loosen's old vines in the Würzgarten give wines packed to bursting point with fruit, spice and extract from the soil. Rich in texture and many-faceted in aroma and flavour, these are great wines by any standards.
Best vintages: '94, '93, '92, '91, '90, '88, '85, '75, '71
Best drunk: Wines as concentrated as these demand to be the centre of attention so food, if served at all, must play a subordinate role. Although they are imposing in their youth, they show their real glory from ten years of age.

Wehlener Sonnenuhr Riesling Spätlese
Weingut Joh Jos Prüm, Wehlen

Vineyard site: Wehlener Sonnenuhr
Site area: 50 hectares, 5 hectares Joh Jos Prüm
Exposure: southwest
Inclination: very steep
Soil: very stony weathered grey slate

Description: Joh Jos Prüm's Sonnenuhrs are classic examples of the way in which the best Mosel wines' natural sweetness magnifies, rather than obscures, their character. These are a perfect marriage of Riesling's peach-like, floral and mineral aspects. White wine cannot be fresher, more vivid and delightful.
Best vintages: '94, '93, '92, '91, '90, '89, '88, '86, '85, '83, '81, '79
Best drunk: Joh Jos Prüm's wines develop more slowly than other Mosel-Saar-Ruwer Rieslings and the Spätlese need two to four years from the vintage to begin giving their best. They can easily stand 20 and more years' ageing.

Unter Mosel

Where the border between the Mittel Mosel and Unter Mosel lies is a matter of some debate. Most experts would contend that it runs through the wine town of Zell, famous for its Schwarzer Katz (Black Cat) Grosslage. However, none would deny that the Riesling wines from the rocky Unter Mosel Valley have a distinctive style. Here the great majority of vineyards are planted on narrow terraces (hence the new alternative name for the area, 'Terrassen-Mosel') giving the landscape a character quite different from the rest of the region. The warm microclimate in the best sites and the extremely stony soils result in wines that are fuller and softer than those of the Mittel Mosel.

The abundant Medieval architecture also gives the towns and villages a completely different appearance from those of the Mittel Mosel. Louis XIV's troops, who occupied the region during the latter part of the 17th century, were less destructive here than further upriver. Burg Eltz, an astonishingly well preserved fairy-tale castle close to Moselkern, should be on any visitor's itinerary.

This little-known part of the region is home to the world's steepest vineyard, the precipitous Bremmer Calmont (part of which belongs to the neighbouring village of Eller). While Reinhold Franzen makes good dry wines from this site and the nearby Neefer Frauenberg, no one is currently making sweet wines that realise the site's full potential. A short distance downstream are several other vineyards capable of yielding fine Rieslings. Heinz Dehren's wines from the Conder Nikolausberg and the tongue-twister Ellenzer Rüberberger Domherrenberg prove that they deserve to recover the reputation they enjoyed during the last century. The Valwiger Herrenberg belongs in the same class.

The most important wine villages here are Lehmen, Kobern-Gondorf and Winningen. Their excellent vineyards, together with a handful of ambitious winemakers, guarantee that we shall hear these names more frequently in the future. The most consistent producer here is Heymann-Löwenstein, though Freiherr von Heddesdorf and Freiherr von Schleinitz frequently make good wines. The sight of the soaring terraces of the Winninger Uhlen next to the Autobahn bridge over the Mosel should be enough to convince anybody that great wine can be made here.

BENCHMARK WINE

Winninger Uhlen Riesling QbA Trocken
Weingut Heymann-Löwenstein, Winningen
Vineyard site: Winninger Uhlen
Site area: 14 hectares, 1 hectare Heymann-Löwenstein
Exposure: southwest
Inclination: very steep; terraced
Soil: greywacke, extremely stony
Description: Quite full-bodied, rich in bouquet and flavour but bone dry, these are hardly typical Mosel wines. But with their full peach- and pineapple-like fruit and intense mineral character they are arguably the Unter Mosel's most distinctive examples.
Best vintages: '94, '93, '92, '91, '90
Best drunk: Unlike most Mosel Rieslings, these wines cry out for food. Their dryness and pronounced acidity enable them to cut through the fat of rich sauces or full-fat cheeses. Unlike most Unter Mosel wines, these need bottle-age to show their best and can live for up to a decade.

Some of the terraced vineyards typical of the area have fallen out of cultivation around Hatzenport on the Unter Mosel.

BEST PRODUCERS

Weingut Clemens Busch

Im Wingert 39,
56862 Pünderich
Owners: Clemens and Rita Busch
Vineyard area: 4.5 hectares
Grape varieties: 84% Riesling,
12% Müller-Thurgau,
4% Spätburgunder
Top site: Pündericher Marienburg

With his long hair and beard Clemens Busch looks like the stereotypical image of an 'alternative' organic vintner. He is an extremely talented young winemaker. Until recently, when the estate began to take public relations seriously, this promise was known only to a handful of insiders. Now Clemens Busch is recognised not only as one of Germany's top organic vintners, but also as the best producer of Rieslings from the excellent Pündericher Marienburg vineyard.

Unlike many organic winemakers on the Mosel there is no trace of dogma in Clemens Busch. Wine quality is no less important to him than the production methods. He developed his own style of dry wine during the late 1980s: Rieslings with a firm backbone of acidity that are so packed with fruit and flavour that the acidity is never dominant. Always extremely fresh as young wines, the best of them need several years' bottle-age for their intensely mineral character to develop fully. The estate's Auslese Trocken and Halbtrocken wines from the Marienburg are some of the few truly outstanding dry Rieslings produced in the Mosel-Saar-Ruwer.

Weingut Joh Jos Christoffel Erben

Schanzstrasse 2,
54539 Ürzig
Owners: Hans Leo and
Hilde Christoffel
Vineyard area: 2.25 hectares
Grape varieties: 100% Riesling
Top sites: Erdener Treppchen,
Ürziger Würzgarten

Compared to many of the Rhine regions' larger estates, that of Hans-Leo and Hilde Christoffel is a miniature – but what a perfect miniature! Holdings in two of Germany's best Riesling vineyards and Hans-Leo's masterly craftsmanship in the cellar makes this one of the top addresses in the Mosel Valley.

The Christoffel estate makes the most elegant of all Ürziger Würzgarten wines, marrying the vineyard's typical power and exotic-spicy character with a lightness of touch that makes them as delightful as they are serious. As young wines they have a dazzling harmony of

strawberry-, peach- and pineapple-like fruit with a vibrancy and clarity that prevents them from being too lush or opulent. They are also capable of long ageing, gaining in subtlety and silkiness as they mature. Although most of the production here is of classic-style Rieslings with natural sweetness, dry wines are also carefully made. Hans-Leo's wines from the Erdener Treppchen are rather sleeker and more discreet than his Würzgarten Rieslings, but no less impressive.

Weingut Fritz Haag

Dusemonder Strasse 44,
54472 Brauneberg
Owner: Wilhelm Haag
Vineyard area: 5.5 hectares
Grape varieties: 95% Riesling,
5% Müller-Thurgau and Kerner
Top sites: Brauneberger Juffer,
Brauneberger Juffer-Sonnenuhr

For more than three decades Wilhelm Haag has dedicated himself to perfecting the wines from Brauneberg's top sites with a passion no less intense than his bone-crushing handshake. The superb Rieslings he has made during this time are not only among the most sought-after in the Mosel-Saar-Ruwer but they have also helped to rebuild the great reputation enjoyed by the Brauneberg a century and more ago.

Wilhelm Haag's wines have a crystalline clarity and raciness that call to mind a brilliant-cut diamond. Their fruit character is both intense and restrained, becoming lush and exotic only in the best Auslese or higher quality Prädikat wines. Even here it is interwoven with subtle mineral notes that give the wines a delicacy

The history of Wilhelm Haag's distinguished estate can be traced to the early 17th century.

remarkable at this elevated level of richness. Although it is with Riesling BAs and TBAs that Wilhelm Haag has made headline prices, the estate's reputation is based no less on the quality of its excellent 'Gutsweine', dry Riesling QbAs which are sold without a vineyard designation. Wine quality here begins with the simplest wines, a reflection of Wilhelm Haag's belief that producers should be judged upon their entire range. By these standards he is unquestionably one of the Mosel-Saar-Ruwer's great winemakers.

Weingut Reinhold Haart

Ausoniusufer 18,
54498 Piesport
Owner: Theo Haart
Vineyard area: 5.75 hectares
Grape varieties: 93% Riesling,
5% Müller-Thurgau,
2% Weissburgunder
Top sites: Piesporter Domherr,
Piesporter Goldtröpfchen,
Wintricher Ohligsberg

Since 1988 Theo Haart has dedicated himself to proving the true

Theo Haart makes ripe and honeyed Goldtröpfchen at his Piesport estate.

worth of the Piesporter Goldtröpfchen. His wines from this most underrated and commercially over-exploited of the Mosel's top sites are among the region's finest. It is hard to imagine how anybody who tastes one of this estate's Rieslings could ever want to see another bottle of the 'sugar-water' sold in supermarkets under the Piesporter Michelsberg Grosslage name.

Riesling can hardly be more ravishingly aromatic than Theo Haart's Piesporter Goldtröpfchens. They are a firework display of blackcurrant-, citrus-, peach- and apple-like fruit. In spite of this there is nothing exaggerated about them; indeed they have a wonderful elegance and refinement. With the increasing recognition won by these wines, the modest and reserved Theo Haart has gained in confidence. Since 1991 he has taken up the challenge of making great wines from another top site whose reputation had also slipped during recent decades: the Wintricher Ohligsberg. Wines from here are intense, compact and have a spicy-mineral character in complete contrast to the baroque extravagance of his Goldtröpfchen Rieslings.

Weingut Heymann-Löwenstein

Bahnhofstrasse 10,
56333 Winningen
Owner: Reinhard Löwenstein
Vineyard area: 4 hectares
Grape varieties: 86% Riesling,
6% Spätburgunder,
4% Weissburgunder
Top sites: Winninger Röttgen,
Winninger Uhlen

Through the texts in his price lists and his frequent public statements Reinhard Löwenstein has gained the reputation of being an *agent provocateur* among the Mosel-Saar-Ruwer's younger vintners. However, his controversial public face has tended to distract from the fact that he is also a highly talented winemaker.

After making interesting but rather hard wines during the late 1980s, Löwenstein rethought his winemaking methods. The resulting dry Rieslings have a power and depth reminiscent of wines from much further south. They do not have the immediate fruity charm typical of the region but are more complex, having many nuances of aroma and flavour and needing time in the bottle and in the glass for their character to unfold. It is hard to imagine a more intense expression of the stony soils of Winningen's precipitous terraced vineyards than the Heymann-Löwenstein's wines.

Weingut Von Hövel
Agritiusstrasse 5–6,
54329 Oberemmel
Owner: Eberhard von Kunow
Vineyard area: 10.5 hectares
Grape varieties: 98% Riesling,
2% Weissburgunder
Top sites: Oberemmeler Hütte
(wholly owned), Scharzhofberg

Jovial Eberhard von Kunow has none of the stuffiness and pomposity projected by some German vintners. As seriously as he takes the work in both vineyard and cellar, his guiding principle is that his wines should give the maximum pleasure. This philosophy is fully reflected in the appealingly fruity, harmonious von Hövel Rieslings.

Although the estate has sizeable holdings in the world-famous Scharzhofberg vineyard, many of its best wines come from Eberhard von Kunow's wholly-owned Oberemmeler Hütte site. In good vintages the Kabinett and Spätlese wines from here have a floral delicacy that is rare among Saar wines, while the Auslese are at once luscious and refreshing. Von Hövel Scharzhofberg Rieslings are richer and more powerful with a slight earthiness. Even the estate's QbA wines, which are marketed under the 'Balduin von Hövel' name are full of fruit and character.

Weingut Karlsmühle
Lorenzhof,
54318 Mertesdorf
Owner: Peter Geiben
Vineyard area: 12 hectares
Grape varieties: 92% Riesling,
3% Müller-Thurgau, 3% Findling,
2% Weissburgunder
Top sites: Kaseler Kehrnagel,
Kaseler Nies'chen, Lorenzhöfer Felslay
(wholly owned), Lorenzhöfer
Mäuerchen (wholly owned)

In his old jeans, pullover and sandals vintner Peter Geiben cuts a most unlikely figure as the rising star

of the Ruwer. However, since the mid-1980s he has been making some of the most expressive wines in the valley. Their dramatic fruit aromas span from apricot-like through blackcurrant and pineapple to grapefruit and his best wines have an almost supernatural intensity. The vivid acidity gives them a mouthwatering vibrancy and great ageing potential.

Until recently the estate's production was dominated by wines from its two wholly-owned Lorenzhöfer sites, but in 1994 Peter Geiben was able to expand his vineyard holdings in the two top sites of Kasel: the Nies'chen and Kehrnagel. Wines from here have a mineral-herbal character in addition to the explosive fruit typical of the estate. Somehow between cultivating the vineyards, the cellar work, wine tastings and hunting, Peter Geiben also finds the time to help run the family's rustic hotel and restaurant which also bear the Karlsmühle name.

Gutsverwaltung Rautenstrauch'sche Karthäuserhof
Karthäuserhof,
54292 Eitelsbach
Owner: Christoph Tyrell
Vineyard area: 19 hectares
Grape varieties: 97% Riesling,
3% Weissburgunder
Top site: Eitelsbacher
Karthäuserhofberg (wholly owned)

When Christoph Tyrell took over the Karthäuserhof estate with the 1986 vintage its reputation was in tatters and changes in both the vineyard and cellar were long overdue. Within remarkably few years Tyrell has succeeded in turning this situation around and introducing a distinctive new style of wine at the estate. Much credit for this is due to his energetic and committed cellar-master Ludwig Breiling.

Today the Karthäuserhof wines are crisp, clean and vibrantly fruity; model 'modern' Mosel-Saar-Ruwer Rieslings. As young wines they rarely fail to impress although some recent examples from the estate have not fulfiled the promise of their youth. On top form, the Kabinett and Spätlese wines with some natural sweetness are among the best wines of the Ruwer Valley. The Auslese and higher quality Prädikat wines are less consistent in quality. The Eisweins have been the estate's most impressive dessert wines in recent years. Dry wines also play an important role here and are consistently good.

Weingut Reichsgraf von Kesselstatt
Liebfrauenstrasse 9–10,

54290 Trier
Owners: Günther Reh family
Vineyard area: 67.5 hectares
Grape varieties: 97.5% Riesling,
2.5% other varieties
Top sites: Bernkasteler Doctor,
Bernkasteler Lay,
Graacher Josephshof (wholly owned),
Kaseler Kehrnagel,
Kaseler Nies'chen,
Piesporter Domherr,
Piesporter Goldtröpfchen,
Scharzhofberg, Trittenheimer
Apotheke, Wiltinger Gottesfuss

Annegret Reh-Gartner, the charming director of the Kesselstatt estate, seems to have been widely underestimated. During the last decade, when so many large wine estates in Germany have had problems maintaining wine quality, she has steadily pushed Kesselstatt up into the first rank of Mosel-Saar-Ruwer producers. The estate now offers a uniquely wide range of high-class Rieslings from many of the region's top sites. From QbA quality upwards, whether vinified dry or with some natural sweetness, the estate's wines are invariably of good to outstanding quality. The Kesselstatt hallmark is a seductive combination of fresh, succulent fruit and silky acidity.

The estate's best wines are from areas where its vineyard holdings are concentrated: Wiltingen Scharzhofberg and Oberemmel on the Saar, Kasel on the Ruwer, Graach and Piesport on the Mosel. They are comparable with the best wines from each respective area, which makes cellar-master Bernward Keiper a leading candidate for the title of best winemaker in the Mosel-Saar-Ruwer. No doubt he would point out that

Annegret Reh-Gartner appraises the vintage at home in Oberemmel.

Kesselstatt's state-of-the-art winery at Schloss Marienlay in the Ruwer makes his job somewhat easier.

Weingut Peter Lauer
Weinhaus Ayler Kupp,
Trierer Strasse 49,
54441 Ayl
Owner: Peter Lauer
Vineyard area: 4 hectares
Grape varieties: 100% Riesling
Top site: Ayler Kupp

The popularity of the stylish hotel and fine restaurant run by Peter Lauer and his wife Julia makes selling the wines from his small estate relatively easy. Thus he can concentrate on developing a wine style unlike any other in the Saar valley. In the cellar almost no concessions are made to modernity. The wines are made using methods similar to those common 50 years ago. The resulting Rieslings have remarkable depth and character for a region so far north and the estate's QbA, Kabinett and Spätlese wines are among the best on the Saar.

Their intense spice, mineral and floral aromas make Peter Lauer's wines distinctive. Their supple, round character is remarkable even in vintages that generally give tart, lean wines. Harmony, as opposed to the steeliness typical of the Saar, is his goal. Disappointingly, the production of Auslese and higher quality Prädikat wines is not a priority, so they are made only rarely.

Weingut Carl Loewen
Mathiasstrasse 30,
54340 Leiwen
Owner: Karl Josef Loewen
Vineyard area: 5.75 hectares
Grape varieties: 94% Riesling,
4% Müller-Thurgau, 2% Kerner
Top site: Leiwener Laurentiuslay

Karl Josef Loewen may not be the

best-known of Leiwen's many young winemakers but during the last five years he has proved himself to be among the most talented. His best Spätlese and Auslese wines in the dry and naturally sweet styles are arguably the most sophisticated Rieslings in the Mosel Valley between Trier and Piesport.

Although the estate house is unpretentious and modern and the estate has only recently joined the region's wine elite, it is difficult to avoid the word 'classic' when describing the wines. While they have abundant fruit and a floral charm there is nothing showy or superficial about them. It is rather their subtlety and perfectly proportioned harmony that makes them so impressive. The best are the rich, filigree Rieslings from the Leiwener Laurentiuslay, from which vineyard this estate makes the best wines. However, Karl-Josef Loewen also produces very good lighter, racier wines from the Detzemer Maximiner Klosterlay and Pölicher Held sites.

Weingut Dr Loosen

St Johannishof,
54470 Bernkastel-Kues
Owner: Ernst Loosen
Vineyard area: 9.5 hectares
Grape varieties: 97.5% Riesling,
2% Müller-Thurgau,
0.5% Weissburgunder
Top sites: Bernkasteler Lay,
Erdener Prälat, Erdener Treppchen,
Graacher Himmelreich,
Ürziger Würzgarten,
Wehlener Sonnenuhr

None of the German estates that came to prominence with the fine vintages of the late 1980s has enjoyed a swifter rise to fame than Weingut Dr Loosen. Since the '87 vintage, Ernst Loosen and his cellar-master Bernhard Schug have created a new style of Riesling. At many Mosel-Saar-Ruwer estates it can be difficult to

Ernst Loosen, talented winemaker at Weingut Dr Loosen in Bernkastel.

taste the difference between wines from the various sites. The Dr Loosen wines are intense and individual: the elegant, floral character of the Wehlener Sonnenuhr is quite distinct from the spicy power of the Ürziger Würzgarten.

This concentration and expressiveness of aroma and flavour owes much to the maturity of the estate's vineyards which average over 50 years of age and give the lowest yields in the region. Natural yeast is used in the exceptionally slow fermentation and the handling of the wines in the cellar is kept to a bare minimum. The methods used here are so extreme that a professor of oenology once declared them impossible! The best proof of their effectiveness are the sensational Auslese wines from the Erdener Prälat site, which are among the greatest white wines in the world. Hardly less impressive is the consistently good quality of the simple wines produced here, QbA and Kabinett wines marketed under the Dr Loosen name without a vineyard designation.

Weingut Meulenhof

Zur Kapelle 8,
54492 Erden
Owner: Stefan Justen
Vineyard area: 4.5 hectares
Grape varieties: 66% Riesling,
34% Müller-Thurgau and Kerner
Top sites: Erdener Prälat,
Erdener Treppchen

The general level of wine quality varies quite considerably from one Mosel wine village to the next. Happily, Erden is blessed with many good small wine estates. As a consequence there are many possible sources of Riesling from the great Erdener Treppchen site. The most reliable of these is currently the Meulenhof estate.

Since the 1990 vintage when Stefan Justen took over the winemaking from his father, Heinz Justen, Meulenhof wines have become considerably richer and more powerful. While they could sometimes benefit from a touch more of the floral delicacy for which the estate was once well known, they are still some of the most expressive wines made in this part of the Mosel Valley. Wines from both the Erdener Treppchen and Prälat are also often among the best. Sadly only two hectares of the estate's vineyard holdings lie in top sites.

Weingut Egon Müller-Scharzhof and Weingut Le Gallais

Scharzhof,
54459 Wiltingen
Owners: Egon Müller (Egon Müller-Scharzhof);
Egon Müller and Gerald Villanova

(Le Gallais)
Vineyard area: 12 hectares
Grape varieties: 97.5% Riesling,
2.5% other varieties
Top sites: Scharzhofberg,
Wiltinger braune Kupp
(wholly owned)

Volumes could be written in praise of the many great late-harvest wines produced by this famous estate. Anyone wishing to experience the ultimate in Riesling nobility should look no further: few sweet wines made anywhere in the world can come close to matching the Müller's Auslese, BA, TBA and Eiswein wines. They marry the highest concentration of honeyed flavours with the greatest possible finesse. The finest of them are capable of ageing for many decades.

The Müllers' enormous success with these wines, which have frequently achieved record prices at the Trier auctions of the Grosser Ring (Mosel-Saar-Ruwer VDP) has made the estate's other wines among the most expensive in Germany. Müller's Kabinett and Spätlese wines are very good but the estate name adds a premium to their price.

The difference in character between elegant, classically proportioned Rieslings from the Scharzhofberg and the slightly richer, broader wines from the Wiltinger braune Kupp is clear to any interested wine-drinker, whether Kabinett wines from these two sites or Beerenauslese wines are being compared.

Thankfully, under the direction of Egon Müller Jr the estate seems to be all but abandoning the rather drab, dry wines produced during the late

Egon Müller's Scharzhofbergers are the world's most expensive white wines.

1980s and early 1990s in response to domestic demand.

Weingut Joh Jos Prüm

Uferallee 19,
54470 Wehlen
Owners: Dr Manfred Prüm and Wolfgang Prüm
Vineyard area: 14 hectares
Grape varieties: 100% Riesling
Top sites: Bernkasteler Lay,
Graacher Himmelreich, Wehlener Sonnenuhr, Zeltinger Sonnenuhr

Few estates in the world can claim to have maintained the highest quality standards uninterrupted for half a century and more. Joh Jos Prüm, the most famous of the many Mosel wine estates bearing the Prüm name, is one estate that can. Since the early 1920s its wines have been among Germany's best, Rieslings with the Mosel's vivacious aroma and racy elegance in its highest form.

Dr Manfred Prüm has directed Joh Jos Prüm since 1969, working cautiously to refine the winemaking methods and wine style developed by his father, Sebastian Prüm. Joh Jos Prüm wines have long been distinct from other Mosel Rieslings and as such are sometimes the subject of heated debate. They develop unusually slowly, often showing a slightly yeasty character when young, which can be confusing for those unfamiliar with the wines. However this dissipates with age as the fruit, floral and mineral characters unfold.

The estate's most seductively rich and filigree wines usually come from

The rich, substantial wines from Brauneberg's top sites, the Juffer and Juffer-Sonnenuhr, are given the highest priority. However, these often face tough competition from the firm, slightly earthy Graacher Domprobst Rieslings. Perhaps the most unusual of the Richters' wines are those from the Veldenzer Elisenberg whose piquant, racy character is reminiscent of good Ruwer wines. Eiswein is produced almost every year from the Richter's wholly-owned Mülheimer Helenenkloster site.

Weingut Schloss Saarstein
Schloss Saarstein,
54455 Serrig
Owner: Dieter Ebert
Vineyard area: 9 hectares
Grape varieties: 97% Riesling,
3% Weissburgunder
Top site: Serriger Schloss Saarstein
(wholly owned)

Christian Ebert runs this model estate on the Saar with the help of his father Dieter, a refugee from former East Germany, who bought the estate in 1956. Since then its standing has risen steadily until it is now regarded as one of the best on the Saar.

The Schloss Saarstein wines have an immediate fruity charm. Even when they have a high natural acidity, which is not rare, the fruit still triumphs. Christian Ebert's style of winemaking could be called modernist: sometimes clarity and polish are achieved at the expense of some depth and structure. Although this limits the ageing potential of his dry wines, the Schloss Saarstein Riesling Kabinett and Spätlese wines gain considerable subtlety and elegance with bottle-age. The estate's Auslese and higher quality Prädikat wines are among the most powerful and concentrated on the Saar, packed with exotic fruit, honey and spice. This is perfectly balanced with acidity and richness, giving them a dazzling brilliance and enormous ageing potential.

Weingut Willi Schaefer
Hauptstrasse 130,
54470 Graach
Owner: Willi Schaefer
Vineyard area: 2 hectares
Grape varieties: 100% Riesling
Top sites: Graacher Domprobst,
Graacher Himmelreich,
Wehlener Sonnenuhr

This tiny estate has made excellent wines since at least the 1940s and during the last decade it has become one of the leading Riesling producers on the Mittel Mosel. Willi Schaefer Jr, who has made the estate's wines since 1971, is a perfectionist with a sure feel for the needs of each individual wine. Extremely pale in colour, with a crystalline purity of

The magnificent headquarters of the Joh Jos Prüm estate in Wehlen.

the Wehlener Sonnenuhr, directly across the river from the Art Nouveau estate house on the river bank in Wehlen. In the right vintage the firm, slightly less fine wines from the Graacher Himmelreich can almost match these. The peach-like fruit and supple acidity of the Zeltinger Sonnenuhr wines makes them well suited to being vinified dry.

Weingut Johann Peter Reinert
Alter Weg 7a,
54441 Kanzem
Owner: Johann Peter Reinert
Vineyard area: 3.5 hectares
Grape varieties: 76% Riesling,
8.5% Elbling, 6.5% Ortega,
6% Müller-Thurgau, 3% Bacchus
Top site: Ayler Kupp

This small estate has long been known to a privileged few as a source of excellent Saar Rieslings. Only very

recently has it begun to be more widely recognised, owing to its success at auctions of the Bernkasteler Ring association of Mosel-Saar-Ruwer wine estates. The impressive quality standard is the result of Johann Peter Reinert's systematic, almost scientific, approach to viticulture and winemaking. There is however nothing clinical about the results. The wine's emphasis is on fruit: the apple, peach and pineapple flavours always clean and absolutely clear. The acidity is refreshing without having the hard edge found in many Saar wines. Appealing in their youth, they also age well. During the last few years Reinert has devoted increasing energy to the wines from his best vineyard site, the Ayler Kupp, with impressive results.

Weingut Max Ferd Richter
Hauptstrasse 85,
54486 Mülheim
Owner: Horst MF Richter
Vineyard area: 14.75 hectares

Grape varieties: 85% Riesling,
8% Müller-Thurgau, 5% Kerner,
2% other varieties
Top sites: Brauneberger Juffer,
Brauneberger Juffer-Sonnenuhr,
Erdener Treppchen, Graacher
Domprobst, Graacher Himmelreich,
Wehlener Sonnenuhr

Well-known internationally, this important Mosel estate is hardly recognised within Germany itself. The Richters produce a wide range of Riesling wines of good to outstanding quality from vineyard holdings in many of the top sites between Brauneberg and Traben-Trarbach. Although both Horst Richter and his son Dr Dirk Richter (who now directs the estate) both prefer Mosel Rieslings with some natural sweetness, they have invested a great deal of energy in the estate's drier-style wines. As a result it is difficult to single out which of the Richter's various styles to call the best.

aroma and flavour, his racy wines are neither extrovert nor showy. They seem to embody the northerly coolness of the Mosel Valley's climate and the stoniness of its slate soils. They are delightful and fascinating drunk young and yet his intensely mineral wines from the great Graacher Domprobst vineyard do not reach their peak until their second or third decade.

Although the vaulted cellars beneath the Schaefer's house are well equipped, the first principle here is respect for each wine's inherent character, regardless of whether it is a 'simple' QbA or a concentrated Beerenauslese.

C Von Schubert'sche Gutsverwaltung, Maximin Grünhaus

Grünhaus,
54318 Mertesdorf
Owners: Dr Carl and Andreas von Schubert
Vineyard area: 33 hectares
Grape varieties: 97% Riesling, 3% Müller-Thurgau and Kerner
Top sites: Maximin Grünhäuser Abtsberg (wholly owned), Maximin Grünhäuser Herrenberg (wholly owned)

Widely recognised as one of Germany's finest wine estates, Maximin Grünhaus wines seem to epitomise all that is great about German Riesling. They have a combination of aromatic intensity, delicacy and crispness that no other wine-growing nation can match. Both as fresh young wines and as mature wines of ten, 20 and more years of age they possess a charm and sophistication that make them delightful and fascinating. The estate's hallmark floral, herbal and mineral notes can be found even in the QbA wines of below-average vintages. In the Auslese wines of top vintages this character is married to peach and apricot flavours that are at once rich and fine. Dry wines are taken as seriously as those with natural sweetness and exceptional results are achieved in both styles.

Unlike most German wine estates whose vineyards are typically scattered around several villages, Maximin Grünhaus' vines cover a single slope. This is divided into three wholly-owned vineyards, each of which gives distinctly different wines. The finest of these are usually those from the Abtsberg, which possess a classical elegance and great subtlety of flavour. The red slate soil of the Herrenberg makes these wines more extrovertly aromatic. In years with very hot summers their slightly more pronounced acidity can give them an edge over the Abtsberg wines. The

Dr Carl von Schubert's family bought the Maximin Grünhaus estate in 1882.

less well-exposed Bruderberg gives much lighter wines that are tart and fresh.

Dr Carl von Schubert's first principle in making the estate's wines is to maintain their distinct personalities. With this in mind, the modernisations of the last decade have been circumspect.

Weingut Selbach-Oster and Frühmesse Stiftung

Uferallee 23,
54492 Zeltingen
Owner: Johannes Selbach
Vineyard area: 8.25 hectares
Grape varieties: 100% Riesling
Top sites: Graacher Domprobst, Wehlener Sonnenuhr, Zeltinger Schlossberg, Zeltinger Sonnenuhr

Johannes Selbach is currently recognised as one of the most talented young winemakers of the Mittel Mosel, just as his father, Hans Selbach, was 20 and more years ago. Between 1966 and the late 1980s Hans Selbach built up the estate from a quarter of its current size, making it by far the most important in the village of Zeltingen. When Johannes returned to the Mosel in 1988, having worked in the United States for several years, a new chapter in the short history of Selbach-Oster was opened. Today the Selbach's goal is not only to make their estate one of the best on the Mittel Mosel, but also to place it firmly among Germany's

wine elite and to make the Zeltinger Sonnenuhr vineyard as famous as the neighbouring Wehlener Sonnenuhr.

Selbach-Oster wines are classic Mittel Mosel Rieslings: richly fruity and filigree, deep and elegant. These qualities are most clearly displayed in Johannes Selbach's wines from the Zeltinger Sonnenuhr vineyard, but in good vintages the slightly lighter, racier wines from the Zeltinger Schlossberg can come close to matching them. Although Selbach-Oster has a small holding in the Wehlener Sonnenuhr, it is more often the firm, powerful wines from the Graacher Domprobst that offer real competition.

Weingut Wwe Dr H Thanisch

Saarallee 31,
54470 Bernkastel-Kues
Owners: Mechthild Thanisch and Sofia Spier
Vineyard area: 6.5 hectares
Grape varieties: 100% Riesling
Top sites: Bernkasteler Doctor, Bernkasteler Graben, Bernkasteler Lay, Brauneberger Juffer-Sonnenuhr, Graacher Domprobst, Graacher Himmelreich

This estate was first brought to prominence with the legendary '21 Bernkasteler Doctor Riesling TBA, the first wine of this quality ever made in the Mittel Mosel, and the series of late-harvest masterpieces that followed it. The Thanisch estate still holds the record for the most

expensive Mosel-Saar-Ruwer wine ever bought, a single bottle having been sold at the VDP rarities auction in November 1985 for DM 11,500. Many of the estate's recent top Auslese and higher quality Prädikat wines are worthy successors to those legendary wines.

Thanisch wines of recent vintages are sleek and pure, with a delicate fruit and mineral character. Their strength is elegance and refinement rather than opulence or power; the qualities which have made Bernkastel one of the best-known of all German wine towns. Nevertheless, many of the estate's Bernkasteler Doctor wines of Kabinett and Spätlese quality are not significantly better than comparable wines from the Bernkasteler Lay and Graben sites, in spite of their being much more expensive.

Weingut Dr Heinz Wagner

Bahnhofstrasse 3,
54439 Saarburg
Owner: Heinz Wagner
Vineyard area: 9 hectares
Grape varieties: 100% Riesling
Top sites: Ayler Kupp, Ockfener Bockstein, Saarburger Rausch

Heinz Wagner is a born vintner who seems always to have known what kind of wines he wanted to make. The sureness of his hand in the vineyard and cellar is reflected in wines of consistently high quality whether nature is kind or not. His Rieslings are solid and substantial yet beautifully balanced and refined. As well as abundant subtlety they have plenty of immediate sensual appeal.

It is hard to determine exactly why this estate's wines are so good but two important factors are the rigorous selective harvesting and a winemaking philosophy based upon patience and caution. In the cavernous cellars as little as possible is done to disturb the wines as they mature in barrel. It is often difficult to judge between the richer, spicier wines from the Saarburger Rausch vineyard and the elegant, filigree Rieslings from the more famous Ockfener Bockstein site, all of which, in both the dry and naturally sweet styles, are among the Saar's best wines.

Weingut Dr F Weins-Prüm

Uferallee 20,
54470 Wehlen
Owner: Bert Selbach
Vineyard area: 4 hectares
Grape varieties: 97% Riesling, 3% Müller-Thurgau
Top sites: Erdener Prälat, Graacher Domprobst, Graacher Himmelreich, Ürziger Würzgarten,

Wehlener Sonnenuhr

Bert Selbach makes classical, racy Rieslings from half a dozen of the Mittel Mosel's top sites as well as some extremely pretty lighter wines from the estate's holdings at Waldrach in the Ruwer. A high standard is maintained throughout the wide range produced here: even the estate's QbA wines (most of which are marketed without vineyard designation as 'Gutsweine') are well crafted.

Weins-Prüm's widely scattered vineyards allow Bert Selbach an objective view of various sites' comparative merits. He would be the first to concede that not every good vintage favours the Wehlener Sonnenuhr over his other sites and that his best wines often come from the Erdener Prälat and Ürziger Würzgarten. These are among the finest expressions of the sites' uniquely spicy and exotic character. Selbach's wines from the Domprobst and Himmelreich vineyards of Graach also deserve to be taken seriously, having the firm, slightly earthy personality typical of the village.

Weingut Forstmeister Geltz Zilliken

Heckingstrasse 20,
54439 Saarburg
Owner: Hans-Joachim Zilliken
Vineyard area: 10 hectares
Grape varieties: 100% Riesling
Top sites: Ockfener Bockstein, Saarburger Rausch

Hanno Zilliken makes some of the most uncompromising wines in the Mosel-Saar-Ruwer. Intensely steely, tightly wound in their youth and capable of living for many decades, they are the ultimate expression of Saar Rieslings' unique personality. This extreme style follows from Hanno Zilliken's belief that Saar wines show their true greatness only when they age as slowly as possible. His marvellously fresh, super-elegant wines

from the '83, '79, '76, '75 and '71 vintages are compelling evidence in support of his theory.

Zilliken has recently come to the surprising conclusion that his young wines can show better when drunk with spicy food than when drunk by themselves; an idea which has caused some eyebrow-raising among his colleagues. Certainly their typical high natural acidity makes even his Kabinett and Spätlese wines with natural sweetness taste virtually dry. This applies particularly to his wines from the Saarburger Rausch, which are as mineral and piquant as Saar Riesling can be. Eisweins from this site are among the greatest in Germany.

OTHER WELL KNOWN PRODUCERS

Weingut Dr Pauly Berweiler and Weingut Peter Nicolay
Gestade 15,
54470 Bernkastel-Kues
In the right vintage this important twin estate, with holdings in almost all the top sites between Bernkastel and Ürzig, can make wines that combine richness with clarity and elegance.

Bischöfliche Weingüter
Gervasiusstrasse 1,
54290 Trier
The famous clerical estates of the Hohe Domkirche, Bischöfliche Priesterseminar and Bischöfliches Konvikt form the Bischöfliche Weingüter: 100 acres of vineyard scattered throughout the region. The best sites include substantial holdings in the first-class Scharzhofberg and Erdener Prälat. Wines are still vinified in wooden *Fuder* casks in labyrinthine cellars below Trier. After a low period during the 1980s wines improved significantly during the early 1990s. Not yet up to its former high standards, this is still a dependable source of good-quality Riesling.

Weingut Jos Christoffel Jr, Christoffel-Prüm
Moselufer 1,
54539 Ürzig
Although often rather sweet, in good vintages this small estate makes some classic wines from the Erdener Treppchen, Ürziger Würzgarten and Wehlener Sonnenuhr.

Weingut Ernst Clüsserath
Moselweinstrasse 67
54349 Trittenheim
Ernst Clüsserath's wines have improved in leaps and bounds during recent years. His Rieslings from the Trittenheimer Apotheke combine richness and subtlety.

Weingüter Dr Fischer
Bocksteinhof,
54441 Ockfen
The estate's best wines are the succulent Spätlese and Auslese from the wholly-owned Wawerner Herrenberg. Sadly, Ockfener Bockstein Rieslings can be a little rustic.

Weingut Grans-Fassian
Römerstrasse 28,
54340 Leiwen
Gerhard Grans' least successful wines are as unharmonious as his best wines are racy and filigree. Here the dry wines and the Spätlese with natural sweetness tend to be the best. Eiswein is an important speciality.

Weingut Willi Haag
Hauptstrasse 111,
54472 Brauneberg
Some of the ordinary-quality wines here can lack liveliness and elegance, but the best Riesling Spätlese and Auslese can be rich and impressive.

Weingut Jordan und Jordan (Van Volxem)
Dehenstrasse 2,
54459 Wiltingen
Judging by its first wines under Peter Jordan, this once-famous estate is set to become a new star in the region. Its main strengths seem to be substantial dry wines and complex, mineral-toned Auslese.

Weingut Kees-Kieren
Hauptstrasse 22,
54470 Graach
During recent years the wines of this small Graach estate have been steadily improving. Clean, pure and crisp, the only thing they lack is a little depth and persistence of flavour.

Weingut Heribert Kerpen
Uferallee 6,
54470 Wehlen
Although the performance of this fine estate has slipped a little during recent years, its Spätlese and Auslese wines

from the Wehlener Sonnenuhr can still be impressively rich and silky.

Weingut Lauerburg
Graacher Strasse 24,
54470 Bernkastel-Kues
In good vintages this estate makes excellent Rieslings from its Bernkastel vineyards. They have the region's typical raciness and delicate fruit.

Weingut Lehnert-Veit
In der Duhr 10,
54498 Piesport
This small estate has become a dependable source of clean, crisp, fruity Rieslings from the great Piesporter Goldtröpfchen vineyard.

Weingut Schloss Lieser
Am Markt 1,
54470 Lieser
With his first two vintages at this revitalised estate Thomas Haag has proved that he has the potential to match the success of his father, Wilhelm Haag of Weingut Fritz Haag.

Weingut Merkelbach
Laurentiushof,
54349 Trittenheim
Brothers Alfred and Harald Merkelbach make marvellously old-fashioned wines from the Erdener Treppchen and Ürziger Würzgarten. The wines are full of character and never too sweet.

Weingut Piedmont
Saartal 1,
54329 Filzen
Claus Piedmont specialises in light, crisp Saar wines of QbA, Kabinett and Spätlese quality. In recent years many have been clean and appealingly fruity.

Weingut S A Prüm
Uferallee 25–26,
54470 Wehlen
After several difficult years during the 1980s, this estate seems to be back on its way to the top. The hallmarks of Raimund Prüm's Rieslings are purity of flavour, restrained sweetness and refreshing acidity.

Weingut Reuscher-Haart
Sankt-Michael-Strasse 22,
54498 Piesport
Although its future is uncertain, this estate has made many impressively powerful wines from the Piesporter Goldtröpfchen in recent years.

Weingut Sankt Urbanshof
St Urbanshof,
54340 Leiwen
Always clean and clear, this large estate's wines from the Saar and Mittel Mosel sometimes lack a little structure and subtlety. Dry wines are an important speciality.

Hanno Zilliken's Rieslings, steely and intensely mineral, are classic Saar wines.

Weingut Freiherr Von Schleinitz
Kirchstrasse 15,
56330 Kobern-Gondorf
Although quality is at times erratic, at their best this estate's wines are among the finest Rieslings in the Unter Mosel. Full of fruit, elegance and harmony they deserve to be better known.

Weingut Carl Schmitt-Wagner
Mülenstrasse 3,
54340 Longuich
Bruno Schmitt is a dedicated individual and it shows in the marvellous Rieslings he often makes from the Longuicher Maximiner Herrenberg vineyard. Richly aromatic and succulent, they are hard to resist.

Weingut Bert Simon
Herrenberg,
54455 Serrig
This substantial estate makes some classic Saar Rieslings from its wholly-owned Serriger Herrenberg and Würzberg sites, but such exceptional vineyards should have the potential to do even better.

**Weingut Stein/
Haus Waldfrieden**
Klosterkammerstrasse 14,
56858 St Aldegund
Peter and Dr Ulrich Stein make some astonishingly good wines from rather average vineyards. Dry wines predominate; Eiswein is a speciality.

**Weingut Studert-Prüm/
Maximinhof**
Hauptstrasse 150,
54470 Wehlen
Judged solely on its most successful wines, this estate is one of the best in the Mittel Mosel. Unfortunately, some of its wines tend to tire quickly or lack the area's typical filigree character.

Weingut Geheimrat J Wegeler Erben
Marterthal 1,
54470 Bernkastel-Kues
Since 1993 this 30-hectare estate has made some good dry wines and some fine Auslese from its extensive holdings in the Mittel Mosel (which include the Bernkasteler Doctor and Wehlener Sonnenuhr). Eiswein has long been a speciality, as have Sekt (sparkling) wines from top sites.

Weingut Weller-Lehnert
St Michaelstrasse 27–29,
54498 Piesport
Jörg and Petra Matheus' estate in Piesport is one of the most reliable producers from its great Goldtröpfchen vineyard. Everything produced here is at least good quality.

Travel Information

PLACES OF INTEREST

Bernkastel-Kues This famous wine town in the Mittel Mosel is full of history – and often almost as full of tourists. The marketplace is surrounded by large 17th-century half-timbered houses and the town's back streets are lined with interesting buildings. From the ruined Burg Landshut castle, a stiff climb from the town, there are magnificent views of vineyards and the surrounding countryside. An impressive row of buildings on the river front date largely from the turn of the 19th century. In Kues on the opposite bank is the St Nikolaus Hospital, founded by Nikolaus Cusanus in 1458 and still in use as an old people's home. The chapel and the library, which houses 300 handwritten books, both date from 1465. The house where Cusanus was born is nearby and all these landmarks are well preserved.

The streets of Old Kues give a feeling of what the region must have been like centuries ago. In late summer there are two annual wine festivals held here, the Kueser Strassenfest being a rather more restrained affair than the Bernkastel festival (held during the first weekend in September) at which the chief preoccupation appears to be the consumption of large quantities of indifferent-quality wine. The wine

The 11th-century Reichsburg, towering above Cochem, was rebuilt in the 1870s.

served in most of the town's bars and restaurants can also be disappointing.

Burg Eltz The sheltered position of the Elzbachtal in a side valley of the Mosel is largely what has preserved this magnificent Medieval castle. Its construction was begun around 1150 and Gothic and baroque elements were added later. It can be reached from either Moselkern or Müden but the last stretch must be undertaken on foot or by bicycle. The walk takes 30 to 40 minutes and is worth every step.

Cochem Like Bernkastel, this attractive old town with its 17th-century marketplace can be rather overwhelmed with tourists. Its Reichsburg, the most important landmark here, was destroyed by French troops in 1698 but restored some 200 years later.

The Eifel The Eifel Hills to the north of the Mosel Valley, a region volcanically active until a few thousand years ago, are more dramatic than the Hunsrück Hills to the south. A number of craters have become beautiful lakes or *Maares*, in which bathing is popular in warm weather. The most attractive is perhaps the Meerfelder Maar.

Enkirch This village has long been a Protestant island in a profoundly Catholic region and as a result has developed somewhat differently from its neighbours. It is not spectacular but there are many fine 16th- and 17th-century buildings.

The Hunsrück The Hunsrück Hills to the south of the Mosel Valley are for the most part covered with forest Given fine weather this is beautiful country but walkers should be aware that the weather can change very rapidly. Just off the A1 motorway on the B327 is the Hermeskeil Air Museum: large models of Concorde and the Saturn V moon rocket suddenly loom up by the roadside, apparently in the middle of nowhere. The sight is bizarre to say the least!

Igel The finest Roman monument outside Trier can be seen at Igel, just across the Mosel from Konz. The 23-metre high Igel Pillar is carved with scenes of everyday Roman life and mythological tableaux. In the Landesmuseum at Trier there is a full-sized reproduction which has been painted in the original gaudy colours.

Kastel-Staadt High above the twin village of Kastel-Staadt lies the Mönchsklause chapel, designed by the architect Schinkel in 1835. From here there is a magnificent view of the Saar Valley and its vineyards.

Kobern-Gondorf Kobern is perhaps the most interesting town on the Unter Mosel. Many of its half-timbered houses date from the 15th

Zeltingen is the biggest wine-growing commune on the Mosel, with vineyards that range from the mediocre to the excellent. Its first-class Sonnenuhr is named after the sundial (to the right of the church).

A carved keystone at Enkirch, part of the Mosel Valley's rich architectural legacy.

and 16th centuries and its ruined Niederburg castle was built in the 12th century. The Mathiaskapelle, a beautifully preserved late-Romanesque chapel dating from just before 1300, is said to have been built over the burial site of the head of the apostle Matthew (whose body is believed to lie in Trier).

Koblenz Together with Trier this is the most important regional centre, but Koblenz has nothing like the wealth of antiquities that are to be found in Trier. Nevertheless the old town is worth a detour. Its finest surviving building is arguably the church of St Florin, which dates from around 1100 and has some beautiful 14th-century stained-glass windows. Deutsches Eck, or 'German Corner', a monument situated at the point where the Mosel flows into the Rhine, is also worth a visit. The statue of Kaiser Wilhelm I was erected by his grandson Kaiser Wilhelm II in 1897 to underline Germany's right to the provinces on the left bank of the Rhine. Much more recently another monument to German unity was erected nearby in the form of three sections of the demolished Berlin Wall.

Completed only a few years before the French invasion of 1794, the classical-style Kurfürstliches Schloss is the town's most imposing building. On the opposite bank of the Rhine is the fortress of Ehrenbreitstein, constructed by the Prussians shortly after 1815 when the region came under their administration.

Konz In Konz, just upstream from Trier and close to the church of St Nikolaus, lies the excavated Kaiservilla. This is the former residence of Caesar Valentinian I (364–375).

Kröv This town is famous for its Grosslage Kröver Nacktarsch, literally Kröv's Bare Bottom (usually graphically depicted on the wine labels). However the town can also boast some marvellous old buildings, including the Dreigiebelhaus which dates from 1658, perhaps the finest example of the half-timbered style in the Mosel Valley.

Longuich Although not the most attractive of the Mosel Valley's many wine villages, Longuich has an impressive reconstruction of a Roman villa from the 3rd century AD.

Mehring On the right bank of the Mosel at Mehring is a reconstructed Roman Villa from the 3rd century AD.

The River Mosel The Mosel winds 206 kilometres from the French-German-Luxembourg border to its confluence with the Rhine at Koblenz. Its canalisation, principally for the barge transport of freight, was completed in 1964. It now passes through 12 locks and falls 75.5 metres during its course. Only from the river can the beauty of the valley be fully appreciated. The best points for picking up river boats are in Trier, Bernkastel-Kues and Koblenz. In recent years cycle paths have been created which extend almost the length of the valley. In addition to the many bridges criss-crossing the river (which often floods during winter months, making roads impassable) a few ferries continue to operate, mostly on the Unter Mosel.

Nennig At Nennig, in the Ober Mosel close to the French border, the remains of a large Roman villa from the 2nd century AD have been excavated, including a magnificent mosaic, the largest of its kind north of the Alps.

Piesport This idyllic village on the left bank of the Mosel is set in the centre of the Piesporter Goldtröpfchen's great amphitheatre of

vines. Here the largest surviving Roman wine press has been excavated and partially reconstructed. During the first weekend in October local vintners recreate a Roman wine harvest, including the treading of the grapes. The village's rococo church of St Michael dates from 1777 and has magnificent painted ceilings. The view from the top of the Goldtröpfchen remains almost exactly as described by the Roman poet Ausonius in his *Mosella* of 371AD.

The River Saar The vineyards of the Saar all lie within the state of Rheinland-Pfalz rather than in the Saarland. The canalisation of the river, whose course is divided between these two states, was completed in 1987 and the scars left across the countryside are now healed. The river traffic is not as heavy here as it is on the Mosel. The most beautiful stretch of the Saar Valley lies upstream of the point where the vineyards end, at Serrig. One of the best ways to see this is from the train which runs from Saarburg to Saarbrücken.

Saarburg Saarburg's history goes back at least 1,000 years, the town having become an important regional centre during the 13th century (its town charter dates from 1291). Although little from this period remains except the ruined castle which gave the town its name, there are some impressive Renaissance and baroque buildings in the centre. The 18-metre high cascade at the heart of the old town is an attractive feature.

Traben-Trarbach This small town was the centre of the wine business on the Mittel Mosel during the region's Golden Age at the end of the 19th and the beginning of the 20th centuries. It is full of beautiful buildings from this period, not least a series by the Jugendstil or Art Nouveau architect Bruno Möhring (Moselbrücke 1899, Hotel Bellevue 1901, Kellerei Julius Kayser 1907). There are also the remains of two fortresses, the Grevenburg on the Trarbach side and the gigantic Mont Royal above Traben. The latter was constructed in 1687 as a stronghold on the orders of Louis XIV in an attempt to guarantee his annexation of the region. It was destroyed by his own troops as they retreated only a few years later in 1698.

Treis-Karden The 13th-century Romanesque church of St Kastor is perhaps the most impressive on the Unter Mosel.

Trier Trier is by far the most interesting town in this part of Germany. Founded by the Emperor Augustus in 16AD, it became the largest city north of the Alps during the 4th century. Its population was then 80,000, not far from today's figure of 100,000. Almost too much remains from this period to be preserved and virtually every building

project in the vicinity has to be interrupted so that archeologists can work. There is certainly plenty to see.

The amphitheatre dates from around 100AD and would be more imposing had not so much of the masonry been removed for use as building material during the Middle Ages. The Porta Nigra, the only surviving Roman city gate, was built slightly later and is better preserved. The basalt pillars of the Römerbrücke, which is still in regular use, are of a similar age. The only remaining sections of the 6.5-kilometre town wall can be found close to the Rheinisches Landesmuseum, which houses a stunning collection of artefacts, sculptures and architectural fragments from the Roman period. Virtually next door is the Roman basilica, or more correctly Palastaula, which was constructed as the throne room for the Roman Emperor Constantine, then served as the residence of the Prince-Bishops of Trier during the Middle Ages.

The Kaiserthermen and Barbarathermen are well preserved Roman baths which give an impression of the grandeur of the Roman Empire's effective capital during its last years. The Dom, or cathedral, also belongs to this period, construction having been begun in 325AD.

Much of Trier's fascination lies in the combination of these Roman remains with the buildings from later centuries. The 13th-century Dreikönigshaus on Simeonstrasse is the finest Romanesque secular building in Trier. The most impressive building of all from this period,

however, must be the St Mathias basilica which was constructed during the 12th century, supposedly on the site where the body of Saint Matthew was buried.

The Hauptmarkt, the modern centre of the city, is a mixture of Gothic, Renaissance and baroque buildings. Trier is well endowed with rococo buildings, the most magnificent being Balthasar Neumann's St Paulin church and the Kurfürstliches Palais, which was the Trier residence of the city's Prince-Bishops during the height of their power. Karl-Marx-Haus, birthplace of the political philosopher, is also worth a visit.

Ürzig With its spectacular vineyards and many fine houses this is one of the most attractive of all Mosel wine villages. Views from the vineyards high above the Mosel are breathtaking.

HOTELS AND RESTAURANTS

Weinhaus Ayler Kupp
Trierer Strasse 49,
54441 **Ayl**
Tel: (06581) 3031, Fax: (06581) 2344
Although Peter Lauer's hotel was built in the 19th century its rooms are modern and stylish. In the restaurant his wife Julia cooks in a traditional style to a consistently high standard. The excellent wines are from the Lauer's own estate.

Hotel Zur Post
Gestade 11,
54470 **Bernkastel-Kues**
Tel: (06531) 2022,
Fax: (06531) 7387
Bernkastel's most comfortable hotel and one of the best places to stay on the Mittel Mosel. Rooms at the rear

are quieter. The restaurant can be disappointing.

Restaurant zur Malerklause
54413 **Bescheid**
Tel: (06509) 558,
Fax: (06509) 1082
Behind what looks like a public bar is one of the best restaurants in the Mosel-Saar-Ruwer. Herr and Frau Lorscheid's restaurant offers beautifully prepared French-German cuisine at modest prices. The excellent wine list is also good value.

Stone carvings with a wine motif adorn many of Traben Trarbach's great old houses.

This ancient crane on the Krahnenufer in Trier was built for lifting wine barrels in and out of river boats.

In spite of its cool climate the Mosel-Saar-Ruwer often enjoys magnificent summers.

Hotel Nicolay zur Post
Uferallee 7,
54492 **Zeltingen**
Tel: (06532) 2091, Fax: (06532) 2306
Unpretentious cooking and a modestly priced selection of good Mosel-Saar-Ruwer wines make this hotel restaurant a good venue for lunch or dinner. In spite of the hotel's less-than-captivating exterior, the rooms are comfortable and pleasant.

Hotel St Stephanus/ Restaurant Le Petit
Uferalle 9,
54492 **Zeltingen**
Tel: (06532) 2055, Fax: (06532) 3970
A stylish restaurant.

USEFUL ADDRESSES

Mosellandtouristik
Gestade 12–14, Postfach 1310,
54470 **Bernkastel-Kues**
Tel: (06531) 2091, Fax: (06531) 2093
The most important source of travel information for the Mittel Mosel. The Moselland-Radwanderführer is essential for anyone planning to take advantage of the region's numerous cycle paths.

Rhein-Mosel-Eifel-Touristik
Bahnhofstrasse 9,
56068 **Koblenz**
Tel: (0261) 14024, Fax: (0261) 14025

Fremdenverkehrsgemeinschaft Ober Mosel-Saar
Granastrasse 24,
54329 **Konz**

Tourist Information Roemische Weinstrasse
Brückenstrasse 26,
54338 **Schweich**
Tel: (06502) 407117

Weinwerbung Mosel-Saar-Ruwer
Gartenfeldstrasse 12a,
54295 **Trier**
Tel: (0651) 45967,
Fax: (0651) 545443

Wittlicher Land Fremdenverkehrsverein
Altes Rathaus,
54516 **Wittlich**
Tel: (06571) 4086, Fax: (06571) 6417

Landhaus Mühlenberg
54313 **Daufenbach**
Tel: (06505) 8779
The Stoebe family runs one of the region's best restaurants in an attractive old country house between the villages of Kordel and Daufenbach. The cooking is modern with some Italian touches; the wine list dominated by the region's top estates.

Restaurant Halterschenke
Hauptstrasse 63,
56332 **Dieblich**
Tel: (02607) 1008
This recently restored slate-built house from the first half of the 19th century houses perhaps the best restaurant on the Unter Mosel. Imaginative modern cooking and a good list of local wines make it well worth a visit.

Waldhotel and Restaurant Sonnora
Auf dem Eichenfeld,
54518 **Dreis**
Tel: (06578) 406, Fax: (06578) 1402
Helmut Thieltges' superb cooking puts this restaurant among Germany's top ten. The good wine list and friendly service also contribute to its popularity. Booking is essential. The hotel is less grand than the restaurant but its quiet situation in a pine forest gives it considerable appeal.

Historischer Weinkeller
Mehlgasse 16,
56068 **Koblenz**
Tel: (0261) 14626
This is one of Germany's best wine bars, built into a 13th-century vaulted cellar. A wide selection of wines from each of Germany's 13 regions is complemented by a range of regional specialities.

Hotel Mehn zum Niederberg
Moselstrasse 2,
54470 **Lieser**
Tel: (06531) 6019
A comfortable hotel with a central location in the Mittel Mosel but with little traffic noise. The restaurant offers simple fare.

Restaurant Auf der Festung
Maximiner Strasse 30,
54340 **Longuich**
Tel: (06502) 4920,
Fax: (06502) 6313
This beautifully restored house from the turn of the century is now a pleasant restaurant serving regional cooking. The wine list is short but contains a good selection of local Rieslings.

Gutshotel Reichsgraf von Kesselstatt
Balduinstrasse 1,
54347 **Neumagen-Dhron**
Tel: (06507) 2035, Fax: (06507) 5644
Easily the most comfortable hotel in this part of the Mittel Mosel. Dishes featuring local ingredients (pike, eel, game) are particularly good.

Burgrestraurant
Schlossberg 12,
54439 **Saarburg**
Tel: (06581) 2622
When not too crowded this beautifully situated restaurant in a restored wing of Saarburg's ruined castle offers some of the best cooking on the Saar. The fish dishes are particularly good and the wine list

features an excellent selection of Saar wines.

Hotel Bellevue
Acherstrasse 1,
56841 **Traben-Trarbach**
Tel: (06541) 2065, Fax: (05641) 2551
This beautiful Art Nouveau hotel on the river bank is perhaps the best place to stay in this part of the Mittel Mosel. Although the restaurant is not among the region's best, it is entirely dependable.

Europa Parkhotel (Ramada)
Kaiserstrasse 29,
54290 **Trier**
Tel (0651) 71950,
Fax (0651) 7195801
Probably the most comfortable of Trier's large modern hotels.

Restaurant Pfeffermühle
Zurlaubener Ufer 76,
54292 **Trier**
Tel: (0651) 26133
Trier's best restaurant is situated right on the bank of the Mosel just north of the town centre. The cooking is a mixture of classic French and German and the wine list (Mosel-Saar-Ruwer and French) is excellent.

Restaurant Scheid
Reinigerstrasse 48,
54332 **Wasserliesche**
Tel: (06501) 13958,
Fax: (06501) 13959
The most creative cooking in the Trier area is found behind the rather drab exterior of this remarkable restaurant. The sensational wine list is full of rarities from the Mosel-Saar-Ruwer and France at modest prices.

Ahr

It would be hard not to fall in love with the beautiful landscape of the Ahr Valley. The wooded hills and steep vineyards of this rocky terrain are no less impressive than the more famous wine landscapes of the Mosel-Saar-Ruwer and the Rhine. Anyone familiar with those regions will immediately recognise that the cliffs and vine-covered terraces of the Middle Ahr Valley not only present a beautiful prospect, but also offer the right conditions for making great wines. Large numbers of tourists flock to the town of Bad Neuenahr-Ahrweiler each year, and happily the town has so far managed to resist attempts to modify it for their benefit, its original charm remaining largely intact.

If one's acquaintance with the region begins with its wines, however, a rather less appealing picture emerges. One of the main reasons for this is that although the Ahr's 450 hectares of vineyards are among the most northerly in Germany, 85 percent of them are planted with red grape varieties: varieties which require plenty of warmth to give good results. Taste a broad range of Ahr wines and it is hard to avoid the conclusion that, without the day-trippers from Cologne and Bonn, many of them simply would not find a market. Pale sweet reds and thin characterless rosés are hardly in demand in a discerning international market.

While many of the region's inferior wines come from the lowly Portugieser grape, even the noble Spätburgunder (Pinot Noir) can yield disappointing wines here. This should hardly be surprising, considering the fact that this grape, from which the great red wines of Burgundy's Côte d'Or are made, is widely regarded as one of the most fickle and demanding. Here, at commercial viticulture's northern limit, it presents wine-growers with a severe challenge.

Thankfully, a band of ambitious young winemakers in the Ahr have recognised the problems and are determined to remedy them, first by producing serious reds with a distinctive character. The Spätburgunder reds from Deutzerhof, Kreuzberg, Meyer-Näkel and Sonnenberg illustrate that in spite of the vicissitudes of the climate, there are sound reasons for producing red wine here. With good depth of colour, plenty of cherry- and blackberry-like fruit and a pleasant touch of oak, these examples are among the best red wines in Germany. Their elegance distinguishes them from the powerful, weighty Spätburgunders made in more southerly regions.

Ahrweiler, the region's centre, sprawls beneath its steeply sloping vineyards.

Kloster Marienthal, home of the Ahr's state-owned wine domaine, under winter's first dusting of snow.

The Ahr's best vineyards enjoy an astonishingly warm microclimate for their northerly situation. This has much to do with their location in a narrow valley which protects them from cold winds, and the southerly aspect which gives them maximum exposure to the sun. The stony slate, greywacke and basalt soils also play an important role, storing the heat of the day and radiating it back at night. A similar combination of factors is responsible for the great Rieslings of the Mittel Mosel, but few Ahr Rieslings come close to matching the quality of their Mosel-Saar-Ruwer counterparts.

The reason for the dominance of red wine production here is due at least in part to historical accident. Until the late 17th century, red wine production played a significant role in every German wine-growing region. During Louis XIV's occupation of the left bank of the Rhine during the late 17th century, large quantities of French red wines were imported. As the local reds could not compete with them, vineyards growing red wine varieties began to be replanted with white wine grapes: a trend which continued into the 19th century. The Ahr is one of few red wine areas that survived the process. No doubt this has much to do with the popularity enjoyed by the region's wines during the 18th and 19th centuries. Rosés, then sold as *Ahrbleichert,* and sparkling wines both had good

reputations, the latter at one stage selling for prices comparable with those of the best champagne.

The low-point for the region was during the 1960s and 1970s when the fashion for sweet wines swept across Germany. The introduction of high-yielding vine clones resulted in larger crops and these, coupled with misconceived winemaking methods, resulted in pale red wines lacking any real fruit or substance. They were then sweetened according to the fashion of the day. Equally feeble reds were produced in many other regions and, sadly, Ahr wines along with German reds as a whole became something of an international joke.

During the early 1980s a new generation of German vintners arrived who were aware that deep-coloured, full-bodied red wines had been produced in Germany 30 or so years previously. This observation and their work experiences in the leading red wine regions of France, Italy, and the New World convinced them it was at least possible to produce serious red wine in Germany. The '85 vintage brought the first successful examples of a new style. The wines were fully fermented on the skins and matured in small, new oak *barrique* casks like all great reds.

Werner Näkel, a former school teacher and self-taught winemaker, was the first to master this style at the Meyer-Näkel estate based in Dernau. His success spurred other local vintners to experiment. Even when Ahr reds achieve an alcoholic content that is

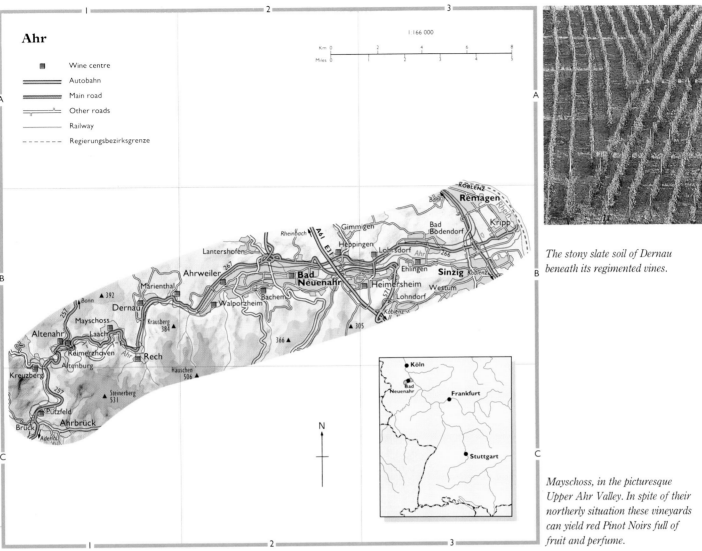

Ahr

- ▪ Wine centre
- ▭ Autobahn
- ▭ Main road
- ▭ Other roads
- ▭ Railway
- ----- Regierungsbezirksgrenze

1:166 000

The stony slate soil of Dernau beneath its regimented vines.

Mayschoss, in the picturesque Upper Ahr Valley. In spite of their northerly situation these vineyards can yield red Pinot Noirs full of fruit and perfume.

comparable with red wines from more southerly regions, they taste lighter and less mouth-filling than those from the Pfalz, Baden and Württemberg. This is a result of the region's light stony soils as much as of its climate. A successful Ahr red should marry the rich fruit and velvety texture typical of high-quality Pinot Noir with a delicacy of aroma and flavour and a subtle mineral character, making it quite distinctive. Those looking for modestly priced alternatives to red burgundy should look to the Pfalz, Baden and Württemberg. Those who favour light, perfumed reds full of character and charm, however, may be pleasantly surprised by Spätburgunders from the Ahr's best producers.

Wines of this kind are most easily produced from the south-facing vineyards on the left bank of the Ahr: Mayschoss, Dernau, Marienthal and Walporzheim in the Mittel Ahr valley, the region's most sheltered sites. On sunny days, temperatures on their terraced slopes rise rapidly, often reaching Mediterranean levels in summer. However, even here strict control of the yield is vital in order to achieve the intensity of fruit and the ripe tannins that are the foundation of all high-quality Pinot Noirs.

As far as possible the wines' alcohol (at least 12 degrees is essential) should also be natural and come from fully ripe grapes. As in Burgundy, the Ahr's leading vintners do not hesitate to chaptalise their red wines, should it be necessary, to build up their alcoholic content.

Roads and walls carved through the Fluerbereinigt *or reorganised vineyards of Heimersheim dramatically reduce the cost and difficulty involved in cultivating the vines.*

Whether these wines should be matured in the traditional *Stück* and *Halbstück* casks (1,200 and 600 litres respectively) which are too old to give much oak flavour to the wine, or in the smaller new oak *barriques* (225–300 litres), is a matter of some debate. Good Ahr Spätburgunder can be made in either type, or by using a judicious combination of the two, but most of the region's best winemakers choose new oak for their top wines. The resulting Spätburgunders may not have the weight of high-quality Pinot Noirs from Burgundy or the New Word but they do have the typical spice and toast aromas imparted by the new oak. Competition among the region's best estates is fierce, which should mean that quality will improve further as more producers take up the challenge.

BENCHMARK WINE

Spätburgunder 'S', QbA Trocken
Weingut Meyer-Näkel, Dernau
Vineyard site: Bad Neuenahrer Sonnenberg
Site area: 15 hectares, 1.2 hectares Meyer-Näkel
Exposure: south
Inclination: sloping
Soil: loam-loess with greywacke
Description: Though not Germany's most powerful red, this Pinot Noir should convince any sceptics that the Ahr must be taken seriously. Bright ruby in colour with intense cherry-like fruit in the bouquet and on the palate, this medium-bodied wine has a fascinating mineral character. The elegant interplay of rich fruit and supple tannin has a long, subtle finish.
Best vintages: '94, '93, '90, '88
Best drunk: The wines' optimum harmony is reached between two and five years of the vintage. Like all Pinot Noirs, Meyer-Näkel's 'S' cries out for red meat, though strong game or spicy dishes are best avoided.

BEST PRODUCER

Weingut Meyer Näkel

Hardtbergstrasse 20,
53507 Dernau
Owner: Werner Näkel
Vineyard area: 6 hectares
Grape varieties: 77% Spätburgunder,
8% Riesling, 5% Portugieser,
5% Dornfelder,
5% Frühburgunder
Top sites: Dernauer Pfarrwingert,
Bad Neuenahrer Sonnenberg

Many of Germany's best young winemakers planned completely different careers before wine got under their skin. Since self-taught winemaker Werner Näkel gave up his job as a high-school teacher at the beginning of the 1980s he has revolutionised the red wines of the Ahr. With his excellent '88 vintage wines he proved that, like Baden, the Pfalz and Württemberg, the Ahr can produce deep-coloured Spätburgunder reds with enough depth and substance to gain considerably from maturation in new oak. Since then his Pinot Noirs have gone from strength to strength. Seldom big and powerful, they possess an intense cherry- and blackberry-like fruit interwoven with a subtle spiciness from new oak. It is in the precise balancing of fruit and oak that Werner Näkel's real genius lies. While several of his colleagues on the Ahr have learned to produce deeply coloured rich red wines, Meyer-Näkel's have a degree of sophistication and subtlety that puts everything else from this tiny region in the shade.

The estate has an idiosyncratic classification system for its Spätburgunder reds. 'G' wines are the lightest and develop the most quickly, the 'Blauschiefer' wines from vineyards with blue slate soil are the most elegant and perfumed and the 'S' wines are the richest, most muscular and slowest to develop.

OTHER WELL KNOWN PRODUCERS

Weingut Deutzerhof

53508 Mayschoss
Few winemakers in the Ahr have made such progress during recent years as Wolfgang Hehla. This is definitely an estate to watch. The best Spätburgunder reds are sold as 'Selektion Caspar C'.

Weingut Kreuzberg

Benedikt-Schmittmann-Strasse 30,
53507 Dernau
In spite of owning only 3.5 hectares of vineyard since 1990, Hermann-Josef Kreuzberg has been making some of the best Spätburgunder and Frühburgunder red wines in the Ahr.

Weingut Sonnenberg

Heerstrasse 98, 53474
Bad Neuenahr
Norbert Görres and his son-in-law Manfred Linden have rapidly built up this small estate up from nothing. Their richly fruity Spätburgunders are model Ahr wines.

Staatliche Weinbaudomäne Marienthal

Klosterstrasse,
53507 Marienthal
The Ahr State Domain makes deliberately old-fashioned Ahr red wines. However, they have plenty of character and depth owing to the low yields.

Former high-school teacher Werner Näkel, the Ahr's self-taught winemaking genius, of Weingut Meyer-Näkel.

Travel Information

PLACES OF INTEREST

Ahrweiler In 1689, Louis XIV's soldiers did their best to raze this attractive town to the ground. Fortunately they were not entirely successful, and many years' painstaking work has restored much of Ahrweiler to its former glory. The town walls, parts of which date back to the 13th century, have been rebuilt, as have the four imposing stone gate-houses which mark the points of the compass. The most important monuments are the Gothic church of St Laurentius, built in the 14th and 15th centuries and the old Town Hall, a marvellous example of late rococo architecture.
Bad Bodendorf This spa village part-way up the Ahr Valley boasts many beautifully preserved half-timbered houses.
Bad Neuenahr Although somewhat distinguished by the fact that Beethoven spent his summers here between 1786 and 1792, Neuenahr was an inconsequential village until the discovery of its spring waters in 1861. Within a few decades it had become an important and fashionable spa town, as it still is today. Its most impressive landmark is the Art Nouveau spa house but it also has numerous imposing private residences built at the end of the 19th and beginning of the 20th century.
Heimersheim Technically a suburb of the twin town Bad Neuenahr-Ahrweiler (which is itself only a bureaucratic creation) Heimersheim boasts a beautiful late-Romanesque church with stained-glass windows from the 13th century.
Mayschoss With its precipitous terraced vineyards, cliffs and forested hill-tops the picturesque village of Mayschoss is the centre of the Mittel Ahrtal. The scenery alone makes this is a most attractive part of the region.
Sinzig The fertile fields of Sinzig on the left bank of the Rhine have been cultivated since Celtic times. Its Romanesque *Petrikirche* (Church of St Peter) has some marvellous 13th-century wall-paintings. The Schloss Sinzig museum, a 19th-century building on medieval foundations, is also worth a visit.

HOTELS AND RESTAURANTS

Wein-Gasthaus Schäferkarre

Brückenstrasse 29,
53505 **Altenahr**
Tel: (02643) 7128
This beautifully restored vintner's house from 1716 is now a fine wine restaurant which boasts the best wine-list in the region.

Steigenberger Kurhotel

Kurgartenstrasse 1,
53474 **Bad Neuenahr**
Tel: (02641) 2291,
Fax: (02641) 7001
This is the most luxurious hotel in the region, with swimming pool and direct access to the spa baths.

Steinheuer's Restaurant-Zur Alten Post

Landskroner Strasse 110,
53474 **Heppingen**
Tel: (02641) 7011,
Fax: (02641) 7013
This is probably the region's best restaurant. It serves sophisticated dishes with an Italian influence.

Romantik-Restaurant Brogsitter's Sanct Peter

Walporzheimer Strasse 134 (B267),
53474 **Walporzheim**
Tel: (02641) 97750
Fax: (02641) 977525
The regional cooking here may not be the most adventurous, but a high standard is maintained. Local game and fish are a regular feature of the menu. The wines from the eponymous wine estate are not among the region's best.

USEFUL ADDRESSES

Verkehrsverein Altenahr

53505 **Altenahr**
Tel: (02643) 8448
Altenahr's tourist information office is situated in the former railway station.

Kur- und Verkehrsverein Bad Neuenahr

53474 **Bad Neuenahr-Ahrweiler**
Tel: (02641) 2278,
Fax: (02641) 29758
For on-the-spot guidance the local tourist information body has offices at the Bad Neuenahr railway station and the Ahrweiler Marktplatz.

Mittelrhein

Ask anyone who does not originate from the Rheinland what they associate with the river Rhine, and they will probably describe the narrow Rhine Gorge between Koblenz and Bingen, the castles studded along the river's course, the rocks and reefs of the Loreley and vineyards clinging to precipitous slopes and ledges. So many painters and poets (Joseph MW Turner, Heinrich Heine...) have depicted this landscape that it has become a cliché of German culture. But few are aware – even within Germany – that this stretch of the Rhine Valley is also the Mittelrhein wine region. It is often wrongly assumed that this romantic landscape is the location of the Rheingau. The fact that Mittelrhein Rieslings can match the finest from the neighbouring Mosel-Saar-Ruwer, Nahe or Rheingau regions is even less well known. If any German wine-growing region can claim that it is misunderstood, or at least that its achievements are unrecognised, then this is it.

The main reason for this ignorance is that almost all the region's vintners earn their living either from selling wine in bulk to sparkling wine producers (Deinhard of Koblenz, for example) or from selling it by the glass and bottle to tourists. Vintners dependent upon such sales simply could not make a living if they produced top-class Rieslings. The combination of the small crops essential to make high-quality wine and the low prices expected for the area's wines would rapidly force them out of business. Only those vintners who are able to sell most of their product outside the region are in a position to strive for the highest quality. There are barely a dozen such estates in the entire Mittelrhein.

Decent, drinkable wines are not difficult to find but Rieslings that capture the full potential of the region's steep stony vineyards are few and far between. Where they do exist they are remarkable. Combining the succulence of ripe peach with the crispness of green apple, fine Mittelrhein Rieslings possess a tense balance between richness and tartness without ever becoming opulent or severe. With more weight than Mosel-Saar-Ruwer wines and more elegance than most other Rhine wines they combine the virtues of Germany's northerly and more southerly regions.

These qualities are the result of the conflicting forces which shape the region's climate. As in the Mosel-Saar-Ruwer, it would hardly be possible to produce quality wines here at all were it not

An inviting terrace overlooks the bustling town of Oberwesel.

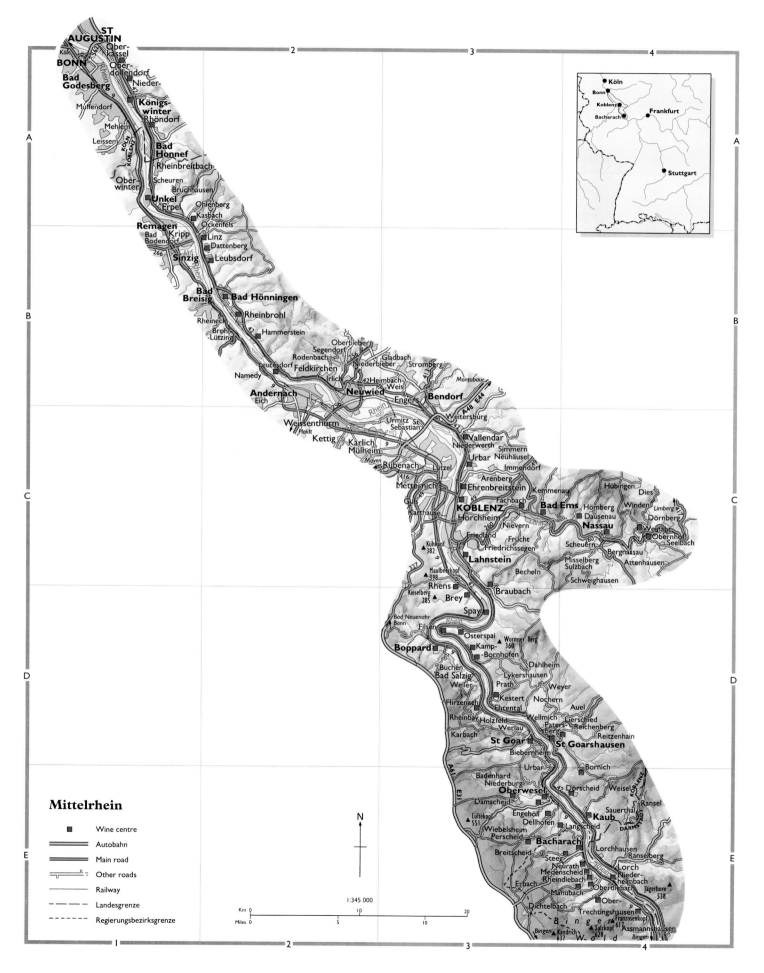

Mittelrhein

- ■ Wine centre
- ═══ Autobahn
- ═══ Main road
- ═╪═ Other roads
- ─── Railway
- ─ ─ Landesgrenze
- ┄┄ Regierungsbezirksgrenze

N

1:345 000

Km 0   10   20
Miles 0   5   10

for the river valley. The weather on the hilly plateau above the Rhine can be bitterly cold and windy. Sudden snow flurries during the spring and autumn are not unusual. Only the protection of the valley sides and the heat reservoir provided by the river enable noble grape varieties to be cultivated with success.

The steep, narrow valley excludes cold winds, sheltering the vineyards close to the river and enabling the sun to warm both the air and soil rapidly. But there are numerous side valleys which run in to the gorge, and these act as channels down which cold air flows from the hills and forests above. The larger a side valley, the cooler the vineyards in its lower reaches will be. Differences in soil are also significant. Stony soils act as 'storage heaters' and heat conductors to the vines, storing the warmth of the day and radiating it back during the cooler evenings. Where the best of these factors coincide, for example in the perfectly situated Bacharacher Hahn vineyard, Riesling grapes of Spätlese or higher quality can be harvested at almost every vintage. The wines from such sites can have an astonishing richness for a region which lies so far north.

By selecting fully ripe grapes from vineyards such as these it is possible to make dry Riesling wines in the Mittelrhein better balanced than those from the Mosel-Saar-Ruwer, the Upper and Middle Nahe and much of the Rheingau. This became apparent with the fine vintages of the late 1980s and early 1990s and promises much for the region's future.

The slate and greywacke soils in the better vineyards can give wines with as much mineral character as those from the Mosel-Saar-Ruwer or the Nahe. This character can take many forms, ranging from flinty to wet earth notes depending on the depth and stoniness of the soil. Botrytis, or noble rot, develops well in the Rhine Gorge during the autumn because of the high humidity. In good vintages it adds exotic fruit, honey, caramel and spice overtones to the naturally sweet wines. Then Mittelrhein Rieslings can be among the country's most aromatically complex whites. Unfortunately, too few vintners in the region selectively harvest the botrytized grapes to make Auslese and higher quality Prädikat wines. Were more of them produced the region would start to earn the recognition it deserves.

The medieval town of Bacharach, one of several wine towns in the region with first-class vineyards, can boast a clutch of fine estates. Fritz Bastian, Toni Jost, Dr Randolph Kauer, Lieschied-Rollauer, Helmut Mades and Jochen Ratzenberger are among them. Their winemaking achievements have succeeded in raising local wine prices to realistic (though still relatively modest) levels, so securing the future of quality wine production.

The town's involvement with the wine trade is centuries old. Bacharach was the centre of the Rheingau wine trade until the Palatinate War of Succession during the 17th century, mainly because of its location. Before that time it was not possible for ships to negotiate the Rhine's 90-degree bend at Bingen – the Binger Loch – except during high water in spring. Bacharach was the last town that vessels from the north could reach safely all year round. With the French occupation of the Rhine's left bank under Louis XIV Bacharach's importance waned because the town could no longer function as a marketplace for wine from the unoccupied Rhine bank. By the 18th century the navigability of this section of the Rhine had improved: wine could be dispatched directly up- or downriver and Bacharach could be routinely bypassed.

In many respects Bacharach is a typical Mittelrhein wine town, with the well preserved medieval fortifications and cobbled streets familiar along this stretch of the river. It has managed to retain much of its original character, perhaps because it is the only part of the region so far that attracts tourists specifically for its wines.

The best Rieslings from Bacharach and its *Ortsteil*, or suburb, Steeg have vibrant fruit character and an acidity that is always crisp but rarely aggressive. They bear a family resemblance to the Rieslings of the Mittel Mosel but are distinguished by their slightly fuller body and rounder texture. At their most powerful, in the wines from the great Posten and Hahn sites, they can possess an intense apricot- or pineapple-like fruit. At their most elegant, in the wines from the Steeger St Jost, they are piquant, racy and intensely mineral. Though the potential to make comparable wines exists in other part of the region, Bacharach currently stands alone, making the best Spätlese and Auslese wines from these sites.

The richest Mittelrhein wines come from the Toni Jost estate, which now owns virtually all the best parcels of vineyard in the Bacharacher Hahn site. The wines are lush and seductively aromatic, but rarely tip into opulence. It is easy to appreciate why these are best known Mittelrhein Rieslings. The Jost's wines from the Oberdiebacher Fürstenberg vineyard are marketed under the Grosslage name of Bacharacher Schloss Stahleck and approach the same high standard, having a vivid fruit and floral character and considerable elegance.

Ratzenberger's wines from Steeg's vineyards are typical racy Mittelrhein Rieslings which have a balance similar to good Saar wines, but more body. Fritz Bastian's wines seem to combine the best of both worlds, being rich, aromatic and very clean. Dry wine

Most of the Mittelrhein's first-class vineyards lie on the undulating slopes above Steeg (in the foreground) and Bacharach.

Tree-lined promenades along the riverside set off the steep vine-clad hills above Bacharach. River traffic includes cargo barges and passenger steamers.

specialist Helmut Mades is a newer arrival in Bacharach's elite, making wines with plenty of fruit and charm. Dr Randolph Kauer's Rieslings are unusual in being very slow to develop, with a mineral piquancy and intense fruit that is more akin to top Mittel Mosel wines than to those of his neighbours. The friendly competition among these vintners has already done much to improve the quality standard in Bacharach.

The contrast between Bacharach and Boppard, further north, is stark, and says much about the region's strengths and weaknesses. The Bopparder Hamm, technically a suburb of Boppard, is a gigantic amphitheatre of vines covering the east-, southeast- and south-facing slopes of the most dramatic bend on the Rhine's course northward from Bingen to Koblenz. This is the largest single expanse of top-class vineyards in the region, and only the best sites of Bacharach and Kaub have a comparable potential for yielding great Rieslings. The Bopparder Hamm has seven subsites whose names appear after its own on wine labels. Of these Mandelstein, Feuerlay and Ohlenberg ought to guarantee good to outstanding quality wine but, sadly, this is often not the case.

The reason why Bopparder Hamm wines are virtually unknown outside the area around Koblenz is simple, but disappointing to anyone with an interest in German wines. Unlike the vintners of Bacharach, those of Boppard and neighbouring Spay seem to be competing with one another — not to produce the best but to produce the cheapest wines. By mechanising the cultivation of the vines as far as is possible here, harvesting ever-larger crops and employing the minimum workforce or none at all, Boppard's vintners have repeatedly undercut each other's prices. In years when nature is generous and harvests are large, Boppard wines taste thin and bland. Among the current producers only Walter and August Perll in Boppard and Adolf Weingart in Spay make wines that regularly stand out from the crowd.

At least in Boppard most of the better vineyards are still in cultivation. From Koblenz south to the Loreley, vineyards that used to be a common sight punctuating the cliffs and castles are steadily falling out of cultivation. Terraces where the vines were pruned last year are now a chaotic mass of shoots, and those which were abandoned the year before are already reverting to scrubland. If these wasted vineyards lacked the potential to produce good wine such a development would be understandable, but they do not. Their position and make-up make them far better suited to wine

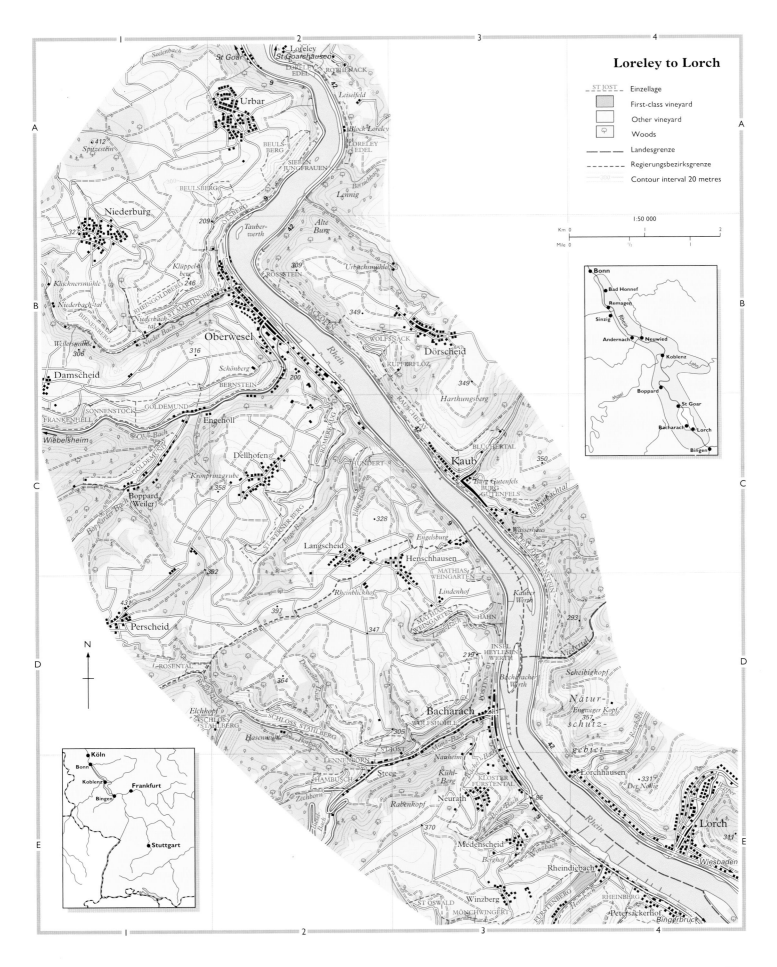

Loreley to Lorch

ST JOST Einzellage

First-class vineyard

Other vineyard

Woods

Landesgrenze

Regierungsbezirksgrenze

—300— Contour interval 20 metres

1:50 000

Km 0   1   2

Mile 0   ½   1

Medieval castles perch precariously in the forest above vine-covered hills.
Per hectare, the almost impossibly steep Bacharach vineyards (right) can take
four times longer to cultivate than those in Rheinhessen's mechanised plains.

growing than the large expanses of over-cropped vines in some of the side-valleys, whose inferior product is used for an increasing proportion of the region's wine.

Happily, the top vineyards of Kaub have not yet fallen into neglect. With punishingly steep slopes their cultivation is both backbreaking and expensive, but with dedicated management they could easily give wines to match the best from Bacharach. Such vineyards have a future only if their potential is fully realised, and the resulting wines sold for realistic prices. The Heinrich Weiler estate, which once made magnificent Rieslings from the Kauber Rosstein and Kauber Backofen vineyards, unfortunately no longer belongs to the region's quality elite.

Along the length of the Mittelrhein are scattered steep vineyard sites with excellent exposure and stony soils. But their potential, like that of the Siebengebirge vineyards north of Neuwied for example, is untried, since no attempts have been made to make high-quality Riesling here in recent years. The best that can be expected from many of these vineyards under the present circumstances is good Sekt, or sparkling wine.

Mittelrhein sparkling Riesling can be very good indeed. Although made from blends that include components from other regions, Deinhard of Koblenz's 'Lila' Sekt has plenty of Mittelrhein character in spite of the large volume produced and its moderate price. While Deinhard's best Sekt, 'Geheimrat J', comes from the Rheingau, several other sparkling wine houses make high-class Sekt from Mittelrhein base wines. The best of these come from the small company Geiling just outside Bacharach. Using the champagne method, Geiling's elegant 'Oyster Cuvée' (Extra Brut) and 'Salmon Cuvée' (Brut) show what is possible. Only Ratzenberger's Riesling Sekt Brut can better this in the Mittelrhein.

This region stands at a crossroads. For Bacharach the future looks positive, competition among its best estates suggesting that quality will only improve. Elsewhere the future looks less bright for quality wine production, though the quantity of indifferent produce is growing every year.

BENCHMARK WINES

Bacharacher Hahn Riesling Auslese
Weingut Toni Jost, Bacharach
Vineyard site: Bacharacher Hahn
Site area: 5 hectares, 4.3 hectares Toni Jost
Exposure: southeast
Inclination: very steep
Soil: weathered grey slate, very stony
Description: Packed with peach-like fruit yet subtle and elegant, these wines are conclusive proof of the Mittelrhein's ability to make top-notch Riesling. In spite of their power and the hint of lush exotic fruit character from botrytis, they still have the sleekness and long, clean aftertaste of the best Rieslings from the northerly regions.
Best vintages: '94, '93, '92, '91, '90, '89, '88, '83
Best drunk: As young wines, rich Auslese of this kind are best by themselves or with liver pâté or blue cheese. When they mature, from five to seven years of age depending on the vintage, they are also delicious with duck, goose or sautéed calves' liver.

Bacharacher Kloster Fürstenthal Riesling Spätlese Halbtrocken
Weingut Dr Randolph Kauer

Vineyard site: Bacharacher Kloster Fürstenthal
Site area: 5 hectares, 0.5 hectares Dr Randolph Kauer
Exposure: southeast
Inclination: steep
Soil: weathered slate
Description: Brimming with floral and mineral aromas and rippling with ripe apple- and peach-like fruit, these are some of the Mittelrhein's most sophisticated and elegant Rieslings. They should not be rushed, however, as Dr Kauer's wines develop new nuances of flavour with each year in bottle and continue to improve for at least a decade, if not two. They are the best example of the region's dry wine potential.
Best vintages: '94, '93, '92, '91
Best drunk: Juicy and harmonious enough to be drunk by themselves, these dry wines are even better with food. Try with richer fish dishes in rich , such as salmon with Sauce Hollandaise.

Steeger St Jost Riesling Spätlese
Weingut Jochen Ratzenberger

Vineyard site: Steeger St Jost
Site area: 10 hectares, 2. hectares Ratzenberger
Inclination: very steep
Exposure: south
Soil: slate with a yellow sandy sub-soil
Description: These Rieslings with their redcurrant and spice bouquet are sleek, tightly wound when young, racy, fruity and refreshing. Although not full-bodied or rich, good vintages of these archetypical Mittelrhein Rieslings can age for 20 years and more.
Best vintages: '94, '93, '90, '89, '88, '83
Best drunk: They have some natural sweetness but taste almost dry due to their piercing, steely acidity. They are ideal aperitif wines, but also accompany smoked fish and ham well.

BEST PRODUCERS

Weingut Fritz Bastian
Oberstrasse 63,
55422 Bacharach
Owner: Friedrich Bastian
Vineyard area: 5.5 hectares
Grape varieties: 90% Riesling,
5% Scheurebe, 5% other varieties
Top site: Bacharacher Posten
　Fritz Bastian Snr is just as likely to be found rowing across the Rhine to tend his wholly-owned Insel Heyles'en Werth vineyard as serving wine in the family's ancient wine restaurant, Zum Grünen Baum. Friedrich Bastian Jr is a gifted musician as well as a talented winemaker and with the help of his tireless father is pursuing two careers, making the wines at the family estate and studying singing.
　This unusual father-and-son team made some of the best Rieslings in the Mittelrhein during the early 1990s. With their rich peach- and apricot-like fruit, pronounced mineral character,

Fritz Bastian in contemplative mood.

racy acidity and 'spritz' of natural carbon dioxide they bear a strong resemblance to high-class Mittel Mosel wines. The estate's substantial vineyard holdings in the great Bacharacher Posten site mean that even better wines could be possible. With luck, Friedrich Bastian Jr's musical ambitions will leave him enough time to realise this potential.

Weingut Toni Jost
Oberstrasse 14,
55420 Bacharach
Owner: Peter Jost
Vineyard area: 9.5 hectares
Grape varieties: 80% Riesling,
15% Spätburgunder,
5% other varieties
Top sites: Bacharacher Hahn,
Oberdiebacher Fürstenberg
　Peter Jost produces the most consistently impressive wines of the Mittelrhein from his vineyards in Bacharach as well as excellent Rheingau Rieslings from three hectares of vines in Walluf. It is difficult to resist making comparisons and usually the

Successful vintners Peter and Linde Jost.

wines from the Bacharacher Hahn are the better. This small, perfectly situated vineyard just north of Bacharach is almost exclusively in the Josts' ownership. Its Rieslings have an opulent peach- and pineapple-like fruit and a rich, creamy texture that makes them seductive whether they are vinified dry or with some natural sweetness. The estate's Rheingau Rieslings are firmer and more reserved, but just as full of character.

Having won numerous 'blind' tastings and wine competitions, Peter Jost and his equally dedicated wife Linde are well aware of the quality of their wines but also of the competition they face from Bacharach's other leading vintners. In recent years changes have been made in the cellar, with the result that the Jost Rieslings have gained in elegance without losing anything in richness and depth. Everything from the standard-quality QbA wines up to the luscious Riesling Trockenbeerenauslese can be wholeheartedly recommended as exceptional value for money.

Weingut Dr Randolph Kauer

Blücherstrasse 87,
55422 Bacharach
Owners: Dr Randolf & Martina Kauer
Vineyard area: 2.0 hectares
Grape varieties: 100% Riesling
Top site: Bacharacher Wolfshöhle

Considering that his wine estate is a part-time occupation for Dr Randolph Kauer he produces some remarkably sophisticated Rieslings. Intensely racy with a strong mineral and floral character, they need some time in the bottle for their subtle fruit aromas to develop but they have excellent ageing potential. His QbA and Kabinett wines are always light and crisp, and the estate's dry Riesling Spätlese, naturally sweet Auslese and sparkling wines are among the best produced in the Mittelrhein. With a scintillating vibrancy and many layers of flavour

they are both expressive and elegant. This miniature estate makes wines of absolute clarity using entirely organic methods. Randolph Kauer's doctorate was based on a comparison between organic viticulture and conventional methods, experiments which he continues to conduct in the day-to-day running of his estate. He plans to expand the estate gradually as good vineyards in Bacharach's best sites come onto the market. He has no plans, however, to compromise his minimalistic winemaking methods. He rejects cultured yeast in favour of natural yeast for fermentation and uses only a single filtration to clarify the wines before bottling. Such techniques require attention to detail and strong nerves, both of which Dr Kauer can bring to bear in abundance.

Weingut Ratzenberger

Blücherstrasse 167,
55422 Steeg
Owner: Jochen Ratzenberger
Vineyard area: 6 hectares
Grape varieties: 70% Riesling,
20% Spätburgunder,
10% Müller-Thurgau
Top sites: Steeger St Jost,
Bacharacher Posten
Bacharacher Wolfshöhle

Although it produced some slightly disappointing wines in the early 1990s this estate is one of the most important in the region. From small beginnings in 1956, Jochen Ratzenberger has steadily built up the estate, establishing a reputation for sleek, racy Rieslings. Apart from the Auslese and higher quality Prädikat dessert wines, all the estate's Rieslings are either completely dry or just off-dry. Often they need several years' maturation in the bottle before they show their full character; they can all age a decade without losing their charm and the best are still fresh and vigorous at 20 years of age. Jochen Ratzenberger Jr, who has recently taken over responsibility for the winemaking, will benefit from more

experience and shows every sign of being able to build upon his father's achievements.

OTHER WELL KNOWN PRODUCERS

Weingut Liescheid Rollauer

Blücherstrasse 88,
55422 Bacharach
Hermann Rollauer's wines are somewhat variable in quality but his best dry Rieslings are crisp and fruity with plenty of character.

Weingut Mades

Borbachstrasse 35–36,
55422 Steeg
During recent years the quality standard at this small estate has improved in leaps and bounds. Helmut Mades' wines have plenty of fruit and substance and are particularly impressive in the dry style.

Weingut Walter Perll

Ablassgasse 11,
56154 Boppard
In good vintages Perll makes juicy, elegant Rieslings with some sophistication. They are the best produced from the Bopparder Hamm.

Weingut Bernhard Prass

Blücherstrasse 132,
55422 Steeg
Still finding his style, part-time winemaker Bernhard Prass has already made some very good Rieslings. In particular he maintains an excellent standard with his QbAs and Kabinetts.

Weingut Adolf Weingart

Mainzer Strasse 32,
56322 Spay
While few of Adolf and Helga Weingart's wines are outstanding, they are consistently good. Always fresh, clean and fruity, these Rieslings offer remarkable value.

Travel information

PLACES OF INTEREST

Bacharach Bacharach's name comes from the Latin *Bacchi ara*, the altar of Bacchus. The Romans established a substantial area of vineyards here. From the late-Roman period until the late-17th century it was an important trading centre, a history which has left an indelible mark upon the town. Nine of the 16 watch towers and much of the medieval fortification wall remains, the Gothic *Peterskirche* built in the town centre between the 12th and 14th centuries is beautifully preserved as are many fine half-timbered houses dating from the 17th and 18th centuries. Above the town lies the 12th-century Schloss Stahleck, which is now the town's youth hostel. Just to the south of the town are the late-19th-century premises of the Georges Geiling sparkling wine company. Above Oberdiebach stand the ruins of the 13th-century Burg Fürstenberg.

Bad Ems Only 17 kilometres from Koblenz in the forested valley of the Lahn lies the elegant idyll of Bad Ems. The 18th-century Kurhaus and the Kurpark (Spa House and Park) have an air of stylish timelessness. The area's wines, however, are rather less exciting.

Bendorf The *Giesshalle* or Foundry Hall of the Sayner Iron Foundry, dating from 1830, is one of the oldest and most graceful steel constructions in Germany.

Bonn The former capital of Germany and soon-to-be former seat of its government forms the northern limit of the Mittelrhein and viticulture on the Rhine as a whole. The town has two contrasting faces, one in the many magnificent official buildings and private residences built during the 18th and 19th centuries, the other in the dramatic modernistic buildings of more recent decades. The most important examples of the former are the Prince-Bishops' Palace, which now houses part of the university, and the rococo Town Hall. The futuristic Bundeskunsthalle, the national gallery of modern art, represents the other extreme. There are many other attractions, including the house where Beethoven was born (Bonngasse 20), the Romanesque-Gothic cathedral and the Rheinische Landesmuseum (Colmanstrasse). Smaller museums and the streets of the old town offer plenty of diversion for those with with time to explore.

Boppard First inhabited by the Celts, then the site of a Roman fortress, Boppard lost much of its former importance after the Thirty Years' War (1618–48), during which it was badly damaged. Boppard now attracts as many tourists as anywhere on the Rhine. The finest and the most prominent of its many historic monuments is the late-Romanesque church of St Severus, whose twin towers dominate the skyline. Many of the town's extensive fortifications are preserved, as are numerous fine old houses. The huge amphitheatre of vines that make up the Bopparder Hamm vineyard sites are a glorious sight. These can be seen from the river or from a train, but a hike through them and the forest above gives a fuller impression of their grandeur.

Engers Now officially a suburb of Neuwied, Engers possesses one of the many Schlosses built by the Prince-Bishops during the 18th century.

Kaub The 14th-century toll castle Burg Gutenfels on the island of Pfalzgrafenstein can be visited by boat from Kaub (there are daily tours) although the views of it from the river are more impressive than inside the castle itself.

Königswinter The slopes of the Drachenfels above Königswinter are renowned for their red wine, once sold as 'Drachenblut', or dragons' blood. The wine is unremarkable but the view from the ruined Drachenfels castle is one of the most spectacular on the Rhine. It may be worth taking the funicular railway or a horse-pulled carriage to the top, since the walk and 250-metre climb are pretty taxing.

Laacher See One of the largest volcanic crater lakes in the Eifel (two kilometres across) the Laacher See lies a short distance to the west of Neuwied.

Leutesdorf
One of the most attractive wine villages in northern Mittelrhein, Leutesdorf boasts many imposing houses dating from the 16th, 17th and 18th centuries.

Linz There are many beautifully carved and painted 17th- and 18th-century half-timbered houses in the old town of Linz; a medieval Rathaus built in 1392, two gate houses and other remnants of medieval fortifications.

Neuwied Established by the Romans, Neuwied was an unimportant small town which was left in ruins by the Thirty Years' War (1618–48). Almost

immediately afterward rebuilding began and the symmetrical plan of the old town dates from this period of baroque absolutism. The Schloss dates from the early 18th century.

Oberwesel Of the many towns in the Rhine Gorge that retain their medieval fortifications, none can match Oberwesel. The town wall is preserved in its entirety and 16 watch-towers remain. The Liebfrauenkirche and neighbouring St Martins-Kirche are the finest Gothic churches in the Mittelrhein.

Rhens This small town once enjoyed considerable political importance, since it was here that the seven Prince-Bishops of Germany elected German kings at the *Königsstuhl* or King's Throne. The town has a fine Gothic *Rathaus* or Town Hall, a baroque church and many fine half-timbered houses. Although not unique in the region, the towers, gates, and walls of the town's 15th-century fortifications are impressive.

Rhöndorf This village at the foot of the Drachenfels was made famous by Konrad Adenauer, the first Chancellor of the modern Bundesrepublik, who wrote his memoirs here and is buried in the Waldfriedhof.

St Goar Above the attractive wine town of St Goar lie the ruins of the massive Rheinfels castle which was built in 1245. It was destroyed by Napoleon's troops in 1797. Recorded in all its glory by Albrecht Dürer, the castle was also painted after its fall by William Turner. The ruined castle is now partly restored and home to a hotel and local museum. The doll, teddy-bear and toy museum in St Goar houses a fascinating collection.

St Goarhausen Directly across the Rhine from St Goar on the river's right bank, St Goarhausen is best known for the legendary Loreley cliffs. The view along the Rhine Valley from the terrace at their summit is spectacular.

Siebengebirge Directly above the vineyards of the Siebengebirge just south of Bonn, the Siebengebirge National Park begins. Forested peaks rise to 460 metres and offer many spectacular views for hikers.

RESTAURANTS AND HOTELS

Kurhotel
Römerstrasse 1,
56130 **Bad Ems**
Tel: (02603) 7990,
Fax: (02603) 799252
This is the best and grandest hotel in the Lahn Valley, where visitors can take the waters, bathe and be massaged at their leisure.

Halbedel's Gasthaus
Rheinallee 47,
53173 **Bad Godesberg**
Tel: (0228) 354253,
Fax: (0228) 354253
The restaurant serves the best and most creative cooking in the Bonn area. Prices are moderate, considering the number of corporate guests entertained here.

Günneweg Residence Hotel
Kaiserplatz,
53113 **Bonn**
Tel: (0228) 26970,
Fax: (0228) 2697777
A comfortable modern hotel with a central location and little traffic noise.

Hotel Bellevue
Rheinallee 41,
56154 **Boppard**
Tel: (06742) 1020,
Fax: (06742) 102602
Boppard's finest hotel offers marvellous views of the Rhine as well as having its own tennis courts and swimming pool.

Gästehaus Petersberg
53639 **Königswinter**
Tel: (02223) 744040,
Fax: (02223) 24313
The German government converted this building into a luxury hotel for state visitors. It has wonderful views of the Rhine Valley and lies within the boundaries of the Siebengebirge National Park.

Burghotel Auf Schönburg
Schönburg,
55430 **Oberwesel**
Tel: (06744) 7027, Fax: (06744) 1613
Situated 230 metres above Oberwesel in the Rhine Gorge this fine hotel lies within the remains of a 1,000-year-old castle and enjoys unrivalled views.

Schlosshotel auf Burg Rheinfels
Schlossberg 47,
56329 **St Goar**
Tel: (06741) 8020, Fax: (06741) 7652
One of the best of the many castle-hotels in the Rhine Gorge.

The legendary siren who lured sailors to their deaths at the foot of the Loreley cliffs.

Some of the remarkable properties of Mittelrhein Riesling still defy scientific explanation.

USEFUL ADDRESSES

Städtisches Verkehrsamt Bacharach
Oberstrasse 1,
55420 **Bacharach**
Tel: (06743) 2968

Gästeinformation Bad Ems
Römerstrasse 1,
56130 **Bad Ems**
Tel: (02603) 4041

Tourist Information Bonn
Münsterstrasse 20,
53111 **Bonn**
Tel: (0228) 773466

Städtisches Verkehrsamt Boppard
Oberstrasse 118,
56154 **Boppard**
Tel: (06742) 3888,
Fax: (06742) 81402

Städtisches Verkehrsamt Königswinter
Drachenfelsstrasse 7,
53639 **Königswinter**
Tel: (02244) 889325

Nahe

Paradoxically, the most famous wine estates and vineyards in the Nahe are better known than the region itself. The Schlossböckelheimer Kupfergrube vineyard, for example – difficult as it is to pronounce – is a name more familiar to wine enthusiasts than that of the Nahe Valley. The Riesling wines from Weingut Hans Crusius & Sohn, Schlossgut Diel auf Burg Layen and Weingut Hermann Dönnhoff have excellent international reputations but many of those who buy and drink them are hardly aware that they come from the Nahe, one of Germany's most dramatic and fascinating wine regions.

The twisting river valley with its cliffs, its bizarre rock formations and forested hills is certainly one of the most remarkable landscapes in Germany and yet in the minds of wine-drinkers – even within Germany – it is not identified with the region's name. Even the Nahe State Domain, the leading producer of quality wine during the 1970s and early 1980s, did more to promote the names of its best vineyards than that of the region itself. In spite of local wine growers' attempts to publicise it, the Nahe remains stubbornly unknown and undervalued, both at home and abroad.

To some extent this is because the region has existed as a precisely delimited wine-growing region only since the introduction of the 1971 Wine Law. While the previous law of 1935 referred to it as a distinct entity, its borders were not defined. Its wines were generally marketed as 'Rhine Wines' or as 'Hock' in the English-speaking world, as they had been for centuries.

Although they lacked a specific identity, however, this was by no means a reflection of their quality. During the late 19th century and the first half of the 20th, they were as successful as Rheingau wines. Price lists from the period show that they commanded prices higher than those of top Bordeaux.

As in all Germany's classic wine-growing regions the vineyard area was then much smaller; the market honoured good quality with higher prices and the production of 'Rhine Wines' and 'Hock' could hardly satisfy demand. The use of these names did have a certain logic since the River Nahe flows into the Rhine at Bingen, where the Rheingau, Rheinhessen and Nahe wine-growing regions meet, but Nahe Rieslings have at least as much affinity with those of the Mosel as they do with those from the Rhine.

The mighty Rotenfels cliffs tower over the winding River Nahe.

It is generally thought that the style of Nahe wines must lie somewhere between the styles of Mosel and Rheingau wines: exactly what one would expect expect of an area lying geographically halfway between between the two. To some degree this is the case. Most Nahe vintners would not be offended if their wines were compared with the best of those neighbouring regions. But on closer examination, a much more varied picture emerges. The wines of the Nahe Valley and its tributaries are as diverse as the complex geological formations on which they are grown.

The most important differences in style are those between the wines of the Lower, or Unter Nahe, which stretches from the river's confluence with the Rhine to Bad Kreuznach; those of the Mittel Nahe from Bad Kreuznach to Schlossböckelheim and those of the Upper or Ober Nahe above Schlossböckelheim. The wines are so distinct that they could come from three entirely different regions. The wines from various side valleys, of which the Alsenz is the most important, diversify the picture even further.

While all three sub-areas can produce top-class Rieslings, those from the Mittel Nahe with their intense mineral smell and taste have the most obvious claim to greatness. From the jagged contours of the scenery it is not difficult to read the history of volcanic activity that formed the Mittel Nahe's melaphyre and porphyry rocks. The almost pungent mineral character they give the Riesling often pushes the wine's fruit aromas into the background. It might

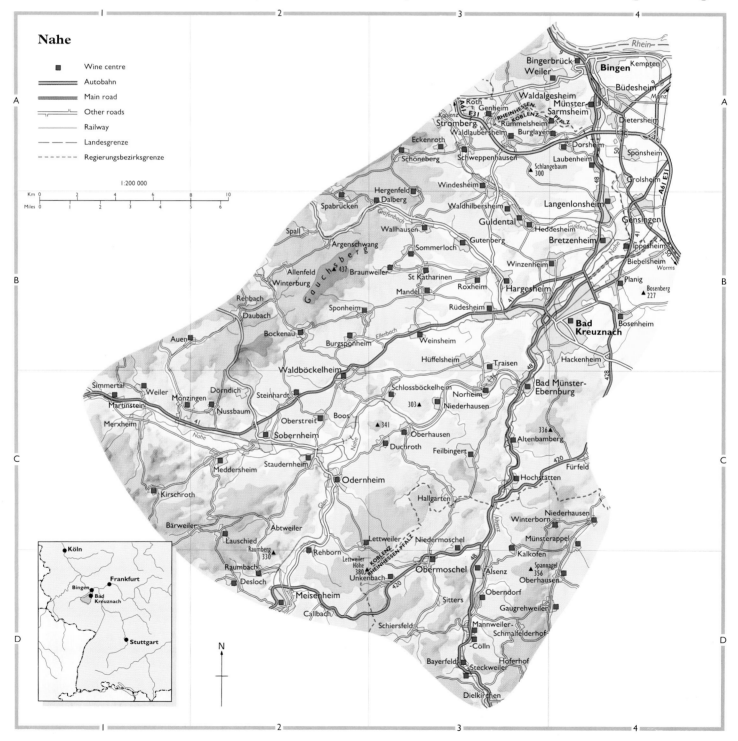

have been these wines that the Roman Emperor Hadrian was thinking of when he wrote that 'wine initiates us in the volcanic mysteries of the soil'.

The reputation of Mittel Nahe wines was already established during the second half of the 19th century and it reached a glorious peak during the heyday of the August Anheuser and Reichsgraf von Plettenberg estates between the early 1920s and late 1960s. The Niederhausen-Schlossböckelheim State Domain reached its zenith between the late 1940s and the mid-1980s, producing wines whose balance of fresh acidity and fruity sweetness was as scintillating and delightful as that of great Mosel wines. German State wineries were founded as model estates whose role was to provide

an example to the producers in their respective regions, promoting viticultural and winemaking techniques for quality wine production. But commercial considerations have begun to erode this ideal, with the result that the Nahe State Domain's vineyards on the Unter Nahe are being sold.

Until recently these estates' nobly sweet Auslese and higher quality Prädikat wines enjoyed reputations as great as those of top Rheingau wines, but none is making such remarkable wines today. Several small family-owned estates, however, of which Weingut Hans Crusius & Sohn in Traisen and Weingut Hermann Dönnhoff in Oberhausen are the most prominent, continue to make wines that realise the great vineyards' potential. Rieslings from the Mittel

Top: Sponheim, a typical Nahe wine village, surrounded by fields, woodland and vines.
Above: Painstaking attention to detail is required when laying out a new vineyard.

Left: The first-class Traiser Bastei clings dramatically to scree at the foot of the Rotenfels. The volcanic rhyolite rock is believed to give Rieslings their pungently intense mineral character.

Spa town Bad Münster-am-Stein and the Mittel Nahe, seen from the Rotenfels.

Nahe's top sites can still be found that combine racy elegance with as much fruit, spice and charm as this noble grape can give.

Some of the most exciting Mittel Nahe wines come from the vineyards of Traisen, the best of these being the Traiser Bastei, or 'Bastion', one of the most dramatic vineyard sites in the world, on a narrow strip of scree at the base of the gigantic Rotenfels cliffs. The Rotenfels is a 200-metre high mass of porphyry, the highest rock-face in Europe north of the Alps. In the evening light the ruddy glow of its huge bulk can be seen from up to 50 kilometres away. It provides a barrier against cold northerly winds and acts as a massive heat reservoir.

The Bastei's steep, south-facing slopes between the river and the cliffs enjoy a warm microclimate which results in full-bodied wines with a pronounced mineral character. The neighbouring Traisen Rotenfels site produces similar but slightly less dramatic and rather tarter wines. Weingut Hans Crusius & Sohn is the best source of wines from both these sites.

The potential of Norheim, a wine village a little further upstream, is almost completely unrealized. The narrow terraces of its top site, the Dellchen, are well tended but produce no wines of any consequence. This is a sad reflection on the current state of the region: many of the best sites seem to be in the hands of poorly managed or declining estates, while ambitious young vintners are struggling to make exciting wines from second-rate vineyards. At Norheim the vines must be tended entirely by hand, making them extremely expensive to cultivate. In spite of this Dr Hans Mittermeier, a professor of mathematics in Munich, recently

bought one of the site's best portions. Helmut Dönnhoff has been taken on as winemaker, which is promising for the future of Norheimer Dellchen Rieslings. The Crusius holdings in the less-favoured Klosterberg site currently produce the best Norheimers.

Niederhausen's top sites are the best in the Mittel Nahe. The Hermannshöhle is the greatest, having a combination of perfect southerly exposure and a complex soil in which slate, porphyry and sandstone are mixed. This geological 'cocktail' results in wines with an extraordinary range of fruit aromas from apple to redcurrant, peach to exotic fruits. Racy but never aggressive, the wines marry richness with the greatest finesse.

A breathtaking panorama is visible from the vine-clad slopes of the Hermannshöhle: the river snaking along the valley and a deciduous forest clinging to the steep slopes of the opposite bank. Taste a Hermannshöhle from Weingut Hermann Dönnhoff, or an older example from the State Domain and it is easy to understand how the site earned the highest rank in the Prussian classification of the Nahe's vineyards, which was published in map form in 1901.

Rieslings from the neighbouring Niederhäuser Hermannsberg and Oberhäuser Brücke sites (the former wholly owned by the State Domain, the latter by Weingut Hermann Dönnhoff) are similar, but slightly more powerful and less fine. In warmer years the wines from the Steinberg, Klamm, Kertz, Felsen-Steyer and Rosenheck sites of Niederhausen can come close to matching those from their more famous neighbours. Steinbergers are lighter and sleeker than Hermannsbergers, while wines from the Felsensteyer are piquant and creamy. Rieslings from the Kertz site are so pungently mineral that the porphyry itself could be in the glass. In addition to the State Domain, the Crusius, Oskar Mathern

A vineyard prepared for an Eiswein harvest. The necessary freezing conditions rarely occur before the third week in November and risk of failure is high.

and Wilhelm Sitzius estates produce good Niederhausen wines, but not all the village's vineyards are to be recommended. The Pfingstweide, for example, is not steep nor does its soil contain much of the stone typical of the area. Its wines are correspondingly unremarkable.

Across the Luitpold bridge on the right bank of the Nahe lies the unspectacular village of Oberhausen. Confusingly, its top site, the Hermann Dönnhoff estate's wholly-owned Oberhäuser Brücke, is on the left bank just below the Niederhäuser Hermannsberg. In this tiny 1.1-hectare vineyard examples of four different soil types can be found. The wines are similar to those of the Hermannsberg, while those from Oberhausen's Felsenberg, Kieselberg and Leistenberg sites on the right bank are lighter and racier.

The vineyards of neighbouring Schlossböckelheim are even steeper and rockier than those of Niederhausen. Rieslings from its best sites, the Felsenberg and Kupfergrube, offer Niederhausen serious competition. The Kupfergrube, or Copper Mine, is planted on former copper workings that were cleared and planted using convict labour during the first years of the 20th century. Its reputation for piquant, steely Rieslings with exceptional ageing potential was secured by the State Domain which owns most of this site. At the highest levels of concentration – BA, TBA and Eiswein – the wines can be breathtaking.

The Felsenberg's richer, more succulently fruity wines are traditionally regarded as superior to those from the Kupfergrube. Like the Bastei, the Felsenberg is a narrow strip of vines on a steep, south-facing slope sandwiched between the river bank and the cliffs. Here too the soil is little more than scree, in this instance of melaphyre rock. Recent vineyard reorganisation resulted in the

entire site's being replanted and the young vines will not reach maturity until the early 21st century. In the meantime, Crusius and Dönnhoff are the most important producers. Schlossböckelheim's Königsfels and Mühlberg sites can also yield racy Rieslings with plenty of mineral character.

Although local vintners do not share the widespread enthusiasm for the Weissburgunder and Grauburgunder vines cultivated by their colleagues further downstream, these varieties are beginning to establish themselves in the Mittel Nahe. Dönnhoff and Hehner-Kilz have found that wines of these grapes give more fruit and character than those of Müller-Thurgau, even when planted in mediocre vineyards. The Paul Anheuser estate has produced some fairly serious dry Weissburgunders from the Schlossböckelheimer In den Felsen site. They promise much for the variety, especially if it is culivated in good vineyard land. Other producers look set to follow suit and begin replacing their inferior varieties with Weissburgunder.

The scenery further upstream is less spectacular; the vineyards are less rocky than those of Traisen and Schlossböckelheim and the forest less dense than at Niederhausen, but the Ober Nahe still has its own rural charm. The wines are broadly similar to those of the Mittel Nahe but reflect the softer landscape, being more supple, simple and less expressive.

One important exception to this general characterisation is Monzingen, whose steep slopes can give Rieslings with just as much stony piquancy as those from further downstream. The best

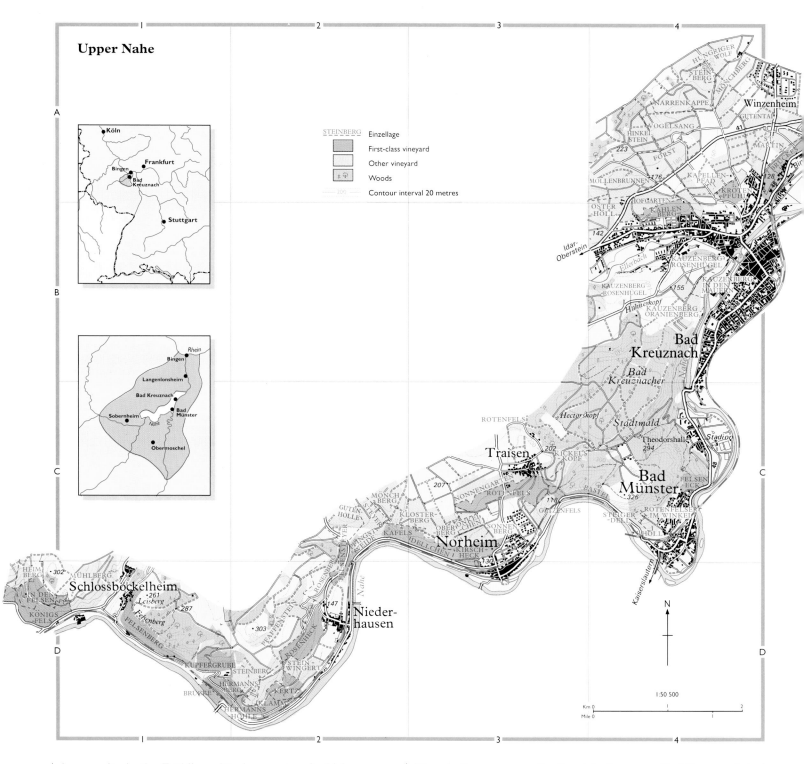

Upper Nahe

STEINBERG　Einzellage

First-class vineyard

Other vineyard

Woods

Contour interval 20 metres

1:50 500

known site is the Frühlingsplätzchen, parts of which are very good indeed. However, the steeply-sloping Halenberg, with its slate soil, is even better. Its wines can resemble the best from the Mittel Mosel. This little-known site has found a worthy champion in the Emrich-Schönleber estate, perhaps the region's most important rising star.

The region's centre is the spa town of Bad Kreuznach. Although heavy traffic mars some parts of the town, the narrow streets and old houses around the Eiermarkt and the elegant Kurviertel or Spa Quarter are both worth a visit. The Kurpark (Spa Park) offers walks through a beautiful wooded stretch of river bank that lies virtually in the town centre. The magnificent Roman mosaics in the

Römerhalle are among the finest in Germany. Bad Kreuznach is also the traditional site for the region's wine auctions. The Nahe section of Germany's VDP Wine Estates Association holds an annual auction at the Hotel Kurhaus in late September.

The best of the town's vineyards – the renowned Kreuznacher Brückes, Kahlenberg, the Kauzenberg sites and the Krotenpfühl – can produce wines as exciting as those from the Mittel Nahe's classic vineyards. The Rosenheck site of neighbouring Winzenheim, which is now technically a suburb of Bad Kreuznach, is in the same class. Richer and more substantial than the wines from further upstream, at their best they can match the elegance of good Rheingau wines. Most of Bad Kreuznach's vineyards however are land were turned over to viticulture during the 1960s and 1970s. Wines from the Unter Nahe's best vineyards can be intense and characterful but those from inferior sites are often simple and bland. The better vineyards begin in Langenlonsheim, especially the Königsschild and Rothenberg estates. Langenlonsheim Rieslings are not the most subtle or elegant but they have plenty of body and juiciness. Wilhelm Schweinhardt is the best producer here. Tesch also makes good wines in some years from both Langenlonsheim and neighbouring Laubenheim's vineyards. Laubenheim's wines, particularly the Rieslings from the Fuchsen and Karthäuser sites, can be finer than Langenlonsheim's, but successful examples from these sites are still rare.

The Unter Nahe's top vineyards are as steep as those of the Mittel Nahe, generally occupying the south-facing slopes in side valleys. The first of these, moving downstream, lie in the Trollbach Valley. The magnificent steep, rocky slopes of the Dorsheimer Goldloch and Pittermännchen can be seen from the A61 Autobahn. Driving past this spectacular corner of the Nahe a number of extra-ordinary sights meet the eye. First there is the Medieval fortified tower of Burg Layen, under which stands a large, rather gaudy sign emblazoned with the words 'Schlossgut Diel' in gothic script. At night this sign is illuminated, making it look like a piece of Piccadilly circus marooned in the middle of nowhere. As this disappears the vineyards swing into view, in the midst of which are two further signs, this time painted in vivid colours with the names 'Goldloch' and 'Pittermännchen'. These signs are in fact paintings by the artist Johannes Helle.

Schlossgut Diel is by far the most important producer of Rieslings from Dorsheim's top sites, but recently the estate has attracted at least as much attention for its artistic statements as for its wines. The buildings and vineyards are now the Unter Nahe's most significant landmark. In 1988, Johannes Helle created a sensation in the cellars by painting the walls, floors, ceilings and even a battery of steel fermentation tanks in rather less than traditional style. The present Schloss, built by the Diel family shortly after they acquired the property in 1802, has also been decorated by Helle, though in a rather more subtle style. Armin Diel has only recently been able to restore the tower of the original ruined Burg, or castle, to its full glory. The combination of these extremely heterogeneous elements produces an effect that is almost dizzying, but somehow it does form an extraordinary whole.

Dorsheim's top-site Rieslings have a citrus-like intensity and an explosive vibrancy that makes them seem larger than life: they are unlike anything else on the Nahe. Those from the Dorsheimer Goldloch add a pronounced apricot-like fruit to this picture while those from the Dorsheimer Pittermännchen are even racier, often having a blackcurrant note similar to that found in some fine Mosel Rieslings. If the Pittermännchen wines represent one side of Nahe Riesling's personality, then the wines from the Goldloch represent the other, often having been described as Rheingau-like.

Other Dorsheim sites, particularly the Burgberg, also have the potential to make interesting Rieslings. Schlossgut Diel, Krüger-Rumpf and Michael Schäfer make good examples with considerably more body and a less pointed acidity than the wines of the Mittel Nahe. These are much better suited to being vinified dry than their more famous cousins from upstream. Indeed, it is a moot point whether the Rieslings from the Unter Nahe are better as dry wines or wines with some natural sweetness. Ample evidence exists to support both arguments.

Some of the Untere Nahe's most interesting drier-style Rieslings come from Münster-Sarmsheim (only the first half of the town's name appears on its wine labels). It is blessed with the two most

The village of Mandel, just northwest of Bad Kreuznach, nestling below its precipitous vineyards in the Hunsruck hill-country.

planted on deep, rather heavy soils that give less distinguished wines. Largely for this reason Bad Kreuznach produces its finest wines in middling vintages, with Rieslings from years with hot summers often tasting rather broad and heavy.

Bad Kreuznach's name is most strongly associated with the August Anheuser, Paul Anheuser, Carl Finkenauer and Reichsgraf von Plettenberg estates. While they all make some good wines, none has been on top form in recent years. As a result Bad Kreuznach's standing as a wine-growing centre has slipped somewhat during the last decade.

The wines of the Unter Nahe are as much a mixed bag as those from around Bad Kreuznach. Here too considerable areas of arable

Münster-Sarmsheim, where excellent drier-style Riesling is produced, with Bingen's top vineyards behind.

famous sites in the area: the Münsterer Dautenpflänzer and Pittersberg, whose fame rests largely upon the wines made here until the mid-1980s by the Nahe State Domain. Unlike Dorsheim's best vineyards, which are tucked away in the Trollbach Valley, these sites lie relatively close to the river. The sweep of their steep slopes can be seen from down in the valley or from the main road on the right bank of the river.

The Münsterer Dautenpflänzer and Pittersberg wines have even more spice and mineral flavour than those of Dorsheim and their fruit character can be positively extravagant. Blackcurrant, strawberry and raspberry notes are no less typical for these wines than peach or apricot. These 'wild' aromas are less pronounced in the Pittersberg wines, which are sleeker and more elegant than Dautenpflänzer Rieslings. The Dautenpflänzer gives the Unter Nahe's biggest, most powerful wines but they can also possess a remarkable balance and persistence of flavour. For some these wines are too much, but for others they represent a further exciting facet of German Riesling's complex personality. Today Krüger-Rumpf of Münster-Sarmsheim makes the best wines from these top sites and owns the best restaurant in the neighbourhood, which shares the estate's name.

The less steep and rocky vineyards in the Unter Nahe, where the soil is deeper and loamier, are ideally suited to the Pinot varieties, most importantly Weissburgunder and Grauburgunder. They give dry wines that can be just as good as the area's Rieslings. Although they can achieve 13 and more degrees of alcohol in years with hot summers, they almost always have a more elegant harmony than wines made from the same grapes in more southerly regions. Their intense but never opulent apple-, pear- and melon-like fruit and crisp acidity make them easy to enjoy.

Several vintners have tried vinifying these wines in new oak. So far, Schlossgut Diel's experiments have enjoyed the greatest success, particularly with a cuvée of Grauburgunder and Weissburgunder called 'Victor'. Michael Schäfer and Wilhelm Sitzius also make good examples. Experiments with Chardonnay are at an early stage and few of the leading vintners have risked planting it. Of those who have, only the Krüger-Rumpf estate is so far offering un-oaked Chardonnay wines on the market. It seems doubtful that the grape will play a significant role in the region as it surely will in Baden, the Pfalz and Württemberg. German Chardonnay has not turned out to be the runaway success predicted by some members of the trade.

Spätburgunder rosé is another wine with which the region seems certain to make its name. Styles range from the pale, clean 'Blanc de Noir' wines of Krüger-Rumpf that are almost white, to Schlossgut Diel's richer, salmon-coloured wines. One of the most important rosé specialists, the Prinz zu Salm-Dalberg estate, lies out to the west of the Unter Nahe at Wallhausen in the Gräfenbach Valley.

A visit to Wallhausen and the Prinz zu Salm-Dalberg estate is almost like a journey back through several centuries and, ignoring the presence of cars and the odd satellite dish, gives a good idea what the region must have been like generations ago. Schloss Wallhausen, one of the homes of the Princes of Dalberg since 1565, is a well preserved Renaissance castle with magnificent vaulted cellars reminiscent of a cathedral crypt. However the Dalbergs' original seat, Dalburg Castle, a few kilometres upstream, was far more imposing. Built around 1150 but now in ruins, this massive fortress was the base from which the family ruled a small but important kingdom. The current owner, Michael Prinz zu Salm-Salm, presides over a small wine kingdom, having recently added the Villa Sachsen estate of Bingen in Rheinhessen to his family estate. Here, as at Wallhausen, Riesling will remain the most important variety.

Another impressive Medieval castle lies a short distance from Wallhausen up in the Hunsrück: the Stromburg of Stromberg. Austrian chef Johann Lafer, who worked previously at the superb

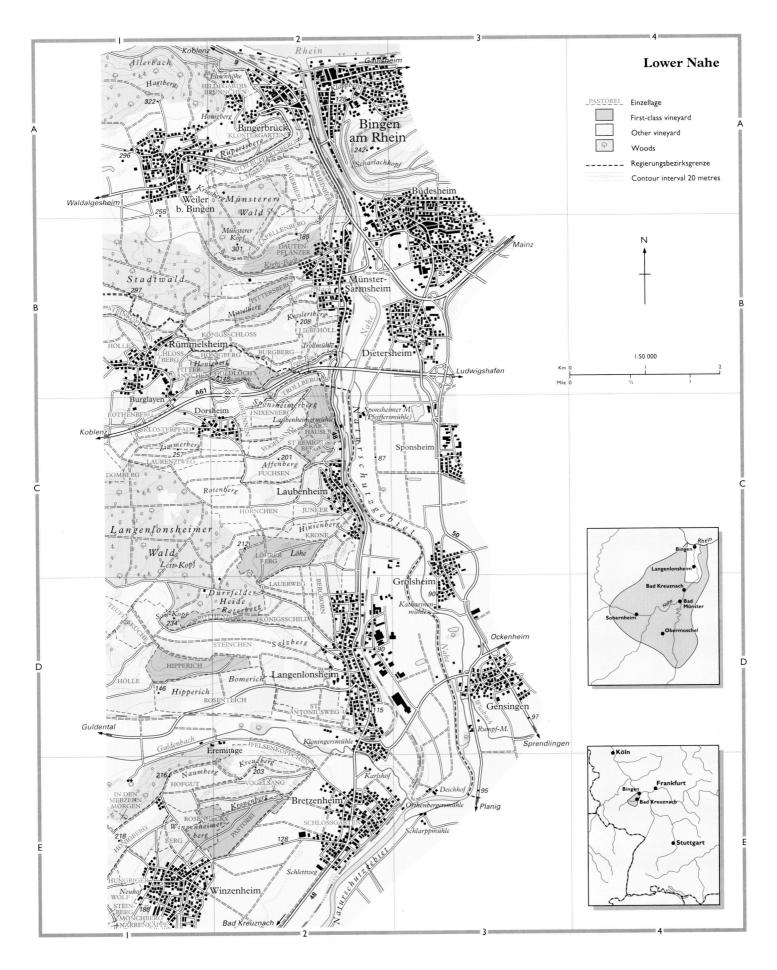

Lower Nahe

PASTOREI — Einzellage

First-class vineyard

Other vineyard

Woods

– – – – Regierungsbezirksgrenze

Contour interval 20 metres

1:50 000

Km 0   1   2

Mile 0   1/2   1

N

Val d'Or restaurant in Guldental on the Unter Nahe, has recently converted this historical monument into a new luxury hotel and restaurant. Despite its being so far from any of Germany's urban centres, it looks certain to become one of the gastronomic highpoints in this part of the country.

The Nahe region certainly has a bright future, notwithstanding one or two unresolved issues such as whether or not red wine production is to play a significant role. Although the climate is rather cool for successful red wine grapes to grow, the region does have the advantage of being much drier than the Mosel or Rheingau. Since rot is one of the biggest problems for red wine producers, a plausible argument can certainly be made for red Nahe wines. A few producers, such as Hahnmühle of Mannweiler-Cölln in the Alsenz Valley, have proved that good Spätburgunder reds can be made, but interesting results have so far been achieved only in years with very hot summers.

The Alsenz Valley is one of many outlying parts capable of producing marvellous white wines, and this is where dynamic young vintners are needed if viticulture is to forge ahead. Here there is a small group of family-owned estates making good wines, and of these Hahnmühle (Peter & Martina Linxweiler), Erich Wilhelm Rapp of Bad Münster-am-Stein and Schmidt of Obermoschel are the best.

Silvaner, which was the dominant variety in the Nahe for centuries, stands at the opposite pole to Spätburgunder. It used to account for most of the vineyards that were too cool for Riesling grapes to ripen regularly. Now Silvaner occupies only 12 percent of the vineyard area. Although its wines are never remarkable, they can be appealingly fresh and fruity in both the dry and off-dry styles. Krüger-Rumpf make the best examples in a bone-dry style. Whether such wines are good enough to secure a long-term place for the grape as one of the region's important varieties is not clear, especially when several other regions, most obviously Franken and Rheinhessen, can achieve significantly better results.

It seems certain that Riesling and the Pinot family of grapes will account for virtually all high-quality Nahe wines in the future and that Müller-Thurgau will become the only significant grape for everyday drinking wines. As elsewhere in Germany, the long-term commercial viability of bulk wine production is questionable. Even

Above: Distinctive red slate soil dominates Roxheimer Berg, one of the Nahe's first-class vineyards.
Right: Springtime at Wallhausen, home of Germany's oldest wine estate Prinz zu Salm-Dalberg.

Below: Snow highlights the bizarre rock protrusions in Langenlonsheim. Similar volcanic formations are scattered throughout the Nahe.

with full mechanisation and the maximum yield allowed by law, production costs are higher here than for comparable wines from other mass-producing countries such as those in Eastern Europe and the Ukraine.

The numerous other, mostly inferior, modern grape varieties cultivated in the region rarely yield anything special. For some inexplicable reason even Scheurebe, which in other parts of Germany can yield dessert wines that match the best Rieslings, does little noteworthy here. In Rheinhessen and the Pfalz Huxelrebe can also give rich dessert wines with marvellous balance, but few such wines have been made on the Nahe. Kerner can achieve reasonably pleasant, fruity wines, but it has had little success here. Other *Neuzuchtungen* are simply a waste of time and effort, since the wines they give are unremarkable and could even be held partly responsible for the region's confused image. The slogan devised to promote the Nahe, *Probierstübchen der Deutschen Weinlande* (Germany's tasting room), was hardly a great success. Most of the other grape varieties cultivated serve only to divert attention from the great Nahe Rieslings, which truly belong among the world's white wine elite.

BENCHMARK WINES

OBER NAHE

Niederhäuser Hermannshöhle Riesling Spätlese
Weingut H Dönnhoff, Oberhausen

Vineyard site: Niederhäuser Hermannshöhle
Site area: 8.5 hectares, 1.3 hectares Dönnhoff
Exposure: south
Inclination: very steep
Soil: weathered slate, porphyry and sandstone, very stony
Description: A ravishing bouquet in which peach, berry and exotic fruit aromas mingle with sweet floral and mineral notes. Not the most powerful Nahe Riesling, but certainly the most subtle. Layer upon layer of fruit interwoven with a vibrant acidity makes the mineral flavours shimmer in the lingering aftertaste.
Best vintages: '94, '93, '92, '91, '90, '89, '83
Best drunk: Too complex and subtle to accompany food, Nahe wines of this exalted quality are best enjoyed by themselves. They show best either during the first two years after the vintage or after at least five years of ageing in the bottle.

Schlossböckelheimer Felsenberg Riesling Spätlese Halbtrocken
Weingut Crusius, Traisen

Vineyard site: Schlossböckelheimer Felsenberg
Site area: 25 hectares, 1.5 hectares Crusius
Exposure: southwest
Inclination: very steep
Soil: melaphyre, very stony
Description: The rich apricot, orange and mango aromas at first suggest these wines will be sweet, but they are rich and dry. Unusually for high-class Mittel Nahe Rieslings, it is the fruit character that stands in the foreground, mineral flavours coming through only in the long, clean aftertaste. They are a perfect marriage of the serious and sensual aspects of Nahe wine.
Best vintages: '94, '93, '92, '90, '89, '88, '86, '85, '83
Best drunk: These are marvellous wines to drink with all kinds of light, savoury food. They can just as easily be matched with meat dishes as with fish, as long as garlic does not come into play.

UNTER NAHE

Dorsheimer Goldloch Riesling Spätlese
Schlossgut Diel, Burg Layen

Vineyard site: Dorsheimer Goldloch
Site area: 15 hectares, 4 hectares Schlossgut Diel
Exposure: south
Inclination: very steep
Soil: gravelly loam top-soil, porphyry sub-soil
Description: Diel's Goldloch Rieslings are a unique expression of the combination of power and elegance that typifies the wines of the Unter Nahe. Apricot and citrus aromas leap from the glass and the vibrant acidity drives the full fruit flavours across the palate to the clean, crisp aftertaste. Dramatic and forceful at first, the subtle earth and mineral notes reveal themselves with each successive sip.
Best vintages: '94, '93, '92, '90, '89, '83
Best drunk: In their youth these are wines to drink by themselves or with canapés. After five or more years' ageing in the bottle they taste dry enough to drink with a wide range of lighter dishes.

Münsterer Dautenpflänzer Riesling Spätlese Trocken
Weingut Krüger-Rumpf, Münster-Sarmsheim

Vineyard site: Münsterer Dautenpflänzer
Site area: 6 hectares, 0.9 hectares Krüger-Rumpf
Exposure: southeast
Inclination: very steep
Soil: loess top-soil, slate sub-soil
Description: Full-bodied and very dry, with intense flavours of blackberry or raspberry, these are about as far from the stereotyped image of German Riesling as a wine can get. They may not be the most subtle wines produced on the Nahe, but they are always full of character with a satisfying harmony of fruit, mineral flavours from the soil and crisp acidity.
Best vintages: '94, '92, '90, '89
Best drunk: These are ideally suited to the hearty country-style cooking served in the Rumpf's own restaurant. They have enough body and flavour to cope with strong cheese, mushrooms – even sausages.

BEST PRODUCERS:

Weingut Crusius
Hauptstrasse 2,
55595 Traisen
Owner: Dr Peter Crusius
Vineyard area: 12.5 hectares
Grape varieties: 75% Riesling,
10% Weissburgunder,
10% Müller-Thurgau,
3% Spätburgunder, 2% Silvaner
Top sites: Niederhäuser Felsensteyer,
Schlossböckelheimer Felsenberg,
Traiser Bastei

Through the 1970s and 1980s Hans Crusius made supremely elegant intensely mineral Rieslings which, together with the wines of the State Domain, epitomise Nahe wine. The estate's Auslese, Beerenauslese and Eiswein dessert wines were among the best in the country. Since taking over the estate in the early 1990s Dr Peter Crusius has had to struggle to maintain his father's impeccable standards, but he now seems to have found his feet. Further improvements are necessary, however, if the Crusius name is once again to symbolise all that is good about German Riesling.

The estate's traditional hallmarks are expressive fruit, a mineral character and perfect balance. While the family presents the wines from the Traiser Bastei as its best, Rieslings from their substantial holdings in the Schlossböckelheimer Felsenberg vineyard have been more impressive in recent years. These are usually vinified in the Halbtrocken style, matching the rich fruit with an appealing dry harmony.

Peter Crusius (left) and his father Hans quietly produce elegant, well balanced Rieslings from land that the family has owned since the 16th century.

Armin Diel, enfant terrible of the German wine and food scene.

Schlossgut Diel

55452 Burg Layen
Owner: Armin Diel
Vineyard area: 12.5 hectares
Grape varieties: 70% Riesling,
15% Grauburgunder,
5% Weissburgunder,
5% Spätburgunder, 5% other varieties
Top sites: Dorsheimer Goldloch,
Dorsheimer Pittermännchen

Armin Diel is a dramatic character, working as a restaurant and wine critic as well as running Schlossgut Diel. Regardless of the apparent conflict of interests, there is no denying the excellence of the estate's classic-style Rieslings or new-oak-aged wines from the Pinot family of grapes. Although the estate is best known for its dry wines, in recent years the naturally sweet and dessert Rieslings have been making headlines. They have an explosive fruitiness and an almost electric interplay of racy acidity and sweetness which reaches the highest intensity in the estate's sensational Eisweins, some of the finest in Germany. However, even a Riesling Spätlese from one of Dorsheim's top sites has impressive aroma and flavour. Although their style deliberately reflects Armin Diel's love of top-class Mosel-Saar-Ruwer wines, the distinctive personality of these long-underrated vineyards shines through every time.

While the estate's new-oak-aged Weissburgunder and Grauburgunder cannot match the richness of comparable wines from Baden or the Pfalz, they have an excellent harmony of fruit, subtle oak and an elegance that predestines them for the dinner table. The best is 'Victor', a concentrated cuvée of both grapes with pronounced toast and vanilla elements from the wood. More recently Spätburgunder rosé has been

added to the list and tentative experiments with red wine have also been made. Although this estate has seen dramatic developments during recent years, there should be still more to come.

Weingut Hermann Dönnhoff

Bahnhofstrasse 11,
55585 Oberhausen/Nahe
Owner: Helmut Dönnhoff
Vineyard area: 9.5 hectares
Grape varieties: 75% Riesling,
15% Weissburgunder and
Grauburgunder, 5% Müller-Thurgau,
5% other varieties
Top sites: Oberhäuser Brücke
(wholly owned),
Niederhäuser Hermannshöhle,
Schlossböckelheimer Felsenberg

Helmut Dönnhoff is the opposite of the stereotypical image of the great winemaker, never blowing his own trumpet and keeping to himself all the tension and doubts involved in making wines of the highest calibre. His estate long stood in the shadow of the Nahe State Domain which dominates the hillside directly across the Nahe from Dönnhoff's small winery in the village of Oberhausen. However, since the late 1980s he has been making wines with all the qualities once associated with those of his famous neighbour. They marry aromatic intensity with the highest elegance and are as expressive and refined as German Riesling can be.

It is difficult to decide whether the Rieslings from the estate's wholly-owned Oberhäuser Brücke site or those from the famous Niederhäuser Hermannshöhle are the greater. The Hermannshöhle wines have a more intense mineral and spice character and finer fruit, while those from the Brücke are more succulent and piquant. One vintage favours the former while the next brings out the best in the latter. Helmut Dönnhoff's dry Rieslings need several years to

Modest Helmut Dönnhoff produces intensely aromatic, elegant wines.

reach their optimum harmony and the best Spätlese and Auslese with natural sweetness can age for 20 years or more.

Weingut Krüger-Rumpf

Rheinstrasse 47,
55424 Münster-Sarmsheim
Owner: Stefan Rumpf
Vineyard area: 14 hectares
Grape varieties: 65% Riesling,
10% Silvaner, 5% Weissburgunder,
5% Müller-Thurgau, 5% Scheurebe,
3% Chardonnay, 3% Spätburgunder,
4% other varieties
Top sites: Münsterer Dautenpflänzer,
Münsterer Pittersberg

This estate on the Unter Nahe, founded by Karl Krüger in 1790, was once one of the largest and most important wine producers in the region. However, by the time Stefan Rumpf took it over in 1984 it had shrunk to a fraction of its former 60 hectares. Rumpf has done a remarkable job of rebuilding the estate's vineyard holdings and its reputation. Although Rieslings are its most highly regarded wines, the dry Silvaner, non-oaked Chardonnay and white Spätburgunder ('Blanc de Noirs') all enjoy a healthy demand. The Krüger-Rumpf Rieslings have a style unlike that of any other Nahe wine. Crystal-clear, sleek yet intensely aromatic, they possess a strong bouquet of blackberry or blackcurrant. The other whites are fresh and fruity with more discreet aromas. The dry wines that make up the bulk of the production often have plenty of alcohol (12 degrees is common). Only since the '90 vintage has Stefan Rumpf made a few Riesling Spätlese and Auslese wines with natural sweetness.

On the ground floor of their home the Rumpf's have opened a restaurant

serving good country food and a wide selection of their wines.

Weingut Prinz zu Salm-Dalberg

Im Schloss,
55595 Wallhausen
Owner: Michael Prinz zu Salm-Salm
Vineyard area: 9.5 hectares
Grape varieties: 65% Riesling,
8% Silvaner, 8% Müller-Thurgau,
7% Spätburgunder, 6% Kerner,
3% Grauburgunder, 3% Scheurebe
Top site: Roxheimer Berg

First recorded in 1200, this is the world's oldest wine estate that has remained in the uninterrupted ownership of a single family. However, it does not blindly follow tradition. The current owner, Michael Prinz zu Salm-Salm (also national president of the VDP) has made many important changes. He has converted the estate's vineyards to organic viticulture, removed vineyard names from all labels except those of the top-sites' Rieslings and, most recently, purchased the vineyards of the Villa Sachsen estate of Bingen in Rheinhessen. (Their wines will be made at Wallhausen but marketed under the Villa Sachsen name.)

The estate's best wines are the Rieslings with natural sweetness. Through late and selective harvesting Auslese and Beerenauslese wines are made in every good vintage. They have abundant fruit and a mineral acidity that is refreshing in spite of the wines' richness. The estate has also established a good reputation for fresh and vibrantly fruity dry Spätburgunder rosé.

Staatliche Weinbaudomäne Niederhausen-Schlossböckelheim

55585 Niederhausen
Owner: State of Rheinland-Pfalz
Vineyard area: 37 hectares
Grape varieties: 96% Riesling,
3% Müller-Thurgau, 1% Kerner
Top sites: Niederhäuser Hermannsberg (wholly owned), Niederhäuser Hermannshöhle, Schlossböckelheimer Felsenberg, Schlossböckelheimer Kupfergrube, Traiser Bastei

Dogged by problems since the departure of its great winemaker Karl-Heinz Sattelmayer in 1987, the owners, the state of Rheinland-Pfalz, decided to make radical changes here. Kurt Gabelmann has been appointed director and winemaker, and the vineyards in Dorsheim and Münster-Sarmsheim on the Unter Nahe are to be sold. Perhaps these moves will help the estate to regain its position among the region's wine elite. Anyone lucky enough to find Nahe State Domain wines of the '83 vintage or before will appreciate the exceptional quality of their wines from the great

Niederhausen and Schlossböckelheim vineyards. Naturally sweet Riesling Spätlese, Auslese and higher quality Prädikat wines have always been the State Domain's greatest strength.

Weingut Emrich Schönleber
Naheweinstrasse 10a,
55569 Monzingen
Owners: Hanne and Werner Schönleber
Vineyard area: 11.25 hectares
Grape varieties: 76% Riesling, 7% Kerner, 6% Grauburgunder, 6% Müller-Thurgau, 5% Bacchus
Top site: Monzinger Halenberg

This estate has been the rising star of the Nahe during the last decade, making ever-better dry and naturally sweet Rieslings. Werner Schönleber is determined to make further improvements and has recently expanded his holdings in the excellent Monzinger Halenberg vineyard in order to increase the estate's potential for producing top-class wines. The slate soil gives wines with fine peach-like fruit, pronounced mineral character and a racy acidity which resemble fine Mittel Mosel Rieslings. The estate's best wines, the Frühlingsplätzchen and Halenberg Riesling Auslese, are also the best of this style in the region.

OTHER WELL KNOWN PRODUCERS

Weingut Paul Anheuser
Stromberger Strasse 15–19,
55545 Bad Kreuznach

Standards at this large, well known estate seem to have slipped during the early 1990s and its Rieslings can lack the combination of ripe fruit and elegant acidity that once made them so attractive.

Weingut Bürgermeister Willi Schweinhardt
Heddesheimer Strasse 1,
55450 Langenlonsheim
One of the most reliable producers of dry Riesling, Weissburgunder, Grauburgunder and Gewürztraminer on the Unter Nahe. The BA and TBA dessert wines can be magnificent.

Weingut Carl Finkenauer
Salinenstrasse 60,
55545 Bad Kreuznach
This is another large estate whose performance has been somewhat erratic in recent years. While some wines are appealingly juicy, others can be a touch rough and rustic.

Weingut Hahnmühle
67822 Mannweiler-Cölln
Within only five years Peter and Martina Linxweiler have established a good reputation for organically grown dry Riesling and Traminer and the best Spätburgunder reds in the Nahe.

Weingut Hehner-Kilz
Hauptstrasse 4,
55596 Waldböckelheim
Holdings in the best vineyards of Schlossböckelheim give Georg and Helmut Hehner the potential to make Rieslings of the highest quality, a goal

they come closer to realising with each successive vintage.

Weingut Oskar Mathern
Winzerstrasse 7,
55585 Niederhausen
Young Helmut Mathern has produced some excellent Niederhausen Rieslings from the good vintages of the early 1990s and looks set to be the new star winemaker on the Nahe.

Weingut Reichsgraf von Plettenberg
Winzenheimer Strasse,
55545 Bad Kreuznach
This famous 40-hectare estate makes a wide selection of wines, some of them among the Nahe's best, from its excellently placed vineyards. Some of the most interesting wines are from Kreuznach. The sweet Riesling Auslese

are good but still do not quite match the spreme quality of those produced between the 1920s and 1970s.

Weingut Michael Schäfer
Hauptstrasse,
55452 Burg Layen
Alfred Schäfer makes dependable but rarely outstanding Rieslings and Weissburgunders from the Burg Layen and Dorsheim vineyards.

Weingut Wilhelm Sitzius
Naheweinstrasse 87,
55450 Langenlonsheim
From his vineyards at Langenlonsheim, Niederhausen and Oberhausen Wilhelm Sitzius has been making increasingly impressive dry and naturally sweet Rieslings. This newcomer is one to watch.

Travel Information

PLACES OF INTEREST

Bad Kreuznach The largest and most interesting town in the Nahe, Bad Kreuznach is the region's natural centre. Once a Roman fortress, it now has 40,000 inhabitants, though this number is swollen during summer months by the thousands of visitors who come to visit its famous spa. The Kurviertel or spa quarter is situated on the Wörth island between the

river Nahe and the Mühlenteich (an ancient diversion of the river designed to power water mills). Great old plane trees lining the Kurhausstrasse and the imposing Kurhaus give this corner of town a noble air. Bad Kreuznach's springs are rich in Radon, which can be inhaled in underground galleries or in the Kurpark. The walk through the Kurpark along the wooded left bank of the river is one of the most beautiful on the Nahe. Above this pathway lies the Kauzenburg castle which was built during the 12th century, destroyed by Napoleon's troops and recently restored as a hotel and restaurant. On the Alte Nahe Brücke or Old Nahe Bridge, built in 1311, stands a row of houses built between the 15th and 17th centuries. The Eiermarkt with its well preserved half-timbered buildings is also worth a visit.
Bad Münster-am-Stein-Ebernburg This spa town is five kilometres upstream from Bad Kreuznach at the confluence of the Alsenz with the Nahe. It is dominated by the beautifully maintained Ebernburg castle and the ruined 11th-century castle which stands on the 135-metre Rheingrafenstein cliff. On the opposite (left) bank of the Nahe lies the far greater mass of the Rotenfels, cliffs that soar over 200 metres almost vertically from the river bank. Below them is the narrow strip of vines which form the Traiser

The spectacular vineyards of Schlossböckelheim, famous for their great Rieslings.

The Alte Nahe Brücke in Bad Kreuznach. The bridge was built in 1311 and the houses added later.

Bastei site. The plateau above offers stunning views of the valley.

Idar-Oberstein Fifty kilometres upstream from Bad Kreuznach, some distance beyond the last vineyards of the Nahe region, the town of Idar Oberstein nestles among the first hills of the Hunsrück. The dual-carriageway passing through town is none too attractive but the national gem and precious stone museum is worth a detour in spite of its being housed in an ugly concrete tower block. The 15th-century *Felsenkirche* or cliff church, built into the side of a cliff face, is a short walk from the marketplace of Oberstein.

Meisenheim This beautiful historic village is in the Lower Glan Valley, a short drive from Sobernheim. The Obergasse and Untergasse are lined with well preserved houses dating from the 15th to 18th centuries, including the oldest surviving half-timbered house of region, the Gelbes Haus, built around 1490.

Monzingen There are beautiful Gothic and half-timbered houses in the centre of Monzingen. Good wine is also made here.

Niederhausen No visit to the Nahe would be complete without driving from Bad Münster-am-Stein to Schlossböckelheim along the left (northern) bank of the Nahe. From here there are unrivalled views of the vineyards of Niederhausen. The State Domain between Niederhausen and Schlossböckelheim is open for wine-tasting during the week from 8am to 4.30pm and in the morning of the first Saturday in each month.

Schlossböckelheim The massively buttressed terraces of the Kupfergrube site and other magnificent vineyards abut the State Domain's cellars in Schlossböckelheim. The town also has the ruins of the oldest castle on the Nahe, which dates back to at least 824.

Simmerntal A short distance upstream from the famous vineyards of Monzingen lies the small town of Simmerntal at the confluence of the Simmern and Nahe rivers. The iron foundry museum here can be visited by appointment. Telephone (06754) 8423.

Stromberg The drive to Stromberg from Rheinböllen along the Guldenbachtal passes through some of the most beautiful countryside in the Hunsrück. The village takes its name from the 11th-century Stromburg castle which has for many years been a hotel and restaurant but has recently been re-styled by chef Johann Lafer.

HOTELS AND RESTAURANTS

Im Gütchen
Hüffelsheimer Strasse 1,
55545 **Bad Kreuznach**
Tel: (0671) 42626
This is perhaps Bad Kreuznach's best restaurant. Good modern dishes are served in a beautifully restored old building.

Insel-Hotel
Kurhausstrasse 10,
55545 **Bad Kreuznach**
Tel: (0671) 43043, Fax: (0671) 27234
Less expensive than the Kurhaus Hotel (below) but also highly recommended for visitors wanting a central location.

Landhotel Kauzenburg
Auf dem Kauzenburg,
55545 **Bad Kreuznach**
Tel: (0671) 25461, Fax: (0671) 25465
Nestling among vineyards above the town, this hotel in a restored 12th-century castle has a good if slightly ostentatious restaurant.

Der Quellenhof
Nachtigallenweg 2,
55545 **Bad Kreuznach**
Tel: (0671) 2191, Fax: (0671) 35218
In its secluded position within Bad Kreuznach's Kurpark on the left bank of the Nahe, this luxury hotel offers an ideal location for complete relaxation.

Steigenberger-Avance Hotel Kurhaus
Kurhausstrasse 28,
55545 **Bad Kreuznach**
Tel: (0671) 2061, Fax: (0671) 35477
This is the grandest and most luxurious hotel in Bad Kreuznach and has direct access to the spa facilities.

Kurhotel Krone
Berliner Strasse 73,
55583 **Bad Münster-am-Stein**
Tel: (06708) 840, Fax: (07808) 84189
One of Bad Münster's best hotels, with sauna and swimming pool.

Metzler's Gasthof
Hauptstrasse 69,
55546 **Hackenheim**
Tel: (0671) 65312
Though the cooking is not the most imaginative, this restaurant is still a cut above many in nearby Bad Kreuznach.

Hotel-Restaurant Trollmühle
Rheinstrasse 199,
55424 **Münster-Sarmsheim**
Tel: (06721) 44066,
Fax: (06721) 43719
The most comfortable hotel on the Unter Nahe and, in spite of its proximity to the A61 Autobahn, quiet and secluded.

Val d'Or
Schlossberg,
55442 **Stromberg**
Tel: (06724) 93100
In 1994 talented Austrian chef Johann Lafer moved his superb Val d'Or restaurant from cramped premises in Guldental to the more spacious and imposing surroundings of the Stromberg's medieval castle. This enabled him to add a second, more rustic restaurant, Der deutsche Michel and a *Vinothek* or wine bar. The hotel rooms are good; the wine list superb.

USEFUL ADDRESSES

Kurverwaltung Bad Kreuznach,
Kurhausstrasse 23,
55543 **Bad Kreuznach**
Tel: (0671) 8360050
The tourist information office is easy to find in the colonnades close to the Kurhaus.

Verkehrsverein Bad Münster-am-Stein-Ebernburg
Berliner Strasse 56,
55583 **Bad Münster-am-Stein-Ebernburg**
Tel:(06708) 3993,
Fax: (06708) 3999

Städtische Verkehrsamt Idar-Oberstein
Bahnhofstrasse 13,
55743 **Idar-Oberstein**
Tel: (06781) 27025

Rheingau

The illustrious wine history of the Rheingau, in terms both of its own achievements and its influence upon other regions in Germany and beyond, makes it one of the most important wine regions in the world. Without the Rheingau the potential of the Riesling grape might never have been realised and the style of German wine, which has been widely copied throughout the world, might never have developed. Although the Rheingau does not always live up to its great traditions and its Rieslings do not always possess the nobility for which its best examples are renowned, its contribution to the wine world has been immeasurable.

As in the Mosel-Saar-Ruwer, viticulture in the Rheingau began with the Romans, as evidenced by archeological sites scattered from Wicker in the east to Rüdesheim in the west. Roman viticulture was probably on a modest scale here compared to other parts of Germany, perhaps because for several centuries the Rhine marked the boundary of the area under Roman administration. It was primarily the Church that set out the Rheingau as it is today, following the foundation of the monasteries of Johannisberg around 1100 and Kloster Eberbach in 1136.

In this stretch of the Rhine Valley the river flows from east to west, creating many sunny south-facing slopes. By the 13th century the monks of Kloster Eberbach had planted large areas of vineyards that took advantage of these and turned the Rheingau into one of Europe's most successful wine-growing regions. Their estate became the largest commercial wine producer in the world.

A wealth of architecture from this period remains, and much of it is still well preserved. The awe-inspiring monastery of Kloster Eberbach is perhaps the most impressive example, nestling between forested hills above the village of Hattenheim. Within and around these finely crafted walls the monks worked hard to improve viticultural and winemaking methods, selecting the best vine material and developing cellar equipment and techniques.

Extensive records survive from the period. By 1496 the monks of Kloster Eberbach and Schloss Johannisberg had developed a primitive filtration system and in 1500 they first used the 70,000-litre *magnum vas* cask, the largest in the world, for storing wine. The low surface-area-to-volume ratio meant that the wine it contained aged more slowly than that stored in the typical 600-litre

Evening sunlight on the busy River Rhine, a vital part of life in the Rheingau.

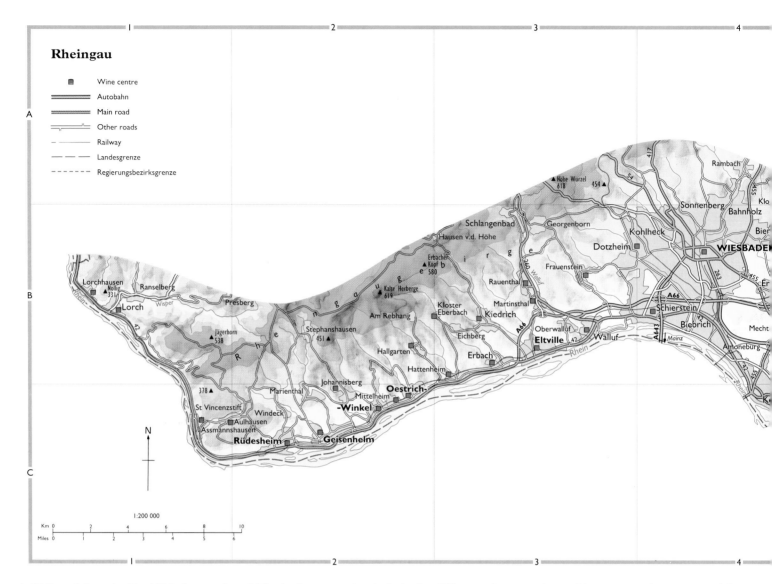

Rheingau

- ■ Wine centre
- ══════ Autobahn
- ═════ Main road
- ───── Other roads
- ─────── Railway
- ─ ─ ─ Landesgrenze
- ‑‑‑‑‑ Regierungsbezirksgrenze

1:200 000

N

Halbstück barrels. By 1603 the monks of Eberbach were using pipes to convey the grape must from the presses down into barrels in the cellar and during the 17th century they introduced the Dockenkelter wine press, examples of which can still be seen in the Laienrefektorium of Kloster Eberbach. Huge and unwieldy as they look now, they were a great improvement on the enormous *Baumkelter,* or tree presses, used until then.

During the 18th century the monks of Eberbach were the first to experiment with the late harvesting of 'rotten' grapes, to see if this could improve wine quality. In 1753 they harvested one 1200-litre *Stück* of such wine and in 1760, 15 of these barrels, which would suggest that the first experiment was a success. It was however the monks of Schloss Johannisberg who claimed the glory for the introduction of varietal Riesling wines and perfected late-harvesting techniques.

In 1720–21 on the slopes of Johannisberg the monks planted the first Riesling monoculture, that is the first recorded vineyard planted solely with Riesling. Until then mixed plantings of anything from two to a dozen vine varieties had been the norm. This strategy had been adopted to combat the effects of vintage variations, fungal diseases and insect pests. If one variety suffered from a particular problem one year, other unaffected varieties would be available to make up the yield. Blends of different grapes would mask individual varietal imperfections – the softness of Traminer and

the body of Silvaner, for example, would counteract the sourness of Riesling in a poor vintage. This was also the period when bottling was introduced: hitherto all wine had been stored and sold in barrel. It soon became apparent that while most wines faded within a few years of being bottled, Riesling could retain, or even improve, its character in glass. By the end of the 18th century the late-ripening Riesling had found its place as the Rheingau's noble grape.

There was then a further, almost accidental, discovery which surely changed the course of wine history. The wine harvest at Schloss Johannisberg could not begin until the order was given by the Abbot of Fulda. In 1775 the messenger conveying the order was delayed and as a result the harvest began considerably later than normal. The autumn of 1775 was fine and the Riesling grapes became over-ripe and began to rot. We now know that this was *Botrytis cinerea* or noble rot, but at the time the anxious monks could not have known that, for centuries to come, generations of vintners around the world would wait and watch and hope and pray for exactly such a 'rotten' harvest in their own vineyards.

The 1775 Schloss Johannisberg wines caused a sensation. In April 1776 the estate manager, Johann Michael Engert, wrote in his diary, "These 1775 wines in the seigniorial cellars receive such extraordinary approval from all manner of true connoisseurs that you often hear nothing else said at tastings than: 'I've never had such a wine in my mouth before'." So the first 'Spätlese', or late-

harvested wine, was produced by a happy accident. During the following years the monks systematically repeated the experiment, picking botrytized grapes separately to produce the first Auslese, or selectively harvested, wine in the 1780s.

These designations, which have been a part of German wine culture for two centuries and are now part of its Wine Law, were not printed on labels until rather later. Coloured sealing wax over the cork was used to signify the differing qualities of bottled wines. Several of the Rheingau's aristocratic estates, notably Schloss Johannisberg, Schloss Vollrads and Langwerth von Simmern still use coloured capsules to indicate wine quality. This system came into general practice at the region's great estates in 1811, the first year in which the entire Rheingau wine harvest was deliberately delayed to improve quality and many noble estates experimented with selective harvesting.

The results were an enormous international success. By the 1820s Rheingau Rieslings already enjoyed an exceptional reputation in Europe. Even in the best Parisian restaurants they outpriced the Montrachets of Burgundy. During the 19th century the Rheingau established an international reputation as the world's number one producer of quality white wines. This was almost entirely the work of the region's aristocratic and church estates, notably Schloss Johannisberg, Schloss Schönborn and the Prussian State Domain (now the Staatsweingüter Kloster Eberbach).

Erwein Graf Matuschka-Greiffenclau of Schloss Vollrads, a tireless promoter of Rheingau wines. The family has owned estates in Winkel since at least 1100.

A glance at the price lists of leading wine merchants from the end of the 19th century shows that Rheingau Rieslings were then the most expensive wines in the world. The November 1896 list of Berry Bros & Rudd of London offers 1886 Marcobrunn 'Cabinet' and 1862 Rüdesheimer Hinterhaus (now Berg Rottland) for 200 shillings per dozen bottles, while the most expensive champagnes are Cliquot and 1880 Binet for 100 shillings per dozen and the highest-priced red Bordeaux is the 1870 Château Lafite at 144 shillings per six magnums. Only the the very best Château d'Yquem matched Rieslings' price. Everywhere merchants and connoisseurs regarded Kiedricher Berg, Marcobrunn, Rauenthaler Baiken, Rüdesheimer Berg, Schloss Johannisberger and Steinberger as the best white wines that money could buy.

Making such wines, however, involved taking enormous risks in the vineyard and devoting great attention to detail in the cellar. In their *Handbook of Wine-growing and Winemaking* (1893) August von Babo and Edmund Mach wrote, 'On the Rhine [Rheingau] the harvest of the Riesling grapes, particularly in the best vineyard sites when the weather allows, takes place very late, often starting in late November or even December. Naturally this results in a considerable quantitative reduction in the yield and is

97

only possible where a very high quality can be achieved. If the autumn is dry then the nobly-rotten berries gradually shrivel to raisins, which can be selectively harvested and from which the most precious Auslese wines are made.'

The words 'noble' and 'aristocratic' could have been coined to describe the finest Rieslings of the Rheingau. In them richness and austerity are precisely matched, power and elegance perfectly balanced. There is rarely anything playful or superficially charming about great Rheingau Riesling as there often is about the finest Mosel-Saar-Ruwer wines. Rheingau wines are firmer and have more body than comparable Mosel Rieslings: their fruit character is more forcefully marked by flavours from the soil; their acidity firmer and more assertive. While their youthful verve can be marvellous, they need several years in the bottle to reach their best harmony and display their full glory. Examples of such perfection might be found in a Spätlese of the '83, '79, '75, or '71 vintages from one of the famous estates. These are now in their best form, still lively, but with the subtlety and equilibrium of maturity. For anyone not blinded by the vibrant fruit of young wines, these Rieslings can bestow one of the greatest pleasures the grape has to offer.

It is sad that these words of richly deserved praise must be qualified but, since the late 1960s, the Rheingau's international standing has slipped badly. The 1971 Wine Law must take some of the blame, as in other German wine-growing regions, but many of the Rheingau's great aristocratic estates have clearly lost their way during the last two decades. The thoughtless 'rationalisation' of winemaking techniques to reduce labour costs is one source of problems, another is the apparent decline in the number of dedicated winemakers. Great Rieslings are not a commodity but the result of tremendous commitment, skill and care in the vineyard and cellar and this kind of dedication seems increasingly rare among those involved.

Modern winemakers are attempting to automate the production of something which, when craftsmen and nature work together, can be a sublime natural phenomenon. The use of reliable cultured yeasts in fermentation, to take just one example, has in some cases been introduced to reduce the risk involved in using natural yeast from the vineyard. Many wine scientists suggest that there is nothing to be lost by substituting cultured for natural yeast, but Germany's top winemakers see this very differently. During recent years poor vineyard management and the introduction of mechanical harvesting have also robbed many wines of the elegance and finesse which they once had in such abundance. It is especially sad that this kind of slackness should occur at such illustrious estates as those of the Rheingau's nobility, but the region's recent history reads like a catalogue of such problems. When the Schloss Eltz estate was wound up during the late 1970s and early 1980s as a result of other business difficulties, the region lost one of its finest producers. Since Schloss Johannisberg changed hands (the Oetken group is now co-owner) its performance has been erratic. State

ownership does not seem to have helped the Staatsweingüter Kloster Eberbach during this period either, though some recent wines, the '93 and '90 vintages for example, are an improvement on those of the 1980s. Schloss Groenesteyn and Prinz von Hessen are two further estates which have made few remarkable wines since 1983 and Schloss Vollrads has not shone in recent years either. Even estates whose wines have been consistently good until recently, such as Langwerth von Simmern and Schloss Schönborn, have been slipping during the last few years. It seems that some of the Rheingau's most famous estates can no longer be counted among the nation's wine elite and even the most exalted vineyard names are no longer a guarantee of superior quality.

But there is hope. There are winemakers who care deeply about the future of winemaking in the area. Apart from the large Schloss Reinhartshausen and Robert Weil estates, which have greatly benefited from new ownership since the late 1980s, the new stars of the Rheingau have come from the ranks of the region's modest sized, family-owned estates. Here at least are winemakers with ambition to make wines that can challenge the best in the world. The estates' headquarters may look more like normal suburban houses than castles, but the clarity of vision among the winemakers and the quality of their best wines are anything but parochial. None of the estates has substantial vineyard holdings in the region's top vineyards, but many of their wines from second-class sites still manage to overshadow comparable wines from the most famous vineyards

and estates, making their achievements all the more impressive.

All the Rheingau's new stars are enthusiastic producers of dry Rieslings and most are members of the Charta Estates Association, which is dedicated to promoting high-quality wines of this style. The Charta was founded in 1984 by Dr Hans Ambrosi (then director of the Staatsweingüter), Professor Helmut Becker (now deceased) of the Geisenheim wine school and research station, Bernhard Breuer of the Georg Breuer estate in Rüdesheim and Erwein Graf Matuschka-Greiffenclau of Schloss Vollrads. The Association took its cue from Graf Matuschka's international campaign to promote dry Rheingau Riesling wines as food wines, which began after he took over his family estate in 1977. The Charta declared that dry Riesling was the traditional style of Rheingau wines, set rigorous standards which had to be met before any wine could be sold in the special Charta bottle and began systematically promoting these wines through wine dinners in European and North American cities. So far these efforts have done much to improve the Rheingau's standing within Germany, but have met with only modest success elsewhere.

Heated discussion sparked by the Charta's bold declaration concerning the style of Rheingau wines continues to animate the region. Many feel strongly that Rheingau wines are traditionally dry; others are just as adamant that this is not the case. Both sides of the argument would appear to have some truth. Tastings of Rheingau wines from 50 and more years ago suggest that the majority of them were dry, if not always bone dry. On the other hand, the Auslese and higher quality late-harvest wines that made the Rheingau's international reputation invariably possessed a natural sweetness. Von Babo and Mach give the figure of 10–150 grams per litre of unfermented grape sugar for wines of this category. The lower limit of this range would correspond to modern Halbtrocken wines, while the upper limit is close to the sweetness of a contemporary Trockenbeerenauslese.

This contrasting pair of wine styles – dry and nobly sweet – together with a classification of the region's vineyards and a set of strict rules designed to guarantee high quality, have become a blueprint for the Rheingau's future. A new designation, *Erstes Gewächs* (First Growth) has been created for dry and sweet wines of Auslese and higher quality from the region's classified vineyards. The promoters of this scheme are the Charta and the Rheingau section of Germany's VDP – the Quality Wine Estates Association. Should the new designation receive official ratification from the State of Hessen, as seems likely, it will become the first modern, officially sanctioned German vineyard classification. This would be a momentous event which would have consequences for each of Germany's 13 wine-growing regions.

If this new scheme has a weakness, it is that participation will be optional. For example, the owners of vines in the Erbacher Marcobrunn will be able to continue producing the full range of wine styles from this site without the new designation, or they will be able to opt into the classification and market Erbacher Marcobrunn *Erstes Gewächs* but only as dry or dessert wines. Thus some producers will regularly offer sweet Erbacher Marcobrunn Spätlese without the words *Erstes Gewächs* on the label, while others will never produce Erbacher Marcobrunn wines of this style but will always sell their wines from this site with the *Erstes Gewächs* designation. This is at least fair, since it gives vintners the chance to decide for themselves what suits their wines best. But once again, the result promises to be confusing for consumers.

Many of the Rheingau's finest vineyards, such as Schloss Shönborn's Hattenheimer Pfaffenberg (left), lie directly on the river bank.

One principle widely accepted among the Rheingau's leading vintners is that a vineyard name printed on a label should guarantee that the bottle contains a superior quality wine with a distinctive character. There is no such consensus, however, on whether the dry or sweet style is better for most of the region's wines. Many of the Rheingau's famous estates appear to favour the existing status quo above the new system and it seems certain that, at least initially, any pressure from the association to dictate an approved style would divide the region's vintners just as the Charta did before it.

Although the main body of the Rheingau comprises a strip of land less than four kilometres wide and only 30 kilometres long, the region's wines are remarkably varied. This has as much to do with climatic differences as with differences in the soil composition. The most important microclimatic factors are, first, the half-mile-wide expanse of the Rhine which forms the southern border of the region for most of its length, acting as a huge heat reservoir and second, the hills of the Taunus to the north which shelter the vines from cold winds. The vineyards on the lower slopes benefit most from the river's warming influence, while those on the steeper slopes closer to the Taunus receive abundant sunlight but are noticeably cooler.

The fact that the soil is deeper and composed of loam or marl close to the river, and shallower and stonier on the higher slopes tends to reinforce the effect of the climatic differences, making the wines from the lower vineyards full-bodied, firm and assertive and those from the hills more perfumed, delicate and racy.

Only at Rüdesheim do steep vineyards rise directly from the bank of the Rhine, creating some of the region's greatest sites. Those whose name incorporates the word 'Berg' – Rüdesheimer Berg Rottland, Berg Schlossberg and Berg Roseneck – are all precipitous, with slate and quartzite soils that certainly present vintners with a practical challenge.

In spite of the vineyard reorganisation of the 1970s and early 1980s, which replaced innumerable tiny terraces with several much larger ones connected by a network of roads, tending the vines on these slopes is still arduous work.

In addition to the practical difficulties, in years with very dry summers drought stress can rob the wines of the Rüdesheimer Berg of the silky elegance and delicate fruit which are their usual hallmarks. The extensive replanting involved in the vineyard reorganisation exacerbated this problem, since nearly all the vines here are now young and their roots have not penetrated far enough to tap underground water sources.

Most of Rüdesheim's vineyards lie on the long gentle slope which extends behind the town up to the Niederwald woods and the massive, ugly statue of the Niederwald Denkmal which commemorates the German victory in the Franco-Prussian war of 1870–71. (The statue is so unattractive and visible from such a distance that the French government is still campaigning to have it removed). These are the so-called 'Oberfeld' vineyards and in hot years their wines can be superior to those from the Berg sites. Their deeper, loamier soils rarely lack water, so while the vines on the Rüdesheimer Berg suffer in the heat these flourish, giving rich wines with a lively acidity and a subtle earthy note. However, they can never match the finesse achieved by Berg Schlossberg and Berg Rottland wines when conditions are right. Given a growing season with enough rain, the Rüdesheimer Berg wines have an

The massive Neiderwald Denkmal statue, commemorating German victory in the Franco-Prussian war, dominates the vineyards behind Rüdesheim (top).
Young vines are nurtured at a nursery in Rüdesheim (right).

almost supernaturally fine peach-like fruit intertwined with a slate character as intense as that of the finest Mosel Rieslings.

Georg Breuer and Josef Leitz are the top producers of Rüdesheim, both making very elegant, generally dry Rieslings designed for long ageing. Many of Dr Nägler, Martin Seifried and Wegeler Erben's Rüdesheimers are also impressive but wines of this quality are, sadly, not the norm in Rüdesheim's many tourist restaurants and hotels.

In spite of having been badly damaged during World War II, the town has much character and large numbers of tourists arrive each year, often threatening to overwhelm its narrow streets. The most imposing of its old buildings is the Brömserburg castle which houses the town's excellent wine museum. It was built during the 11th century as one of a series of fortifications guarding this crucial point along the Rhine's course. The ruined Ehrenfels castle in the Rüdesheimer Berg Schlossberg site and the tiny Mouse Tower on an island in the Rhine were both built as toll gates.

Neighbouring Assmannshausen is an exception to the Rheingau norm, Spätburgunder (Pinot Noir) being the most important grape here. Red wine accounted for a sizeable proportion of most Rheingau villages' production until the late 18th and early 19th centuries and this is one of the few sites that was not replanted with white varieties. Local vintners maintain that red varieties are grown in most of Assmannshausen's vineyards because of the slate soil, but to the dispassionate observer the logic of this is hard to follow. Here vineyards just as steep and stony as the Rüdesheimer Berg yield generally rather pale, tart red wines quite unlike the Pinot Noirs of Burgundy.

The top vineyard site is the Assmannshäuser Höllenberg, a name which strikes a chord with many German wine enthusiasts. The red wines from the State Domain Assmannshausen are well made examples of the village's classic style, but the high prices they command disqualify them from an international audience. The best wines from August Kesseler are another matter. These possess a depth of colour and rich fruit remarkable for red wines produced so far north.

Part of the appeal of Assmannshausen's wines stems from the fact that this has long been a favourite destination for affluent visitors from Wiesbaden and Frankfurt. The beautiful Hotel Krone is full of photographs and paintings which illustrate the town's long history of grand hospitality. Assmannshauser Spätburgunder has long been a favourite with German high society.

Beyond Assmannshausen lie Lorch and Lorchhausen, whose sleek, tense Rieslings have more in common with those of the Mittelrhein than with typical Rheingau wines. Out on a limb both geographically and in terms of wine style, these villages have more difficulty in selling their wines than elsewhere in the region. This is unfortunate since although they may not have the depth of the greatest Rheingau wines they can be charming and elegant. The Graf von Kanitz estate is not only the best wine estate of Lorch but also an important landmark. The magnificent Renaissance Hilchenhaus, with its stepped gables, is perhaps the finest example from the period on the entire Rhine.

On the eastern side of Rüdesheim the main body of the Rheingau begins with the vineyards of Geisenheim. Geisenheim is best known for its wine school and research station which were founded in 1872 and are the most famous of their kind in Germany. A century ago the wines from Geisenheim's Rothenberg site were its prime claim to fame, being among the most sought-after and highly priced of all Rheingau wines. The iron-rich red slate soil

Finest Rheingau Riesling has tremendous ageing potential.

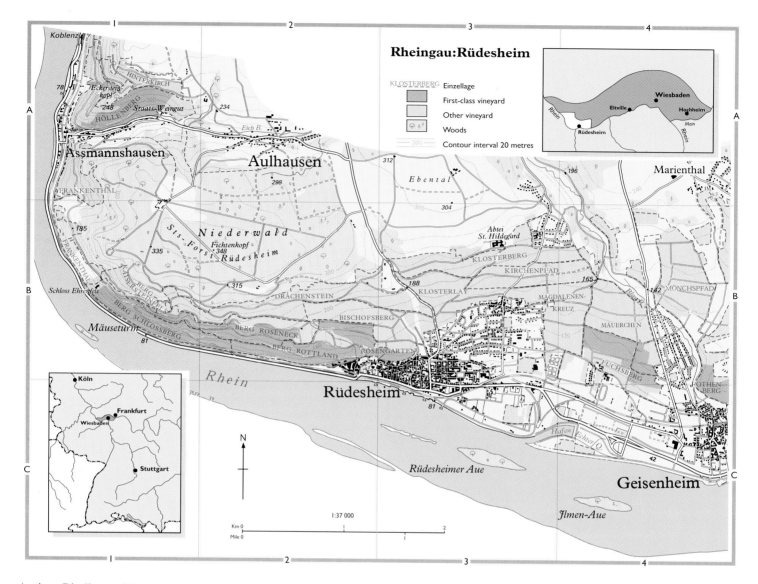

Rheingau:Rüdesheim

KLOSTERBERG Einzellage

First-class vineyard

Other vineyard

Woods

Contour interval 20 metres

1:37 000

Km 0 ____ 1 ____ 2

Mile 0 ____ 1

gives Rieslings with aromas of mango, passion fruit and almond: the wines are positively extravagant compared with the reserve typical of the region. Rich and succulent yet firmly structured, they are hard to resist as young wines and can age magnificently. Wegeler-Erben makes the most authentic examples. Freiherr von Zwierlein and Schloss Schönborn have also made some good Rothenbergers.

Most of Geisenheim's other vineyards give powerful, firm and earthy wines. Those from the Kläuserweg combine these qualities with some real sophistication. They need several years in bottle to show their best, often being rather firm and tart in their youth. The wines from the Fuchsberg are more juicy and appealing in their first years, having as much in common with Rüdesheim's wines as those of Geisenheim. Geisenheim itself is not particularly attractive, due to the light industry and uninspiring flats built there to accommodate students, but the old streets around the town's cathedral and Schloss Kosakenberg (a restaurant and home to the Zwierlein estate) next to the railway station are worth a visit. The wine school has open days several times a year.

The outstanding landmark of the central Rheingau is Schloss Johannisberg which, as Goethe wrote, sits regally on the pinnacle of the vine-clad Johannisberg hill as on a throne. According to legend, the vineyards here were planted on the orders of the Holy Roman Emperor Charlemagne. He is supposed to have looked

across the Rhine from his palace in Ingelheim (in what is now Rheinhessen) and noticed that the winter snow melted first on these slopes. There may well be some truth in the story: a document dated August 4, 817 recording vineyards here bears the seal of Charlemagne's son, Ludwig the Pious.

Under the ownership of the State Chancellor Clemens Wenzeslaus Fürst von Metternich-Winneburg, who was presented with the Schloss and its vineyards at the Vienna Congress of 1815, the estate became one of Germany's greatest and most famous. The Chancellor's work was continued by succeeding generations until the death of his great grandson, Paul Alfons, in 1992. The estate's wines can have the highest elegance and refinement and those of the '71, '64, '59, '53, '49, '47 and '45 vintages have achieved legendary status. All these wines were still in magnificent form in the mid-1990s.

Like the great wine estates of Bordeaux, Schloss Johannisberg is the name of both the wine estate and its vineyard site (which under German Wine Law is an *Ortsteil*, or suburb, of Johannisberg). Looked at objectively, this is one of the most favoured locations for the Riesling vine in the whole Rheingau. The hillside which falls from the terrace in front of the Schloss enjoys perfect southerly exposure and is the steepest vineyard in this part of the region. The loess and loam top-soil is littered with stones from the quartzite cliff that lies just below the surface. This, as much as the

The steep slopes of Rüdesheimer Roseneck (above and below). Terraces were widened in the 1970s, but tending the precipitous vineyards is still no easy task.

dedication of the Bishops of Fulda and the Fürst von Metternich family, is responsible for Schloss Johannisberg's becoming one of the first German estates and vineyards to appear on wine labels from the middle of the 18th century. The origins of the estate's own distinctive style of label go back to the 1822 vintage.

The Schloss itself is a unique monument and one of the essential destinations on any tour of the region. The majestic arc of its cavernous barrel cellar makes it possibly the most beautiful in the country. Like most of the Schloss it is baroque in style but lacks the pomposity associated with so much architecture of the period. The Schloss was almost completely destroyed in 1942 but painstakingly rebuilt between 1945 and 1965. For visitors it has its own restaurant and wine store, but the view from the terrace is reason enough to make a detour. Virtually the entire Rheingau, together with much of Rheinhessen on the opposite bank of the river, is spread before the Schloss.

Schloss Johannisberg's wines face tough competition from Rieslings produced by less renowned estates from the village's other fine sites. Of these the Klaus, Hölle and Mittelhölle are the best, but in years with hot summers the Goldatzel can also give first-class wines with as much racy elegance and finesse as those from the Schloss. The best of these come from the Johannishof estate of Hans Hermann Eser, which is in Johannisberg-Grund at exactly the spot where Johannisberg viticulture was first recorded.

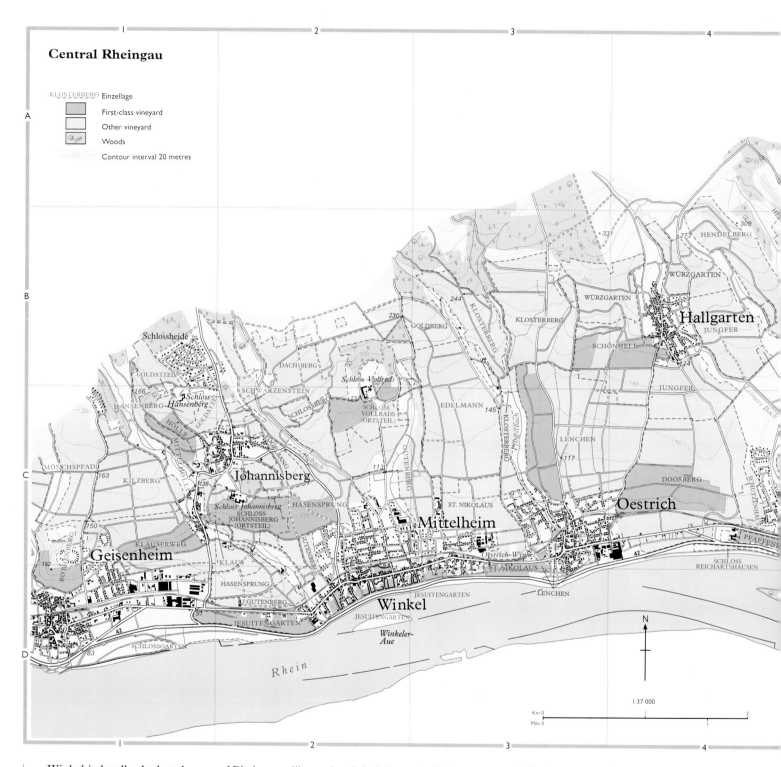

Central Rheingau

KLOSTERBERG Einzellage

First-class vineyard

Other vineyard

Woods

Contour interval 20 metres

1:37 000

Km 0 — 2
Mile 0 — 1

N

Winkel is hardly the best known of Rheingau villages, but it is full of history. The Romanesque *Graues Haus*, or Gray House, which stands close to the bank of the Rhine towards the western end of the town, is almost certainly the oldest stone house in Germany. It served as the home of the Knights of Greiffenclau from the time of its construction around 1050 until 1330 and remains in their ownership. Today it houses the region's finest restaurant. The nearby Romanesque church of Winkel was built at about the same time and is as well preserved as the *Graues Haus*.

The Brentano estate house close to the centre of town, which documents another important period in the region's history, is also worth a visit. The Brentanos were close friends of Goethe and their

home is a living museum full of mementos from the period. Goethe stayed here in September 1814 and sang the praises of the *Eilfer*, or Comet, as the wines of the great 1811 vintage were nicknamed.

The drive up to Vollrads behind Winkel is almost unchanged since Goethe's time, but in contrast to the picture of decay recorded in his diary, the Schloss is the most beautifully restored castle in the region. Its moated tower dates from 1330, although the roof was added when the complex of buildings was radically changed during the late 17th century. As at Schloss Johannisberg, the vineyard and estate names are identical. Traditionally, the Vollrads wines have enjoyed a high standing, although they need years with hot summers to excel. Then they possess a brilliance reminiscent of

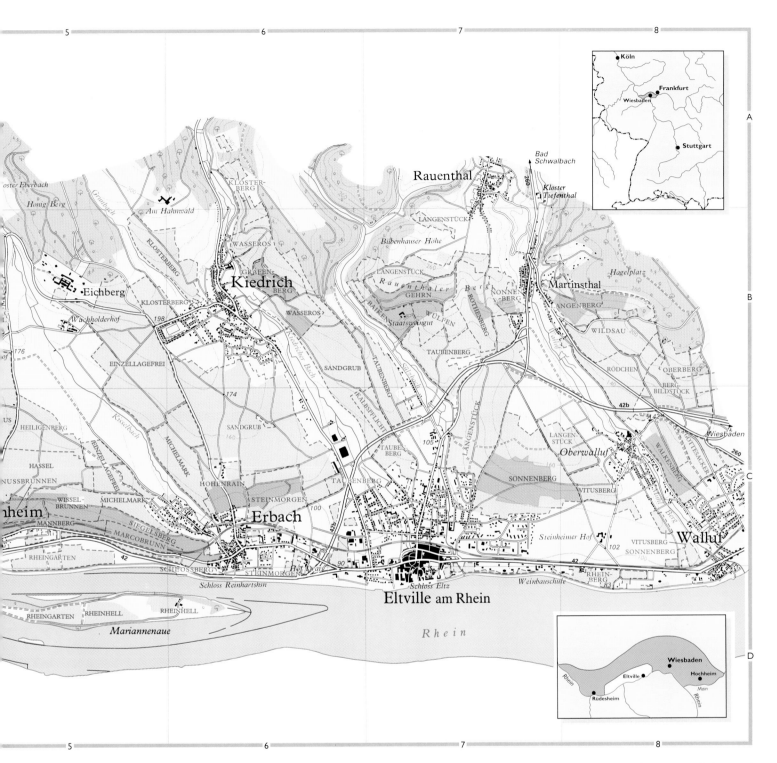

fine Saar Rieslings combined with the body and weight of the Rheingau. The lean, steely dry wines that make up most of the current production, however, sometimes fail to meet the estate's very high standards.

Winkel has two sites capable of giving Rieslings with the subtlety and depth expected of top-class Rheingau wines, the Jesuitengarten and the best part of the Hasensprung. Their wines combine crisp acidity with plenty of fruit and and a touch of earthiness. Those from the Hasensprung are the more powerful, those from the Jesuitengarten are more elegant. August Eser, Johannishof and Wegeler-Erben make the best Winkelers.

Much of the production from the lesser vineyards of Mittelheim

and Oestrich goes into sparkling wine production. Due to their pronounced acidity and relatively light body Rheingau Rieslings are in high demand from the larger sparkling wine companies as base wines. Fully ten percent of the region's product is sold in bulk to sparkling-wine producers. Fürst von Metternich, Reuter & Sturm and Schloss Vaux all specialise in high-quality sparkling Rheingau Riesling. Even better is the Geheimrat J Sekt from Wegeler-Erben, which is one of the finest in Germany.

Oestrich has another string to its bow in the form of the Spätlese and Auslese wines from the best parts of its Doosberg and Lenchen sites. If not the most elegant or refined Rheingau Rieslings, they have plenty of substance and are juicy and full of character in a slightly rustic way. Which of these sites is superior is a much disputed point. The Doosberg is often cited as the better because its wines are firmer and longer-living. August Eser and Wegeler-Erben, whose estates are situated close to one another in the centre of Oestrich, are the most reliable producers. Little else distinguishes the rather drab town.

Above Oestrich lies Hallgarten, perhaps the Rheingau's most under-appreciated wine village. In their youth Hallgarten Rieslings are strong and firm, even stern, but they can blossom magnificently after some years in the bottle. When mature, good examples can be compared to wines from much more famous vineyards. The only problem is to find such wines, since Hallgarten is dominated by co-operatives which produce nothing more than decent everyday wines. In the village itself the mini-estate of Fred Prinz makes the best wines. Though several other producers, such as Fürst Löwenstein, make some good wines from these vineyards, they are marketed without a vineyard designation. The result is that Hallgarten's name hardly ever appears on the label and its poor profile is perpetuated.

The contrast between Hallgarten's obscurity and the fame of neighbouring Hattenheim could not be more dramatic. Clustered around this village are a group of vineyards whose names conjure the noblest associations: Nussbrunnen, Wisselbrunnen, Pfaffenberg, Mannberg and Engelmannsberg. The description of a model Rheingau wine exactly fits the best Rieslings from these sites. They can combine depth and elegance, assertiveness and finesse in a form that certainly deserves to be called noble and aristocratic. In spite of this common thread, each of these sites gives wines with a distinctive personality.

The richest of these are the Rieslings from the Pfaffenberg, a monopoly of Schloss Schönborn, whose extremely warm situation next to the river and light soil give aromatic wines which frequently have a strong exotic fruits character. In spite of this tendency to opulence, they also age well. The Engelmannsberg wines are also charmers in their youth but less full-bodied and racier. The Nussbrunnen and Wisselbrunnen, both named after springs situated within their boundaries, are Hattenheim's most famous vineyards. Both are capable of giving intense wines with great 'breed'. A great Nussbrunnen Riesling is full-bodied with a rich apricot-like fruit, a strong spice and mineral character and firm acidity. It makes a bold statement, while the best Wisselbrunnen wines are altogether more discreet, with a floral delicacy and a racy elegance reminiscent of great Mosel Rieslings. The Mannberg gives wines of comparable quality only in years with hot summers, when they combine full peach-like fruit and a marvellous harmony.

The legendary walled vineyard of the Steinberg, situated high above Hattenheim, is the Rheingau's equivalent to Clos Vougeot of Burgundy's Côte d'Or. Planting of the Steinberg was completed in 1232 by the Cistercian monks of the Kloster Eberbach monastery who, in 1766, also completed construction of the three-kilometre wall that surrounds it. Steinberg was the jewel in the crown of their extensive vineyard holdings until the monastery was secularised in 1803. Under the 1971 Wine Law, Steinberg received the status of an *Ortsteil*, enabling the Staatsweingüter to market the wines from their great monopoly site without the name of Hattenheim.

In vintages with hot summers the Steinberg can yield Auslese wines with an unmatched brilliance and piquancy, but during the 1970s and 1980s few wines of such quality were produced. Sadly, exciting wines from Hattenheim's vineyards as a whole are now

Legendary wines such as the 1811 Steinbergers matured here in the 'Cabinet' cellar of the Cistercian Kloster Eberbach monastery.

rather rare. The best modern examples are probably the Wisselbrunnen Rieslings from Schloss Reinhartshausen. Langwerth von Simmern's wines from the Nussbrunnen and Mannberg are frequently good, as are Schloss Schönborn's wines from the Pfaffenberg, but considering the village's excellent vineyards and glorious history, this is far too few.

Some areas of Hattenheim, especially the old part lying south of the railway line, are still very beautiful. The houses lining narrow cobbled streets seem hardly to have changed since the Rheingau's golden age during the Belle Epoque. With at least four good restaurants, this is also the gastronomic centre of the region. Zum Krug is notable not just for its authentic regional cooking, but also for the beautiful decoration of its half-timbered frontage, the finest example of this traditional style in the Rheingau. The fortified tower of the Hattenheimer Burg, which was the Freiherr Langwerth von Simmern family home and headquarters of the eponymous wine estate from 1472 until 1711, is also impressive.

No trip to the Rheingau would be complete without driving up from Hattenheim to walk through Kloster Eberbach's cloisters, huge hallways, cellars and basilica. Although the contents of the abbey were auctioned off when it was secularised, the buildings themselves retain their timeless beauty.

In neighbouring Erbach a similar situation exists, with renowned vineyards frequently yielding unworthy wines. Erbach's most famous and important vineyard is the Marcobrunn, but it also has excellent vineyards in the Siegelsberg, Schlossberg and Hohenrain sites. The heavy marl soil of the Marcobrunn never dries out however hot the summer, as underground water is abundant here. This, combined with its position close to the warming influence of the river and its excellent southwesterly exposure, results in powerful, imposing wines with enormous depth and breed. More than any other Rheingau Riesling these wines need time in the bottle and the glass for their many layers of flavour to unfold.

The Marcobrunn wines from the principal proprietors – Langwerth von Simmern, Schloss Reinhartshausen, Schloss Schönborn and the Staatsweingüter – are frequently good but seldom equal the best examples from previous decades. Reinhartshausen's wines from their Schlossberg monopoly and the Siegelsberg sites regularly match and sometimes surpass the best Marcobrunners, which says a great deal about the quality of these sites, both direct neighbours of the Marcobrunn. Their Rieslings tend to be a shade lighter than those of their more famous relatives, but have plenty of the complex earthy-spice character of top-class Marcobrunners.

The Marcobrunn's recorded history begins before 1200. In 1726 it became the first vineyard site name to appear on a bottle of German wine. In 1810 the village of Erbach erected the neo-classical monument around the spring which gives the site its name. Marcobrunn means 'the spring on the border', in this instance the border between Hattenheim and Erbach. The inscription on this monument states the claims of Erbach very clearly: 'Marcobrunnen gemarkung Erbach' (Marcobrunn, Parish of Erbach) The people of Hattenheim replied with an inscription on their side of the border, 'Für Erbach das Wasser, Für Hattenheim den Wein' (For Erbach the water, for Hattenheim the wine). The 1971 Wine Law finally settled the question by incorporating Erbach's name into the vineyard designation.

The dispute among connoisseurs as to whether the wines of the Marcobrunn or the Rauenthaler Baiken give the greatest Rheingau wines shows no sign of reaching a conclusion after more than 200 years of debate. Thomas Jefferson sang the praises of the

Marcobrunn two centuries ago and since then the English-speaking world has tended to follow his lead. The Germans have generally preferred the sleek, racy wines from the Baiken, with their haunting mineral spice from the stony phyllite soil. Both sites produce some of the longest-living wines in the region and both have given some of the most astonishing Auslese and higher quality Prädikat dessert wines ever made.

The Rauenthaler Berg is perhaps the most impressive of the vine-clad hills high above the river. In addition to the Baiken, four of its other sites can yield wines worthy of Rauenthal's lofty reputation: Gehrn, Nonnenberg, Rothenberg and Wülfen. There is a family resemblance among these wines, the finest examples possessing a rich yet extremely fine peach- or apricot-like fruit and a strong mineral character. The Staatsweingüter is easily the biggest vineyard owner here, making the lion's share of Baiken and Gehrn wines. While some of their recent Auslese and Eiswein from Rauenthal have been impressive, the best Rauenthalers come from JB Becker, Georg Breuer's monopoly Nonnenberg site, August Eser and Langwerth von Simmern.

Neighbouring Kiedrich offers Baiken stiff competition with its Gräfenberg wines. The Gräfenberg enjoys an exposure similar to that of the Baiken, is also steeply sloping and has a phyllite soil. A century ago, when it was often called simply Kiedricher Berg, the site enjoyed a reputation as great as that of any other vineyard in the Rheingau. The Robert Weil estate sold its 1893 Kiedricher Berg Auslese to Queen Victoria, Kaiser Franz Josef of Austria and Kaiser Wilhelm II of Germany for prices far exceeding their modern equivalent. Since purchasing the Weil estate in 1988, the Japanese drink giant Suntory has invested heavily in renovating the magnificent Neo-Gothic estate house, building a new winery

and expanding the estate's vineyard holdings. It has also given director Wilhelm Weil free rein. As a result of its far-sighted policies, Weil is on course to see its name and that of the Gräfenberg once again among the most illustrious in the Rheingau.

The success of the Robert Weil estate has sent shock-waves through the region. Suddenly there is a large, important Rheingau estate whose wines stand head and shoulders above the general standard in the region. The wines that have caused the greatest stir are the late-harvested Riesling Auslese, BA and TBA, which the estate has produced every single vintage since 1989, a feat without parallel in the recent history of the region. Perhaps, before long, connoisseurs will be debating whether the Marcobrunn or the Gräfenberg gives the greater wine.

The village of Kiedrich is worth a visit not only for the Weil estate, but also for its many other historical and architectural monuments. The now ruined Scharfenstein castle which stands at the top of the Gräfenberg was built during the early Middle Ages as a residence by the Prince-Bishops of Mainz and the elegant Gothic church dates from the 14th century. The most imposing building in the village is the Renaissance palace of Schloss Groenesteyn, home to the eponymous estate. The town hall, which dates from the same period, is remarkably grand for a village of this size.

Below Rauenthal and Kiedrich lies the town of Eltville, which has become much more attractive since heavy traffic has been diverted from its narrow streets to the new bypass. Eltville has many fine Gothic and Renaissance buildings, most notably the beautiful examples in the park-like courtyard of the Langwerther Hof, headquarters of the Langwerth von Simmern estate. The Stockheimer Hof, which stands in the middle of this complex, dates from the 11th century and is still in use as the estate's offices and

The Kiedricher Gräfenberg site, from which the Robert Weil estate produces some of the region's best late-harvested Auslese and higher quality Prädikat wines.

The elegant spire and finials of Erbach's magnificent Gothic church rise above the village, where the small stream of Eberbach joins the Rhine.

tasting room. Eltville's vineyards may not be the very best, but the Sonnenberg regularly produces mid-weight wines that are full of fruit and flavour. These make an ideal introduction to the region's wines since they have all the typical characteristics and are appealing even if drunk very young. The best of these come from JB Becker, J Fischer and Langwerth von Simmern.

Both Martinsthal and Walluf deserve to be better known. Much of their product is sold under the Grosslage name of Rauenthaler Steinmächer, which enables them to take advantage of that village's good name. This is sad, because the best parts of the Martinsthaler Langenberg and Wildsau (meaning 'wild boar') enjoy a similar exposure and soil to the Rauenthaler Berg, whose wines they come close to matching in style and quality. When they are good they offer excellent value for money.

The soil of the Wallufer Walkenberg is deeper and heavier than that of the Martinsthal and results in firm, even steely, wines that require plenty of time in the bottle but can then acquire a remarkable elegance. The village of Walluf has a strong red wine tradition: many of the best Walkenbergers are Spätburgunder. JB Becker makes excellent dry Riesling and Spätburgunder from the Walkenberg, the latter having more depth and a silkier texture than almost all the red wines from Assmannshausen. Here is something reminiscent of good Burgundy. During the summer months the Beckers' wine garden is a popular meeting point for local people as well as wine tourists.

To the east of Walluf the vineyards suddenly become fewer and more widely scattered and farmland begins to dominate. The village of Frauenstein and town of Schierstein have significant areas of vineyard but these produce few wines of special quality and much of the production is sold in bulk. The Neroberg vineyard of Wiesbaden is another matter, the wines from its four hectares of vines selling easily to Wiesbaden residents for healthy prices. In a good vintage these prices can be justified by wines with delicate fruit and considerable elegance.

The last of the Rheingau's great vineyards on this stretch lies about 15 kilometres east of Eltville in Hochheim on the river Main. It is from Hochheim that 'Hock', the English word for Rhine wines, is derived. This is no accident of history. Together with the Rüdesheimer Berg, the top sites of Hochheim enjoy the warmest microclimate of the entire region. Their south-facing slopes benefit from the warming influence of both the Rhine and the Main rivers. Here the bud-break, the flowering of the vines and the beginning of the harvest are several days ahead of most of the Rheingau.

The soils are generally deep and heavy which, combined with other favourable conditions, results in wines with power and richness, a pronounced earthy character sometimes described as smoky and a firm structure. Seldom charming when tasted in their extreme youth, Rieslings from Hochheim's top sites can age magnificently. This was the style of white wine preferred by the Victorians, hence the high prices achieved by Hochheim Rieslings during the 19th century when they were among the best regarded of all German wines.

Domdechaney, the most famous site in Hochheim, with the Domdechant Werner estate and the town church in the background.

Wines from the Hölle site represent the most extreme expression of Hochheim's unique style, this site being closest to the warming influence of the Main and possessing the heaviest soils of all. Here drought stress is virtually unknown, enabling the vines to take full advantage of hot summers such as those of '89 and '83. They are the most powerful and massive wines in the whole region. Good examples have a full apricot-like fruit and are packed with an earthy mineral character from the marl soil. While they can be almost too much to take as young wines, they gain considerable elegance with some bottle-age. Franz Künstler is the best producer, but the organic Biason estate can also make good examples.

The Königin Victoriaberg site, which is wholly owned by the

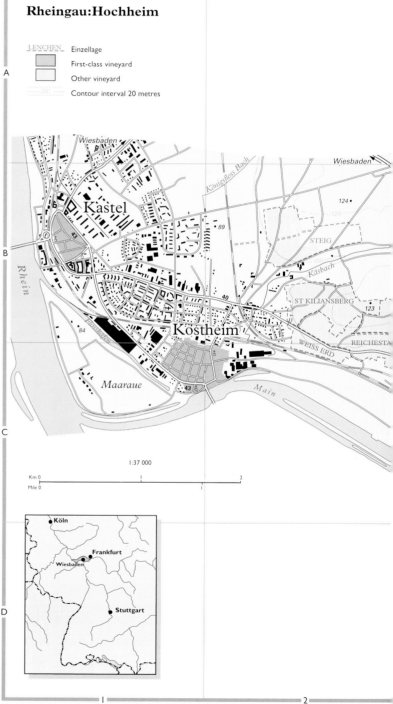

Rheingau:Hochheim

LENCHEN — Einzellage

First-class vineyard

Other vineyard

Contour interval 20 metres

1:37 000

Hupfeld estate of Mittelheim, has a similar soil and microclimate to the Hölle but gives slightly lighter, less earthy wines. Its name commemorates Queen Victoria's visit to Hochheim in 1850. An extraordinary mock-tudor monument to the Queen's visit stands among the vines, looking so extravagant and incongruous that it could be part of a film set. Depending upon one's point of view, the Neo-Gothic label under which the vineyard's wines are sold is either bombastic in the extreme or a masterpiece of Victorian design.

The most famous and highly regarded vineyard in Hochheim is the Domdechaney. Its wines resemble those from the Hölle, being powerful almost to the point of heaviness and strongly marked by the heavy marl soil upon which they grow. In good vintages they are considered more subtle than the Hölle wines. Certainly many historic wines came from this site, which includes the Staatsweingüter, Schloss Schönborn and Domdechant Werner. Of these estates, Domdechant Werner has the highest success rate.

The wines from the Kirchenstück are almost as well known, but are of a different style, being much sleeker and more elegant. With their delicate floral and mineral flavours they make a surprising contrast to Hochheim Riesling, especially since these vineyards lie directly next to one another and enjoy almost identical exposure. The Franz Künstler and Domdechant Werner estates are the best producers.

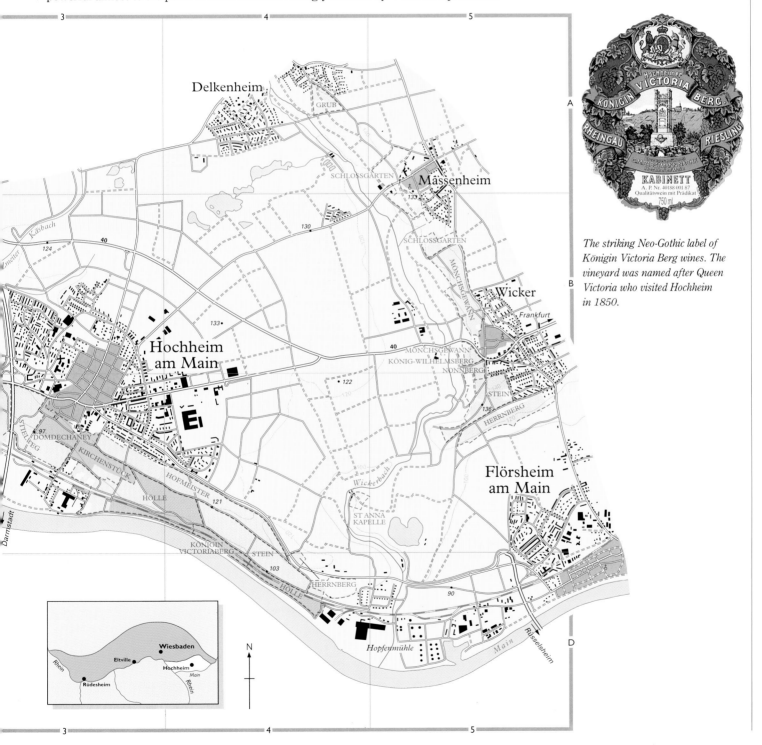

The striking Neo-Gothic label of Königin Victoria Berg wines. The vineyard was named after Queen Victoria who visited Hochheim in 1850.

The Stein, Stielweg, Reichestal and Herrnberg sites can also give good wines. Those from the Stein and Stielweg are powerful, thoroughbred Hochheimers while those from the lighter soils of the Reichestal and Herrnberg are more immediately appealing. Wine from the small Herrnberg site, one of Franz Künstler's specialities, can show fruit aromas such as strawberry and passion fruit, which makes them more like Mosel Rieslings than Hochheimers. Neighbouring Flörsheim and Wicker make lighter wines that are completely overshadowed by Hochheim's best Rieslings.

It is perhaps appropriate that a description of the Rheingau's vineyards and Riesling wines should conclude with Hochheim, since it was very close to here in Rüsselsheim that the Riesling vine was first recorded in 1435. There has been much speculation as to whether the vines were intended for Hochheim's vineyards, but there is no decisive evidence one way or another. Hochheim as a wine town mirrors the situation of the Rheingau as a whole, having marvellous vineyards with the potential to give great dry and nobly sweet wines, but too few vintners who can translate this potential into fine wines.

Substantial new investment has given the recently-restored Schloss Reinhartshausen hotel and wine estate a new lease of life.

BENCHMARK WINES

Assmannshäuser Höllenberg Spätburgunder QbA Trocken
Weingut August Kesseler, Assmannshausen
Vineyard site: Assmannshäuser Höllenberg
Site area: 43.5 hectares, 7 hectares August Kesseler
Exposure: south
Inclination: very steep
Soil: quartzite and slate
Description: These are deep ruby red wines which shade to amber at the rim when they are mature. Hardly a hint of oak intrudes in the pure cherry- and blackberry-like fruit of these medium-bodied but intense Pinot Noirs. Although the tannins are a little edgy when the wines are young, a couple of years in the bottle are enough to give them an elegant harmony. Their real class shows in the long, subtle aftertaste.
Best vintages: '94, '93, '90, '88
Best drunk: These are definitely food wines and make an excellent match for game, lamb or firm cheese such as mature Gouda. This is a personal favourite with red mullet and ratatouille.

Geisenheimer Rothenberg Riesling Spätlese 'Charta'
Weingüter Geheimrat J Wegeler Erben, Oestrich
Vineyard site: Geisenheimer Rothenberg
Site Area: 27 hectares, 6.5 hectares Geheimrat J Wegeler

Exposure: south
Inclination: steep
Soil: iron-rich red slate and quartzite
Description: For dry German Rieslings these are remarkably seductive wines, rich in texture and packed with ripe apricot- and mango-like fruit. The acidity is masked by this opulence, but forms a firm backbone, giving excellent balance. After waves of fruit, the clean aftertaste is a subtle blend of almond and minerals.
Best vintages: '94, '93, '92, '90, '89, '88, '85, '83
Best drunk: These have the richness to cope with strong flavours and a fresh acidity to cut through fatty foods. Try with Lobster à l'Armoricaine or veal in a cream sauce with morel mushrooms.

Kiedricher Gräfenberg Riesling Auslese 'Gold Cap'
Weingut Robert Weil, Kiedrich

Vineyard site: Kiedricher Gräfenberg
Site area: 10.5 hectares, 7.5 hectares Robert Weil
Exposure: southwest
Inclination: steep
Soil: weathered phyllite
Description: Wines like these late-picked masterpieces made the Rheingau's reputation. Honey, exotic fruits, caramel and spice pour from the glass. Extremely rich and intense, they have a perfect balance of sweetness and acidity. Waves of honeyed flavours pour across the palate, ending in a persistent spicy aftertaste.
Best vintages: '94, '93, '92, '91, '90

Best drunk: Although sweet and powerful enough to drink with rich desserts, blue cheese or liver pâté, these wines are best drunk by themselves in place of dessert.

Hattenheimer Wisselbrunnen Riesling Auslese
Schloss Reinhartshausen, Erbach

Vineyard site: Hattenheimer Wisselbrunnen
Site area: 17 hectares, 7 hectares Schloss Reinhartshausen
Exposure: south
Inclination: steep
Soil: marl
Description: Rheingau elegance in its highest form. Currant-like fruit, flowers and a hint of honey mingle in the subtle bouquet. Though full and sweet, the wines have a cleanness of flavour and a lightness of touch that make them lively and animating. Vibrant acidity runs through them, binding together their many elements in a perfectly harmonious whole.
Best vintages: '94, '93, '92, '90, '89
Best drunk: These are perfect wines for simple fruit desserts, blue cheese or liver pâté

Hochheimer Hölle Riesling Auslese Trocken
Weingut Franz Künstler, Hochheim

Vineyard site: Hochheimer Hölle
Site area: 49 hectares, 1.25 hectares Franz Künstler
Exposure: south
Inclination: sloping to steep
Soil: heavy marl
Description: Intense and powerful but not heavy or alcoholic, these are great dry wines. Their rich apricot- and citrus-like fruit is married to ample body and a firm core of mineral flavours from the soil, the interplay of fruit and acidity as fascinating as in any of the region's great sweet wines.
Best vintages: '93, '92, '90, '88
Best drunk: This dry Hochheimer is strong enough to stand up to game – a combination much loved by the Victorians. Try it with roast pheasant.

Rüdesheimer Berg Schlossberg Riesling
Weingut Georg Breuer, Rüdesheim

Vineyard site: Rüdesheimer Berg Schlossberg
Site area: 25.5 hectares, 2.25 hectares Georg Breuer
Exposure: south
Inclination: very steep
Soil: weathered slate and quartzite
Description: It is with refinement rather than power that these wines impress. As they mature, the delicate peach-like bouquet gains subtle mineral overtones from the slate soil. Harmoniously dry, with an elegant balance of racy acidity and ripe fruit, the mineral character echoes in the long aftertaste.
Best vintages: '94, '93, '92, '90, '86, '84, '83
Best drunk: It is hard to imagine a better partner for elegant fish dishes than these wines, but they are also excellent with veal or poultry in light cream sauces.

The beautiful headquarters of Weingut Robert Weil, renovated thanks to the estate's new owner, Japanese drink giant Suntory.

113

BEST PRODUCERS

Weingut JB Becker

Rheinstrasse 6,
65396 Walluf
Owners: Maria and Hans-Josef Becker
Vineyard area: 13 hectares
Grape varieties: 81% Riesling,
17% Spätburgunder,
2% Müller-Thurgau
Top sites: Eltviller Sonnenberg,
Rauenthaler Wülfen,
Wallufer Walkenberg

Firm and austere in their youth, the Becker's unique dry Rieslings need many years of bottle-age before they reach their optimum harmony. With their pronounced mineral character these are classical Rheingau wines of a kind now very rare. Hans-Josef and Maria Becker are no less original than their winemaking style. Rieslings are usually bottled after a year maturing in large wooden casks. The Becker's less well known sweet Riesling Spätlese and Auslese wines are elegant and never too sweet. Their Spätburgunder reds never see new oak, but together with August Kesseler's Spätburgunders are the best full, fruity reds in the region.

Between May and September the Becker's run a wine garden on the bank of the Rhine in Walluf, selling wines by the glass or bottle from 5pm onwards during the week and from 3pm at weekends.

Weingut Georg Breuer

Geisenheimer Strasse 9,
65385 Rüdesheim
Owner: Bernhard Breuer
Vineyard area: 19 hectares
Grape varieties: 88% Riesling,
4% Grauburgunder,
5% Müller-Thurgau,
3% other varieties
Top sites: Rauenthaler Nonnenberg
(wholly owned),
Rüdesheimer Berg Rottland,
Rüdesheimer Berg Schlossberg

The dynamic Bernhard Breuer is a founder member of the Charta Wine Estates Association and an active promoter of the region's vineyard classification system. In recent years he has expanded his estate, adding the 5.7-hectare Rauenthaler Nonnenberg vineyard site to his significant acreage in the Rüdesheimer Berg Schlossberg. Perhaps even more importantly he has found an excellent cellar-master in Hermann Schmoranz, who has helped to raise the estate's quality standard. The dry Rieslings, which account for most of the estate's production, are concentrated and elegant and among the best examples of this style in the region. The Riesling Auslese, BA and TBA dessert wines are somewhat more variable but often excellent.

As well as running his wine estate Bernhard Breuer has a wine store and

Bernhard Breuer of Rüdesheim.

has recently opened a restaurant, Berg Schlossberg, in Rüdesheim in the Grabenstrasse.

Weingut August Eser

Friedensplatz 19,
65375 Oestrich
Owner: Joachim Eser
Vineyard area: 7 hectares
Grape varieties: 94% Riesling,
6% Spätburgunder
Top sites: Hallgartener Schönhell,
Oestricher Doosberg,
Oestricher Lenchen,
Rauenthaler Gehrn,
Rauenthaler Rothenberg

Joachim Eser makes consistently fine dry and naturally sweet Rieslings which are marketed without the 'hype' that is now common in the Rheingau. His wines have their vineyards' typical characteristics: aroma, rich fruit and balance. Their generous style – less 'severe' than many Rheingau examples – and moderate prices have made them increasingly popular. The elegant Rauenthal wines, for which Weingut August Eser is one of few reliable sources, are highly sought-after. The estate's Oestricher Doosberg wines are their richest and most substantial.

Fürst von Metternich-Winneburg'sche Domäne Schloss Johannisberg

Schloss,
65366 Johannisberg
Owner: Johannisberger Weingüter Verwaltung GbR
Vineyard area: 29 hectares
Grape varieties: 100% Riesling
Top site: Schloss Johannisberg
(wholly owned)

Although Schloss Johannisberg has performed rather erratically in recent years, the best bottlings from this world-famous estate are still impressive Rheingau wines. For several years now the wines have been fermented in temperature-controlled stainless steel tanks, the traditional

barrel cellar being used only for maturing selected wines. As a result the wines have a little more freshness than was once the case, but their character remains fundamentally unaltered. With their subtle apple- and white peach-like fruit and racy elegance these can be among the region's finest wines. Their legendary ageing potential is proved by the marvellous condition in which so many old wines emerge from the 'Bibliotheca Subterranea' below the Schloss. With the unquestionable dedication of the estate's director, Domänenrat Wolfgang Schleicher and the new cellar-master, Hans-Hermann Kesseler, wines from this famous estate will once again stand alongside Germany's greatest.

Weingut Johannishof – HH Eser

Im Grund 63,
65362 Johannisberg
Owners: Hans Hermann and Elfriede Eser
Vineyard area: 14 hectares
Grape varieties: 100% Riesling
Top sites: Geisenheimer Kläuserweg, Johannisberger Hölle, Winkeler Hasensprung, Winkeler Jesuitengarten

The Rheingau's renown is no longer attributable to the large aristocratic estates which established its reputation during the 19th century, but to smaller, family-owned estates that strive to produce the best possible wines. The estate run by the family of HH Eser in Johannisberg is a good example. Its sleek, racy wines are not at their most charming as very young wines, needing several years of bottle-age to show their true class, but they are capable of long ageing. Together with Weingut Franz Künstler this estate maintains the highest standard of Charta wines. The Esers produce equally impressive Riesling Spätlese with natural sweetness and their occasional Auslese, BA and Eiswein dessert wines are of the

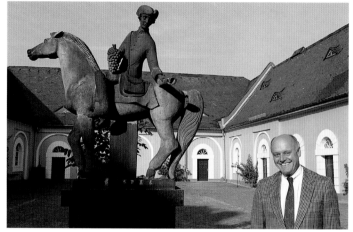

Wolfgang Schleicher in Schloss Johannisberg's magnificent courtyard.

highest quality. Indeed, right across their broad range of wines from Geisenheim, Johannisberg and Winkel, it is hard to find a single example that is not at least of good quality.

Weingut August Kesseler

Lorcher Strasse 16,
65385 Assmannshausen
Owner: August Kesseler
Vineyard area: 14 hectares
Grape varieties: 50% Spätburgunder,
40% Riesling, 10% Silvaner
Top sites: Assmannshäuser Höllenberg, Rüdesheimer Berg Roseneck, Rüdesheimer Berg Schlossberg

August Kesseler's 1988 Spätburgunder reds made his name almost overnight. Since then his red wines have gone from strength to strength and in recent vintages their balance of rich fruit with a touch of oak has been judged near perfect. They may not be the biggest or most powerful red wines in Germany, but they are certainly among the most perfumed and sophisticated.

Having made only dry wines during the 1980s, August Kesseler rediscovered the appeal of Rieslings with natural sweetness in the early 1990s. No doubt this was influenced by his appointment as Director of the Schloss Reinhartshausen estate in Erbach, where there is a long tradition of excellence in this style. The August Kesseler white wines are of consistently good quality but do not yet match the depth and breed of the reds.

Weingut Freiherr zu Knyphausen

Klosterhof Drais,
65346 Erbach
Owner: Gerko Freiherr zu Knyphausen
Vineyard area: 22 hectares
Grape varieties: 96% Riesling,
4% Spätburgunder
Top sites: Erbacher Hohenrain,
Erbacher Marcobrunn,

Erbacher Siegelsberg, Hattenheimer Wisselbrunnen

Perhaps because the estate undertakes no noisy promotion of its wines and because Gerko Knyphausen is the soul of modesty, the consistent high quality of these wines is something of an insider secret. Here the classic virtues of Rheingau Riesling are paramount: an elegant harmony that avoids every kind of excess. The estate is one of the most active members of the Charta Wine Estates Association which aims to promote harmonious dry Rheingau Rieslings. Gerko Knyphausen places as much emphasis on the classic-style Spätlese wines from Erbach and Hattenheim's top sites as upon his dry wines. At this estate there is hardly such a thing as a lesser vintage, the wines of difficult years often being as successful as those from top vintages.

Weingut Franz Künstler

Freiherr-von-Stein-Ring 3,
65234 Hochheim
Owner: Gunter Künstler
Vineyard area: 7 hectares
Grape varieties: 90% Riesling,
10% Spätburgunder
Top sites: Hochheimer Hölle,
Hochheimer Kirchenstück

Few German winemakers have enjoyed such a meteoric rise to fame as Gunter Künstler. With the fine vintages of the late 1980s he

Gunter Künstler with his Hochheimers.

established a reputation for the estate, founded by his father in 1965, as one of Rheingau's finest. Few of the region's wines come close to matching his dry Rieslings which are packed with apricot- and citrus-like fruit and mineral extract. A racy acidity binds this together and the wines need several years of bottle-age to reveal their full depths. Even the simplest will age five years or more, while the best dry Rieslings will retain their charm for between ten and 20 years.

Perhaps because of the estate's tremendous success with its dry wines, its magnificent Auslese and higher quality Prädikat dessert wines from the Hochheimer Hölle and Hochheimer Herrnberg vineyards have tended to be overlooked. Such classic Hochheim wines were highly esteemed by the Victorians. Although they possess the honey and spice character of noble rot this is never dominant. Instead there is a fascinating interplay of botrytis aromas with the special earthy and smoky notes unique to Hochheim's top-site wines. These are remarkable achievements for a winemaker still only in his early thirties.

Freiherrlich Langwerth von Simmern'sches Rentamt

Langwerther Hof,
65343 Eltville
Owner: Friedrich Freiherr Langwerth von Simmern
Vineyard area: 33 hectares

Grape varieties: 95% Riesling,
1.5% Spätburgunder,
0.75% Weissburgunder,
0.75% Chardonnay, 2% other varieties
Top sites: Erbacher Marcobrunn, Hattenheimer Nussbrunnen, Hattenheimer Mannberg, Rauenthaler Baiken, Rauenthaler Rothenberg

Of all the Rheingau's great aristocratic estates, this one has come closest to maintaining its reputation through the difficult 1980s and early 1990s. The hallmarks of the von Simmern style are no less distinctive than its unique (and practically illegible) neo-Gothic label. When they are good, no other Rheingau wines can match the elegance and subtlety of this estate's Rieslings: they are wines to fall in love with at first sip. Since cellar-master Josef Schell arrived in 1958, changes in winemaking techniques have been circumspect and tradition carefully nurtured.

This estate plays a central role in the debate as to whether the greatest Rheingau wines come from the Erbacher Marcobrunn or the Rauenthaler Baiken, as these legendary vineyards are the twin jewels in von Simmern's crown. The Marcobrunn Rieslings are heady with power and depth while the Baiken wines are the ultimate in racy elegance. The richly fruity wines from the Hattenheimer Nussbrunnen and firm, classical Rieslings from the Hattenheimer Mannberg are hardly less impressive. With continuing good management, the consistently high quality that once characterised the estate could surely be achieved again.

Weingut Josef Leitz

Theodor-Heuss-Strasse 5,
65385 Rüdesheim
Owners: Doris, Lydia and Johannes Leitz
Vineyard area: 4.5 hectares
Grape varieties: 90% Riesling,
10% Spätburgunder
Top sites: Rüdesheimer Berg Rottland, Rüdesheimer Berg Schlossberg

Johannes Leitz is arguably the most unlikely new star in the Rheingau's firmament. Although he attended the Eltville wine school he dismisses the experience with a wave of the hand. A stint at the Johannishof estate (HH Eser) in Johannisberg was more important to him in fixing his ideal style of Rheingau Riesling and most of his methods are established as a result of trial and error. The contrast between Johannes Leitz and Rüdesheim's other leading winemaker, the cosmopolitan Bernhard Breuer, could not be more dramatic.

Although the Leitz family (which also runs a florist shop and an idiosyncratic wine bar in the back streets of Rüdesheim) has a tradition

of making superior wines, Johannes is the first to approach winemaking systematically. This shows in the clarity, freshness and expressiveness of his Rieslings. The style shows influences as diverse as those of Burgundy, the Mosel and Austria. Yields are kept low for maximum ripeness and flavour; the grapes pressed without being pre-crushed (as in Champagne); fermentation is slow and intervention in the cellar kept to a minimum to retain the maximum fruit and aroma. This is Leitz's recipe for wines of individuality and elegance.

Weingut Prinz

Im Flaschsgarten 5,
65375 Hallgarten
Owner: Fred Prinz
Vineyard area: 1.5 hectares
Grape varieties: 88% Riesling,
12% Spätburgunder
Top site: Hallgartener Schönhell

With his almost absurdly small wine estate Fred Prinz is currently the only vintner waving the flag for Hallgarten. His firm, slightly earthy Rieslings have more fruit and raciness than Hallgarten wines from any of the large estates with vineyards in this underrated village. Within five years he has made his miniature estate one of the best sources of both dry and naturally sweet Rheingau Rieslings. If and when Fred Prinz has enough vineyards at his disposal to make dessert wines regularly, he should prove that Hallgarten can make some of the most vivid and longest-living examples in the Rheingau.

Weingut Schloss Reinhartshausen

65346 Erbach
Owners: Friedrich Prinz von Preussen and the Leibbrand heirs
Vineyard area: 76 hectares
Grape varieties: 89% Riesling,
4% Weissburgunder,
4% Spätburgunder, 3% Chardonnay
Top sites: Erbacher Marcobrunn, Erbacher Schlossberg (wholly owned), Hattenheimer Nussbrunnen, Hattenheimer Wisselbrunnen, Rauenthaler Wülfen

With August Kesseler as director, a magnificent state-of-the-art winery and an abundance of first-class vineyard, this exemplary estate could not be better prepared for the 21st century. The excellent wines made since the estate came into the Leibbrand family's majority ownership in late 1988 that show this is one of the Rheingau's most important producers. Here elegance is prized above all else and whether sweet or dry the wines have a racy acidity that gives even the richest of them a marvellous brilliance. Consistency is not entirely reliable yet, but the problem is being addressed.

The Erbacher Rheinhell and Hattenheimer Rheingarten sites on the Mariannenaue island in the middle of the Rhine are organically cultivated. Their wines are sold under a white and orange label while those from the mainland sites have a Prussian blue and gold label. The most important of the latter are the Erbacher Marcobrunn, the estate's wholly-owned Erbacher Schlossberg, the underrated Erbacher Siegelsberg and the Hattenheimer Wisselbrunnen, where Reinhartshausen is the largest vineyard owner. The estate's wines from these vineyards almost always live up to standards expected of such first-class sites.

Domänenweingut Schloss Schönborn

65347 Hattenheim
Owner: Dr Karl Graf von Schönborn-Wiesentheid
Vineyard area: 50.5 hectares
Grape varieties: 90% Riesling, 5.5 % Spätburgunder, 4.5 % Weissburgunder
Top sites: Erbacher Marcobrunn, Geisenheimer Kläuserweg, Geisenheimer Rothenberg, Hattenheimer Nussbrunnen, Hattenheimer Pfaffenberg (wholly owned), Hattenheimer Wisselbrunnen, Hochheimer Domdechaney, Hochheimer Hölle, Hochheimer Kirchenstück, Lorcher Krone, Oestricher Doosberg, Rauenthaler Baiken, Rauenthaler Wülfen, Rüdesheimer Berg Rottland, Rüdesheimer Berg Schlossberg

Of all the Rheingau's famous wine estates, Schloss Schönborn has perhaps the richest endowment of excellent vineyards. However, such abundance does present practical problems since the estate's vines are scattered throughout the region from Lorch to Hochheim and there is a serious shortage of vineyard workers in Germany. Given these difficulties it is perhaps surprising that so many of the wines are so good. Low yields result in wines with ample substance and power but all too often at the expense of subtlety and finesse. Some are excellent but others fall far short of the quality expected from such famous vineyards. With luck the new director Günter Thies will apply renewed energy to solving these problems and the estate will achieve its former high standards more regularly.

Weingüter Geheimrat J Wegeler Erben

Friedensplatz 9,
65367 Oestrich
Owner: Deinhard and Co, Koblenz

Vineyard area: 59 hectares
Grape varieties: 98% Riesling, 2% other varieties
Top sites: Geisenheimer Kläuserweg, Geisenheimer Rothenberg, Hallgartener Schönhell, Oestricher Doosberg, Oestricher Lenchen, Rüdesheimer Berg Rottland, Rüdesheimer Berg Schlossberg, Winkeler Hasensprung, Winkeler Jesuitengarten

Best known for its 'Geheimrat J' luxury dry Riesling, a blend created by director Norbert Holderrieth in 1983, this is one of the most dependable producers in the region. The Wegeler estate, an active members of the Charta Wine Estates Association virtually since its inception, has played a leading role in promoting the Rheingau's recently launched vineyard classification system. If it could boast a fine castle or an aristocratic owner rather than occupying unpretentious premises in the centre of Oestrich and being owned by a large company (Deinhard) then it would surely enjoy the same kind of renown as Schloss Johannisberg or Langwerth von Simmern. However, it is still one of the Rheingau's most successful estates, principally because of the consistently high quality of its wines which combine the region's typical elegance with a great deal of fruity charm.

Weingut Robert Weil

Mühlberg 5,
65399 Kiedrich
Owner: SG-Weingüterverwaltungs-gesselschaft (Suntory)
Vineyard area: 38.5 hectares
Grape varieties: 96% Riesling, 4% Spätburgunder
Top sites: Kiedricher Gräfenberg, Kiedricher Wasseros

The purchase of this famous estate, previously known as Weingut Dr Weil, by the Japanese drink giant Suntory in 1988 was viewed with considerable scepticism in the Rheingau. However, the praise heaped upon the wines made since by director Wilhelm Weil has justified Suntory's investment in modernising the winery and purchasing further vineyards, and proved Wilhelm Weil's unswerving commitment to quality. Continuing the estate's long history of excellence with dessert wines, the finest now are the lusciously sweet Auslese, BA, TBA and Eiswein from the Kiedricher Gräfenberg. Crammed to bursting point with dried fruit, honey and spice notes they are widely regarded as the best in the Rheingau. While the drier-style wines are less spectacular, they are still of a high standard.

Having extended its holdings in the Kiedricher Gräfenberg, one of the best half-dozen sites in the Rheingau, the estate's ability to produce top-class

Wilhelm Weil enjoys some older Gräfenberg wines.

dry and sweet Rieslings is significantly increased. The restless ambition of Wilhelm Weil and cellar-master Michael Thien to refine winemaking techniques still further suggests that the coming years will bring even better wines.

Domdechant Werner'sches Weingut

Rathausstrasse 30,
65234 Hochheim
Owner: Dr Franz Werner Michel
Vineyard area: 12 hectares
Grape varieties: 96% Riesling, 2% Spätburgunder, 2% other varieties
Top sites: Hochheimer Domedechaney, Hochheimer Kirchenstück

Dr Michel is best known as the co-director of the Deutsches Weininstitut, the official body charged with the international promotion of German wines. At home in Hochheim, however, his own estate – long the unchallenged leader among Hochheim's producers – deserves to be better known. Many of the estate's wines still meet the high standards set during the 1970s and 1980s. Substantial vineyard holdings in the Domdechaney and Kirchenstück sites give the best wines. Rieslings from the former are made with some natural sweetness, while those from the latter are usually fermented to complete dryness. For several years now wines from all the estate's other vineyards, even those from the excellent Hölle site, have been marketed simply as Hochheimer Rieslings.

OTHER WELL KNOWN PRODUCERS

Staatsweingut Assmannshausen

Höllenbergstrasse 10,
65385 Assmannshausen
The red wines from Assmannshausen's most important estate have gained in colour, body and depth in recent

years. Drunk young, their fresh cherry-like fruit can give much pleasure.

Weingut Hans Barth

Bergstrasse 20,
65347 Hattenheim
Barth's wines may not be remarkable but the estate's Sekts are the best sparkling wines in the Rheingau. The best of them is 'Barth Ultra' made from white Spätburgunder grapes.

Winzergenossenschaft Erbach

Ringstrasse 28,
65337 Erbach
Erbach is by far the best of the Rheingau's co-operative wineries. Its fresh, fruity wines offer good value for money in a region famous for its high prices.

Weingut der Forschungsanstalt

Von-Lade-Strasse 1,
65633 Geisenheim
Wines from the Geisenheim research station and wine school have improved considerably during recent years, largely owing to the conscientious efforts of Wolfgang Pfeiffer.

Weingut Schloss Groenesteyn

Suttonstrasse 22,
65399 Kiedrich
Most of this estate's Kiedrich vineyards had to be sold in 1994. Its remaining 17 hectares are spread around Rüdesheim and include holdings in the first-class Berg Roseneck, Berg Rottland and Berg Schlossberg sites. Its Schloss in Kiedrich and baroque winery in Rüdesheim are important architectural monuments. During recent years Groenesteyn Rieslings have failed to achieve their usual high standard of elegance and refinement.

Weingut Graf von Kanitz

Rheinstrasse 49,
65389 Lorch
The quality of this estate's firm, lean wines has slipped somewhat in recent years. During the 1970s and 1980s marvellous racy wines were produced in this neglected corner of the region.

Weingut Hans Lang

Rheinallee 6,
65347 Hattenheim
Not the most subtle wines in the Rheingau, Hans Lang's Rieslings are big and rich. Dry wines dominate the production.

Weingut Dr Hans Nägler

Friedrichstrasse 22,
65385 Rüdesheim
During the 1980s this was the most consistent producer in Rüdesheim, but more recently the quality has been erratic. Some wines are a little too alcoholic.

Weingut Ökonomierat J Fischer Erben

Weinhöhle 14,
65347 Eltville

Hanni Fischer, now over 80 years of age, has been making this small estate's wines since 1953. Considered old-fashioned by some, the firm Rheingau Rieslings have excellent ageing potential.

Weingut Prinz von Hessen

Grund 1,
65366 Johannisberg

This 50-hectare estate is well known for its wines from the Winkel, particularly the first-class Hasensprung and Jesuitengarten, and those from Johannisberg. High-quality Auslese, BA and TBA dessert wines are the estate's speciality. New director Ronald Müller-Hagen has some work to do if the rest of his wines are to meet the same standard.

Weingut Wilfried Querbach

Dr-Rody-Strasse 2,
65367 Oestrich

With more care to avoid high yields this could be one of the region's leading estates since the quality of its winemaking is undisputed.

Weingut Balthasar Ress

Rheinallee 7,
65347 Hattenheim

Charming, cosmopolitan Stefan Ress has expanded his estate to its present 30 hectares in the best sites between Assmannshausen and Hochheim. The estate is best known for its artist label wines, a new edition of which has been produced annually since 1979. Although wine quality has been variable in recent years, wines from the first-class Hattenheimer Nussbrunnen and Rüdesheimer Berg Schlossberg have often been worthy of these famous names.

Verwaltung der Staatsweingüter Kloster Eberbach

Schwalbacher Strasse 56–62,
65343 Eltville

This 121-hectare estate has a distinguished and ancient winemaking tradition. The estate has sole ownership of the first-class Steinberg, majority ownership of the Rauenthaler Baiken and Gehrn and substantial holdings in other first-class sites including the Rüdesheimer Berg Rottland and Berg Schlossberg, the Erbacher Marcobrunn, Hochheimer Domdechaney and Kirchenstück. The estate's Prädikat wines are often magnificent but the quality of wines up to Spätlese level are often disappointing. New director Dr Karl-Heinz Zerbe was previously at Schloss Reinhartshausen.

Weingut Schloss Vollrads and Fürst Löwenstein

Schloss,
65375 Winkel

Since taking over as director in 1977, Erwein Graf Matuschka-Greiffenclau has been a tireless promoter of quality German wines and Rheingau wines in particular. His restaurant the Graues Haus in Winkel (the best in the Rhine-Main area) puts into practice his well-publicised belief in the suitability of Rheingau wines as partners for fine cuisine. Schloss Vollrads has recently been dogged by financial difficulties but with Graf Matuschka's nephew Markus having recently joined as co-director and with new winemaker Ralph Herke, the estate has the opportunity to recover its reputation for sophisticated, racy Rheingau Rieslings.

Intricate gilded signs vie for prominence along the Rheingau's narrow streets.

Travel Information

PLACES OF INTEREST

Assmannshausen With its late-Gothic church and many half-timbered houses, Assmannshausen is one of the most attractive wine villages in the Rheingau. It can be reached from Rüdesheim by two chair-lifts, between which there is a short walk through forest.

Eltville Originally the site of a Roman villa, Eltville became an important regional centre during the 14th century when the Eltviller Burg (completed in 1348) became the residence of the Prince-Bishops of Mainz. This made it a popular place for aristocratic families to establish their homes and many of the great old houses remain. One of the most important of these is the Langwerther Hof, built in the centre of town between the 12th and 17th centuries and now home to the Langwerth von Simmern estate. Schloss Eltz on the river bank, begun in the 16th century and extended in the 18th, is another impressive example. In Schwalbacher Strasse (numbers 56–62) near the edge of town stands the imposing Staatsweingüter winery (completed 1911) which is open for wine tastings from 9pm to 6pm every weekday and until 1pm on Saturdays.

Geisenheim Geisenheim is best known for its wine school and research station, the Forschungsanstalt und Fachhochschule für Wein-, Obst- und Gratenbau, founded in 1872. Close to the railway station are the fine 18th-century Schloss Kosakenberg, which now houses an attractive Weinstube, and the 16th-century Schönborner Hof. The 15th- to 16th-century Heiligkreuzkirche or Church of the Holy Cross with its 19th-century twin-tower façade is referred to locally as 'the cathedral of the Rheingau'.

Hattenheim The half-timbered, beautifully painted houses on the Hauptstrasse alone make this famous wine village worth a visit, and it also has some good restaurants. The former monastery of Kloster Eberbach (see below) belongs administratively to Hattenheim.

Hochheim On the river Main just upstream from its confluence with the Rhine at Mainz, this village is famous for its exceptional Rieslings. Hochheim is the origin of the traditional English word 'Hock' for all Rhine wines. The Königin Victoriaberg site was so named after a visit by Queen Victoria in the summer of 1850. To commemorate the visit a 'tudor-style' monument was erected among the vines in 1854. Recently restored, it is a consummate example of Victorian extravagance. The narrow streets of the old town have retained much of their original character but, sadly, the A671 Autobahn passes through the town's vineyards (thankfully on a flyover) and several ugly tower blocks have been erected on the western side of town.

Johannisberg Schloss Johannisberg dominates the village in more than one sense. As well as being almost single-handedly responsible for the fame of Johannisberg's wines, it is also a conspicuous part of the Rheingau due to its position and the sheer scale of the building. In fact, only the Romanesque church of St Johannes Bapt (John the Baptist) has survived from the estate's 12th-century foundation. The Schloss and its magnificent barrel cellar are both baroque, dating from around 1720 shortly after the estate was taken over by the the Bishop of Fulda. Fürst Clemens von Metternich-Winneburg then re-styled the Schloss in classical manner in 1826. It was badly damaged by bombing in 1942, since when it has been completely rebuilt. Today the Schloss wine boutique is open for tasting and sales from 10am to 1pm and 2pm to 6pm during the week and from 10am to 1pm on Saturdays. The view from the terrace should not be missed and the Gutsschänke is one of the Rheingau's best wine restaurants. Just below the Schloss, signs indicate where the 50th degree of latitude passes through the estate's vineyards. Below the castle lies the Klaus, a former Benedictine nunnery from which the Johannisberger Klaus site takes its name.

Kiedrich Often referred to as 'the Gothic wine village' Kiedrich has a wealth of marvellous old buildings and has almost completely escaped the attentions of modern town-planners. Its beautiful late-Gothic Valentinskirche justifies the title. However, many of the other fine buildings date from later centuries: the Renaissance Rathaus, the late 17th- and early 18th-century Schloss Groenesteyn and the Robert Weil estate built in the late 19th century.

Kloster Eberbach Founded in 1136 and secularised under Napoleon in 1803, the former monastery Kloster Eberbach is one of Germany's great cultural monuments and an essential stop on any tour of the Rheingau. The serried rows of barrels under the cavernous vault of the Hospitalkeller defy description. The vaults are open for visitors every day from 10am until 5.30pm. Just below Kloster Eberbach lies the legendary Steinberg vineyard, which can be visited by appointment or on one of its open days.

Lorch Lorch, together with its suburb Lorchhausen, is the most northerly wine village in the Rheingau and has a completely different character from the villages in the main body of the region. Its architecture, no less than its wines, belong to the Mittelrhein. The most imposing building, the hallmark of Lorch, is the gabled Hilchenhaus (1524) of the Graf von Kanitz estate. In its cellars is an excellent *Gutsschänke* or wine restaurant (see page 119). Lorch's climate is strongly influenced by the cool air, the *Wisperwind*, that flows into the Rhine Valley through the 30-kilometre-long valley of the Wisp stream. The Wispertal, or valley, offers some of the most picturesque scenery in the Taunus Mountains and is well worth a drive or a day's hike.

Oestrich-Winkel No Rheingau tour could overlook the town of Winkel. It has a wealth of old buildings, not the

Hotel Lindenwirt in Rüdesheim, just a stone's throw from the vineyards.

least of which is the Graues Haus dating from between 1035 and 1075. Behind the town below the Taunus forest stands the painstakingly restored complex of Schloss Vollrads with its 14th-century moated tower and baroque mansion. From more recent times the 18th-century house of Baron von Brentano is a living museum celebrating the friendship of the Brentanos with Goethe. It is best seen at one of the musical or literary evenings which are regularly staged there (booking is essential; telephone 06723 2068). Mittelheim, sandwiched between Winkel and Oestrich, boasts a magnificent basilica, construction of which began in the 10th century. Oestrich would be a rather dull town without its remarkable 16th-century crane which was built on the bank of the Rhine for loading and unloading wine barrels.

Rüdesheim This popular town may be rather over-loaded with souvenir stores and tourist restaurants, but it has much to offer its many visitors. The wine museum in the 12th-century Brömserburg castle (open daily from March until October) and Siegfried's Mechanical Music Cabinet (open daily from April until October) are both worth a detour. For the ultimate traditional German wine experience, the crowded narrow alley of the Drosselgasse is famous for its wine restaurants. The best food and wine is to be found at the Rüdesheimer Schloss, but diners should be prepared to enjoy the accompanying 'oompah' band.

Wiesbaden Elegant, chic Wiesbaden with its luxury hotels, fine restaurants, spa, casino and designer stores is perhaps not the best place for a traveller on a tight budget. However, the town has other attractions. One is the week-long Wiesbaden Weinwoche, held annually during the third week of August, during which many of the city's inner streets are lined with stands serving Rheingau wine, lobster, oysters and other delicacies. The city and its suburbs also contain one of the most important centres of the German sparkling wine industry. Henkell Sekt may not be what it was at the turn of the century, but the Sektkellerei with its extravagant neo-baroque marble hallway is well worth a visit. There are weekday tours at 10am and 2pm. (Biebricher Allee 142, Wiesbaden; telephone 06121 633309).

Traditional carved wooden shutters depict the wine harvest in the narrow back streets of Rüdesheim.

HOTELS AND RESTAURANTS

Hotel-Restaurant Krone
Rheinuferstrasse 10,
65385 **Assmannshausen**
Tel: (06722) 4030,
Fax: (06722) 3049
This is one of Rheingau's best hotels. Its rooms are decorated in the style of the hotel's heyday at the end of 19th century. The staunchly old-fashioned cuisine belongs in the same period. The list of moderately priced mature Rheingau wines, clarets and Burgundies is superb. In good weather there are fabulous views of the Rhine from the tables under the pergola on the terrace.

Hotel Schloss Reinhartshausen
65337 **Erbach**
Tel: (06123) 6760,
Fax: (06123) 676400
Huge investments in the total remodelling of this 18th-century palace have turned it into one of the grandest hotels on the Rhine. Schloss Reinhartshausen now looks like a film set waiting for Greta Garbo; almost over-laden with marble, gilt, antiques and old masters. The Restaurant Marcobrunn does not quite live up to its fabulous location, but the Schlosskeller (second) restaurant has the same extensive international wine list and offers good modern cooking at fair prices.

Hotel-Restaurant Kronnenschlösschen
Rheinallee,
65347 **Hattenheim**
Tel: (06723) 640,
Fax: (06723) 7663
The refined modern cooking is of a high standard and the wine list good, but not exceptional for the region. The Bistro restaurant serves somewhat simpler but equally well prepared food. The hotel rooms are miniature masterpieces of Belle Epoque nostalgia, and make this the premier luxury hotel in the region. It is expensive but not overpriced.

Hotel-Restaurant Zum Krug
Hauptstrasse 34,
65347 **Hattenheim**
Tel: (06723) 2812,
Fax: (06723) 7677
Traditional regional cooking and an extensive list of modestly priced mature Rheingau wines make this a popular restaurant so reservation is essential. As a hotel, Zum Krug is comfortable and excellent value for money.

Gutsschänke Schloss Johannisberg
Schloss,
65366 **Johannisberg**
Tel: (06722) 8538,
Fax: (06722) 7392
Chef Dieter Biesler's team have turned this into one of the Rheingau's best wine restaurants. The cooking has its roots in regional tradition but is lifted with a light, modern touch. The interior is modern and stylish and many rooms give magnificent views over the Rhine. A wide selection of wines from Schloss Johannisberg and the von Mumm estate are available – and the cheese course should not be missed.

Central-Hotel
Kirchstrasse 6,
65385 **Rüdesheim**
Tel: (06722) 3036,
Fax: (06722) 2807
This is perhaps the most attractive and comfortable of the many hotels in Rüdesheim. In spite of its central location there is little traffic noise and the rooms are good value for money.

Zur Hufschmiede (Strauswirtschaft)
Schmidtstrasse,
65385 **Rüdesheim**
The Josef Leitz estate's wine bar is open daily from 4pm until midnight but only during Rüdesheim's 'closed season' from November until March. Difficult to find (look for the iron blacksmith's sign hanging above the door) and usually full of local people, it makes a refreshing change from the familiar face of Rüdesheim.

Jagdschloss Niederwald
65385 **Rüdesheim**
Tel: (06722) 1004,
Fax: (06722) 47970
Set in the forest above Rüdesheim this fine, moderately-priced country hotel has its own swimming pool, sauna and tennis courts.

Restaurant Die Ente vom Lehel (in Hotel Nassauer Hof)
Kaiser-Friedrich-Platz 3–4,
65183 **Wiesbaden**
Tel: (0611) 133666,
Fax: (0611) 133632
Alongside the Graues Haus in Winkel, this famous restaurant is the gastronomic high-point of the region. There are few restaurants in the Mainz-Wiesbaden-Frankfurt area where classic modern cooking can be found to compare with the work of chef Herbert Langendorf. An extensive wine list offers the best from the Rheingau, France and elsewhere. Downstairs in the Entenkeller (telephone 0611 133663) more simple fare is available, also of a good standard. Ask for the full wine list.

Restaurant Graues Haus
Graugasse 10,
65375 **Winkel**
Tel: (06723) 2619,
Fax: (06723) 7086
During the last decade Egbert Engelhardt has made this tastefully restored historic building one of the best restaurants in the region. The creative cooking is of a high standard and the prices, though high, are fair.

The list of Rheingau wines (including a separate list of old wines and rarities) is unmatched.

Schloss Vollrads Gutsschänke
Schloss,
65375 **Winkel**
Tel: (06723) 660,
Fax: (06723) 1848
Schloss Vollrads' wine restaurant shares staff with Graf Matuschka's gourmet restaurant Graues Haus, but here the cooking is regional in style. A wide range of wines from the Schloss Vollrads and Fürst Löwenstein estates is offered. Whether or not the steel and glass atrium marries well with the adjoining 17th-century building is a matter of some debate.

Overlooking the sunny terrace of the Kronnenschlösschen at Hattenheim, one of the best hotel and restaurants in the region.

USEFUL ADDRESSES

Städtischer Verkehrsamt Eltville
Schmittstrasse 2,
65343 **Eltville**
Tel: (06123) 697153,
Fax: (06123) 2244
Also covers Erbach and Hattenheim.

Köln-Düsseldorfer Deutsche Rheinschiffahrt AG
Frankenwerft 15,
50667 **Köln**
Tel: (0221) 20880
This is the Rhine's largest passenger ship company. Timetable details are also available from their Rüdesheim office. Telephone (06722) 3808.

Fremdenverkehrsverband Rheingau-Taunus
Rheinstrasse 5,
65385 **Rüdesheim**
Tel: (06722) 3041

Städtischer Verkehrsamt Rüdesheim
Rheinstrasse 16,
65385 **Rüdesheim**
Tel: (06722) 2962, Fax: (06722) 3485
Also covers Assmannshausen.

Verkehrsburo Wiesbaden
Rheinstrasse 15,
65185 **Wiesbaden**
Tel: (0611) 1729780,
Fax: (0611) 1729799

119

Rheinhessen

With more than 25,000 hectares of vineyards, Rheinhessen is Germany's largest wine-growing region. It stretches from Bad Kreuznach in the west to the Rhine in the east and from Mainz in the north to Worms in the south and accounts for one quarter of the nation's wine production. It is difficult to generalise about the Rheinhessen as a region, not only because of its size but also because of the extraordinary diversity of its vineyards and the wines they produce. Here there are good, indifferent and poor examples of almost every German wine style. Over 20 significant grape varieties, large variations in microclimate and soil composition, plus the radically differing perspectives of numerous vintners result in a picture of dizzying complexity.

Rheinhessen produces wines that scale the same breathtaking heights as the best from the Mosel-Saar-Ruwer, the Rheingau, the Pfalz or the Nahe. Rieslings from the top vineyards of Nackenheim and Nierstein just south of Mainz are among the greatest German wines. At the other extreme are those made from inferior modern varieties planted during recent decades on unsuitable arable land. Somewhere between the two extremes a wealth of good-quality country wines are made from both traditional and modern varieties.

Sadly, the region is still most strongly identified with Liebfraumilch; the industry's export success story of the 1970s and early 1980s. Demand for Liebfraumilch has diminished but together with generic wines sold under the Niersteiner Gutes Domtal and Oppenheimer Krötenbrünnen Grosslage names, it still accounts for a large proportion of Rheinhessen's production, further obscuring the fact that other, completely different, wines are also produced here.

The industry's current restructuring will probably result in a proportion of Rheinhessen's inferior vineyards falling out of cultivation during the next decade. This should simplify the picture as the less fashionable grape varieties all but disappear. Until this is effected, however, the only way to make sense of Rheinhessen is to break it up into its component parts and to consider each one separately. Even this is not easy, since the boundaries between them are often vague.

Rheinhessen is farm country, where vineyards dotted with modest villages stretch as far as the eye can see.

Most top-quality Rheinhessen wines come from the vineyards around a few villages on the left bank of the Rhine between the old towns of Worms and Mainz. This is the only part of the region in which steep, well exposed vineyards are situated close enough to the river to benefit from its warming influence. Hence the traditional name of this area running along the Rheinhessen's eastern boundary, the 'Rheinfront'. The borders of this most important sub-region have never been precisely defined, so where they lie depends upon individual perspective. To a quality-orientated vintner in Laubenheim in the north of the area or Alsheim in the south, it is clear that his or her vineyards belong to the Rheinfront, but to those determined to include in the area only those villages with first-class vineyards, Nackenheim, Nierstein and Oppenheim constitute the entire Rheinfront.

Whichever way the border lines are drawn the vineyards of the 'Roter Hang', or Red Slope, of Nierstein and Nackenheim lie at the heart of the Rheinfront. At the northern end of this breathtaking five-kilometre escarpment the vineyards rise directly from the left bank of the Rhine, while the vines at the equally vertiginous southern end enjoy perfect southerly exposure. Since the end of the 19th century the Riesling Beerenauslese and Trockenbeerenauslese from the vivid red soil of these hillsides have been recognised internationally as some of the finest dessert wines in the world. During the last 15 years several vintners here have also produced dry Rieslings that have won international acclaim. Such success with both dry and sweet wines is unusual in Germany and proves that these are among the best vineyards in the Rhine Valley.

The technical name for this dramatic geological formation is the Niersteiner Horst. It was formed during the Middle Tertiary period when the Upper Rhine Rift Valley collapsed, creating the Mainz

A small chapel overlooks farm land and the vineyards beyond. The warm climate and fertile soil make Rheinhessen an important agricultural region.

Basin and exposing a strip of older red slate from the Permian period between Schwabsburg and Nackenheim. This is a much softer slate than the blue-grey Devonian slate typical of the Mosel-Saar-Ruwer and it weathers quickly to a clay-like consistency. It is a mixture of this material and the local red slate stones, combined with the excellent local microclimate, that give the wines from the Nierstein and Nackenheim top sites their unique character.

It is difficult to compare them with either the wines of the Rheingau to the north, or the Pfalz to the south. While they can easily match the the body and weight of examples from the Pfalz (dry Rieslings with 12 to 13.5 degrees of alcohol are common in the Rheinhessen in good vintages) they never taste heavy or lush as Pfalz wines sometimes do. Equally, while they can match the acidity of Rheingau wines, they taste more elegant – even silky – in better years. Even in lesser vintages Rieslings from the Roter Hang rarely taste hard or aggressive. Good examples possess Riesling's hallmark peach- and apricot-like fruit augmented with almond, exotic fruit, citrus, redcurrant and mineral tones. The resulting wines are seductive, suave and refined.

Six sites account for most of the Roter Hang: Nackenheimer Rothenberg, Niersteiner Pettenthal, Niersteiner Brudersberg, Niersteiner Hipping, Niersteiner Oelberg and Niersteiner Orbel. Although they are all steeply sloping, all possess the same red slate soil and lie directly next to one another, each of their Rieslings has a distinct personality. The contrasts are as great as those between wines from the *Grand Cru* sites of Vosne-Romanée in Burgundy or the classified growths of Pauillac in Bordeaux.

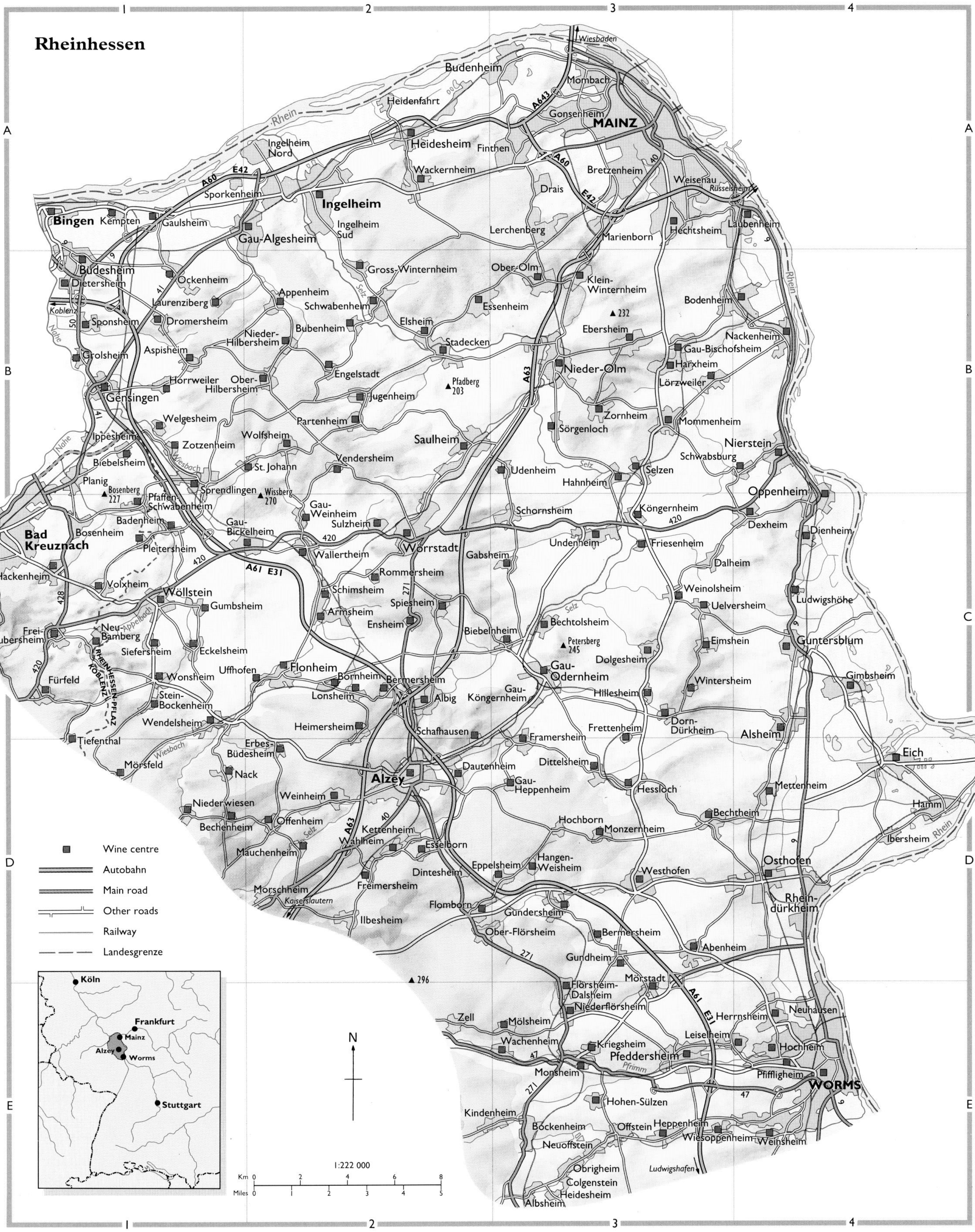
Rheinhessen
Wiesbaden
Budenheim
Mombach
Heidenfahrt
Rhein
Gonsenheim
MAINZ
Ingelheim Nord
Heidesheim
Finthen
Wackernheim
Bretzenheim
Weisenau
Rüsselsheim
Drais
Sporkenheim
Ingelheim
Bingen
Kempten
Gaulsheim
Ingelheim Sud
Gau-Algesheim
Lerchenberg
Marienborn
Hechtsheim
Laubenheim
Büdesheim
Dietersheim
Ockenheim
Gross-Winternheim
Ober-Olm
Klein-Winternheim
Appenheim
Laurenziberg
Schwabenheim
Essenheim
Bodenheim
Koblenz
Sponsheim
Dromersheim
Elsheim
Nackenheim
Nahe
Nieder-Hilbersheim
Bubenheim
Stadecken
Ebersheim
Gau-Bischofsheim
Grolsheim
Aspisheim
Harxheim
Nieder-Olm
Engelstadt
Horrweiler
Ober-Hilbersheim
Pfadberg 203
Lörzweiler
Gensingen
Jugenheim
Welgesheim
Partenheim
Zornheim
Mommenheim
Sörgenloch
Ippesheim
Wolfsheim
Saulheim
Nierstein
Zotzenheim
Schwabsburg
Biebelsheim
Vendersheim
Wiesbach
St. Johann
Udenheim
Selzen
Planig
Hahnheim
Bosenberg 227
Pfaffen-Schwabenheim
Sprendlingen
Wissberg 270
Oppenheim
Gau-Weinheim
Köngernheim
Badenheim
Schornsheim
Sulzheim
Bad Kreuznach
Bosenheim
Gau-Bickelheim
Dexheim
Undenheim
Dienheim
Pleitersheim
Wallertheim
Wörrstadt
Friesenheim
Gabsheim
Dalheim
Hackenheim
Rommersheim
Volxheim
Wöllstein
Schimsheim
Weinolsheim
Gumbsheim
Spiesheim
Uelversheim
Ludwigshöhe
Armsheim
Frei-Laubersheim
Neu-Bamberg
Ensheim
Bechtolsheim
Siefersheim
Biebelnheim
Petersberg 245
Eimsheim
Guntersblum
Eckelsheim
Dolgesheim
Fürfeld
Uffhofen
Flonheim
Gau-Odernheim
Gimbsheim
Wonsheim
Bornheim
Bermersheim
Wintersheim
Stein-Bockenheim
Lonsheim
Albig
Gau-Köngernheim
Hillesheim
Rheinhessen-Pfalz
Dorn-Dürkheim
Wendelsheim
Heimersheim
Schafhausen
Frettenheim
Alsheim
Tiefenthal
Erbes-Büdesheim
Framersheim
Eich
Mörsfeld
Dautenheim
Dittelsheim
Nack
Alzey
Gau-Heppenheim
Hessloch
Mettenheim
Niederwiesen
Weinheim
Hamm
Offenheim
Bechenheim
Kettenheim
Hochborn
Monzernheim
Bechtheim
Wahlheim
Esselborn
Ibersheim
Mauchenheim
Hangen-Weisheim
Eppelsheim
Dintesheim
Osthofen
Westhofen
Morschheim
Kaiserslautern
Freimersheim
Flomborn
Rhein-dürkheim
Ilbesheim
Gundersheim
Ober-Flörsheim
Bermersheim
Abenheim
Gundheim
296
Mörstadt
Flörsheim-Dalsheim
Niederflörsheim
Herrnsheim
Neuhausen
Zell
Mölsheim
Leiselheim
Wachenheim
Kriegsheim
Pfeddersheim
Hochheim
Monsheim
Pfrimm
Pfiffligheim
WORMS
Kindenheim
Hohen-Sülzen
Bockenheim
Offstein
Heppenheim
Wiesoppenheim
Weinsheim
Neuoffstein
Obrigheim
Ludwigshafen
Colgenstein
Heidesheim
Albsheim
A60
E42
A643
A63
A61
E31
Wine centre
Autobahn
Main road
Other roads
Railway
Landesgrenze
Köln
Frankfurt
Mainz
Alzey
Worms
Stuttgart
N
1:222 000
Km 0 2 4 6 8
Miles 0 1 2 3 4 5

The two most northerly of these sites, the Nackenheimer Rothenberg and the Niersteiner Pettenthal (sometimes written Pettental) are also the steepest. They form a single slope running almost exactly north to south, giving them an easterly exposure and the full benefit of the morning sun. The soil is shallow and stony and warms quickly. The disadvantage is that the vines can suffer from drought stress if there are many rainless weeks during the growing season. The first Riesling Beerenauslese and Trockenbeerenauslese wines in Rheinhessen were harvested here in the great 1893 and 1911 vintages by the Franz Karl Schmitt estate of Nierstein and the Gunderloch estate of Nackenheim.

In spite of having so much in common and looking virtually identical, the wines from these two sites are very different. The Pettenthal wines are flatterers, even when very rich and powerful, and show a marvellous peach- and apricot-like fruit from their earliest youth. The finest have a mineral character as intense as any German Riesling, yet remain sleek and graceful. In contrast the Rothenberg Rieslings are slow developers, the Spätlese and higher quality Prädikat wines needing several years' ageing before they reveal their full potential. With time a rich tapestry of fruit, mineral, nut and spice aromas develops, making these some of the most sophisticated Rieslings in the Rhine Valley. Gunderloch's Rothenberg wines currently overshadow everything else produced from this site, while from the Pettenthal top honours are shared among St Antony, Heinrich Braun and Freiherr Heyl zu Herrnsheim.

The tiny Brudersberg vineyard tucked in a side valley is the smallest of Nierstein's top sites and potentially the greatest. It is the only portion of the Roter Hang next to the Rhine that faces due south. Wholly owned by the Nierstein Freiherr Heyl zu Herrnsheim estate, it has yielded some legendary wines. The '53 Riesling Trockenbeerenauslese, still sensational at 35 years of age, is perhaps the most famous of these. The site's Rieslings marry an impressive richness with the elegance typical of Pettenthal and Rothenberg wines.

The virtues of the Niersteiner Hipping, which is effectively identical to the Goldene Luft site, have long been debated. Some of Nierstein's vintners regard this site as the greatest of the Roter Hang while others consider its wines somewhat superficial. Certainly the lower-lying and less steep Hipping vineyard is nothing special compared to the steeper sites higher up, which can produce wines with a rich pineapple and citrus character in their youth

Other crops compete for precious space but vineyards take priority.

and be full and lush even as dry wines. This richness is not always backed up by much power, however, and some Hipping wines lack persistence of flavour. The number of successful Rieslings harvested here will undoubtedly increase as the vines age. They were replanted during the mid-1980s as part of the *Fluerbereinigung* vineyard reorganisation programme, and have not yet reached the optimum age of 15 years and more. Currently the best sources for Hipping Rieslings are St Antony and Georg Albrecht Schneider. The Weissburgunder wines from Freiherr Heyl zu Herrnsheim are the best from this grape in Rheinhessen.

The Oelberg and Orbel sites, which give the southern half of the Roter Hang's best wines, have also been handicapped by their vines' immaturity in recent years. In the mid-1990s they were only just back in production. Young vines whose roots have not yet penetrated the sub-soil are particularly sensitive to drought and the Nierstein area's low rainfall can make this a serious problem in hot dry years. Here again are two neighbouring sites that share many characteristics, such as their southeasterly exposure, steep inclination and a position further from the Rhine than the Roter Hang vineyards to the north, and yet they produce strikingly different wines.

The Oelberg has a gentler slope and a deeper, richer soil than the Orbel, resulting in full-bodied wines with plenty of flesh and substance. Good examples have a full peachy fruit into which are woven subtle almond and earth notes. Even in cool years when most Rhine wines are tart and have too much acidity, Oelberg Rieslings have a certain roundness that makes them ideally suited for vinification in the dry style. When they retain some natural sweetness their high mineral content somehow counters the impression of sweetness. Perhaps these are the qualities that make Oelberg wines consistent: even little-known growers frequently make good wines from this site. The St Antony and Freiherr Heyl zu Herrnsheim estates make the most complete and imposing Oelberg wines.

For reasons that are hard to fathom, the great wines from the Orbel site are little-known compared to those from the Oelberg. The Orbel's precipitous steepness and its shallow stony soil result in intense, racy wines with a vigour that makes them dramatic in their youth but also gives them great ageing potential. Because their acidity is pointed they gain enormously from a touch of sweetness. This acidity can make the Orbel wines of poor vintages rather angular, but in years with hot summers it turns greatly to their advantage. It is then, when some of the town's wines can be a little too broad and weighty, that the unique brilliance of Orbel Rieslings shines.

The only other great site on the Roter Hang is the Heiligenbaum. Its position should guarantee remarkable wines in most years, but though they are frequently good they seldom have either the character or sophistication of those from the neighbouring sites. Perhaps this is because of the soil, which is loamy and therefore heavier than that of neighbouring Oelberg and Orbel. Only the upper third of the site has soil of pure red slate.

Red slate is also the predominant soil type in the steeply sloping Schloss Schwabsburg site to the west of the Orbel. Cooler and more exposed to wind than Nierstein's top vineyards, its wines are light and quite tart, but share the peach-like fruit and elegance of Nierstein's best wines. The best part of the Niersteiner Rosenberg, that within the 180-metre contour line (see page 126), gives wines with a similar balance but an extraordinary bouquet of redcurrants and spice.

Between the Roter Hang and Nierstein lies the isolated hillock of the Kranzberg, upon which are also the tiny Zehnmorgen,

Looking east across the Rhine from the Nackenheimer Rothenberg vineyard towards the flat plains beyond.

Bergkirche and Glöck vineyards. The yellowish colour of its soil is typical of loess, a fine powdery material deposited by the wind in parts of Rheinhessen many thousands of years ago. It holds water well, which enables the vines to sustain an ample crop, but it rarely gives Rieslings of any great sophistication. With their sheltered position close to the Rhine, however, these vineyards are exceptionally well protected from the elements, enabling the Riesling to give medium-bodied wines of some elegance.

The wines from almost all these sites can also be encountered under two Grosslage names: the Rehbach, made up of the Pettenthal, Brudersberg, Goldene Luft and Hipping of Nierstein and the Auflangen, made up of the Kranzberg, Oelberg, Heiligenbaum, Orbel and Schloss Schwabsburg. Small Grosslage like these, composed entirely of superior vineyards, find them-

selves in a very different position from large, heterogenous ones such as Niersteiner Gutes Domtal. In spite of this the Rehbach and Auflangen names appear less and less frequently on labels as local vintners increasingly elect to use the village name for wines of less exalted quality. German Wine Law perversely requires that wine sold under the 'Nierstein' name be produced entirely from the town's vineyards, and yet most wines sold under the Niersteiner Gutes Domtal Grosslage name contain little or no Nierstein wine.

Few of Nierstein's vineyards are included within the borders of the Niersteiner Gutes Domtal. Most of the wine comes from neighbouring villages with inferior vineyards. Needless to say, little of it comes from noble grapes, Müller-Thurgau accounting for the greater part. The large volume of Niersteiner Gutes Domtal on supermarket shelves around the world is anything but good publicity for Nierstein and the same problem affects the town of Oppenheim, whose name has also been shamelessly – but under the Wine Law legally – exploited. The Oppenheimer

125

Top: *A typical German maypole supporting less-than-typical wine advertising.*
Above: *A more straightforward invitation to taste the region's wines.*

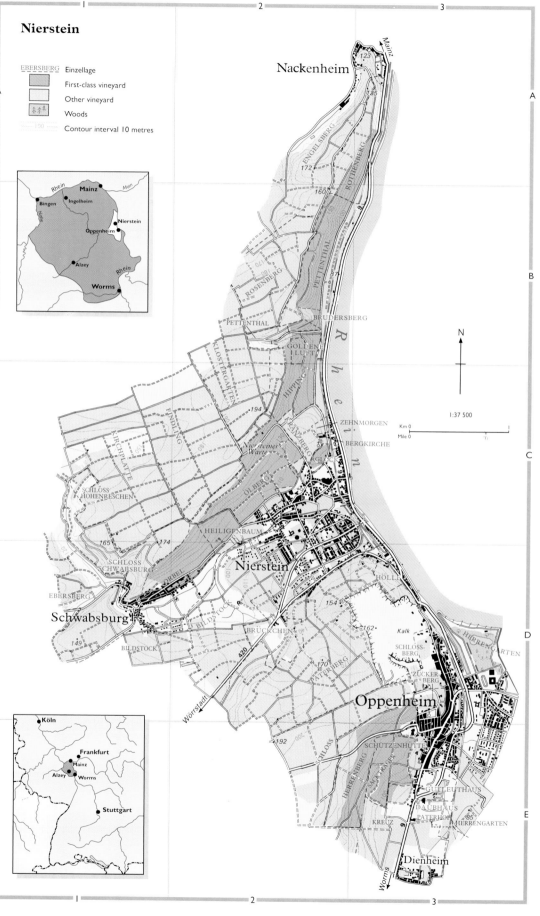

Nierstein

EBERSBERG Einzellage
First-class vineyard
Other vineyard
Woods
Contour interval 10 metres

Nackenheim

Nierstein

Schwabsburg

Oppenheim

Dienheim

N

1:37 500

Km 0
Mile 0

Köln

Frankfurt

Mainz

Alzey   Worms

Stuttgart

Krötenbrünnen Grosslage labours under the same handicap as the Gutes Domtal. All Oppenheim's better vineyards are included within the boundaries of the much smaller Oppenheimer Güldenmorgen Grosslage, only the poorest vineyard land falling within the borders of the Krötenbrünnen. The bizarre legislation that created and condones such misleading nomenclature is not found anywhere else in the world.

Most of Oppenheim's better wines are sold under single vineyard names. They possess a character very different from those of Nierstein, having more opulence and naked power. Although the distance between Nierstein and Oppenheim is only a couple of kilometres, their soil types have little in common. Immediately south of Nierstein lies a series of limestone hills covered in loam, loess and marl soil. Oppenheim's best vineyards are on the southeast-facing side of these hills which, in spite of their steepness, have deep, heavy marl soils.

The best and most famous of these vineyards is the Sackträger. Its superiority can be largely attributed to the bowl-like formation of the surrounding hillsides which shelter the site from cold winds. It can give dry wines as well as rich dessert Rieslings whose succulence, full of apricot flavour and overtones of exotic fruits, belies the firm structure that gives them excellent ageing potential.

While the best vineyards of Nierstein can suffer from drought stress, the opposite problem exists in Oppenheim. The Sackträger's deep soil can easily result in too heavy a crop if the vines are not kept in check. The resulting wines can tend to heaviness if they are not made with the greatest care. Louis Guntrum, Carl Koch Erben, Kühling-Gillot and Dr Alex Senfter all make good Oppenheimers but their wines can rarely match Nierstein's best examples.

The wines of the neighbouring Herrenberg and Schützenhütte sites (the latter wholly-owned by Guntrum) are slightly lighter and

Looking south across the great sweep of first-class sites Niersteiner Pettenthal and Niersteiner Hipping. The town of Nierstein lies in the distance.

more playful, while the Kreuz wines are frequently as powerful as those of the Sackträger but lack some of their sophistication. During the last decade the Carl Koch Erben estate has proved that these vineyards are ideally suited to Weissburgunder, making wines with an almost burgundian richness. The Dienheimer Tafelstein, which lies immediately to the south, is less steep than Oppenheim's best vineyards but has a similar soil. Here the Dr Becker estate produces good, generally dry wines from half-a-dozen grape varieties. What they lack in finesse they make up for in firm, earthy character.

Further south this ridge of hills becomes lower and less steep and the soil changes to loess and sand. The vines in the sloping and terraced vineyards to the west of the B9 road can yield appealingly juicy, medium-bodied Rieslings but these should be enjoyed for their youthful charm rather than kept for long. The vineyards of Gau-Bischofsheim, Bodenheim and Laubenheim to the north of the area are a different matter. Here the soils range from light loam to calcareous clay, and the latter is well suited to Riesling. Vineyards are planted on a range of low hills that give them good southeasterly exposure.

The story of Rheinhessen Riesling would not be complete without mentioning Bingen, whose best vineyards are shown on the detailed map of the Unter Nahe (see page 87) since they are situated in the extreme northeast of Rheinhessen. A succession of elegant, racy Rieslings was made by the Villa Sachsen estate during the 1970s and 1980s from the Binger Scharlachberg's stony terraces. They had more in common with the wines of the Rheingau's Rüdesheimer Berg, just across the Rhine, than they did with anything else produced in Rheinhessen.

After a troubled period in the early 1990s the vineyards and estate name were acquired by Michael Prinz zu Salm-Salm, owner of the Prinz zu Salm-Dalberg estate of Wallhausen in the Nahe. Hopefully he will restore Bingen's reputation to its rightful place alongside that of Nierstein.

Nierstein's principal challenger with the Riesling grape is an unlikely one: the walled town of Flörsheim-Dalsheim in the opposite corner of the region to Bingen, the far southeast. At a glance there seems little to distinguish this area from the rest of the region. Indeed, the soil here includes all the types found in the region's *Hügelland* or hill country: loess, loam, clay and marl. However, these vineyards stand in the rain shadow of the Donnersberg, at 687 metres the highest peak of the Nordpfälzer Bergland. Consequently the rainfall is the lowest in the region and almost the lowest in Germany. This limits yields naturally and those vintners who adjust their vineyard management accordingly can harvest Rieslings with almost as much depth as those from Nierstein. Wines from the sloping marl vineyards are particularly expressive. Here Keller makes the best Rieslings in Rheinhessen.

Keller and the neighbouring Schales have also demonstrated the potential of such diverse grape varieties as Weissburgunder and Huxelrebe. Unlike Riesling, these are less discriminating about soil and microclimate. As long as they have enough warmth and sunshine, the vintner's commitment is a more decisive factor than the soil or vineyard exposure. Weissburgunder is much easier to ripen than Riesling in Rheinhessen's hill country and is the ideal grape for dry white wines in most of the region. Such wines are typically medium bodied with 11 to 12 degrees of alcohol and they can resemble good-quality Pinot Blancs from Alsace. With Weissburgunder, the vintner's challenge is focused more on harvesting healthy grapes than with Riesling, where the battle is more likely to be against excess acidity in the grapes. The vintner must take considerable trouble tending Weissburgunder vines, but a healthy crop almost invariably results in harmonious dry wine.

Huxelrebe is different again, its often sharp, citrus-like acidity and Muscat-like bouquet making it unsuitable for dry wines. Compare an ungainly dry Huxelrebe with a Huxelrebe BA or TBA dessert wine, however, and it is difficult to believe that they are the product of the same grape. With their intense grapefruit, exotic fruit, honey and spice character they can be as lavish and many-faceted as Rieslings of comparable quality. The combination of power, richness and mouthwatering acidity makes them some of Germany's most remarkable dessert wines. Because Huxelrebe is one of the unfashionable *Neuzuchtungen*, however, these wines suffer from an image problem domestically and internationally. As a consequence, prices are very reasonable such excellent wines.

Both Keller and Schales produce elegant Huxelrebe dessert wines with none of the rough edges that often come with high acidity. Their aromas are pure and clean. With the '89 vintage, Schales went so far as to name their Huxelrebe TBA a '100-Year Wine', guaranteeing that with careful cellaring it would live for a century. Old Huxelrebe wines are hard to find, but the rare examples that have appeared at tastings suggest that Schales' claim is not unrealistic. The Geil estate of Bechtheim makes a much more powerful, pungently spicy style of Huxelrebe dessert wine. It has enough concentration of aroma and flavour to stand comparison with Riesling BA and TBA from anywhere along the Rhine.

The Geil estate's wines are fine examples of what is possible, given strict quality control, in relatively undistinguished parts of Rheinhessen. The estate makes not only first-class Huxelrebe but also good wines from a handful of other varieties. One of its biggest successes is with dry Silvaner, Rheinhessen's traditional country wine. This grape once accounted for more than two-thirds of the region's vineyard plantings, but since extensive new vineyards were planted with Müller-Thurgau, Kerner and modern grape varieties during the 1970s the figure has fallen below 15 percent. Traditionally bone-dry and tart with a rustic apple and earth character, Silvaner is a wine for quaffing rather than studying. Taste a few average examples and it is not difficult to understand why local vintners and farmers opted for modern grape varieties that give more superficially appealing wines. However, a top-class example such as the Spätlese Trocken from Geil is a different matter: a unique dry wine that is both wine and fruit, substantial but not heavy and very well balanced. Other producers of superior Silvaners are Brüder Dr Becker, Freiherr Heyl zu Herrnsheim, Sander and Georg Albrecht Schneider.

During the late 1980s the trend back to traditional grape varieties resulted in a significant revival of interest in Silvaner. Rheinhessen vintners, sampling good wines from this grape grown in Franken, were convinced that they could produce similar wines and the prices commanded by Franken Silvaners made this an appealing prospect. A worthy initiative called 'RS', devised to promote the production and appreciation of quality dry Rheinhessen Silvaners, got off to a promising start. However, the initiative was rather too ambitious and the participating producers too disparate in size and structure. Some of the larger participants undercut the planned price structure, which undermined the entire exercise. RS now operates on a more modest scale.

Recently however a more stringently defined and tightly controlled regional initiative called 'Rheinhessen Selektion' has been introduced to promote dry wines from the Silvaner and other traditional varieties. 'Rheinhessen Selektion' wines may be produced only from old vineyards that are cropped at a very low level. The wines must also pass a 'blind' tasting test to confirm that the policy has resulted in a wine of superior quality. The first releases

The undulating plateau west of the Rheinfront, where the Silvaner flourishes. Traditionally used for Rheinhessen's country wines, the variety enjoyed renewed attention in the late 1980s when winemakers began to develop its potential for making quality dry wines.

were of an impressive standard and suggest that this initiative will achieve more than its predecessor.

The new varieties that most successfully replaced Silvaner in producing the region's everyday wines are Scheurebe, Kerner and Bacchus. They are all capable of producing fruity, aromatic wines in Rheinhessen, but only if their yield is kept low and their harvest carefully timed. Unfortunately, strict crop management is still not commonplace in Rheinhessen's hill-country. Decades spent mass-producing generic wines have left a legacy that inhibits the development of quality wine production. Thankfully, however, the region does have its complement of forward-thinking vintners. There are those determined to establish a new identity for the region with wines completely different from those made during the 1960s and 1970s. The era of cloyingly sweet, crudely aromatic Rheinhessen wines is coming to an end as they are increasingly replaced with high-quality dry and dessert wines.

that is the hallmark of this estate's wines. These are botrytis masterpieces of a kind rare on the Rhine.
Best vintages: '94, '93, '92, '90
Best drunk: As young wines these are too sweet to drink with savoury food apart from Foie Gras or Roquefort, but there seems little need for food with wines as rich and irresistible as this.

Niersteiner Hipping Weissburgunder Spätlese Trocken
Weingut Freiherr Heyl zu Herrnsheim, Nierstein
Vineyard site: Niersteiner Hipping
Site area: 31 hectares, 1.5 hectares Heyl zu Herrnsheim
Exposure: east-southeast
Inclination: sloping
Soil: deep weathered red slate
Description: Ripe pineapple, melted butter and caramel mingle in these full-bodied dry whites. Much richer and rounder than the wines of this grape from Alsace or Italy, they have depth and balance to compare with many good-quality Chardonnays. The healthy acidity prevents the substantial alcoholic content from ever becoming dominant and gives them a long clean finish.
Best vintages: '93, '92, '90, '89, '88
Best drunk: This style is ideal for richer fish dishes and for pork and veal with glazed vegetables. It is also well suited to a wide range of cheese.

Niersteiner Oelberg Riesling Spätlese Trocken
Weingut St Antony, Nierstein
Vineyard site: Niersteiner Oelberg
Site area: 60 hectares, 2.5 hectares St Antony
Exposure: southeast
Inclination: steep
Soil: deep weathered red slate
Description: Some of the most opulent dry Rieslings in Germany, these remarkable wines are a succulent cocktail of fruit and mineral aromas and flavours. With the kind of richness and concentration normally associated with the best whites of Alsace or even Burgundy, they are the opposite of the thin, acidic style once typical of dry German wines.
Best vintages: '94, '93, '92, '91, '90, '89
Best drunk: Dry Riesling of this kind demands rich food such as lobster or veal in a morel cream sauce. Large wine glasses are also important to allow the wine's aroma to expand.

BENCHMARK WINES

Huxelrebe Trockenbeerenauslese '100 Jahre Wein'
Weingut Schales, Flörsheim-Dalsheim
Vineyard site: Dalsheimer Steig
Site area: 80 hectares, 12.5 hectares Schales
Exposure: south-southeast
Inclination: gently sloping
Soil: limestone and loess-loam
Description: Luscious and tart aromas are intertwined in these distinctive dessert wines. With their grapefruit, lime, exotic fruits and honey character they are at once lavishly rich and racy. They have the intensity, elegance and ageing potential to stand comparison with top Riesling dessert wines, Sauternes or Tokay.
Best vintages: '94, '93, '90, '89
Best drunk: These wines have the power, sweetness and acidity to stand up to all but the sweetest dessert (or chocolate). The best combination is with exotic fruit desserts.

Nackenheimer Rothenberg Riesling Auslese Gold Cap
Weingut Gunderloch, Nackenheim
Vineyard site: Nackenheim Rothenberg
Site area: 20 hectares, 7 hectares Gunderloch
Exposure: east-southeast
Inclination: very steep
Soil: weathered stony red slate, very stony top-soil
Description: Their enveloping bouquet of hibiscus, exotic fruit, honey and almond makes these some of the most ravishing Auslese dessert wines in Germany. More mouth-filling and intense than many Beerenauslese, they retain the elegance and silkiness

BEST PRODUCERS

Weingut Heinrich Braun

Glockenstrasse 9,
55283 Nierstein
Owner: Peter Braun
Vineyard area: 25 hectares
Grape varieties: 70% Riesling,
10% Müller-Thurgau,
5% Silvaner, 15% other varieties
Top sites: Niersteiner Oelberg,
Niersteiner Orbel,
Niersteiner Pettenthal

Peter Braun's Rieslings from the best Nierstein sites may not be the most powerful or intense wines in the region but they frequently possess an elegance and charm reminiscent of the Mosel. Indeed, Mosel-Saar-Ruwer wines provided the ideal that Braun has been pursuing for more than 20 years. While some of his neighbours have reduced yields to concentrate their wines, he has replanted the estate's vineyards with Riesling clones from the Nahe and Mosel in order to make filigree and floral medium-bodied wines. He has also experimented with the ageing of Riesling in new-oak *barriques* and endeavoured to imitate the style of Italian white wines, but most of the estate's wines successfully realise his principal goal. Dry and sweet wines are equally well made and the estate enjoys an excellent reputation for its Riesling BA and TBA dessert wines, which are among the best in the region.

Weingut Brüder Dr Becker

Mainzer Strasse 3,
55278 Ludwigshöhe
Owner: Lotte Pfeffer
Vineyard area: 9 hectares
Grape varieties: 42% Riesling,
20% Silvaner, 20% Scheurebe,
5% Müller-Thurgau, 5% Kerner,
5% Spätburgunder, 3% Grauburgunder
Top site: Dienheimer Tafelstein

Helmut Pfeffer switched to organic cultivation nearly 20 years ago and now this estate is one of the country's most serious organic producers. Helmut's daughter Lotte Pfeffer and her husband Hans Müller have now taken over but continue to run the business with the same combination of idealism and down-to-earth practicality. Theirs are traditional Rheinhessen wines in the best sense. With plenty of fruit and substance the racy dry Rieslings are full of character. The hearty dry Silvaners with their full apple-like fruit, subtle earthiness and crisp acidity are among the best wines from the grape in the region. Top examples from both grapes are sold under the 'Rheinhessen Selektion' designation. No less impressive are the estate's dry and sweet Scheurebe wines which possess a fascinating blackcurrant and spice character with no sign of the loud cattiness often associated with the grape. The Brüder Dr Becker wines are neither dramatic nor showy, but have excellent ageing potential, improving for many years as they age in the bottle.

Weingut Gunderloch

Carl-Gunderloch-Platz 1,
55299 Nackenheim
Owner: Agnes Hasselbach
Vineyard area: 10 hectares
Grape varieties: 85% Riesling,
5% Silvaner, 5% Müller-Thurgau,
5% other varieties
Top site: Nackenheimer Rothenberg

Until the late 1980s the wines of this historic estate were of good but not exceptional quality. Since then, husband-and-wife team Fritz and Agnes Hasselbach have pushed the estate to the forefront of the region and it now belongs among the country's wine elite. Though they are packed with succulent fruit, the beautifully balanced Gunderloch wines retain a silky elegance. Their apricot, hibiscus, grapefruit and almond character is seductive when they are young but they can also age for many years. While the Hasselbachs have invested a great deal of energy in their dry wines, their greatest success is with their naturally sweet style. Considering the estate's great tradition for noble sweet wines, this is hardly surprising. Their 1911 Edelbeerenauslese (a designation between BA and TBA which was abolished by the 1971 Wine Law) was the most expensive wine ever produced in Rheinhessen. Like that wine, the magnificent Auslese, BA and TBA wines currently produced here all come from the slopes of the Nackenheimer Rothenberg. Here the Hasselbachs harvest more selectively than any other estate in the region, passing through each parcel of vines many times in order to pick the grapes at exactly the right level of ripeness. In the cellar they use an idiosyncratic mixture of high-tech and old-fashioned methods developed by former wine-school lecturer Fritz Hasselbach after he threw out the textbooks he used to teach from. 'These books are all about reducing the risks in winemaking, but you cannot make great wines without taking risks,' he says. This estate takes the maximum possible risks in pursuit of optimum quality.

Weingut Freiherr Heyl zu Herrnsheim

Langgasse 3,
55283 Nierstein
Owners: Isa von Weymarn and Valckenberg
Vineyard area: 33 hectares

Fritz and Agnes Hasselbach with their aromatic Rieslings.

Grape varieties: 60% Riesling,
15% Silvaner, 15% Müller-Thurgau,
10% other varieties
Top sites: Niersteiner Brudersberg (wholly owned), Niersteiner Hipping, Niersteiner Oelberg,
Niersteiner Pettenthal

This great estate was long the Rheinhessen's undisputed champion, its beautifully crafted traditional-style dry Riesling, Silvaner and Weissburgunder wines unmatched. It was also Germany's leading producer of organic wines, achieving a quality standard that astonished many critics. In recent years, however, competition in Rheinhessen to produce top-quality wines has intensified and, like many large wine estates in Germany, the von Weymarns have faced business difficulties. However, since entering a partnership with the Worms-based wine-export house of Valckenberg in 1994, they have consolidated their position as one of the region's leading dry wine producers. Part of this deal involves their taking over the 12 hectares of vineyards in the Wormser Liebfrauenstift-Kirchenstück vineyard which is owned by Valckenberg. This historic site in the centre of Worms is the birthplace of Liebfraumilch and its wines enjoyed a high reputation until well into this century. As demand for Liebfraumilch became overwhelming, wines from all over Rheinhessen, the Pfalz, Nahe and even the Rheingau were sold as Liebfraumilch and this is when the wine's reputation began to suffer. Peter von Weymarn is in the process of converting this vineyard to organic cultivation. Only the best wines from the Liebfrauenstift-Kirchenstück will be marketed under this site name, following the system of internal classification introduced by Heyl zu Herrnsheim. Now only the very best wines from the top sites, such as Niersteiner Brudersberg Riesling Spätlese, are sold with vineyard designations. Good-quality wines such as Niersteiner Riesling or Niersteiner Silvaner are sold under the village names and everyday wines are labelled with only the name of the grape. The von Weymarns consider that, given the unhelpful Wine Law of 1971, this is the only way to indicate clearly to consumers the real quality of each wine.

Weingut Keller

Bahnhofstrasse 5,
67592 Flörsheim-Dalsheim
Owners: Klaus and Hedwig Keller
Vineyard area: 12 hectares
Grape varieties: 25% Riesling,
11% Huxelrebe,
11% Müller-Thurgau,
6% Rieslaner, 6% Scheurebe,
6% Silvaner, 6% Weissburgunder
29% other varieties

No vineyards in the hill-country of Rheinhessen have the potential to give Rieslings comparable to those of Nackenheim, Nierstein, and Oppenheim. This makes the Kellers' achievements of recent years all the more remarkable. Not only have they produced a string of increasingly impressive dry and sweet Rieslings but they have also made some very good dry Weissburgunder and Silvaner and some magnificent Rieslaner and Huxelrebe dessert wines. Their winemaking has steadily improved and now this estate is the top quality wine producer in Rheinhessen outside the Rheinfront. This success is achieved through modest yields and professional vineyard management; selective harvesting and winemaking that aims for crystalline clarity with maximum fruit and character. The Kellers' love of Mosel-Saar-Ruwer wines can be clearly read in their Rieslings. Their aromatic, racy Auslese and higher quality Prädikat dessert wines are among the best in the Rheinhessen.

Peter von Weymarn: classic Niersteiner.

Dr Alex Michalsky: dry Rieslings.

Weingut St Antony

Wörrstadter Strasse 22,
55283 Nierstein
Owners: MAN AG
Vineyard area: 22.5 hectares
Grape varieties: 60.5% Riesling,
12.5% Silvaner, 5.5% Kerner,
4.5% Dornfelder, 3% Müller-Thurgau,
2% Weissburgunder,
2% Spätburgunder, 1.5% Scheurebe,
1.5% Portugieser, 7% other varieties
Top sites: Niersteiner Hipping,
Niersteiner Oelberg, Niersteiner
Orbel, Niersteiner Pettenthal

Since the late 1980s Dr Alex
Michalsky has dedicated himself to
making the best dry Rieslings in
Germany. Now only two or three
estates in the country make
comparable rich, aromatic and
complex dry Rieslings from the slopes
of Nierstein's Roter Hang. Their
concentrated pear-, peach- and
apricot-like fruit is interwoven with an
intense mineral character to create a
complex and perfectly harmonious
whole in spite of up to 13.5 degrees
of natural alcohol. The difference in
character between the wines from the
estate's four top sites is clear. Since
the '92 vintage Dr Michalsky has also
produced some marvellous Rieslings
with natural sweetness, including
some magnificent BA and TBA
dessert wines. Together with
Gunderloch this is now the top wine
estate in Rheinhessen. Dr Michalsky
would not have been able to make
such dramatic improvements in the
estate's wine quality were it not for
the support and advice of his wife,
leading oenological consultant Dr Ute
Michalsky. The free hand Dr Alex
Michalsky has been given by the
owners, the MAN truck company, has
also been crucial. With increasing
support from MAN and a
determination not to rest on his
laurels, we can expect great things
from Dr & Dr Michalsky during the
coming years.

Weingut Schales

Alzeyer Strasse 160,
67592 Flörsheim-Dalsheim
Owners: Arno, Heinrich and
Kurt Schales
Vineyard area: 35 hectares
Grape varieties: 30% Riesling,
18% Müller-Thurgau,
15% Weissburgunder,
7% Siegerrebe, 6% Kerner,
6% Scheurebe, 18% other varieties

This large estate run by the Schales
brothers is one of the most consistent
producers of dry and sweet wines in
the Rheinhessen hill country. With
their stylish modern packaging,
uncluttered labels (vineyard
designations have been abandoned
since the '89 vintage) and excellent
promotional material they are also
sophisticated wine marketers. Like the
neighbouring Keller estate, the quality
achieved here with Riesling is
remarkable considering the
undistinguished vineyards in which
they grow. The dry Rieslings, like the
dry Weissburgunders and
Grauburgunders, are substantial and
full of character. The best wines are
the intensely piquant dessert wines
made from the Huxelrebe grape. The
best of these, always of TBA quality
with explosive grapefruit- and
pineapple-like aromas and flavours,
are marketed as '100-Year Wines'.
Such is their structure and the
excellence of the brothers'
winemaking that this is no hollow
claim.

Weingut Georg Albrecht Schneider

Oberdorfstrasse 11,
55283 Nierstein
Owner: Albrecht Schneider
Vineyard area: 16 hectares
Grape varieties: 45% Riesling,
25% Müller-Thurgau, 8% Kerner,
4% Scheurebe, 2% Silvaner,
16% other varieties
Top sites: Niersteiner Hipping,
Niersteiner Oelberg, Niersteiner
Orbel, Niersteiner Pettenthal

Albrecht Schneider once told a
journalist that he was a useless
salesman. The modest prices of this
estate's excellent wines suggest there
is some truth in his claim. However,
what is less well known and the
modest Schneider would never tell a
journalist, is that he is one of the best
winemakers in Rheinhessen. His wines
may not be the most subtle in
Nierstein, but they are certainly
among the most appealingly fruity:
even when bone dry they are
succulent and juicy. The best usually
come from the Schneiders' extensive
parcels in the Niersteiner Hipping.
These rich, elegant Rieslings are a
credit to the professionalism with
which Ulrike Schneider tends the
vineyards and to the excellence of the
winemaking. The full-bodied dry
Silvaners and Grauburgunders are
among the best from these grapes in
the region.

Weingut Ökonomierat J Geil Erben

Kuhpfortenstrasse 11,
67595 Bechtheim
Owner: Karl Geil-Bierschenk
Vineyard area: 25 hectares
Grape varieties: 25% Riesling,
15% Müller-Thurgau,
15% Kerner, 7% Ortega,
5% Silvaner, 5% Huxelrebe,
5% Bacchus,
5% Scheurebe, 5% Faberrebe,
3% Traminer, 3% Weissburgunder,
7% other varieties

This estate, with its range of grape
varieties including many
Neuzuchtungen planted in
unexceptional locations, may be
typical of the Rheinhessen but the
consistently high quality achieved by
Monika and Karl Geil-Bierschenk
across their wide range of wines is
exceptional. This is not the result of
driving ambition for fame as
winemakers or great commercial
success, rather of a straightforward
belief that good wine can be made
only through conscientious attention
to detail in vineyard and cellar.
Whether dry or sweet, light or rich,
Geil wines are all clean, fruity and well
balanced. Together with the Freiherr
Heyl zu Herrnsheim estate the Geils
make the best dry Silvaner in
Rheinhessen, producing exceptionally
aromatic wines from this normally
neutral grape. While Karl Geil-
Bierschenk's favourite wines are the
Rieslings, which are invariably of good
quality, these are overshadowed by
the concentrated Huxelrebe dessert
wines. Packed with fruit, spice and
honey, they prove that excellent wines
can be made from this grape in
Rheinhessen.

OTHER WELL KNOWN PRODUCERS

Weingut Balbach Erben

Mainzer Strasse 64,
55283 Nierstein
Although this well known estate
makes some good wines from the
Pettenthal vineyard, the general
standard is not as high as it once was.

Weingut Jean Buscher

Wormser Strasse 4,
67595 Bechtheim
Michael Buscher's dry and sweet
wines, some of which have interesting
artist labels, are consistently good.

Weingut Louis Guntrum

Rheinallee 62,
55283 Nierstein
During the 1980s this important
estate with over 60 hectares of
vineyard around Nierstein and
Oppenheim produced some fine dry
Rieslings and Gewürztraminers,
particularly the 'Guntrum Classic'
wines from its holdings in the first-
class Oppenheimer Sackträger and
Niersteiner Dalberg sites. 'Hajo'
Guntrum makes many good wines but
quality has been less consistent since
the early 1990s.

Weingut Carl Koch Erben

Wormser Strasse 62,
55276 Oppenheim
Young Carl Stieh-Koch is making good
Rieslings, Weissburgunders and
Gewürztraminers at Oppenheim's
finest estate but the excellent vineyard
holdings should have the potential to
make even better wines.

Weingut Kühling-Gillot

Ölmühlstrasse 25,
55294 Bodenheim
Roland Gillot has a good reputation
for his dessert wines, which are
excellent. His dry Rieslings are good,
though more intensity and elegance
would improve them.

Niersteiner Winzergenossenschaft

Karolingerstrasse 6,
55283 Nierstein
This is one of Germany's best
co-operative wineries, making some
good Rieslings and excellent
Huxelrebe dessert wines.

Sektkellerei Menger-Krug

An der Königsmühle 7,
55239 Gau-Ordenheim
From base wines produced at their
Pfalz and Rheinhessen estates, Regina
and Klaus Menger-Krug make some of
Germany's best champagne-method
sparkling wines. Their still wines are
less impressive.

Weingut Rappenhof
Bachstrasse 47,
67577 Alsheim
The wine quality has not kept pace with this growing estate. The Riesling and Gewürztraminers are solid but the new-oak-aged wines less good.

Weingut Dr Alex Senfter
Wörrstädter Strasse 10,
55283 Nierstein
Talented Jost Senfter makes some very promising dry and sweet Riesling.

Weingut Villa Sachsen
C/o Weingut Prinz zu Salm-Dalberg,
55595 Wallhausen
After having been purchased by Michael Prinz zu Salm-Salm in 1994 a new era is beginning for this once highly regarded Riesling producer.

Weingut Wittmann
Mainzer Strasse 19,
67593 Westhofen
Clean almost to the point of neutrality, Günter Wittmann's dry Rieslings are good but unexciting. The sweet wines can be more impressive.

Travel Information

PLACES OF INTEREST

Alzey The castle of Alzey was destroyed by Louis XIV's troops in 1689 but restored during the early 20th century. Today it houses the local courts. A range of wines from the town's vineyards can be tasted in its 12th-century cellars. Alzey is also home to the Sichel wine-export house, whose modern winery is situated just outside the town. There are well preserved 16th- to 18th-century half-timbered houses around the Fischmarkt and Rossmarkt.

Bingen Bingen is not the prettiest town on the Rhine but it has several important monuments. The 11th-century Nahebrücke is the oldest bridge in Germany and survives almost in its original state. No less well preserved is the Mäuseturm toll tower (constructed 1208 and originally called the Mautturm) in the middle of the Rhine. The

Rochuskapelle above the great Scharlachberg vineyard appears in Goethe's memoirs.

Bodenheim This is one of the most attractive villages in Rheinhessen, with numerous fine vintners' houses built between the 15th and late-19th centuries.

Ingelheim The remains of Charlemagne's palace can be visited in Nieder-Ingelheim. The 15th Burgkirche or fortified church and the remains of the town fortifications can be found in Ober-Ingelheim.

Mainz Founded by the Romans in 38BC as a base from which to conquer Germany, Mainz is one of the oldest towns in the country. From the late 8th century it became an important centre of power from which the Archbishops (later the Prince-Bishops) of Mainz ruled a wide expanse of country including the whole of Rheingau and Rheinhessen. It was here that Johannes Gutenberg

developed printing with moveable type in 1445 and the first German republic was founded in 1792/3.

Just as it was 1,000 years ago, the town is still dominated by the Dom or cathedral, the exterior of which has hardly changed since the 13th century. Among other fine churches in Mainz are the Gothic Johanneskirche and the Stiftskirche on the Stephansberg (with modern stained glass windows by Marc Chagall). Completely rebuilt after its destruction in February 1945, the church of St Peter is one of Mainz's many fine rococo buildings. The Osteiner Hof and Bassenheimer Hof are also impressive rococo palaces. The Kurfürstlichen Marstall or Prince-Bishop's stables now house the Landesmuseum which has a magnificent collection of architectural fragments from the Roman and early-medieval periods. The Kurfürstliche Schloss, or Prince-Bishop's palace houses the Römisch-Germanische

The village of Bechtheim, whose wines are often found under its Grosslage name, Pilgerpfad.

Zentralmuseum which exhibits artifacts from the Roman and Medieval periods. The Gutenberg museum on the Liebfrauenplatz holds the first Gutenberg Bible, printed between 1452 and 1455. A stroll through the old town will reveal many other surprises. The Kupferbergmuseum houses the Art Nouveau German wine pavilion from the Paris World Fair of 1900. Visits are by appointment only: Sektkellerei Kupferberg, Kupferberg-terrasse, telephone (06131) 555.

Nierstein The view of Nierstein from its vineyards is marred by ugly maltings which stand on its northern side. But the old town is a different matter: many of its narrow streets look as though they have not changed for centuries. The Langgasse and imposing houses of the Heyl zu Herrnsheim and Heinrich Braun estates are magnificent.

Oppenheim Given the destruction wrought by Louis XIV and his troops in 1689 it is astonishing how many fine old buildings remain in Oppenheim. The 13th-century Gothic

Katharinenkirche, the fine 17th- and 18th-century houses and the Rathaus in the centre of town are among many attractive examples.

Worms While Worms' origins go back to a Stone Age settlement, the imposing Romanesque cathedral takes its visible history back to the 12th century. Of equal interest for wine visitors is the Liebfrauenkirche surrounded by the Liebfrauenstift-Kirchenstück vineyard, the original source of Liebfraumilch until demand exceeded production at the turn of the century. The late-Gothic church and the famous Madonna and Child statue date from the 14th and early-15th centuries. Both were built by the monks of the Capuchin monastery of Our Lady (Liebfrauenstift). The monastery buildings and the greater part of the vineyards have belonged to the Valckenberg company of Worms since 1808 (see Weingut Freiherr Heyl zu Herrnsheim, page 130). The oldest synagogue in Germany (built in 1034), the Jewish cemetery Heiliger Sand with graves from as far back as the 11th century

and the lovingly restored Jewish quarter document the important part played for many centuries by the Jewish community in Worms.

HOTELS AND RESTAURANTS

Wesp (in Hotel Krause)
Gartenstrasse 2,
55232 **Alzey**
Tel: (06731) 6181,
Fax: (06731) 45613
Rustic but with a rare lightness of touch, Michael Wesp's cooking overshadows almost everything else in Rheinhessen's hill-country.

Weingut Nack
Pfarrstrasse 13,
55296 **Gau-Bischofsheim**
Tel: (06135) 3043
No longer filled with wine barrels, the cellars of Weingut Nack now house a rather grand restaurant which has prices to match. While the cooking is not uniformly remarkable, within Rheinhessen this is still one of the better places to eat.

Alter Vater Rhein
Grosse Fischergasse 4,
55283 **Nierstein**
Tel: (06133) 5628,
Fax: (06133) 5440
It may be kitsch but this restaurant tucked in the back streets of Nierstein offers good country cooking at modest prices.

Hotel Villa Spiegelberg
Hinter Saal 21,
55283 **Nierstein**
Tel: (06133) 5145,
Fax: (06133) 57432
Nierstein's best hotel is situated at its eastern edge and has marvellous views of the town's great vineyards. It is secluded and stylish but fairly priced.

Rotisserie Dubs
Kirchstrasse 6,
67550 **Worms-Rheindürkheim**
Tel: (06242) 2023,
Fax: (06242) 2024
Serge Dubs runs one of the best restaurants in Rheinhessen in this suburb of Worms. While the interior is not to everyone's taste the cooking is creative, always good and sometimes sensational. Among the regional wines offered is a series made under Derge Dubs' supervision. France and Italy are also well represented.

USEFUL ADDRESSES

Städtische Verkehrsamt Alzey
Fischmarkt 3,
55232 **Alzey**
Tel: (06731) 6503,
Fax: (06731) 495555

Städtische Verkehrsamt Bingen
Rheinkai 21,
55411 **Bingen**
Tel: (06721) 184205

Rheinhessenwein eV
An der Brunnenstube 33–35,
55120 **Mainz**
Tel: (06131) 681058,
Fax: (06131) 682701

Rheinhessen-Information
Schillerstrasse 44,
55116 **Mainz**
Tel: (06131) 263 419

Verkehrsverein Worms
Neumarkt 14,
67547 **Worms**
Tel: (06241) 853560

The majestic town gates of Worms, whose Liebfrauenstift-Kirchenstück vineyard is the birthplace of the widely-exported Liebfraumilch.

Pfalz

Warmer and sunnier than almost anywhere in Germany, the Pfalz could have been designed specifically for growing vines. Undulating vineyards run more than 80 kilometres from Worms to the French border at Wissembourg along the eastern flank of the forested Haardt mountains. Vines cover gentle slopes around a succession of half-timbered and stone-built villages as far as the Rhine Rift Valley.

The Pfalz, or Palatinate, may lack the Mosel's precipitous vineyards and the Rheingau's liberal scattering of castles, but its verdant charm and friendly people have won it many friends.

The region's strength lies not in the glamour of world-beating prices or Michelin-starred restaurants but in its unpretentiousness. Good cooking and good wine with plenty of regional character are the region's lifeblood and can be found in the Pfalz in abundance.

Here, as in Alsace immediately to the south, the mountains are a decisive climatic factor. Shielding the region against inclement weather and providing a rain shadow, they are chiefly responsible for the favourable climate. Here figs ripen easily outdoors and citrus trees and oleander bushes are common in local gardens.

The region has much in common with Alsace in its climate, its architecture and in the grape varieties it favours, but Pfalz wines are distinctly Germanic even when full-bodied and dry like those of Alsace. The emphasis is on ripe fruit flavours and a refreshing acidity prevents even the region's most powerful wines from being heavy, alcoholic or cloying. The difference between the wines of the two areas is not only the result of winemaking traditions that have developed separately for centuries, but also it seems to reflect the differing character and outlook of the people themselves.

A significant proportion of the Pfalz's 22,000 hectares of vines is devoted to quality wine production, using a wider range of grapes than any other region. This is possible not only because of the climate but also because of the extraordinary range of soils. Light soils of sand, loam and loess dominate, but there are also areas with sandstone, limestone, marl, clay, granite, red and grey slate and gravel.

As in the other Rhine regions, Riesling is the most important grape for quality wine production, accounting for 20 percent of the vineyard area and most of the best wines. However, its close

Sheltered by the Haardt mountains, Pfalz vineyards bask in spring sunshine.

relatives Scheurebe and Rieslaner offer stiff competition in similar wine styles. Together with Baden, the Pfalz produces the best German wines from the Pinot family: Weissburgunder, Grauburgunder, Spätburgunder and, more recently, Chardonnay. The traditional aromatic grapes Gewürztraminer and Muskateller also retain a significant foothold as specialities. More recent arrivals are the red Dornfelder and St Laurent grapes, the former already enjoying commercial success.

Even some of the grapes planted primarily for the mass-produced wines can be induced to give something more serious here. Müller-Thurgau, with 23 percent of the vineyard area, is the most widely planted vine. Most of it, along with the Kerner and Silvaner, ends up either in Liebfraumilch blends or as a varietal wine in litre bottles on German supermarket shelves, although all are capable of giving more characterful wines. The same is true of the red Portugieser grape, which accounts for nine percent of the region's vines. Most Portugiesers are pale and thin, but when vinified with care can give deeply coloured serious reds.

This seems to be a favourable climate not only for vines but also for ambitious young vintners. During the last decade more new winemaking talent has emerged here than in almost any other region and so many excellent wines are produced that the Pfalz has emerged as arguably the quality leader among the Rhine regions. Many of these vintners come from towns and villages which

traditionally sold their wines in barrel at very modest prices. Now they are being sold in bottle for more realistic prices and concerted efforts are being made to build national and international reputations for such wines.

The region was at one time sub-divided into three parts, one of which, the Mittelhaardt around Bad Dürkheim, was the centre for Riesling and quality wine production. To the north lay the Unterhaardt and to the south the Oberhaardt where the mass production of everyday drinking wines was the norm. These divisions are now less clear-cut – there are as many good estates outside the boundary of Mittelhaardt as there are within it. However, in a historical context it is easy to see how they developed.

The first Pfalz vineyards were planted by the Romans. The Roman wine press in the vineyards of Ungstein is smaller than many found in the Mosel Valley but very well preserved. In the labyrinthine cellars of the the Dr von Bassermann-Jordan estate in Deidesheim there is a remarkable private collection of Roman amphora and sculptures. Roman glassware, including the oldest known bottle of wine, found in the vineyards of Deidesheim, are displayed in the estate house. A century ago vineyard workers ploughed up a bottle of Roman wine intact, close to the village of Grosskarlbach in the north of the region. Apparently they drank

Basalt stones and deep sub-soils add complexity to the wines of Forst.

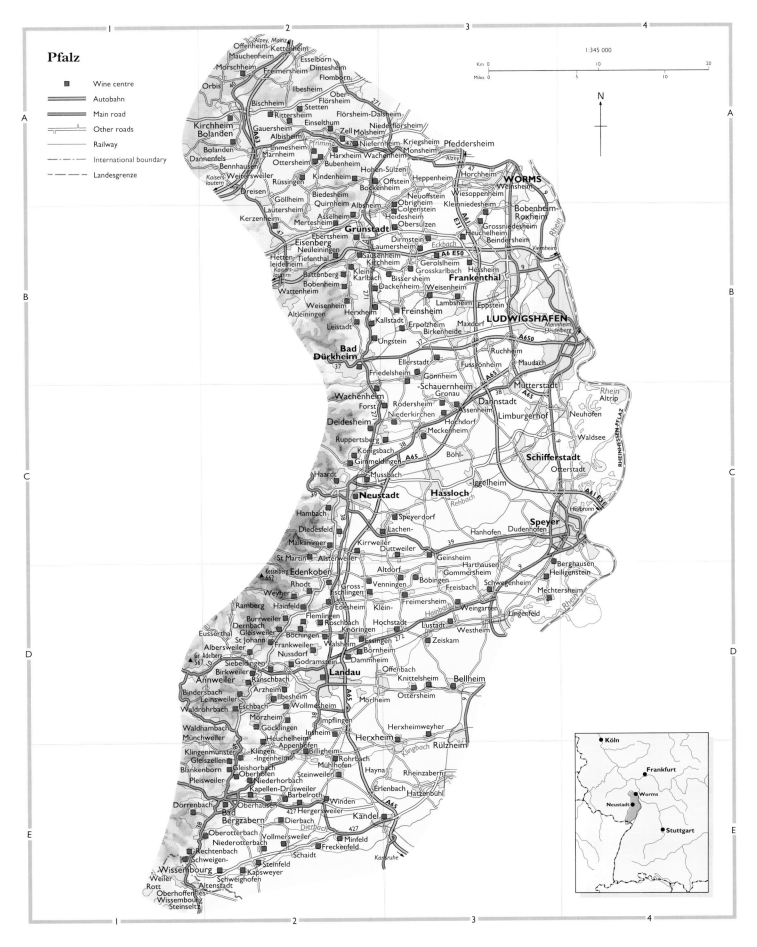

Pfalz

- ■ Wine centre
- Autobahn
- Main road
- Other roads
- Railway
- International boundary
- Landesgrenze

1:345 000

Km 0   10   20
Miles 0   5   10

N

Alzey, Mainz
Offenheim · Kettenheim
Mauchenheim
Morschheim · Esselborn
Freimersheim · Dintesheim
Orbis · Flomborn
Ilbesheim · Ober-
Flörsheim
Bischheim · Stetten
Rittersheim · Flörsheim-Dalsheim
Gauersheim · Einselthum · Niederflörsheim
Kirchheim · Albisheim · Zell Mölsheim
Bolanden · Immesheim · Nieffernheim Kriegsheim · Pfeddersheim
Bolanden · Marnheim · Harxheim Wachenheim · Monsheim
Dannenfels · Ottersheim · Bubenheim · Alzey
Bennhausen · Weitersweiler · Hohen-Sülzen · Horchheim
Kaisers-lautern · Rüssingen · Kindenheim · Heppenheim · WORMS
Dreisen · Weinsheim
Göllheim · Biedesheim · Offstein · Wiesoppenheim
Kerzenheim · Quirnheim · Bockenheim · Neuoffstein · Kleinniedesheim
Lautersheim · Albsheim · Obrigheim · Bobenheim-Roxheim
Mertesheim · Colgenstein · Grossniedesheim
Ebertsheim · Heidesheim · Heuchelheim
Grünstadt · Obersülzen · Beindersheim
Eisenberg · Dirmstein · Eckbach
Neuleiningen · Laumersheim
Hetten-Tiefenthal · Sausenheim · A6 E50
leidelheim · Kirchheim · Gerolsheim · Hessheim
Kaisers- · Battenberg · Klein- · Grosskarlbach · Frankenthal
lautern · Bobenheim · Karlbach · Bissersheim
Wattenheim · Dackenheim · Weisenheim
Weisenheim · Lambsheim · Eppstein
Altleiningen · Herxheim · Freinsheim · LUDWIGSHAFEN
Leistadt · Kallstadt · Erpolzheim · Maxdorf · Mannheim, Heidelberg
Ungstein · Birkenheide · A650
Bad · 37 · Ruchheim
Dürkheim · Ellerstadt · Fussgönheim · Maudach
Friedelsheim · Gönnheim
Wachenheim · -Schauernheim · Mutterstadt · Rhein Altrip
Forst · Gronau · A65
Rödersheim · Dannstadt · A65
Deidesheim · Niederkirchen · Hochdorf · Limburgerhof · Neuhofen
Ruppertsberg · Meckenheim · RHEINHESSEN-PFALZ
Königsbach · Böhl- · Waldsee
Haardt · Gimmeldingen · A65
Mussbach · -Iggelheim · Schifferstadt
Neustadt · Hassloch · Otterstadt
Hambach · Rehbach · Heilbronn
Diedesfeld · Speyerdorf
Maikammer · Lachen · Hanhofen · Speyer
St Martin · Kirrweiler · Dudenhofen
Alsterweiler · Duttweiler · Geinsheim · Harthausen · Berghausen
Altdorf · Gommersheim · Heiligenstein
Kesselberg · Edenkoben · Venningen · Böbingen · Schwegenheim
Rhodt · Gross- · Freisbach · Mechtersheim
Weyher · fischlingen · Weingarten
Ramberg · Hainfeld · Edesheim · Klein- · Freimersheim · Lingenfeld
Burrweiler · Flemlingen · Roschbach · Hochstadt · Lustadt
Dernbach · Böchingen · Knöringen · Westheim
Eusserthal · Gleisweiler · Frankweiler · Essingen · Zeiskam
Albersweiler · St Johann · Walsheim · Bornheim
Gr Adelberg · Nussdorf · Dammheim
Siebeldingen · Godramstein · Landau
Birkweiler · Ranschbach · Knittelsheim · Bellheim
Annweiler · Arzheim · Offenbach
Bindersbach · Ilbesheim · Mörlheim · Ottersheim
Leinsweiler · Eschbach · Wollmesheim
Waldrohrbach · Mörzheim · Impflingen · Herxheimweyher
Waldhambach · Göcklingen · Insheim · Herxheim
Münchweiler · Heuchelheim · Rülzheim
Klingenmünster · Appenhofen · Billigheim · Klingbach
Gleiszellen · Klingen · Rohrbach
Blankenborn · -Ingenheim · Mühlhofen · Hayna · Rheinzabern
Oberhofen · Gleishorbach · Steinweiler · Erlenbach
Pleisweiler · Niederhorbach · Hatzenbühl
Dörrenbach · Kapellen-Drüsweiler · Rhein
Bad · Oberhausen · Barbelroth · Winden
Bergzabern · Hergersweiler · A65
Oberotterbach · Dierbach · Kandel
Niederotterbach · Vollmersweiler · 427
Rechtenbach · Minfeld
Schweigen- · Steinfeld · Freckenfeld
Weiler · Wissembourg · Schaidt · Karlsruhe
Rott · Kapsweyer
Oberhoffen-lès- · Schweighofen
Wissembourg · Altenstadt
Steinseltz

Köln
Frankfurt
Worms
Neustadt
Stuttgart

the wine, but history does not record whether they went back to look for the rest of the case.

Quality wine production began in the area almost exactly 200 years ago at the turn of the 19th century. Andreas Jordan (1775–1848), the founder of what is now the Dr von Bassermann-Jordan estate in Deidesheim, took over the estate upon the death of his father in 1797 and immediately began to follow the example set by the great aristocratic and clerical estates of the Rheingau during the last decades of the 18th century. He replanted extensive areas of the family's best vineyards with Riesling and produced the region's first varietal Riesling wine (which was also the first wine in the region to be sold under a vineyard name) in 1802. Up to this point *Gemischte Satz,* or mixed plantings, of Silvaner and Riesling, sometimes with other varieties included, had been the norm. In 1811 Andreas Jordan harvested the region's first Auslese from his Deidesheim vineyards. From this point on the Pfalz was to be the Rheingau's prime challenger for quality leadership among the Rhine regions.

Upon Andreas Jordan's death the estate was divided among his three children. His daughters married FP Buhl and F Deinhard, their shares becoming the foundations of the neighbouring Reichsrat von Buhl and Dr Deinhard estates. Ludwig Andreas Jordan (1811–1883) followed his father's footsteps, causing a sensation with his 1852 Auslese wines which achieved record prices. Jordan's neighbours took up the gauntlet and a struggle ensued between the large estates of Deidesheim and Wachenheim, competing to produce the best possible Riesling from Mittelhaardt vineyards. The rivalry lasted more than a century and resulted in some of the greatest German wines ever made. The 'Three Bs' of the Pfalz, the Dr von Bassermann-Jordan, Reichsrat von Buhl and Dr Bürklin-Wolf estates, became the most famous and highly regarded white wine producers in the world.

Such an achievement would not have been possible but for the exceptional quality of their best vineyards. Many experts believe there is a direct relationship between the quality of a Pfalz vineyard and the height of the mountains immediately to its west. Directly to the west of the famous wine villages of Wachenheim, Forst, Deidesheim and Ruppertsberg lies the Drachenfels, at 571 metres one of the highest peaks of the Mittelhaardt. Together with the surrounding hills it forms a massive barrier preventing cold air from flowing down into the vineyards from the Pfalz Forest, and at the same time pushes storms approaching from the west either to the north over Bad Dürkheim or to the south past Neustadt. To the east on the opposite side of the Rhine Valley lie the Odenwald mountains, which provide good protection from cold easterly weather. The gentle vine-clad slopes around these villages all enjoy favourable southerly or easterly exposures and their light top-soils warm quickly.

These factors combine to make these vineyards some of the most climatically favoured along the length of the Rhine, a fact that was recognised long ago. When Bavaria's agricultural land was classified by the Royal Surveyors' Office in 1830, the Kirchenstück vineyard of Forst was rated in the highest of the 65 classes. A series of official valuations during the following decades confirmed this judgement; in 1924, for example, the vineyard was valued at 20,000 gold marks per hectare, making it some of the most expensive vineyard land in Germany beside the Mosel's Bernkasteler Doctor and the Rheingau's Rauenthaler Baiken.

With its cobbled main street and large stone-built houses, the village of Forst is one of the Pfalz's most attractive wine villages. It also has a rare serenity: even at mid-day during the week there is nothing approaching bustle on the streets. Only the

The first-class Dürkheimer Spielberg site, with Kallstädter Annaberg in the top left-hand corner. The first great dessert wines from the Scheurebe grape were harvested here in 1945.

Gutsschänke (wine restaurants) of Achim-Magin and Heinrich Spindler show any liveliness. None of the wine estates here is particularly famous, but the village name has a considerable cachet and the local vintners need no marketing gimmickry to help sell their wines. Perhaps it is this, as much as the village's appearance, that is reminiscent of Burgundy's Côte d'Or.

The vineyards covering the gentle slope running from Forst's main street up to the edge of the forest to the west are perhaps the region's best. Although the soil type here, mostly weathered sandstone, is common in the Mittelhaardt, two additional factors make this a unique spot. The first of these involves the basalt stones, carried into the vineyards from the quarries above Forst as part of a long-term 'vineyard enrichment' programme. Much of the dark stone, which has improved not only the heat-retention capability of

the soil but also its structure, making it more open, was transported by horse and cart. A similar operation was undertaken at Ürzig in the Mosel Valley. The other factor is the deep, heavy sub-soil of the best sites: Kirchenstück, Jesuitengarten, Freundstück, Ungeheur and Pechstein. Even in the hottest summers the vines here never suffer from drought stress, since there is always subterranean water available.

The Rieslings from Forst's top sites combine the substance and aromatic intensity of Pfalz wines with racinesss and intense mineral character of a kind more normally associated with cooler, more northerly regions. The character of Kirchenstück Rieslings, which have the most finely nuanced fruit and the most elegant harmony of all Forst wines, has often been compared to the tall, graceful spire of the village's church. Full appreciation demands patience, however, since they also need the longest ageing in order to show their best. Jesuitengarten wines can match them, having a similar character but often more charm. In contrast, the Pechstein wines can be more severe, with an acidity that can be steely in lesser

vintages but gives the wines from hot years a marvellous vibrancy. Rieslings from the Freundstück vineyard are different again: both filigree and juicy, they have a personality completely different from that of the powerful wines from the Ungeheuer site. Ungeheur means 'giant' and, as Bismark once remarked, *Dieses Ungeheuer schmeckt mir ungeheuer*, (this giant tastes enormously good).

With their combination of peach- and citrus-like fruit and subtle earthiness, the Ungeheur Rieslings are the best suited of Forst's wines to vinification in the dry style. Georg Mosbacher, Eugen Müller and Wegeler-Deinhard make excellent examples. The other outstanding dry wines produced here are the Kirchenstück Rieslings from the Eugen Müller estate, which owns the only remaining old vines in this site, and the Jesuitengarten Rieslings from Dr Deinhard. The Forst vineyards were reorganised between the mid-1970s and mid-1980s, a process which involved the replanting of almost all the vines. It will therefore be several more years before they give their best, as vines less than 15 years old are normally still growing too vigorously to produce top-quality fruit.

The real glories of Forst are the Spätlese and Auslese wines that have a modest amount of natural sweetness. It is they who are responsible for the village's exceptional reputation. Some Pfalz Rieslings in this style can be rather plump and even a little clumsy, the sweetness somehow failing to integrate fully within the wine. A Riesling Auslese from Forst should marry power and elegance and possess layer upon layer of aroma and flavour, the aftertaste remaining in the mouth for some time after the wine is swallowed. The '76 or '71 Auslesen from Dr Bürklin-Wolf are perfect examples of this style.

Forst's problems stem from the current scarcity of wines that live up to this ideal. Vineyard reorganisation is partly to blame, but a certain degree of complacency and lack of commitment is also evident among local vintners. Georg Mosbacher is the only estate regularly making Forst wines at this sublime level, although in good vintages Eugen Müller, Wegeler-Deinhard and Werlé also make classic Forst Spätlese and Auslese wines. Some wines from Dr von Bassermann-Jordan, von Buhl and Dr Bürklin-Wolf are good but they do not match the great wines the estates made from Forst's vineyards in earlier decades.

The best vineyards of neighbouring Wachenheim, which cover the slopes on the southern side of the town to the west of the B271 road, can also give magnificent wines. The Dr Bürklin-Wolf estate is by far the biggest vineyard owner here and was almost solely responsible for establishing the sites' reputations. The wines from the Gerümpel, Goldbächel and Rechbächel (the last wholly owned by Bürklin) are less dramatic than those of Forst, but possess a wonderful subtlety of flavour. They remain fine and elegant even at the highest levels of richness.

The finest Wachenheimers are the Rieslings from the Gerümpel site, which yields equally remarkable dry and sweet Rieslings. The typical qualities of the village's wines are found in their highest form in these examples. Wines from the Goldbächel and Rechbächel also possess a filigree peach- and apricot-like fruit but they usually lack the multi-dimensional character of Gerümpel wines. The Altenburg, Böhlig and Belz vineyards can all give lighter wines that can be impressive in top vintages. Josef Biffar of Deidesheim, Dr Bürklin Wolf and Karl Schaefer of Bad Dürkheim make the best wines from these vineyards.

Deidesheim is perhaps the most attractive wine town of the Mittelhaardt. Among its many historic buildings the Renaissance Town Hall is perhaps the finest example, and there is much to be

Above: Preparing vines for the growing season.
Right: Springtime arrives early in the Mittelhaardt area of the Pfalz.

seen around the extensive residences of the town's leading wine estates, especially those of Dr von Bassermann-Jordan, Josef Biffar, Reichsrat von Buhl and Dr Deinhard/Wegeler-Deinhard. It is worth taking the time to explore the winding back streets, as almost every corner has something to offer. There are several excellent hotels dotted about the town and it boasts the region's best restaurant, the Schwarzer Hahn in Hotel Deidesheimer Hof. These attractions and more draw many visitors to Deidesheim.

Deidesheim's wines are renowned for their seductively rich fruit and the supple, even silky, texture that makes them extremely appealing as young wines. In good vintages it is frequently difficult to decide whether the Deidesheim, Forst or Wachenheim has produced the most successful wines, but in an average or lesser vintage Deidesheimers nearly always stand head and shoulders above the rest. The light, sandstone soils here are free draining and rapidly warmed by the sun. The vines are therefore able to make the best of a cool, wet summer while those in Forst's top sites are forced to stand in cold, waterlogged soil.

For some reason, perhaps the distinctiveness of its name and the fact that so many large estates own vines here, the Herrgottsacker is probably Deidesheim's best known vineyard site. In fact it is far from being the top-quality producer and rarely gives wines of outstanding quality or much individuality. These are typical, aromatic Pfalz Rieslings but no more.

Rieslings from the very small Kalkofen and Grainhübel sites, however, are a different matter, being rich, powerful wines with strong personalities. Situated on a south-facing terraced slope at the edge of town, the vines enjoy an extremely sheltered position and flourish in a chalky sub-soil. This combination of factors results in wines with exotic aromas of pineapple, guava and passion fruit which make them easy to enjoy. However, beneath the lush exterior is the firmest structure of any Deidesheim wine, making them among the most long-living. With a shade less power the Grainhübel Rieslings are less imposing but possess a ravishing apricot and passion fruit character and an extremely elegant harmony. The best wines from here are made by Josef Biffar and Dr Deinhard, who generally vinify them dry.

The Hohenmorgen vineyard, ownership of which is divided between Dr von Bassermann-Jordan and Dr Bürklin-Wolf, is traditionally regarded as being at least on a par with the sites mentioned above. However, in recent vintages few wines from here have been on the same level as those from the Grainhübel and Kalkofen. The reputations of the Langenmorgen, Leinhöhle and Kieselberg vineyards are hardly less exalted, yet the same problem applies. Rieslings with the fabulously succulent fruit and perfect balance which made these names famous are few and far between.

Again, this has much to do with the vineyard reorganisation of the 1980s, which resulted in almost all the vines being replanted. The vineyards' extremely light soils (Kieselberg means 'hill of gravel') results in frequent drought stress for the shallow-rooting young vines. With time this problem will ameliorate and good examples of the wines should become more common. The substantial vineyard holdings of Bassermann-Jordan and von Buhl in these sites should enable them to make magnificent wines.

A glance at the detailed map of the Mittelhaardt on page 143 shows that the top vineyards of Deidesheim, Forst and Wachenheim lie on virtually flat ground to the west of the B271 main road, but that there is an even larger acreage under vines to the road's eastern side. In hot years, these vineyards can give good wines simply because the soil here retains enough water to sustain the vines through the heat. However, this does not mean that the land will ever yield wines with anything like the sophistication or ageing potential of those from the top sites. Good, everyday drinking wine is the best that can be expected, hence Dr Bürklin-Wolf's laudable decision to market everything the estate produces from these less-favoured vineyards under a second label, Villa Eckel.

The only exception is Ruppertsberg, where much of the vineyard land east of the B271 is higher, with lighter soil and better exposure than sites down on the plain. The strengths of Ruppertsberg wines are their floral charm and delicate fruit: their playfulness. Rarely powerful and alcoholic or thin and acidic, year after year they are some of the region's most appealing wines. There could hardly be a better introduction to Mittelhaardt Rieslings than one of these Spätlesen. While a great Forst Riesling needs several years' ageing in the bottle for its full character to develop, even the very best Ruppertsberg wines can be enjoyed from the summer after the vintage. The Nussbien and Reiterpfad sites tend to give wines with more character, spice and citrus being the most common notes, but differences between the various sites here are not dramatic.

Bad Dürkheim was once as grand as Deidesheim is pretty, but it suffered terrible damage during the spring of 1945. Some of the imposing mansion houses that once dominated the town, fashionable residences for the wealthy during the 19th and early 20th centuries, can still be seen on its southern side but the town centre is marred by several ugly modern buildings in prominent

Bad Dürkheim, capital of the Mittelhaardt proper and home of some first-class estates, but also producer of cheap, pale red wines.

positions. Today the town is best-known for its spa, for the *Riesenfass* or giant wine barrel which now contains a restaurant, and its Wurstmarkt, which is a wine fair rather than the sausage market its name suggests.

Although it has some first-class vineyards and excellent estates, Bad Dürkheim does not enjoy the same renown as its southerly neighbours. This is in part due to its large-scale production of cheap wine for everyday drinking: litre-bottles of pale red or rosé wines from the Portugieser grape sold in German supermarkets under the Bad Dürkheimer Feuerberg Grosslage name do nothing for the town's reputation. There are also no large estates with long-established international reputations here. The very best Dürkheim wines can match those of the famous wine towns and villages immediately to the south, but this is a fact known only to a small number of German connoisseurs. Blessed with a marvellously fine apricot-like fruit combined with a subtle earthiness, they are slower to develop than most Mittelhaardt Rieslings.

Together with the best wines of neighbouring Ungstein, Dürkheimers come from vineyards that cover a limestone ridge running north to south between the town and the village of Ungstein. The terraced southern tip of this is the Michelsberg, the steep western flank (also partly terraced) is the Spielberg and the eastern flank the Ungsteiner Herrenberg. A century ago all were well regarded, but now only the Herrenberg enjoys a reputation for its excellent Riesling and Scheurebe wines from the Pfeffingen estate, situated at the foot of this magnificent vineyard. The best Michelsberg and Spielberg wines are made by Karl Schaefer, but

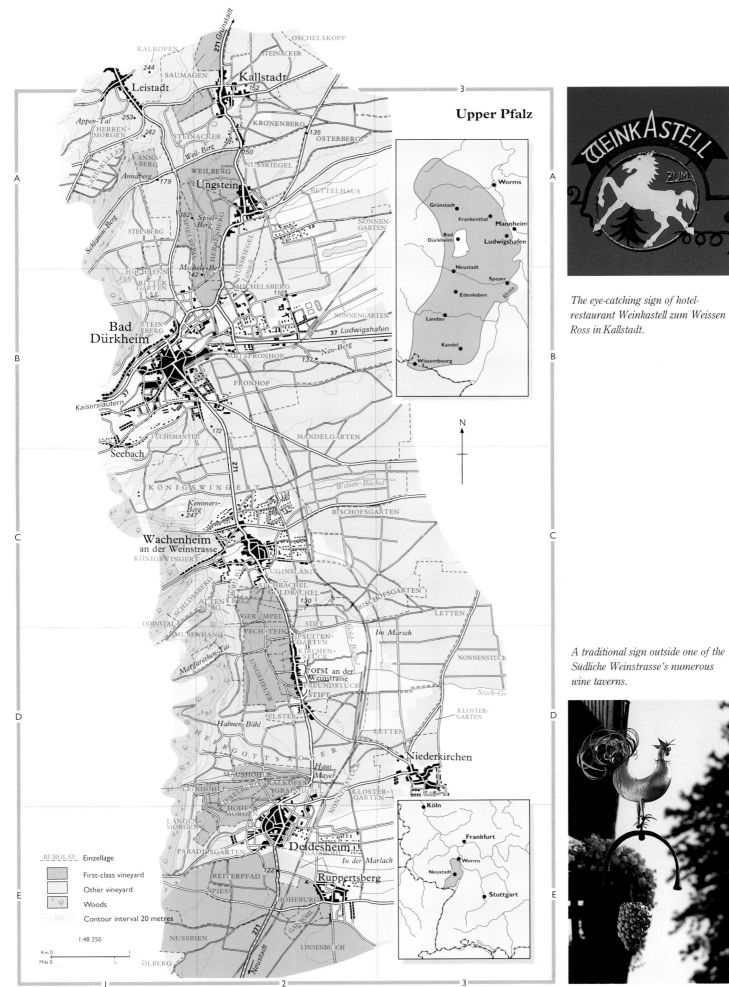

Upper Pfalz

Worms
Grünstadt
Frankenthal
Mannheim
Bad
Dürkheim
Ludwigshafen
Neustadt
Speyer
Edenkoben
Rhein
Landau
Kandel
Wissembourg

N

KALKOFEN
SAUMAGEN
STEINACKER
OSCHELSKOPF
244
Leistadt
Kallstadt
152
Appen-Tal
253
KRONENBERG
HERREN-
MORGEN
242
STEINACKER
OSTERBERG
135
150
Annaberg
Weil-Berg
WEILBERG
NUSSRIEGEL
179
Ungstein
182
BETTELHAUS
Spiel-
Berg
NONNEN-
GARTEN
STEINBERG
Michels-Berg
142
SCHLAMM-BERG
Schlamm-Berg
MICHELSBERG
110
Bad
Dürkheim
STEIN-
BERG
NONNENGARTEN
37 Ludwigshafen
ABTSFRONHOF
Neu-Berg
Kaiserslautern 37
FRONHOF
137
172
FUCHSMANTEL
MANDELGARTEN
Seebach
271
KÖNIGSWINGERT
Weisen-Bächel
Kemmers-
Berg
247
BISCHOFSGARTEN
Wachenheim
an der Weinstrasse
KÖNIGSWINGERT
LUGINSLAND
RECHBÄCHEL
GOLDBÄCHEL
BISCHOFSGARTEN
SCHLOSSBERG
BÖHLIG
130
LETTEN
ALTEN-
BURG
GERÜMPEL
STIFT
Im Marsch
ODINSTAL
MUSENHANG
PECHSTEIN
JESUITEN-
GARTEN
KIRCHEN-
STÜCK
NONNENSTÜCK
Forst an der
Weinstrasse
UNGEHEUER
FREUNDSTÜCK
Stech-Gr
STIFT
ELSTER
Hahnen-Bühl
KLOSTER-
GARTEN
LETTEN
Niederkirchen
HEERGOTTSACKER
Haus
Mayer
MAUSHÖHLE
KALKOFEN
LEINHÖHLE
GRAINHÜBEL
KLOSTER-
GARTEN
KIESELBERG
HOHEN
MORGEN
LANGEN-
MORGEN
Deidesheim
PARADIESGARTEN
In der Marlach
REITERPFAD
122
Ruppertsberg
SPIESS
HOHEBURG
271
NUSSBIEN
Neustadt
LINSENBUSCH
ÖLBERG

Köln
Frankfurt
Worms
Neustadt
Stuttgart

BURGLAY Einzellage
First-class vineyard
Other vineyard
Woods
Contour interval 20 metres
1:48 250
Km 0
Mile 0

143

Above: Weingut Pfeffingen, one of the star producers of the Pfalz.
Right: Ungstein, where the best vineyards benefit from limestone soil.

this estate tends to put the spotlight on its wines from Forst and Wachenheim.

Limestone is also responsible for the top Rieslings of Kallstadt, where the great vineyard is the Saumagen or 'pig's stomach'. Saumagen, a distant cousin of the haggis, is a traditional Pfalz dish: a pig's stomach stuffed with a mixture of pork, potatoes, herbs and spices. One can only speculate that the vineyard, which was once a limestone quarry, was named after the dish because of its shape. Certainly the flavours are entirely different from, though complementary to, the regional speciality. The fat of the dish is perfectly cut by the acidity of the wine, whose power is enough to stand up to Saumagen's spicy flavours. Visitors should sample Saumagen with Kallstädter Saumagen Riesling: a perfect Pfalz combination.

Saumageners are big, muscular Rieslings packed with fruit, minerals from the soil and a firm acidity. They usually need several years of ageing in the bottle for all these elements to integrate fully, after which they slowly blossom during a lifetime that can last more than 20 years. They are ideally suited to vinification as dry wines, gaining an almost burgundian aromatic richness as they mature, with beeswax, almond and honey notes overlaying the rich peach and passion fruit character of their youth. Saumagen Riesling Auslese dessert wines are dense and powerful but never overbearing, and seem almost immortal. While many Pfalz Rieslings from light, sandy soils start to taste tired after three or four years of age, a 50-year-old Saumagen Auslese can still be vigorous and fruity.

The Saumagen's warm microclimate and the limestone soil also have considerable potential for the Pinot family of grapes, not least for Spätburgunder. Until recently this potential was unrealized since few of Kallstadt's vintners had experience of making red wine. However, Koehler-Ruprecht, who produce the best Saumagen Rieslings, has recently made enormous strides in this field. Winemaker Bernd Philippi's deep, powerful Spätburgunders from the '93 and '92 vintages have demonstrated that the Pfalz can produce red wines up to the highest standards and that the Saumagen is as great a vineyard for Pinot Noir as it is for Riesling.

Kallstadt's other famous vineyard is the Annaberg, whose name was made by the eponymous estate between 1945 and the late 1970s. Sadly this estate is now only a shadow of its former self. Annaberg was a dessert-wine specialist which, in addition to making some of the best sweet Rieslings in the region, discovered the noble possibilities of the Scheurebe grape. This variety is a cross of Riesling and Silvaner dating from 1916 and is named after its creator, Georg Scheu of Alzey in Rheinhessen. On the heavy soils and in the rather cool climate there it showed little potential. It was only when the Stump-Fitz family planted the vine on the warm slopes of the Kallstädter Annaberg that it revealed an entirely unexpected aspect of its personality.

Scheurebe is one of the best grape varieties for dessert wines made from botrytized grapes. The catty flavour and aggressive acidity of unripe Scheurebe are transformed into a cocktail of exotic fruit, grapefruit and spices when the grapes turn golden and are attacked by botrytis. As a BA or TBA dessert wine Scheurebe is the ultimate in honeyed decadence, the opulent dried-fruit and spice flavours never cloying, the balance of sweetness and acidity often dazzling. The 1945 Scheurebe TBA from the Annaberg was the wine that proved that this grape can give wines comparable with the best Riesling BA and TBA dessert wines. Since then a

Pretty shuttered windows at the Ökonomierat Rebholz estate in Siedbeldingen.

number of the region's best estates have planted Scheurebe in their top vineyards and created considerable excitement in the wine world, especially since this is a *Neuzuchtung* making headlines, and not a traditional variety.

One of the leading such 'Scheu' specialists is the Lingenfelder estate of Grosskarlbach. This estate is typical of the region's new generation of top producers, situated well away from its traditional quality wine centres and having no holdings in its famous vineyards. The Lingenfelders were among the pioneers of a new style of Scheurebe made during the 1970s and early 1980s. Together with the Pfeffingen and Müller-Catoir estates they proved that given ripe grapes without too much botrytis it was possible to produce rich, full-bodied dry wines from Scheurebe. More supple and substantial than comparable dry Rieslings, they make excellent partners to food. Unlike even the best dry Pfalz Rieslings, which need a year or two in bottle before they are harmonious enough to drink with food, these succulent wines have excellent balance

from the beginning. In this respect they certainly fit Rainer Lingenfelder's description of them as 'dry wines for the post-Chardonnay era'.

The area's best Rieslings come from the Goldberg site of Freinsheim and Weisenheim am Sand. The slope's graceful arc makes it look like a sand dune, an impression confirmed by the appearance of the 'soil' here, which appears exactly like beach sand. It gives exceptionally aromatic wines with grapefruit and exotic fruit notes that make them easy to mistake for Scheurebes. The best of them age well but they are most impressive in their intense youth.

To the north of Kallstadt, in the neighbouring village of Laumersheim in what used to be called the Unterhaardt, the Knipser estate also makes a remarkable range of wines, many of which are red. The strong red wine tradition in this area has enjoyed a renaissance during the last decade. This estate's speciality is red wine and, while Spätburgunder tends to attract most attention, the vineyards of Grosskarlbach and Laumersheim also yield some deep-coloured rich reds from the Portugieser, Dornfelder and St Laurent grapes that are just as serious as the Pinot Noirs.

The leader of this new generation of Pfalz vintners is Hans-Günther Schwarz, winemaker at Weingut Müller-Catoir in the Neustadt suburb of Haardt. Since joining the estate in the early 1960s, when Heinrich Catoir took control, he has developed a wine style entirely different from anything previously seen in the region. His example did much to prompt the quality revolution which brought the younger generation of vintners to prominence during the 1980s.

The hallmarks of the Müller-Catoir wines are an explosion of ripe fruit aromas with an absolute clarity and precision of flavour. They are uncompromising wines, even the least of which is full of character, the greatest of which can seem almost to overwhelm the nervous system. Matching the purity and intensity of these wines has become a goal for dozens of ambitious young winemakers throughout the region. The non-interventionist or 'hands-off' winemaking methods employed have set an example for vintners throughout Germany.

Müller-Catoir's vineyards are in the Gimmeldingen, Haardt and Mussbach sites which, like the vineyards of the region's most famous wine villages, stand immediately to the east of one of the highest peaks of the Haardt mountains, the 553-metre Weinbiet. In its rain shadow the vines enjoy ample warmth and sunshine, but can also lack adequate water during the growing season. While Hans-Günther Schwarz is best known for his winemaking philosophy, his viticultural ideas are no less revolutionary. He believes in improving the soil structure to maximise its water-retention capabilities so that the vines can reap the full benefit of the area's microclimatic advantages.

For Schwarz, wine quality can come only from the vineyard and wines can achieve the maximum intensity of fruit only when the vines enjoy optimum conditions. He spends far more time in the vineyard than he does in the cellar. His first principle is to allow the grapes' character its full expression in the wine by intervening as little as possible once they reach the cellar.

Before Hans-Günther Schwarz came on the scene no one had established these vineyards' real potential. Now that a number of other growers, such as Christmann in Gimmeldingen, are also working to make top-quality wines here it is possible to distinguish the special characteristics of each site. The lightest soils are in the Mussbacher Edelshaut vineyard, which gives Rieslings with the blackcurrant and grapefruit aromas normally associated with Scheurebe and an exciting marriage of richness and racy acidity. The Rieslings from the heavier soils of the Gimmeldingen Mandelgarten and Haardter Herzog are more powerful and have an enormous depth of peach- and apricot-like fruit.

This part of the Pfalz is well suited to a range of grapes and it could be argued that Riesling does not always give the best wines here. To give just one example, Müller-Catoir has received more acclaim for its wines from aromatic varieties (Scheurebe, Muskateller and Gewürztraminer) and from the Pinot family of grapes (Weissburgunder and Grauburgunder) than it has for its Rieslings. The Kaiserstuhl area of Baden might claim it grows the best Weissburgunder and Grauburgunder wines in Germany, but it faces tough competition from Neustadt and the Südpfalz.

Here both Weissburgunder and Grauburgunder give dry wines with a high alcoholic content. They achieve 13 degrees easily and, given a good vintage and vineyard, 15 degrees is possible. With anything less than the most cautious treatment in the vineyard and cellar, such wines can become heavy, hot and bitter, problems that are more common in the Kaiserstuhl than they are in the Pfalz.

The most impressive super-charged wines from these grapes are made by Müller-Catoir and Bergdolt and Geissler of Duttweiler, just south of Neustadt. The density and concentration of fruit flavours in these 'monsters' is almost too much for the palate to bear. They could easily be mistaken for Chardonnays matured in new oak barrels, since they frequently have a melted butter and caramel character, sometimes even a touch of vanilla. Bergdolt and Geissler have both now begun to experiment with fermenting and maturing these wines in new wood and have discovered that, inexplicably, it makes them more elegant rather than more opulent.

While these giants are not the easiest of wines to combine with food – they are so concentrated that they overwhelm most dishes – most Weissburgunder and Grauburgunder wines from the Südpfalz are ideally suited to the dining table. Medium- to full-bodied without being too alcoholic, they have plenty of fruit and an acidity that is at once fresh and supple. The best producers include Herbert Messmer, Münzberg (Kessler), Thomas Siegrist, Dr Wehrheim and Wilhelmshof. Fritz Becker of Schweigen, at the southern tip of the region, also makes excellent Pfalz wines from both these grapes, though many of his best vineyards are on the French side of the border. Being vinified in Germany, they are legally Pfalz wines rather than qualifying for the Alsace AC.

For Fritz Becker and many of his colleagues in the Südpfalz, red wine plays an important role. Vintners here seem less influenced

Top: Little-known Leinsweiler, almost hidden among the vineyards.
Above: The magnificent carved oak gateway to Weingut Müller-Catoir in the Neustadt suburb of Haardt.

by the ideas promulgated by German wine schools during the 1960s and 1970s which overturned Germany's red wine traditions in so many parts of the country. Here some of the best red wines are made without the fashionable use of new oak, but they are still deep in colour with real body and substance.

Further north, red wines tend either to be pale or to have had the full oak treatment, often to the point where the oak dominates the fruit. Here too Portugieser, most prominently at Fritz Becker, and St Laurent at Herbert Messmer, give serious wines with rich fruit that can challenge many of the region's Pinot Noirs.

The Pinot varieties are also being used to produce interesting

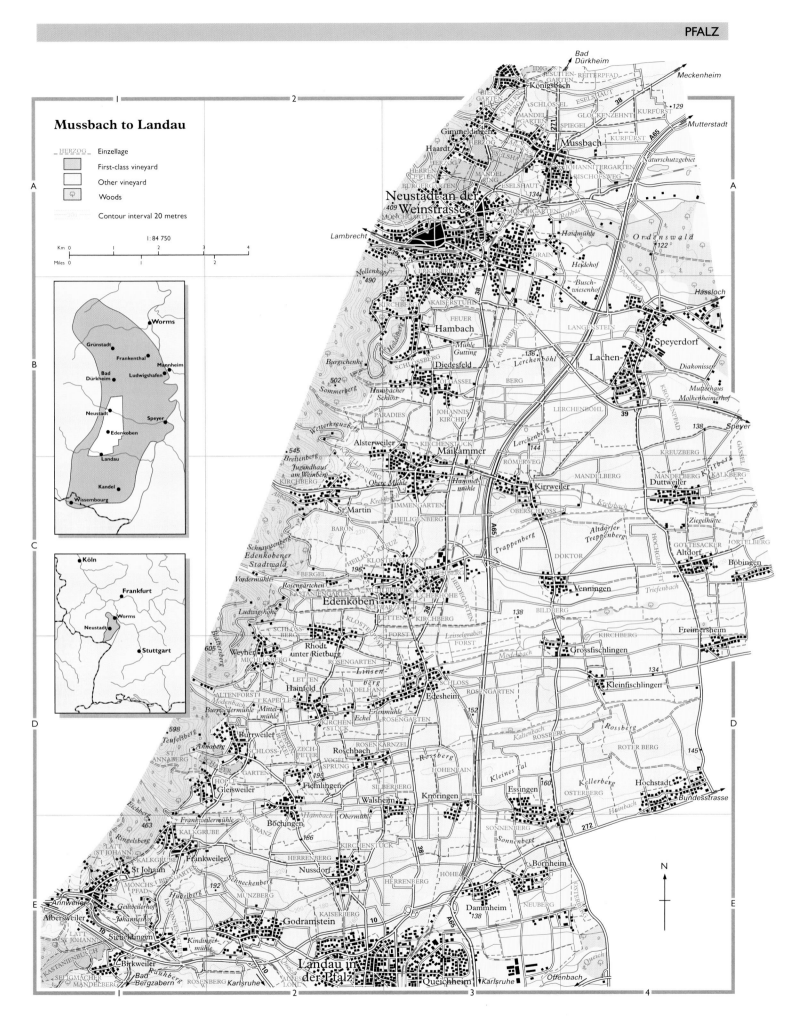

Mussbach to Landau

HERZOG	Einzellage
	First-class vineyard
	Other vineyard
	Woods
	Contour interval 20 metres

1:84 750

Km 0 1 2 3 4
Miles 0 1 2

champagne-method sparkling wines. The recently-formed VSR producers' association aims to promote these and has established minimum standards that are as strict as those for champagne itself. The best examples, such as the 'Blanc de Noirs' Brut from Wilhelmshof in Siebeldingen, made from the white juice of red Spätburgunder grapes, already puts many champagnes in the shade. The Koehler-Ruprecht estate in the Mittelhaardt is another producer beginning to release top-class sparklers from Pinot grapes. With more experience in producing and selecting base wines, even better results should be possible.

Although Gewürztraminer and Muskateller are the region's traditional varieties, in the north at least, Riesling has tended to push them out of the best vineyards they once dominated. However, a number of estates in the Südpfalz still take them seriously. The most important is Ökonomierat Rebholz in Siebeldingen, which has long been the area's quality leader. While Gewürztraminer can give rather exaggeratedly perfumed, broad and bitter wines, in Hans-Jörg Rebholz's hands it gives wines with a discreet bouquet of roses and spice and a perfect balance of fruit, alcohol and clean acidity. Similarly, Muskateller can yield loud wines that are aggressive, tart and rather green, but at this estate its wines are both grapey and racy and so lively that the fruit seems to dance on the palate.

Like Müller-Catoir, which is Hans-Jörg Rebholz's principle source of inspiration, this estate seems to do everything well. Its wines prove that the Südpfalz can shine with a wide range of grape varieties. As well as making fine aromatic wines, it produces some of the best Spätburgunder reds and rosés in the region and excellent dry Weissburgunders and Grauburgunders. Rebholz has also

Birkweiler, on the southern edge of the Pfälzerwald, whose Kastanienbusch site is one of only two first-class vineyards in the Südliche Weinstrasse.

shown that the dry Rieslings from the Pfalz's less fashionable half need not be overshadowed by their cousins from the north.

In the Südpfalz, the Haardt mountains do not form such a continuous barrier to inclement weather as they do in the Mittelhaardt. They have been carved into a row of jagged peaks between which cold air flows from the forest down into the vineyards and through which storms from the west can easily pass. As a result there are relatively few vineyards here that are ideally suited to Riesling. Siebeldingen is lucky in this respect, since the neighbouring Birkweiler Kastanienbusch vineyard, 300 metres above sea level and close to the forest, is one of few favoured locations. The Rieslings made by both Rebholz and Dr Wehrheim from this dramatic site possess a combination of rich fruit and raciness similar to that of the best Mittelhaardt examples. The red slate soil gives them distinctive almond and mineral tones.

The only other location in the Südpfalz capable of producing Rieslings with comparable character is the Burrweiler Schäwer. Schäwer means 'slate' in the Pfalz dialect and this is the only vineyard in the region to have a slate soil that resembles parts of the Mosel-Saar-Ruwer. The Herbert Messmer estate of Burrweiler, which was founded only in 1960, can with some justification claim to have discovered the site's potential for producing wines with the delicate fruit and subtle mineral character expected from top-class examples. As the young vines mature and winemaker Gregor Messmer gains experience, these wines will surely consolidate the estate's growing reputation.

One quarter of Pfalz wines are made by co-operatives; a modest proportion compared with regions such as Baden and Württemberg. Even the largest co-operatives in the Pfalz, however, Rietburg in Rhodt and Deutsches Weintor in Ilbesheim, produce a good many solid wines. The former was the first to demonstrate the huge international appeal of the region's dry Weissburgunders

Deidesheim, one of the most beautiful and historic wine towns in the Pfalz and an essential stop on any tour of the region.

and the latter has proved that Dornfelder is capable of producing good-quality red wines in large quantities. The Vier Jahreszeiten co-operative, along with those of Deidesheim, Forst, Herxheim am Berg and Hoheburg of Ruppertsberg, have all established good reputations as quality wine producers.

Although its southern half still suffers somewhat from its image as the producer of large quantities of cheap, sweet wines – it was long nicknamed the Süssliche Weinstrasse (Sweet Wine Street) – during the last decade the region has managed to establish an international reputation for producing quality rather than quantity. Unlike the Rheingau, the Pfalz suffers from the disadvantage that many of its vineyards can give only simple wines. However, it has been much more effective than its neighbour Rheinhessen in separating wines of differing quality levels for the consumer. Prices remain moderate even for the region's best wines and value for money is the norm rather than the exception. This healthy situation, combined with the new winemaking talent which is still emerging, makes the Pfalz's future look extremely bright. The region has everything it takes to become a world leader.

BENCHMARK WINES

Forster Ungeheuer Riesling Auslese
Weingut Georg Mosbacher, Forst
Vineyard site: Forster Ungeheuer
Site area: 38 hectares, 1.5 hectares Georg Mosbacher
Exposure: east
Inclination: gently sloping
Soil: deep weathered sandstone
Description: These are among the biggest and most powerful Rieslings in Germany. Packed with layers of mango, grapefruit, honey and earth flavours that seem to pour over the palate in waves, they have the unique combination of richness and 'breed' that made Forst the region's most famous wine village.
Best vintages: '94, '93, '90, '86, '83
Best drunk: Auslese wines with this kind of power and richness should easily stand up to a wide range of fruit desserts but they probably give their best when drunk with liver pâté or roast game.

Deidesheimer Kieselberg Riesling Spätlese Halbtrocken
Weingut Josef Biffar, Deidesheim
Vineyard site: Deidesheimer Kieselberg
Site area: 20 hectares, 1.5 hectares Josef Biffar
Exposure: south
Inclination: sloping
Soil: weathered sandstone and gravel
Description: It would be hard to find more typical Pfalz Rieslings than these. Richly aromatic, with full mango-, guava- and citrus-like fruit, they have the immediate sensual appeal typical of the region's wines. There is no lack of subtlety, however, the ripe fruit balanced by a racy acidity that gives the wines the elegance common to all top-class Rieslings.
Best vintages: '94, '93, '92, '91, '90

The entrance to Weingut Koehler-Ruprecht in Kallstadt, where Bernd Philippi makes a range of exciting new wines.

Weingut Müller-Catoir, now recognised as one of the country's best estates, produces intense, expressive wines.

Best drunk: These taste completely dry to anyone not used to drinking German whites. They are ideal for all manner of vegetarian dishes and for light seafood, especially prawns or scampi.

Kallstädter Saumagen Riesling Spätlese Trocken
Weingut Koehler-Ruprecht, Kallstadt

Vineyard site: Kallstädter Saumagen
Site area: 50 hectares, 2.5 hectares Koehler-Ruprecht
Exposure: south
Inclination: steep
Soil: stony, limestone rich loam
Description: Substantial, firm and discrete in their youth, the peach, passion fruit and mineral character of Bernd Philippi's wines blossom as they age. No German Rieslings have more in common with the great white wines of Burgundy.
Best vintages: '93, '92, '90, '89, '88, '86, '85, '83
Best drunk: They can be enjoyed when young but, unusually for dry Pfalz Rieslings, they show much better after five to ten years of bottle-age. Then they are perfect partners for all manner of richer fish dishes, poultry, pork – and Saumagen.

Mussbacher Edelshaut Rieslaner Auslese
Weingut Müller-Catoir, Neustadt-Haardt

Vineyard site: Mussbacher Edelshaut
Site area: 293 hectares, 3 hectares Müller-Catoir
Exposure: southeast
Inclination: gently sloping
Soil: sandy loam
Description: Hold on to your hat! All the Müller-Catoir wines are concentrated, but the estate's Rieslaner wines are almost overwhelming. More like an apricot essence mixed with all kinds of exotic spices, the aromas and flavours have a tremendous intensity. The dazzling acidity is like a lightning bolt shooting through the wine, illuminating its every contour.
Best vintages: '94, '92, '90, '89, '86, '85, '83
Best drunk: Some wines have so much character that even the

spiciest food cannot challenge them. This is one such wine. Not dry, but hardly sweet either, it can handle everything from curry to Crème Brûlée.

Freinsheimer Goldberg Scheurebe Spätlese
Weingut Lingenfelder, Grosskarlbach

Vineyard site: Freinsheimer Goldberg
Site area: 80 hectares, 2 hectares Lingenfelder
Exposure: south
Inclination: terraced slope
Soil: beach sand
Description: All Rainer Lingenfelder's wines are packed with ripe fruit, his Scheurebes being the most complete expression of this seductive style. Lush and creamy in texture, their pineapple and grapefruit flavours are decadently rich. In spite of this the sweetness is subliminal rather than obvious, the aftertaste clean and fruity.
Best vintages: '94, '93, '90, '88, '85, '83
Best drunk: While Lingenfelder's dry Scheurebe are excellent with food, this style of 'Scheu' needs more careful handling. However, it would be hard to find a better wine for salads with blue cheese dressing, or any deep-fried fish or poultry.

Kirrweiler Mandelberg Weissburgunder Spätlese Trocken
Weingut Bergdolt, Pfalz

Vineyard site: Kirrweiler Mandelberg
Site area: 50 hectares, 9 hectares Bergdolt
Exposure: south
Inclination: gently sloping
Soil: loess-loam
Description: In spite of 14 or more degrees of alcohol these enormously powerful dry wines are neither heavy nor alcoholic. Their succulent apricot- and pineapple-like fruit mingles with melted butter and caramel notes to create a lavish but never exaggerated whole.
Best vintages: '94, '92, '90, '89, '88
Best drunk: Such huge dry wines need dishes of comparable character to match their intensity. Most fish dishes have no chance. Lobster or meat dishes with truffles or morrels are possibly the best matches.

Siebeldinger Königsgarten Muskateller Spätlese Trocken
(from '95 marketed as:
Godramsteiner Münzberg Spätlese Trocken)
Weingut Rebholz, Siebeldingen

Vineyard site: Siebeldinger Königsgarten
Site area: c 400 hectares, 2 hectares Rebholz
Exposure: south
Inclination: sloping
Soil: deep sandy loam
Description: Very grapey and delicately perfumed, Hans-Jörg Rebholz's Muskateller wines have all the vivaciousness and crispness this rare grape can give. These charming, medium-bodied, bone-dry whites have spice and mineral notes that make the long aftertaste subtle and fascinating.
Best vintages: '94, '93, '92, '90, '89, '88
Best drunk: Wines with such an intense fruit character as this are difficult to match with food. The best matches are with spicy dishes, but care must be taken here too, since those with sweet or hot flavours will make the wine taste hard and bitter.

Leafy courtyards give welcome relief from the summer heat.

BEST PRODUCERS

Weingut Dr Ludwig von Bassermann-Jordan
Kirchgasse 10,
67142 Deidesheim
Owner: Dr Ludwig von Bassermann-Jordan
Vineyard area: 40 hectares
Grape varieties: 100% Riesling
Top sites: Deidesheimer Grainhübel, Deidesheimer Hohenmorgen, Deidesheimer Kalkofen, Deidesheimer Langenmorgen, Deidesheimer Leinhöhle, Forster Freundstück, Forster Jesuitengarten, Kirchenstück, Forster Pechstein, Forster Ungeheuer, Ruppertsberger Hoheburg, Ruppertsberger Nussbien, Ruppertsberger Reiterpfad, Ruppertsberger Spiess

For two centuries this estate has stood at the forefront of quality wine production in the Pfalz. Although the wines made during the early 1990s were not quite up to the high standards of the 1970s and 1980s, it remains one of the region's most important traditional estates. All the Rieslings ferment and mature exclusively in wooden casks of neutral German oak and experiments with other grapes or vinification styles are eschewed. Although dry wines are made, those with a touch of naturally-retained sweetness are generally more successful. In order to differentiate between the dry and sweet wines the former are marketed under the Art Nouveau 'Probus' label designed by Alois Balmer in 1905 and the sweet wines under the label bearing the von Bassermann-Jordan coat of arms designed by Otto Hupp in 1925. The best wines are usually those from the estate's parcels in the top vineyard sites of Forst: Jesuitengarten, Kirchenstück and Ungeheuer.

Weingut Friedrich Becker
Hauptstrasse 29,
76889 Schweigen
Owner: Friedrich Becker
Vineyard area: 12.5 hectares
Grape varieties: 20% Riesling, 20% Müller-Thurgau, 15% Spätburgunder, 10% Silvaner, 10% Weissburgunder, 5% Grauburgunder, 5% Chardonnay 5% Gewürztraminer, 5% Portugieser, 5% Schwarzriesling

Friedrich Becker and winemaker Stefan Dorst make one of the region's best traditional-style reds. In addition to their substantial Spätburgunder reds they also manage to conjure remarkable colour and richness from Portugieser and Schwarzriesling – grapes normally considered only good enough for light red everyday wines. The full-bodied dry Weissburgunder, Grauburgunder and Gewürztraminer are also excellent examples of these grapes' potential in the Südpfalz. In top vintages they give wines with power and substance to match the best from Alsace. This should not be surprising since many of them come from vineyards just over the French-German border south of Schweigen. Becker and Dorst still have to master the maturation of red and white wines in new oak. Their first experiments with this style were not particularly successful.

Weingut Bergdolt

Klostergut Sankt Lamprecht,
67435 Duttweiler
Owners: Rainer and Günther Bergdolt
Vineyard area: 17.75 hectares
Grape varieties: 35% Riesling,
30% Weissburgunder,
7% Silvaner, 7% Spätburgunder,
4% Dornfelder,
4% Müller-Thurgau,
13% other varieties

During the last decade, quietly determined Rainer Bergdolt has worked to make his one of the leading estates south of the Mittelhaardt area. He is perhaps the only vintner in the Pfalz to have built his reputation with dry Weissburgunders. His specialities are dry Spätlese and Auslese from this grape with 13–15 degrees of alcohol and hugely concentrated flavours. They are crammed full of peach, pineapple, butter, smoke and vanilla flavours that disguise the high alcohol content. In the Pfalz only Müller-Catoir can match this astonishing balancing-act of alcohol, fruit and acidity to make such remarkable 'monster' dry wines from Pinot Blanc. However, Rainer Bergdolt has also made considerable progress in recent years vinifying Weissburgunder in new oak, giving the wines more elegance, rather than more opulence. Bergdolt's Spätburgunder reds have improved in leaps and bounds and his '92 Riesling was also first class.

Weingut Josef Biffar

Niederkirchener Strasse 13,
67146 Deidesheim
Owner: Gerhard Biffar
Vineyard area: 11 hectares
Grape varieties: 93% Riesling,
7% Weissburgunder
Top sites: Deidesheimer Grainhübel,
Deidesheimer Kalkofen,
Deidesheimer Kieselberg,
Deidesheimer Leinhöhle,
Ruppertsberger Nussbien,
Ruppertsberger Reiterpfad,
Wachenheimer Gerümpel,
Wachenheimer Goldbächel

This estate has always made good wines but since Gerhard Biffar hired winemaker Ulrich Mell in 1990 it has shot to the first rank of the region's wine elite. The wines have gained considerably in fruit and freshness and now resemble Müller-Catoir Rieslings. Biffar's are distinctive, however, always showing the peach- and apricot-like fruit, spice and mineral character

Winemaker Ulrich Mell has helped take Weingut Josef Biffar to the top.

typical of Deidesheim's top sites, Ruppertsberg and Wachenheim. Virtually every vintage has brought dramatic improvements in quality. Alongside the Georg Mosbacher estate, Josef Biffar now produces the best wines in the Mittelhaardt.

The estate's best dry and sweet Rieslings are sold in tall flute bottles. Their elegant modern labels perfectly reflect the character of the wines behind them, clarity and elegance being the estate's hallmarks. Perhaps the best are the firm, intense dry Rieslings from the Wachenheimer Gerümpel site, which need a year or two in bottle. Since the 1992 vintage, excellent sweet Riesling Auslese and BA wines have been produced from Deidesheim's top sites. The medium-bodied dry Weissburgunders, the best of which are bottled 'sur lie' (straight off the lees) are also good quality. Unusually, the Biffars also own a candied fruits company, based next door to the winery. Both product lines are successfully exported.

Weingut Dr Bürklin-Wolf

Weinstrasse 65,
67157 Wachenheim
Owners: Bettina Bürklin-von Guradze
and Christian von Guradze
Vineyard area: 43.5 hectares under Dr Bürklin-Wolf, the remainder under the Villa Eckel second label
Grape varieties: 81% Riesling,
19% other varieties
Top sites: Deidesheimer Hohenmorgen,
Deidesheimer Langenmorgen,
Deidesheimer Kalkofen,
Forster Jesuitengarten,
Forster Kirchenstück,

Forster Pechstein, Forster Ungeheuer, Ruppertsberger Gaisböhl (wholly owned), Ruppertsberger Hoheburg, Ruppertsberger Reiterpfad, Wachenheimer Gerümpel, Wachenheimer Goldbächel, Wachenheimer Rechbächel (wholly owned)

Having gone through a difficult period in the early 1990s when Bettina Bürklin-von Guradze and Christian von Guradze took control, this great estate seemed to be back on course from the '93 vintage. Considerable changes have been made in recent years. Most importantly, only a fraction of the wines produced by the estate – those from vineyards west of the B207 road – are marketed under the Dr Bürklin-Wolf label. At least for these wines a great effort is made in the cellar, with noticeable results in the wine quality. The rest of the estate's production is sold under the Villa Eckel second label at more modest prices.

Since 1945 the estate has produced a string of magnificent Riesling Auslese, BA and TBA dessert wines which are among the best in Germany. It is still the foremost producer of these wines in the region. Extensive holdings in the best Deidesheim, Forst and Wachenheim sites make more refined and expressive dry Rieslings, sweet Riesling Kabinett and Spätlese wines possible. Dry Muskateller and Weissburgunder are important specialities and a high standard is maintained here. The magnificent estate buildings in the centre of Wachenheim and Bürklin-von Guradze's house on the southern

edge of the town could hardly provide a better setting.

Weingut Dr Deinhard / Weingüter Geheimrat J Wegeler Erben

Weinstrasse 10,
67146 Deidesheim
Owners: (Dr Deinhard) Hoch family;
(J Wegeler) Deinhard & Co
Vineyard area: (Dr Deinhard) 26 hectares; (J Wegeler) 15.5 hectares
Grape varieties: (Dr Deinhard)
81% Riesling, 4.5% Müller-Thurgau,
4.5 % Kerner, 3.5% Scheurebe,
3.5% Gewürztraminer,
1.5% Weissburgunder, 1.5% Silvaner;
(J Wegeler) 91% Riesling,
9% Müller-Thurgau
Top sites: (Dr Deinhard) Deidesheimer Grainhübel, Deidesheimer Kalkofen, Deidesheimer Kieselberg, Forster Jesuitengarten, Ruppertsberger Reiterpfad, Ruppertsberger Spiess;
(J Wegeler) Forster Ungeheuer

A single team cultivates the vineyards and makes the wines of these two estates in the extensive, well equipped cellars under the imposing Weinstrasse mansion. Heinz Bauer crafts the wines for both estates in a richly fruity, aromatic and elegant style. Whether dry or sweet, these are classic modern-style Pfalz Rieslings made using a combination of stainless steel and large wooden casks of neutral German oak. There may be more intense or sophisticated Pfalz wines, but none is more typical than these. The consistent quality is impressive given the substantial production. The most impressive wines from the Dr Deinhard estate tend to be Rieslings from Deidesheim's Grainhübel and Kalkofen sites and the Forster Jesuitengarten.

Weingut Knipser

Hauptstrasse 47,
67229 Laumersheim
Owners: Werner and Volker Knipser
Vineyard area: 13 hectares
Grape varieties: 27% Spätburgunder,
23% Riesling, 10% Scheurebe,
9% Portugieser, 7% St Laurent,
5% Weissburgunder,
5% Ehrenfelser, 5% Dornfelder,
9% other varieties

The Knipser brothers make some remarkable wines from the rather unremarkable Laumersheim vineyards in what used to be called the Unterhaardt. New oak is used for the maturation of their best red wines and they are arguably the most reliable producers of fine-quality reds in the Pfalz. While the intense, firmly structured Spätburgunders have attracted the most attention, the Knipsers also make impressive wines from the normally second-class red

Volker and Werner Knipser,
red wine stars of the northern Pfalz.

Dornfelder, Portugieser and St Laurent grapes. Cabernet Sauvignon has recently been added to their portfolio and the first results suggest that the grape has a promising future here. While the white wines are consistently good, they rarely match the quality of the estate's reds. Most of the former are dry and some of the best are fermented and/or matured in new oak. These are marketed as Deutscher Tafelwein.

Weingut Koehler-Ruprecht
Weinstrasse 84,
67169 Kallstadt
Owner: Bernd Philippi
Vineyard area: 8 hectares
Grape varieties: 57% Riesling,
14% Spätburgunder,
7% Weissburgunder,
4% Grauburgunder, 4% Chardonnay,
3% Cabernet Sauvignon,
2% Muskateller, 2% Gewürztraminer,
7% other varieties
Top site: Kallstädter Saumagen

Nobody in Germany makes better dry Rieslings than Bernd Philippi, yet they are only one of the many strings to this polymath's bow. What looked like a series of eccentric winemaking experiments a decade ago has blossomed in to a range of exciting new wines. It now seems almost anachronistic that the core of Bernd Philippi's production is dry Riesling, made in a style remarkably close to that of 50 years ago. It is fermented and stored in large wooden casks of neutral oak, where it matures until at least the September before the following harvest; far longer than is the norm today. This process, together with the top-quality fruit of the great Saumagen vineyard, results in wines with an aromatic complexity and classical elegance unmatched in the Pfalz. They are made for long ageing, showing their best from five to eight years of age depending upon the vintage.

Bernd Philippi's new-oak-aged Spätburgunder reds represent the opposite extreme. These are deep-coloured with a rich blackberry-like fruit and a strong smoke and vanilla character from the new oak in which they are matured. Since the '92 vintage they have been among the best Pinot Noir reds in the country. The estate's new-oak-aged dry whites made from Weissburgunder, Grauburgunder and Chardonnay are also beautifully crafted, with an elegant balance similar to that of good Pouilly Fuissé or St Véran. Even better is Elysium, the best Sauternes-style new-oak-aged dessert wine in Germany. These innovations, along

with the estate's Cabernet Sauvignon and exotic creations such as red Eiswein, are sold in Bordeaux-style bottles under the Philippi name in order to differentiate them from traditional Koehler-Ruprecht wines.

Weingut Lingenfelder
Hauptstrasse 27,
67229 Grosskarlbach
Owners: Rainer and
Hermann Lingenfelder
Vineyard area: 15 hectares
Grape varieties: 36% Riesling,
16% Spätburgunder, 13% Scheurebe,
10% Dornfelder, 5% Silvaner,
20% other varieties

Rainer Lingenfelder is one of the most talented Pfalz winemakers to emerge with the fine vintages of the late 1980s. Perhaps his most important achievement was to bring to the world's attention the excellent quality and unique styles that can be produced with the Scheurebe in the Pfalz. The estate's dry Scheurebes ripple with exotic and grapefruit-like fruit, and are rich in texture yet absolutely clean. They have enough depth to be drunk with substantial, well spiced Pfalz cooking. The Scheurebe dessert wines could hardly be more sensuous, oozing with exotic fruit and honeyed flavours. The Riesling are generally a little more restrained and elegant, with ripe peach, apricot and grapefruit notes. The best Rieslings are the rich wines from the estate's old vines in the Freinsheimer Goldberg, which in recent years have been vinified with a touch of natural sweetness as

Rainer Lingenfelder, promoter
of Sheurebe as 'wine for the post-
Chardonnay age'.

Spätlese or Auslese Halbtrocken. These 'fruit bombs' are the result of meticulous vineyard cultivation rather than exceptional vineyards. In the cellar Rainer Lingenfelder is a disciple of Hans-Günther Schwarz of Müller-Catoir in that, apart from the minimum filtration, he leaves the wines to make themselves.

The estate's red Dornfelder is made in a deliberate Beaujolais style, full of fruit and supple enough for easy drinking. No recent Spätburgunders have quite fulfiled the promise of the fine '86 and '85 vintages.

Weingut Herbert Messmer
Gaisbergstrasse 132,
76835 Burrweiler
Owner: The Messmer family

Vineyard area: 21.5 hectares
Grape varieties: 47% Riesling,
14% Spätburgunder,
10% Weissburgunder,
6% Grauburgunder,
6% Müller-Thurgau,
17% other varieties
Top site: Burrweiler Schäwer

Founded only in 1960, the Messmer estate has rapidly become one of the Südpfalz's leading producers. Herbert Messmer and his son Gregor have attracted the most attention with their Rieslings from the Burrweiler Schäwer. The Schäwer is the only site in the Pfalz with a slate soil comparable with those in the best Mosel-Saar-Ruwer vineyards. It gives dry wines which, even with 13 degrees of natural alcohol, are sleek with mineral notes and a delicate

153

peach-like fruit: quite a contrast to the lush aromatic style typical in the Pfalz. Since Gregor Messmer took over the winemaking during the mid-1980s the estate's Grauburgunder, Weissburgunder and Gewürztraminer wines have improved just as much as its Rieslings. They are all powerful dry wines with rich fruit and excellent harmony, making their resemblance to Müller-Catoir wines, Gregor Messmer's ideal, unmistakable. With the vintages of the early 1990s Gregor Messmer also demonstrated his skill with red wines: his Spätburgunder and St Laurent were deeply coloured with an intense berry fruit character. With a little fine-tuning of the oak element they would be among the region's finest reds.

Weingut Georg Mosbacher
Weinstrasse 27,
67147 Forst
Owners: Richard and
Hildegard Mosbacher
Vineyard area: 9.5 hectares
Grape varieties: 84% Riesling,
4% Müller-Thurgau,
3% Spätburgunder,
2% Dornfelder,
2% Gewürztraminer, 2% Scheurebe,
2% Kerner, 1% Weissburgunder
Top sites: Forster Freundstück,
Forster Ungeheuer

One taste of the superb Forster Ungeheuer wines from the Georg Mosbacher estate demonstrates why the Forst Rieslings enjoy the highest reputation of all Pfalz wines. Winemaker Richard Mosbacher is a perfectionist who has consistently made the best wines in Forst since the late 1970s. His wines are always full of fruit, rich and intense yet perfectly balanced. The estate's Ungeheuer Rieslings are the most complete expression of this style, adding layers of mineral and spice character to the picture. Since the '92 vintage the best barrels of the Mosbacher's Ungeheur wines have been bottled separately and sold as *Selektionsweine*, or 'reserve' wines, and it would be hard to find better dry or naturally sweet Pfalz Rieslings. Since 1992 Richard Mosbacher has been assisted by his son-in-law Jürgen Düringer and his daughter Sabine, who are to take over the estate during the coming years. Their aim is to refine the wine style still further and to consolidate its position as one of the region's quality elite.

Weingut Müller-Catoir
Mandelring 25,
67433 Neustadt-Haardt
Owner: Heinrich Catoir
Vineyard area: 16 hectares
Grape varieties: 51% Riesling,

11% Scheurebe, 8% Weissburgunder, 6% Rieslaner, 5% Grauburgunder, 5% Gewürztraminer, 5% Muskateller, 5% Spätburgunder, 2% Müller-Thurgau, 2% Kerner
Top sites: Gimmeldinger Mandelgarten, Haardter Mandelring, Haardter Bürgergarten, Haardter Herrenletten, Haardter Herzog, Mussbacher Eselshaut

Showered with praise during the last decade, this estate is now widely recognised as one of the country's best. Few white wines are made that can match the intensity or expressiveness achieved by Hans-Günther Schwarz with an astonishing variety of grapes. Each wine is like an essence of its grapes yet, however dense and powerful, Müller-Catoir wines possess an excellent harmony. Schwarz's extraordinary majestically rich dry Weissburgunders and Grauburgunders have no hint of heaviness in spite of their 14 or 15 degrees of alcohol. Similarly sensational are the estate's wines from the Riesling crosses Scheurebe and Rieslaner. The former yields opulent dry wines that have seen off the toughest international competition in 'blind' tastings, the latter gives some of the most explosively rich dessert wines in Germany. The dry Muskateller and Gewürztraminer, still relatively unknown, are marvellously elegant expressions of their grapes.

Since the '89 vintage Müller-Catoir has made dramatic improvements to its dry and sweet Rieslings and these are now in the same class as the estate's other wines. Any sweetness in the Riesling Halbtrocken and dessert wines is entirely natural and always beautifully integrated with the racy acidity, a prominent feature of all the estate's wines. In spite of increasingly

Winemaking genius Hans-Günther Schwarz of Weingut Müller-Catoir.

Doris Eymael of Weingut Pfeffingen, one of Germany's leading women winemakers.

intense competition in this dynamic wine region this is still one of the premier wine estates along the length of the Rhine.

Weingut Ökonomierat Rebholz
Weinstrasse 54,
76833 Siebeldingen
Owner: Christine Rebholz
Vineyard area: 9 hectares
Grape varieties: 40% Riesling,
22% Spätburgunder,
9% Gewürztraminer,
8% Müller-Thurgau,
7% Weissburgunder, 5% Chardonnay,
5% Muskateller, 4% Grauburgunder
Top site: Birkweiler Kastanienbusch

Since the late 1940s the Rebholz family have made the finest wines in the Südpfalz and done much to promote the quality wine movement which bore such abundant fruits here during the 1980s and 1990s. In 1949 the estate produced the first ever Trockenbeerenauslese from Müller-Thurgau and the first in a series of remarkable dessert wines to which Hans-Jörg Rebholz regularly adds new examples. However, as his grandfather and father did before him, he places his prime emphasis upon dry wines. These have a reputation for being uncompromisingly dry and acidic, which hardly seems a fair description. The dry Rieslings do have a pronounced acidity but this is always counterbalanced by vibrant pear- and peach-like fruit. The Weissburgunder, Grauburgunder and Gewürztraminer wines are medium- to full-bodied, bone dry but rich in texture. Together with Müller-Catoir, the estate makes the best wines in the Pfalz from the Muskateller. Just as racy as the Rebholz Rieslings, these are intensely grapey and delicately perfumed and make perfect apéritif wines.

Since the late 1980s Hans-Jörg Rebholz has invested a great deal of time and energy in improving the estate's Spätburgunder reds. They have since gained in colour, depth and structure and now number among the best in the Pfalz. Interesting experiments have also been made with champagne-method sparkling wines from red Pinot Noir grapes (what the French call Blanc de Noirs) and these are the only part of the estate's extensive range where improvements could still be made.

Weingut Pfeffingen-Fuhrmann-Eymael

Weinstrasse,
67098 Bad Dürkheim-Pfeffingen
Owner: Doris Eymael
Vineyard area: 10.5 hectares
Grape varieties: 70% Riesling,
10% Scheurebe, 9% Müller-Thurgau,
6% Gewürztraminer,
3% Weissburgunder and
Chardonnay, 2% Silvaner
Top sites: Ungsteiner Herrenberg,
Ungsteiner Weilberg

Nestling at the foot of the Herrenberg vineyard of Ungstein just north of Bad Dürkheim, the Pfeffingen estate has long been one of the star wine producers of the Pfalz. Its unique wines marry two complementary winemaking styles: that of Karl Fuhrmann who built up the estate's reputation from the 1950s to the 1970s, and that of his son-in-law Günther Eymael from Ürzig in the Mittel Mosel, whose influence became apparent during the 1980s. The estate's Rieslings at their best combine the rich fruit of the Pfalz with a Mosel-like elegance and crispness. The dry and sweet Scheurebe wines are frequently excellent and the opulent BA and TBA dessert wines from this grape the best in Germany. Until the 1990 vintage the estate held a steady course with this style. However, since then some of the wines have lost the brilliance which once made them so distinctive. Hopefully Karl Fuhrmann's daughter Doris, who has directed the estate since the late 1980s, will be able to put Pfeffingen back on course.

Weingut Karl Schaefer

Weinstrasse Süd 30,
67098 Bad Dürkheim
Owner: Dr Wolf Fleischmann
Vineyard area: 17 hectares
Grape varieties: 85% Riesling,
3% Silvaner, 2% Müller-Thurgau,
10% other varieties
Top sites: Dürkheimer Michelsberg,
Dürkheimer Spielberg,
Forster Pechstein,
Ungsteiner Herrenberg,
Wachenheimer Gerümpel

The dry and sweet Rieslings of this fine estate in the southern outskirts of Bad Dürkheim have long been among the most elegant and sophisticated in the Pfalz. During the second half of the 19th century this was one of the region's first producers to bottle its own wines to sell to private customers. Little has changed here in decades and most of the vineyards are still planted on narrow terraces in the best sites of Bad Dürkheim and in Wachenheim and Forst. Just as they did 50 and more years ago, most of the wines ferment and mature in wood until bottling in the September after the harvest. In order to prevent

them from maturing too quickly in barrel, the cellar is cooled through the summer, one of few innovations made during recent years. During the 1980s and early 1990s the estate's best dry Rieslings came from the first-class Wachenheimer Gerümpel site, from which only the Josef Biffar estate makes wines of comparable depth and breed. The best sweet Rieslings generally come from the Dürkheimer Spielberg, although they face tough competition from Schaefer's own Rieslaner dessert wines. In the Pfalz only Müller-Catoir makes wines of comparable quality from this fickle grape.

Weingut Dr Wehrheim

Südliche Weinstrasse 8,
76831 Birkweiler
Owner: Karl-Heinz Wehrheim
Vineyard area: 10 hectares
Grape varieties: 40% Riesling,
22% Weissburgunder, 12% Silvaner,
8% Spätburgunder,
8% St Laurent, 10% other varieties
Top site: Birkweiler Kastanienbusch

During the early 1960s Dr Heinz Wehrheim made this fine estate one of the quality leaders in the Südpfalz. Today his son Karl-Heinz Wehrheim makes some of the richest and most succulent dry white wines in the region. Whether from Riesling, Weissburgunder or Grauburgunder, they are opulently aromatic with full apricot- and pineapple-like fruit, substantial yet silky in texture. In spite of alcohol levels that often reach 13 degrees for Riesling and 14 for the Pinot varieties, they show no signs of heaviness or imbalance. The best come from the steep slopes of the Birkweiler Kastanienbusch, the highest and most southerly top site in the Pfalz. Its red slate soil yields not only imposing white wines but also some powerful Spätburgunder reds. Since the '85 vintage these have possessed more than enough power to take on good red Burgundies. All they need now is a touch more elegance and subtlety.

OTHER WELL KNOWN PRODUCERS

Weingut Reichsrat von Buhl
Weinstrasse 16,
67146 Deidesheim
The complex of buildings housing this famous estate is one of Diedesheim's architectural high-points. Since being leased by a group of Japanese investors in 1989, however, it has experienced mixed fortunes. With 55 hectares of vineyards, many of which are in the first-class sites of Deidesheim, Forst and Ruppertsberg, the estate's potential to produce top-quality wines is unquestionable.

Together with new winemaker Frank Hohn (formerly of Heyl zu Herrnsheim in Nierstein) von Buhl's director Stefan Weber is determined to recapture the magic that once characterised von Buhl wines.

Weingut Christmann
Peter-Koch-Strasse 43,
67435 Gimmeldingen
The Christmann's impressive dry Rieslings of recent vintages suggest that this will soon be one of the Pfalz's best estates.

Weingut Kurt Darting
Am Falltor 2,
67098 Bad Dürkheim
Since striking out alone in 1989 the Dartings have made some good dry and dessert wines, some of which represent excellent value.

Weingut Fitz-Ritter
Weinstrasse Nord 51,
67098 Bad Dürkheim
Konrad Fitz and his American wife Alice cultivate 19 hectares of vineyards including holdings in the famous Ungsteiner Herrnberg and the less well known Dürkheimer Michelsberg and Spielberg sites. Their dry Riesling and Gewürztraminers are consistently good.

Weingut Georg Henninger IV
Weinstrasse 93,
67169 Kallstadt
Walter Henninger specialises in fresh dry Rieslings which ably complement the traditional Pfalz cooking in his wine restaurant.

Weingut Julius Ferdinand Kimmich
Weinstrasse 54,
67142 Deidesheim
While this estate's generally dry Riesling from Deidesheim and Forst are rarely exciting, a good general standard is maintained.

Weingut Lergenmüller
Weinstrasse 16,
76835 Hainfeld
During recent years the Lergenmüller brothers have attracted considerable attention with their enormously powerful oaky red wines.

Weingut Lucashof
Wiesenweg 1a,
67147 Forst
The sleek, racy Rieslings of this estate are often of good quality and enjoy a loyal following within Germany.

Weingut Eugen Müller
Weinstrasse 34a,
67147 Forst
Kurt Müller makes some impressive dry Rieslings from the top vineyard

sites of Forst, but also some rather ordinary wines.

Weingut Münzberg
76829 Godramstein
Brothers Rainer and Gunther Kessler are best known for their powerful dry Grauburgunders, which can be excellent.

Weingut Siegrist
Am Hasensprung 4,
76829 Leinsweiler
The rich red wines of this estate are invariably good but the whites are often rather alcoholic or slightly confected.

Winzergenossenschaft Vier Jahreszeiten
Limburgstrasse 8,
67098 Bad Dürkheim
In spite of stiff competition from the Forst and Ruppertsberg village co-operatives, this is probably the best co-operative in the Pfalz. From 310 hectares of vineyards it produces a wide range of traditional Pfalz wines including some good Rieslings and impressive dessert wines.

Weingut Heinrich Vollmer
Gönnheimer Strasse 52,
67158 Ellerstadt
When not in Argentina managing his extensive vineyards there, mountaineer and winemaker Heinrich Vollmer produces a range of excellent-value white and red wines (including Cabernet Sauvignon) at this young estate.

Weingut Werlé Erben
Weinstrasse 84,
67147 Forst
Although quality can be erratic, this estate produces some of the best traditional-style Pfalz Rieslings.

Weingut Wilhelmshof
Queichstrasse 1,
76833 Siebeldingen
Herbert and Christa Roth's estate is best known for its excellent champagne-method sparkling wines.

Travel Information

Top restaurant Weinkastell in Kallstadt serves regional specialities and classic dishes.

PLACES OF INTEREST

Bad Bergzabern For those travelling south to Alsace or from Alsace north to the Pfalz, Bad Bergzabern is a natural stopping point. In the centre of town the most notable of many fine buildings are the Schloss and the magnificent Renaissance Gasthaus zum Engel (Königstrasse 45) the finest example of this period in the region.

Bad Dürkheim Several monstrous modern buildings replace parts of Bad Dürkheim which were damaged during the spring of 1945 but in spite of these the town retains a good deal of charm. The early 19th-century Kurhaus is a most impressive building, and to the south and west are a series of ruined castles, of which the extensive Burg Graf von Leiningen in the suburb of Hardenberg is the most imposing. The Wurstmarkt, originally a pilgrim celebration, takes place annually in the second half of September and is one of the biggest wine festivals in Germany.

Deidesheim Pfalz's most famous wine town is an essential stop in any tour of the region. Apart from the more obvious monuments such as the 15th-century town wall and church of St Ulrich, there is the Renaissance Town Hall and a complex of fascinating narrow cobbled streets. Imposing vintner's houses say much for the reputation of the town's wines from the mid-19th to the mid-20th centuries. The small wine museum cannot compare with that of Speyer, but is still worth a visit. It opens from Wednesdays to Sundays and on public holidays.

Edenkoben The Max Slevogt collection of mainly 19th- and early-20th-century paintings, drawings and sculptures is housed in Schloss 'Villa Ludwigshöhe' just to the west of Edenkoben. From the Schloss a cable car runs to the terrace of the ruined Rietburg castle from which there are magnificent views over the Südpfalz.

Freinsheim Freinsheim is one of the better-kept secrets of the Pfalz. This attractive wine town has a well preserved town wall, a baroque Rathaus and many fine old buildings in the centre.

Leinsweiler Tucked into the Birnbachtal Valley is the most attractive old village of Leinsweiler. Among many beautifully preserved houses the Rathaus (1619) is outstanding. Above Leinsweiler is Schlossgut Neukastell, which was once home of artist and art collector Max Slevogt (1868–1932).

Maikammer Situated immediately below the highest peak of the Haardt Mountains (the 673-metre Kalmit) Maikammer boasts many half-timbered houses dating back to the 16th century.

Neustadt an der Weinstrasse The narrow old streets, early 18th-century Rathaus and 14th-century Stiftskirche of central Neustadt make it one of the most attractive of the region's larger wine towns.

St Martin The half-timbered houses in this beautiful wine village make it a photographer's dream. The festival of St Martin, held annually on

A typically inviting Gutsausschank, or vintners' tavern, in Rhodt on the Südliche Weinstrasse.

November 11, is a fascinating traditional celebration.

Speyer The Dom of historic Speyer, whose foundation stone was laid in 1030, is perhaps the country's greatest Romanesque building. Much of the town was razed to the ground by Louis XIV's troops in 1689, but this masterpiece of medieval architecture survives in almost pristine condition. The cathedral crypt, the oldest part of the building, is the resting place of eight German kings and kaisers. In the grounds a portion of the town wall dating from about 1280 can be seen. The baroque Dreifaltigkeitskirche, or Church of the Holy Trinity (1717), with its painted wooden interior, represents the other extreme of ecclesiastical architecture. Speyer is also home to the magnificent 13th-century Altportal, one of the oldest town gates in Germany and the Historisches Museum der Pfalz (Domplatz) which includes an excellent wine museum (open daily).

Wachenheim The Pfalz's most important large wine estate, Dr Bürklin-Wolf, and the Schloss Wachenheim sparkling wine company are both based in this small wine town. The Schloss premises are the most impressive buildings in town.

HOTELS AND RESTAURANTS

Restaurant Schwarzer Hahn (in Hotel Deidesheimer Hof)
Am Marktplatz,
67146 **Deidesheim**
Tel: (06326) 1811, Fax: (06326) 7685
Manfred Schwarz, one of Germany's best known chefs, is a gastronomic artist of the highest calibre. In the vaulted cellar of the Deidesheimer Hof Hotel he serves some of the finest food in any of Germany's wine regions. His fish dishes are sensational. Upstairs in the *Weinstube* the cooking is more regional but hardly less impressive. The wine list includes a careful selection of the best wines from the Pfalz as well as the best from Bordeaux. The hotel (the same telephone and fax numbers) is also excellent.

Hotel-Restaurant Luther,
Hauptstrasse 29,
67251 **Freinsheim**
Tel: (06353) 2021, Fax: (06353) 8388
Dieter Luther is a talented cook though the quality of the restaurant

food is not entirely consistent. The hotel and its rooms are beautiful.

Restaurant Gebrüder Meurer
Hauptstrasse 67,
67229 **Grosskarlbach**
Tel: (06238) 678,
Fax: (06238) 1007

In fine weather Harry and Wolfgang Meurer's garden restaurant is a most attractive place to eat out-of-doors. The interior, though rustic, is tasteful. The cooking may not be the most imaginative in the region but the standard is always good. The wine list features a selection of local wines at moderate prices.

Restaurant zur Krone
Hauptstrasse 62–64,
76863 **Herxheim-Hayna**
Tel: (07276) 5080,
Fax: (07276) 50814

Since chef Karl Emil Kuntz returned to this out-of-the-way family restaurant in 1985 it has become one of the best in the region. Kuntz's cooking is outstanding for its excellent flavour and texture – but not the best choice for anyone trying to cut down on their cholesterol intake! The restaurant is expensive but not over-priced.

Gutsschänke Henninger
Weinstrasse 101,
67169 **Kallstadt**
Tel: (06322) 63469

Walter Henninger's Weinstube with its timeless interior is perhaps the most authentic in the Pfalz, offering a range of traditional dishes and good dry wines from the Henninger IV estate.

Restaurant-Hotel Weincastell zum Weissen Ross
Weinstrasse 80–82,
67169 **Kallstadt**
Tel: (06322) 5033,
Fax: (06322) 8640

Norbert Kohnke serves a small selection of regional specialities including the most refined Saumagen in the Pfalz and a range of carefully prepared classic dishes. The wine list features a wide selection from the neighbouring Koehler-Ruprecht estate (Jutta Kohnke is the sister of winemaker Bernd Philippi). The vaulted dining room is beautiful. This marvellous restaurant will never get a Michelin star – and does not give a hoot. As a hotel it is comfortable and tasteful without being luxurious.

Top chef Manfred Schwarz in his kitchen at Restaurant Schwarzer Hahn in Deidesheim.

Restaurant Da Gianni
R7 34,
68161 **Mannheim**
Tel: (0621) 20326

Mannheim may no longer be part of the Pfalz, but a restaurant this good cannot be overlooked. Arguably Germany's finest Italian restaurant (and there is plenty of competition) Da Gianni is reason enough to forget German wine and food for one evening.

Restaurant Backmülde
Karmeliterstrasse 11–13,
67346 **Speyer**
Tel: (06232) 71577,
Fax: (06232) 70903

Oenophile Gunter Schmidt is also a talented cook and his restaurant is easily the best in the cathedral city of Speyer. The poultry dishes are particularly recommended.

USEFUL ADDRESSES

Information im Haus des Gastes
67098 **Bad Dürkheim**
Tel: (07726) 666266,
Fax: (07726) 666301

Tourist Information Deidesheim
Bahnhofstrasse (Stadthalle),
67146 **Deidesheim**
Tel: (06326) 5021,
Fax: (06326) 5023

Tourist-Information Neustadt an der Weinstrasse
Exterstrasse 2,
67433 **Neustadt an der Weinstrasse**
Tel: (06327) 855329,
Fax: (06327) 81986

Verkehrsamt Speyer,
Maximilianstrasse 11,
67346 **Speyer**
Tel: (06232) 14395

The village of Siebeldingen, tucked below the foothills of the Haardt range.

Hessische Bergstrasse

The wines of this almost impossibly pretty pocket-handkerchief region are usually spoken of in relation to those of the Rheingau. In fact they have more in common with the wines of northern Baden – the region's vineyards are effectively a continuation of the northernmost vineyards of Baden around Heidelberg. Any confusion surrounding the area and its affiliations is understandable since the region belongs to the state of Hessen, as does the Rheingau. (To confuse matters further, the wine-growing region of Rheinhessen actually belongs to the state of Rheinland-Pfalz, not that of Hessen....) And Hessische Bergstrasse's most famous estate, the State Wine Domain of Bensheim, is closely linked to that of Kloster Eberbach in the Rheingau. This typifies the not uncommon situation in Germany in which political boundaries do not coincide with geological or climatic ones.

Until the introduction of the German Wine Law in 1971, Hessische Bergstrasse was part of the Bergstrasse region which spanned the border between the states of Hessen and Baden. However, Baden's political authorities insisted on their half of the Bergstrasse vineyards' being included in the Baden region and Rheingau vintners were not prepared to have the 400 hectares of Bergstrasse vineyard in Hessen incorporated in their region. There was therefore no option but to turn the area into a separate wine-growing region. Until the reunification of Germany on October 3, 1990, this was the country's smallest wine-producing region.

Since much of Hessische Bergstrasse's wine is drunk by visitors or sold in bottle to tourists, it remains virtually unknown outside the area. Its production is negligible compared to the enormous productions of Baden, the Pfalz and Rheinhessen, and as very little is exported, in international terms it is all but invisible.

On the other hand, treating the region simply as an extension of Baden could easily give the impression that the narrow strip of vineyards around Bensheim and the small island of vines around Gross-Umstadt produce no distinctive wines of their own, which is certainly not the case. Although first-class Bergstrasse wines are few and far between, some excellent Rieslings have emerged. While the region's wines from the Pinot family of grapes bear a strong similarity to the wines from further south, the best Hessische Bergstrasse Rieslings have more in common with wines produced

Sunset over the Rhine Rift Valley in Germany's 'spring garden'.

The sunny vineyards of Heppenheim give lively, juicy dry white wines.

in the north and face little competition from Badische Bergstrasse.

The region's wines sell readily to the large number of visitors drawn to the verdant hills, castles and old towns on the western flank of the Odenwald, a short distance south of Darmstadt and Frankfurt. Many of the region's steep vineyards are dotted with fruit trees in amost Italian-style 'promiscuous cultivation'. Several weeks before winter is over in most other parts of the country, the favourable climate turns its terraced hillsides into a sea of almond, peach, apricot and cherry blossom. Its old towns and villages are well preserved and overwhelmed neither by tourist kitsch nor day-trippers and wine is a natural part of the scene without overriding the many other attractive aspects of country life.

Hessische Bergstrasse also belongs to the 'stockbroker belt' of both the Main-Rhine area conurbation and that of Mannheim-Ludwigshafen. As it is well connected to these urban centres by road and rail, its vintners do not need to cast far afield to find markets for their wines. Local custom is brisk and many producers have opened wine bars and restaurants, adding to the region's appeal to visitors.

In many respects Hessische Bergstrasse's situation is comparable with that of the similarly small and equally attractive Ahr region just south of Bonn. However, it enjoys a considerably better image than the Ahr, perhaps because it produces mostly solid, well made dry and off-dry white wines. As it is situated within a short distance of the Rheingau, Rheinhessen, the Pfalz and Baden, buyers could easily look elsewhere for their wines if they were not satisfied. Hessische Bergstrasse vintners have the advantage of being part of a region with a small but exclusive product. They face seri-

ous competition from their colleagues in nearby regions and this has tended to keep quality standards high, whereas the lack of serious local competition to spur vintners in the Ahr has to some extent led to flagging standards for its red wines.

Hessische Bergstrasse is also home to Domäne Bensheim, currently perhaps the best State Wine Domain in the country. Germany's State Domains belong to those states which make up the federal republic, not to the nation as a whole, so they are not subject to centralised direction. Their official purpose is to act as model estates, demonstrating what can be achieved through uncompromising commitment to quality. They have also traditionally served as testing grounds for new viticultural and winemaking techniques. However, there are in practice huge differences between one State Domain and another, depending on the policies and resources of their respective agricultural ministry. Until the beginning of the 1970s several of Germany's State Domains lived up to the original noble ideals but it is now more difficult to find good examples.

The success of this particular Domain can be attributed to the Hillenbrand family, three generations of which have directed the estate since it was established in 1904. They have run it as if it were a family-owned estate rather than a state-owned company. Decades of dedication to quality have made it the flagship of Hessische Bergstrasse. It comprises almost ten percent of the region's vineyards and a significant percentage of its production.

The Domain's holdings span the entire range of vineyard types to be found in the region. The Odenwald foothills rise steeply on the eastern side of the Rhine Rift Valley and together with the mountains behind them form a massive wall which protects Bergstrasse vineyards from cold easterly air streams. This protection allows spring to begin early here, so extending the growing season and allowing the Riesling grapes to develop their potential for subtle and aromatically intense wines.

The vineyards can be divided between those on lower-lying, gently sloping ground and those on the higher steep slopes. While both enjoy the same generally southwesterly exposure, differences in soil types are dramatic. Deep loess soils are typical of the lower-lying sites, making them very fertile. The higher the site the thinner the loess deposits become until the primary rock is exposed. Sandstone, limestone and granite are all found in the region's top vineyards where the soils are poorer and stonier. It is extremely expensive to work these vineyards and had horizontal terracing

not been introduced during the 1970s, many of them would have fallen out of cultivation.

Given the region's favourable climate and geology it is not surprising that Riesling accounts for more than half the vineyard plantings. It can be found throughout the region, giving wines that vary from medium to full bodied with appealingly juicy fruit and supple but rarely aggressive acidity. Müller-Thurgau and Silvaner still account for a quarter of the Bergstrasse's plantings, giving unspectacular country wines for everyday drinking. Weissburgunder and Grauburgunder/Ruländer are another matter. With these wines the region's association with Baden becomes clear. Both varieties give medium- to full-bodied dry white wines

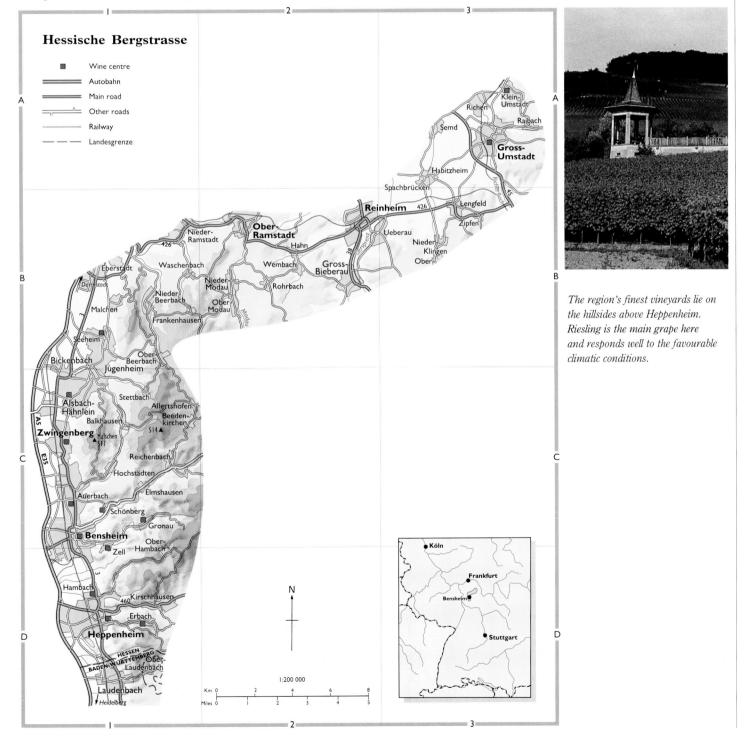

Hessische Bergstrasse

■ Wine centre
Autobahn
Main road
Other roads
Railway
Landesgrenze

The region's finest vineyards lie on the hillsides above Heppenheim. Riesling is the main grape here and responds well to the favourable climatic conditions.

1:200 000

Narrow streets and red-tiled roofs typify the villages of the Hessische Bergstrasse. The vineyards around the small town of Zwingenberg (below and right) are not well known to outsiders but are among the best in the region.

that can compete with northern Baden's best from these grapes. The remaining vineyards, none of which yields anything spectacular, are planted with new grape varieties and Spätburgunder.

The Rieslings are worth considering in some detail since the best of them are certainly among Germany's finest white wines. They all come from high-altitude vineyards which, through a combination of their southerly or southwesterly exposure and their steepness, receive more warmth from the sun than the gentler, lower-lying slopes. The steepest and warmest of these sites is the Steinkopf of Heppenheim, whose recorded history goes back to 1517. Its rocky sandstone soil gives wines which are very different from the Bergstrasse norm. Pungently mineral, with a racy acidity more like that of fine Rheingau wines, they need several years' ageing in the bottle before their wonderful peach- and apricot-like fruit emerges fully. Domäne Bensheim's vineyards in this site were first planted in 1907 on land that had previously been forested. They yield the Bergstrasse's finest Rieslings in both the dry and naturally sweet styles.

The neighbouring Centgericht vineyard of Heppenheim, wholly-owned by Domäne Bensheim, represents the other extreme. Gently sloping with a deep loess soil, it was originally planted as a nursery for propagating American root stock. Only in 1970 was this land turned over to productive vineyard. It gives full, juicy wines that are appealing to drink from the summer following the harvest; wines with the typical character of Bergstrasse Rieslings, if on a

higher level. Such vineyards allow Grauburgunder/Ruländer to give more exciting wines. Full-bodied and rich with a pronounced honey-caramel character, they have a little more elegance than most comparable wines from Baden. Not surprisingly, the vineyard area devoted to these varieties is steadily increasing.

Bensheim's best vineyards, the Kalkgasse and Streichling, could have been predestined for Riesling. Both lie high above the town on south-facing slopes. The Kalkgasse is the more sheltered and as its name suggests (*Kalk* means chalk or lime) it has a light chalky soil. Its supple, spicy wines with ample fruit have made this the best-known of Bensheim's sites. Here the Stadtweingut Bensheim shares the honours with the Domain. Although less well protected by neighbouring hills, the Streichling's weathered granite soil gives medium-bodied Rieslings with a pronounced apricot- or pineapple-like fruit and considerable elegance. The best part of this extensive vineyard and a large slice of the Kalkgasse are in the hands of the Domäne Bensheim, thus giving it the chance to produce a range of different Rieslings.

The wines from Bensheim's suburbs Schönberg and Auerbach are light and fruity. Along with those of Zwingenberg and Alsbach to the north, many are sold under the Zwingenberger Rott Grosslage name and consumed almost entirely within the region. Only Zwingenberg's Steingeröll vineyard (*Stein* means stone) has a reputation for giving Rieslings of special quality: wines with a character and elegance similar to those from the Bensheimer Streichling. Tobias Georg Seitz is the best producer.

Perhaps because so much of the region's wine is drunk in cafés and wine bars, the German tradition of making wines from a mixture of grape varieties has survived here. Although a wide range of solid varietal wines is also produced, a good proportion of the Bergstrasse co-operative's production consists of simple blends of Riesling, Silvaner and Müller-Thurgau. It is surprising that this practice is not more widespread, since in poor vintages it is difficult to produce harmonious dry Rieslings everywhere in Germany. The addition of Silvaner and Müller-Thurgau can soften the hardness characteristic of Riesling in lesser years.

Gross Umstadt's 50 hectares of vineyards form a viticultural island which is closer to the most westerly vineyard of Franken (around Aschaffenberg) than to the rest of Hessische Bergstrasse. The climate here is considerably cooler than around Bensheim and Heppenheim, which gives early-ripening Müller-Thurgau and Silvaner an opportunity to play a leading role.

Klein Umstadt's cooler climate favours earlier-ripening varieties (below).

Since its small area allows it only limited production capabilities, it seems unlikely that Hessische Bergstrasse will ever gain a wider reputation for high-quality wines. But it should not be lightly dismissed. It deserves a respected place among Germany's wine-growing regions.

BENCHMARK WINES:

Heppenheimer Centgericht Riesling Eiswein
Domäne Bensheim, Bensheim

Vineyard site: Heppenheimer Centgericht
Site area: 18 hectares, wholly owned by Domäne Bensheim
Exposure: southwest
Inclination: gently sloping
Soil: deep loess
Description: With their lush dried and exotic fruit aromas, these are some of Germany's most opulent ice-wines. Their acidity is generally a shade softer than in Mosel-Saar-Ruwer, Nahe or Rheingau examples but they still have the intensely sweet-sour character typical of this style. The aftertaste is an explosion of fruit and spice.
Best vintages: '93, '91, '90, '88, '86, '85
Best drunk: With voluptuous sweetness and a good acidity these dessert wines can stand up to all kinds of desserts, even those containing caramel or some chocolate.

Heppenheimer Steinkopf Riesling Spätlese Trocken
Domäne Bensheim, Bensheim

Vineyard site: Bensheimer Steinkopf
Vineyard area: 36 hectares, 3 hectares Domäne Bensheim
Exposure: southwest and southeast
Inclination: very steep, terraced
Soil: weathered sandstone
Description: Anyone sceptical about the mineral character attributed to so many German Rieslings should try one of these remarkable dry examples. Their mineral 'spice' is positively pungent. They also have a fine apricot-like fruit and a racy acidity, making them some of the region's most complex and sophisticated wines.
Best vintages: '94, '93, '92, '90, '88
Best drunk: These subtle and elegant wines are ideal for fish dishes, particularly those with cream sauces.

Heinrich Hillenbrand, following his uncle and Grandfather, is the third generation to direct Domaine Bensheim.

BEST PRODUCER

Domäne Bensheim (previously Staatsweingut Bergstrasse)
Grieselstrasse 43–46,
64625 Bensheim
Owner: State of Hessen
Vineyard area: 24.5 hectares
Grape varieties: 74% Riesling,
9% Weissburgunder,
7% Grauburgunder,
5% Spätburgunder,
5% other varieties
Top sites: Heppenheimer Steinkopf, Bensheimer Kalkgasse

Perhaps because this state-owned winery is run like a family-owned estate it makes far and away the best wines in the Hessische Bergstrasse. Heinrich Hillenbrand is the third member of his family to direct the Domäne Bensheim since its foundation in 1904, following his uncle Josef and grandfather Johann. Little-known outside the Rhine-Main region, this is perhaps the most consistent of Germany's state-owned wineries. The potential of its excellent vineyards on the slopes above Bensheim and Heppenheim is fully realised, even the simplest wines being well made and satisfyingly fruity. The best dry Rieslings, particularly the racy wines from the Heppenheimer Steinkopf, match the quality of top-class Rheingau wines. The dry Weissburgunders and Grauburgunders also compare favourably with the best from Baden. Since 1972 Hillenbrand has regularly produced Eisweins from the estate's wholly-owned Heppenheimer Centgericht vineyard. These fetch high prices at the estate's annual wine auctions in Bensheim each October. Most of the estate's wines represent excellent value for money.

OTHER WELL KNOWN PRODUCERS

Weingut der Stadt Bensheim
Darmstädter Strasse 6,
64625 Bensheim
Cellar-master Ellen Ittner makes rich, well balanced dry-style Rieslings.

Weinbau-Weinkellerei Tobias Georg Seitz
Weidgasse 8,
64625 Bensheim-Auerbach
Fresh, racy Rieslings with excellent ageing potential dominate the production. Most are vinified trocken or halbtrocken.

Travel Information

PLACES OF INTEREST

Bensheim The pedestrian-only area in the centre of Bensheim enables visitors to admire the late-17th- and early-18th-century houses around the marketplace undisturbed by the more obvious signs of modernity. For the energetic, the climb to the 14th-century Schloss Schönberg offers marvellous views of the Odenwald.

Gross-Umstadt Like Bensheim and Heppenheim, Gross-Umstadt has many distinguished late-Gothic buildings and fine houses built by the aristocracy during the 17th, 18th and 19th centuries.

Heppenheim One of the most beautiful towns in the region, Heppenheim is an essential stop on any tour of the region. The Marktplatz with its 16th-century Rathaus and the magnificent Gothic Dom (so called, although it is actually not a cathedral but a church) should not be missed. The 200-metre climb from the centre of town to the ruined Starkenburg castle is more than worth the exertion for a panoramic view of the vineyards, the Rhine Rift Valley and the Odenwald forest.

Jugenheim For those wishing to see the Odenwald without serious exertion, both the the Alsbach and Stettbach Valleys can be reached from the town of Jugenheim.

Reichenbach A hike from the village of Reichenbach to the 501-metre-high Felsberg gives a full and memorable impression of the Odenwald's abundant natural beauty.

Seeheim This small town at the northern tip of the Hessische Bergstrasse retains fragments of its town wall and has a fine 16th-century Rathaus.

Zwingenberg This small wine town, with its many half-timbered houses, is one of Hessische Bergstrasse's less well known beauty spots.

HOTELS AND RESTAURANTS

Weinhaus Blauer Aff
Kappengasse 2,
64625 Bensheim-Auerbach
Tel: (06251) 72958
Peter Poth runs a unique wine restaurant in the picturesque village of Auerbach. The wine list offers not only everything of any note produced in the Hessische Bergstrasse, but also a comprehensive range of French, Italian and other wines at moderate

prices. The food is secondary to the outstanding wine on offer.

Parkhotel Krone
Darmstädter Strasse 168 (B3),
64625 **Bensheim-Auerbach**
Tel: (06251) 73081,
Fax: (06251) 78450
This comfortable hotel has an indoor swimming pool and sauna.

Hotel am Bruchsee
Am Bruchsee 1,
64646 **Heppenheim**
Tel: (06252) 73056,
Fax: (06252) 75729
The best hotel in Heppenheim.

USEFUL ADDRESSES

Städtische Verkehrsbüro Bensheim
Beauner Platz,
64625 **Bensheim**
Tel: (06251) 14117,
Fax : (06251) 14127

Verkehrsbüro Heppenheim
Grosser Markt 3,
64646 **Heppenheim**
Tel: (06252) 13171

Above: Hessische Bergstrasse's winegrowing activity is limited by its size, but it remains one of the most charming wine regions in Germany.

Left: Half-timbered houses feature strongly in the attractive centre of Bensheim. Many were built in the late-17th and early-18th centuries.

165

Franken

With its forests, rolling countryside, magnificent castles and churches, Franken has many attractions quite apart from its rich winemaking tradition. Its position in the centre of Germany surrounded by hill-country has to some extent allowed it to develop culturally and politically in isolation. Franken's geographical situation also has a strong influence on its climate. These factors combine to give the region's wines a character completely different from the stereotypical image of German wine.

Franken seems to have been either very lucky or very far sighted in recent times. During the post-war decades it has been affected by changes in fashion that have eroded much of Germany's wine culture, but a good proportion of its vintners have remained staunchly committed to the traditional style. Franken has always been dry wine country, dedicated to making hearty wines for drinking with the substantial regional cuisine. Full-bodied, with a pronounced earthy flavour and firm acidity, they rarely possess the floral charm found in many Rhine and Mosel wines. Franken is the only wine-growing region in the world making top-quality wines from Silvaner, its traditional quality-wine grape.

Any account of Franken must begin with the baroque city of Würzburg and its Stein wines. Würzburg is one of Europe's great wine cities and has been the region's political centre for centuries. It was the seat of the Catholic Prince-Bishops until the King of Bavaria superseded their rule in 1802. Even now the city is dominated by their two monumental residences. For almost five centuries, from 1253 until 1719, they ruled from the massive Marienburg fortress which stands almost 100 metres above the river Main on its eastern bank. Its huge fortifications and those around the town on the western bank date from the 14th and 15th centuries and were constructed to protect the Prince-Bishops as much from their own subjects as from invaders. These were turbulent times, with peasant uprisings in 1308, 1400, 1476 and 1525.

When Johann Philipp Franz von Schönborn (Prince-Bishop from 1719–24) decided to move his court down into the town, he employed the young architect Balthasar Neumann to design his enormous palace. The result, the mighty Residenz, is the most imposing rococo building in Germany.

Franken's rolling countryside is home to a rich winemaking tradition as well as countless historical and architectural treasures.

The 18th century was the high-point of the region's history. This is reflected in the remarkable architecture from that period. In 1746, through the initiative of Friedrich von Schönborn, the Main became an important commercial highway. It was also during the 18th century that Stein wines became internationally renowned and Würzburg one of Germany's most famous wine cities.

Wine merchants used the name 'Stein Wein' for any wine from Würzburg. But at that time any Stein wine sold in the Bocksbeutel bottle under the vineyard name without any mention of Würzburg or of the grape variety was generally assumed to be a forceful dry wine of a strong savoury character. The grape variety was always Silvaner or a mixture of Silvaner and others. In spite of the changes wrought by succeeding centuries, Stein wines of a similar kind are still produced by the estates that made them famous between two and three centuries ago. These estates are the Staatlicher Hofkeller, the successor of the Prince-Bishops' estate, the Juliusspital Church Foundation which helps finance the eponymous hospital and old people's home and the civil foundation of the Bürgerspital hospital.

The Staatlicher Hofkeller still occupies the cellars beneath the Residenz's magnificent staircases and Tiepolo celestial ceilings. Ancient casks stand in cavernous vaulted galleries which make the cellars even of the great Rheingau estates look insignificant. The Juliusspital's wines mature in comparable surroundings. The main gallery of the estate's barrel cellar extends over 100 metres beneath the frontage of the Renaissance hospital building, which was completed in 1579 under Prince-Bishop Julius Echter von

The rococo splendour of the Würzburg Residenz, designed in the 18th century.

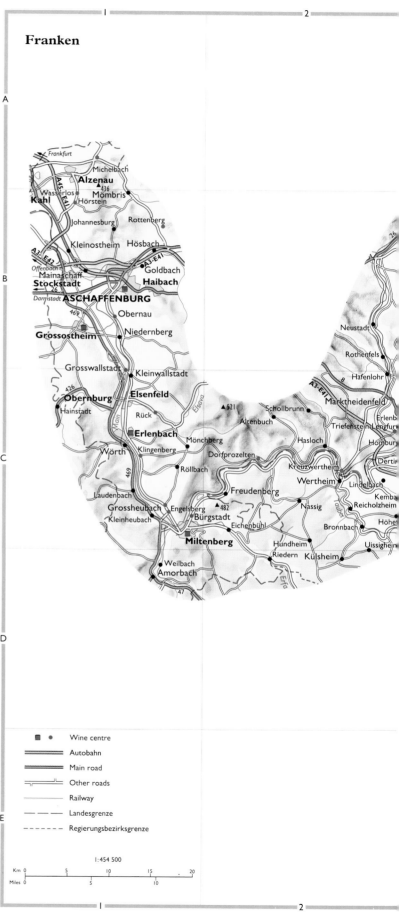

Franken

Wine centre

Autobahn

Main road

Other roads

Railway

Landesgrenze

Regierungsbezirksgrenze

1:454 500

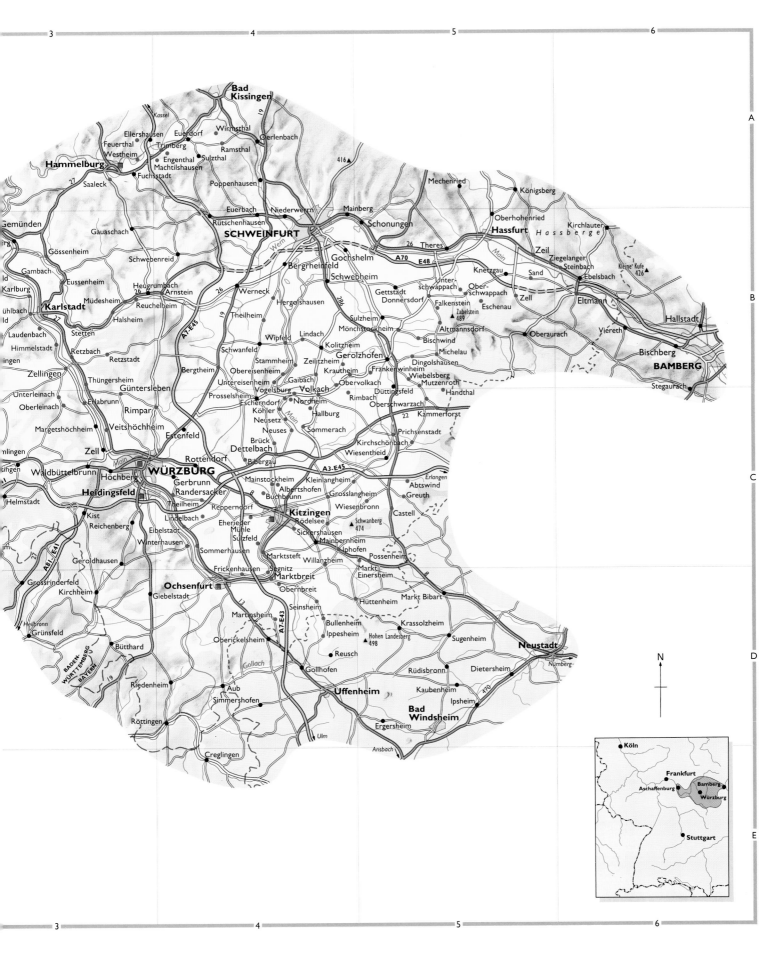

Mespelbrunn. The history of the Bürgerspital zum heiligen Geist goes back another two-and-a-half centuries to its foundation in 1319. Its first vineyards were donated in 1321.

The Bürgerspital is the birthplace of the Bocksbeutel bottle. Paradoxically, this most widely copied and exploited of all bottle shapes was introduced in order to guarantee the authenticity of the region's best wines. Sales of inferior wines being passed off as Stein wines became widespread during the early 18th century, so the Bürgerspital bottled their 1718 vintage in Bocksbeutels with the estate's seal embossed in the glass. From this point the Bocksbeutel became the standard Franken wine bottle. No doubt the origins of this bottle form (which is rather unappetisingly named after the goat's scrotum) lie in the previous century when glass wine bottles were introduced.

The region's most legendary wine, the 1540 Würzburger Stein from the Prince-Bishop's vineyards, tells an interesting story about the technical developments during this period. At that time sweet wines were almost unknown. The only naturally sweet wines were those made from over-ripe fruit, whose high sugar content the yeast could not fully convert into alcohol. Most wines found themselves at the other end of the taste spectrum: thin and acidic, if not sour. This accounts for the almost religious adoration accorded to wines of great vintages; these rarities were full and rich and the most noble of them sweet.

Before the introduction of bottles, wine was stored exclusively in barrels. The life of a wine could be extended only by keeping it in the largest possible barrel and 'topping up' the barrel so that it remained brim-full to minimise the wine's contact with air. When some of the contents were drawn off for consumption it would be replaced with wine of a similar quality and character. The relatively small size of the barrel in which the 1540 Stein was

The mighty Marienburg fortress, for centuries home to the Prince-Bishops of Würzburg, towers over the slopes of the Würzburger Innere Leiste.

stored (the barrel still lies in the cellars of the Residenz) suggests that wine suitable for topping up this vintage was hard to find.

The 1540 Stein was one of the first wines to benefit from the introduction of bottles and corks, a decisive innovation for the development of wine culture throughout Europe. Bottled after 150 years' maturation in barrel (as opposed to the three to 12 months' typical today) the wine must already have been brown in colour and have tasted old. So rich and powerful was this wine, however, that when one of the last remaining bottles was opened in 1961 it was still drinkable, having a character somewhat reminiscent of an old Madeira.

To this day the town's three large estates and the region as a whole are most famous for the wines of the Würzburger Stein. In many respects the Stein is a typical Franken vineyard, since it covers a well exposed slope close to the river Main and has a limestone (*Muschelkalk*) soil. Franken's climate is continental: there are often dramatic differences in temperature between icy winters and warm summers. The average temperature in July is 19°C higher than it is in January. Spring frosts can damage the vines' new growth, greatly reducing the potential harvest and winter often arrives suddenly, making a delayed harvest a risky prospect. For centuries vintners in Franken have concentrated their efforts upon those sites which enjoy the best microclimatic advantages. Most of these are within the valley of the Main and its tributaries where the danger of frost is reduced and the slopes have a sunny, southerly aspect.

The bend in the Main's course as it flows past Würzburg creates perhaps the most famous vineyard sites in Franken: the Stein and the Stein-Harfe sub-site, together almost two kilometres long, the latter wholly-owned by the Bürgerspital. Protected from the wind by the surrounding hills, they enjoy an exceptionally favoured position. Only railway lines stand between the vines and the warming influence of the river. Fifty years ago and more it was suggested that soot from passing trains was responsible for the smoky notes found in some Stein wines, but it is more likely that this originates in the stony limestone soil. Rieslings from here are some of the most elegant in Franken, having a delicate peach- and citrus-like fruit and a racy brilliance. Even at the highest levels of richness they never taste heavy or show their naked power. Altogether more substantial and somehow 'winey', Stein Silvaners have the harmony of a Grand Cru Chablis, and refuse to be weighed down even when (as is not unusual in good vintages) they have over 13 degrees' alcohol.

Some believe that Rieslings from the Innere Leiste vineyard are as good or even better than those from the Stein. Both are certainly exceptional vineyards. The Innere Leiste, on the slopes below the Marienburg's massive fortifications, could hardly enjoy a more dramatic situation and its wines, considerably more muscular and aromatic than Stein Rieslings, seem to reflect this extraordinary location. For centuries the struggle has continued among Würzburg's three great estates to make the best wines from these sites and the glory seems to shift from one to another with each successive vintage. During recent years, however, the Juliusspital has been holding the crown.

Good as the wines from Würzburg's other vineyards are, they rarely scale such heights. The lightest of them are from the Pfaffenberg, which runs over several of the Main's side valleys to the north of the Stein. Both the Rieslings and Silvaners from here are medium-bodied and sleek, generally lacking the opulent fruit aromas characteristic of the top-site wines. The typical gooseberry or green plum notes are a result of the modest degree of ripeness grapes can achieve here even in the best vintages. South of the town on the Main's right bank lies the Abtsleite, whose wines are quite rich, supple and even 'fat', with a pronounced mineral spice note.

Riesling accounts for only four percent of the region's 6,000 hectares of vineyards but the grape plays a disproportionately important role in the vineyards of Würzburg and neighbouring Randersacker. In Franken the total area planted with Riesling has doubled during the last 20 years, but in these particular districts it has shared the glory with Silvaner for generations. In Randersacker, Riesling is perhaps the more important variety, giving elegant wines full of fruit.

Although it has many historic buildings Randersacker is far from being the prettiest or most remarkable wine village in Franken. Its narrow streets give the impression of a people dedicated to the serious business of winemaking. Experiencing a wine-tasting with one or other of the town's leading vintners should confirm this, but should also leave a visitor in no doubt as to the inhabitants' lively wit and enthusiasm.

One good reason for such confidence could be the healthy domestic demand that exists for Franken wines, which enables vintners to develop and refine their own wine style in the sure knowledge that their wines will sell. Randersacker is a good example of the positive effects of such a ready market, since the town's leading vintners are free to make with confidence wines in dramatically contrasting styles. These range from Robert Schmitt's deliberately old-fashioned wines, which need many years' ageing in bottle before they reveal their full character, to the highly polished wines from Schmitt's Kinder, which shine almost from the

Fortifications such as these at Marienburg are typical of many of Franken's towns and villages and often date from the 16th or 17th centuries.

moment they are bottled. The solid, unpretentious wines from Josef Störrlein are at the opposite end of the scale to the lavishly fruity wines of Martin Goebel.

In spite of the diverse personalities of the town's vintners (and their wines) they all acknowledge the greatness of the Randersackerer Pfülben vineyard. They would also agree that at present its superiority is not as clear-cut as it once was. In common with the vineyards of many other wine towns and villages in Franken, the steeply sloping vineyards of Randersacker have been *fluerbereinigt,* or reorganised, in order make their cultivation less arduous and costly. This process requires the replanting of virtually all the vines, and currently the Pfülben has the largest proportion of young vines in the Randersacker. Not until the turn of the millennium will they be mature enough to give optimum-quality grapes. Until then the wines from the excellent Sonnenstuhl and Teufelskeller sites will be able to compete with those from their famous neighbour. Like the Pfülben, the Sonnenstuhl and Teufelskeller vineyards also lie directly on the river Main and have southeasterly slopes facing the sun. Their wines have plenty of fruit and body, but they cannot normally equal the elegance and the mineral spice of a first-class Pfülben Riesling.

Famous as Randersacker Rieslings are, they are sometimes overshadowed by the dramatic, racy wines made by leading vintners from the Rieslaner grape, or the Mainriesling as it was once called. Of all the vine crosses developed in Germany this is closest to the noble Riesling, taking to even higher levels of intensity its characteristic fruit aromas and flavours, racy acidity and vibrancy. It is however a difficult grape to cultivate, since it is very late

The first-class Lump vineyard above Escherndorf produces stunning Silvaner.

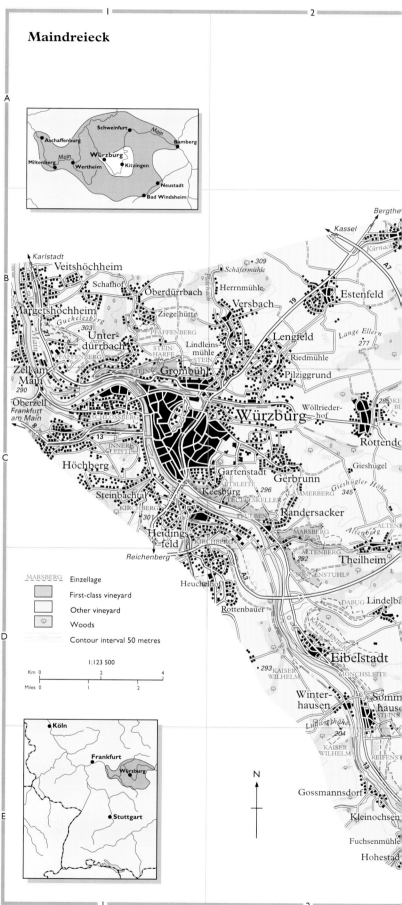

Maindreieck

MARSBERG   Einzellage

First-class vineyard

Other vineyard

Woods

Contour interval 50 metres

1:123 500

Km 0   2   4

Miles 0   1   2

ripening like Riesling and must therefore be planted in the most favoured locations in order to give good results. Indeed, while half-ripe Riesling grapes can still give reasonably harmonious results, anything less than fully ripe Rieslaner grapes will result in thin, raw wine. Rieslaner QbA or Kabinett should be avoided. Thankfully these problems are understood, and the variety's naturally low yields guarantee that it is cultivated only by the most dedicated vintners.

Rieslaner originates from Franken, and here its wines marry the ultimate in power with more elegance than any other white wine grape. Rieslaner Spätlese wines are impressive, both vinified dry and with some natural sweetness, but Rieslaner Auslese, BA and TBA dessert wines truly prove the variety's potential for greatness. In spite of their enormous concentration and opulence these wines have a racy brilliance which makes them animating and refreshing rather than overbearing or tiring. Taste a few of these wines alongside comparable Rieslings and Silvaners and it is hard to avoid the conclusion that Rieslaner gives the region's greatest dessert wines. The best sources are Martin Goebel, Robert Schmitt and Schmitt's Kinder in Randersacker, Juliusspital and Staatlicher Hofkeller in Würzburg, Castell and Johann Ruck in the Steigerwald and Rudolf Fürst in Bürgstadt which is between Würzburg and Aschaffenburg.

The next first-class vineyards on the Main lie a considerable distance upstream at Escherndorf and Volkach. For a brief part of its course the river snakes its way around several extreme bends creating a unique amphitheatre of vineyards. The most famous of these sites is the Escherndorfer Lump (*Lump* means tramp). As in

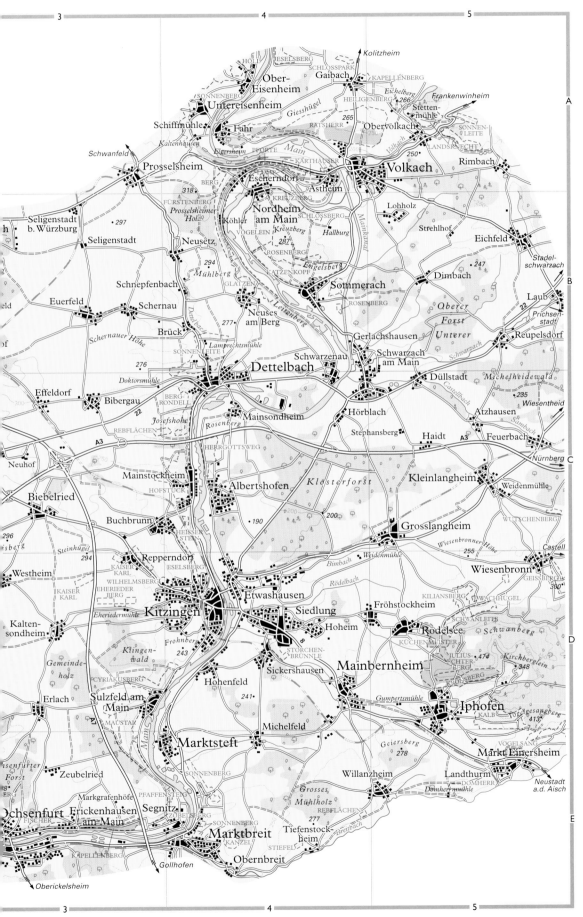

Steeply inclined vineyards provide a dramatic backdrop to the village of Nordheim, east of Würzburg.

Despite the technical advances of recent years, winegrowing here at Escherndorf still involves much manual labour.

the best vineyards of Würzburg and Randersacker, the soil here is limestone. The combination of this soil and a sunny aspect seems to be the key to producing top-class Silvaner. While good examples of Franken Silvaners have a balance similar to that of Chablis made without new-oak ageing, Silvaners from the Lump have an extra succulence in the best years. They acquire ripe fruit aromas such as melon and pear and notes of butter and caramel.

Lump Rieslings fully deserve to be considered alongside the wines from the Würzburger Stein or Randersackerer Pfülben, which they frequently match in richness and substance. This is not the place to seek the ultimate in elegance or delicacy, but certainly here the wines of lesser vintages are more harmonious and less angular than the norm. Rieslings from the nearby Volkacher Ratsherr vineyard, which lies within the same loop of the Main, rarely possess the power and lush fruit of the Lump wines but have plenty of fruity charm. In this corner of the region the best producers are the Juliusspital and Egon Schäffer in Escherndorf.

Although most Franken wines come from vineyards lying in or close to the Main Valley, some of the region's greatest wines come from the forested slopes of the Steigerwald hills, roughly ten kilometres east of Kitzingen in the Main Valley. This is a wild area, very different in character from sophisticated Würzburg. Here it is not unusual to come across cottages with a couple of pigs in the yard, fattening up for the pot. Wandering through small towns and villages it is easy to imagine that time has slipped back three centuries to the region's golden age when, with 40,000 hectares of vineyards, Franken was the country's largest wine-growing region.

Nowhere is this timelessness more apparent than in the fairytale village of Castell. It was independent until it was incorporated into the Kingdom (now state) of Bavaria in 1806. Castell itself was once the capital city of the princedom of Castell and had 500 inhabitants. Among the many fine half-timbered houses stands a church that could make a cathedral look plain, a magnificent baroque Schloss, imposing government buildings and a state archive housing records from seven centuries of viticulture. Castell's vineyards were first recorded in 1258, although there is good reason to believe that the Fürst Castell family has been involved in viticulture for much longer. Records in the Castell archive show that the first Silvaner vines in Franken were planted in Castell by the estate's *Amtmann,* or director, on Wednesday April 6, 1659, six years before the first Silvaner vines were planted in the Würzburger Stein. Such historical precision seems entirely normal within the miniature world of Castell.

Castell's vineyards begin at an altitude of 300 metres and climb to nearly 400 metres in the steepest and best vineyard sites such as the Casteller Schlossberg. Their high altitude gives them a different microclimate from the vineyards along the Main Valley: spring comes later, but autumn can be warm and prolonged. The heavy gypsum marl soils which predominate in the Steigerwald also play an important role in giving these wines their character. They are big-boned and broad-shouldered even at modest quality levels and in the best years can be massive and powerful. They are the antithesis of light, perfumed Mosel-Saar-Ruwer Rieslings.

The most important wine town of the Steigerwald, Iphofen, lies at the western tip below the complex of Schloss Schwanberg. Above the medieval town tower are the slopes of the Julius-Echter-Berg, one of the greatest vineyards in Franken for both Riesling and Silvaner. Named after the Prince-Bishop Julius Echter von

Mespelbrunn, founder of the Juliusspital in Würzburg (which is still the largest landowner here), this site gives the area's most powerful and noble wines. Their grandeur lifts them to a different plane from the typically full, earthy Steigerwald wines. Influenced perhaps by the modern preference for elegance over power, there are those – even within the region – who find the extremely rich Julius-Echter-Berg Silvaners overwhelming. In a good vintage they can have as much depth and persistence of flavour as Grand Cru white Burgundy. Nowhere else in Franken does Silvaner have the exotic and dried-fruit aromas of the best examples.

Rieslings from these sheltered southwest-facing slopes are also the subject of divided opinion. Within Franken, Silvaner is regarded as the best wine for the dining table because of its additional body and its fresh but not dominant acidity. Riesling also may be served with food, but the food should be an accompaniment rather than a partner, as this wine will take centre stage. Julius-Echter-Berg Rieslings have so much body, such lush fruit and abundant mineral power from the soil that they can match all but the spiciest dishes. Alongside Stein Rieslings of the same vintage they taste massive and opulent, the Stein wines seeming almost fragile by comparison. Juliusspital, Johann Ruck and Hans Wirsching make the best Riesling and Silvaner wines here.

The Steigerwald's vintners are not however limited to these varieties and the Riesling x Silvaner cross Scheurebe is more at home here than anywhere else in Franken. Its typical blackcurrant and grapefruit aromas are filled out with an earthy character to give full, pithy wines that are fresh but rarely sour or catty even in less-favoured years. The best dry Scheurebe is made by Hans Wirsching, who shares the honours for best dessert Scheurebes

with Castell. Other new varieties such as Rieslaner and Huxelrebe also give excellent dessert wines.

Wines from the lower reaches of the Main Valley between Aschaffenburg and Marktheidenfeld have a different personality again. These widely scattered vineyards generally have weathered sandstone soils, although islands of granite and gneiss also exist. Their wines are elegant and floral compared to the 'monsters' from the Steigerwald. Such conditions are ill-suited to Silvaner, which rarely yields anything remarkable, but ideal for Riesling and the Pinot family of grapes. Particularly in the south-facing Bürgstädter Centgrafenberg vineyard, Riesling gives wines with a forthright peachiness and discreet earthiness that have more in common with those of the Rhine than with other Franken examples.

At the end of the 1980s the potential of Weissburgunder and Spätburgunder grapes began to be realised as a result of the introduction of new-oak ageing, the principles of which were grasped here more quickly than in most of Germany's wine regions. During the late 1980s both the Städtisches Weingut of Erlenbach and the Rüdolf Fürst estate of Bürgstadt won accolades for their burgundian-style Spätburgunder reds. Since then winemaker Paul Fürst has also become one of the country's leading producers of new-oak-aged Weissburgunder.

Although Aschaffenburg and the region's most westerly vineyards are only a short distance southeast of Frankfurt, Franken has traditionally sold most of its wines in Bavaria because these are the state's only vineyards. During recent decades the region's biggest problem has been an enormous fluctuation in the size of its wine harvest. Favourable weather conditions in years such as 1983 and 1989 result in crops so huge that the vines simply cannot

Above: Many estates sell almost all their wines directly to the consumer and have a Probierstuben, or wine tasting room, set aside for the purpose.

Left: Because of the continental climate winemakers concentrate their efforts on sites around the Main such as Volkach, where there is less likelihood of frost.

Opulent Silvaners come from Iphofen's Julius-Echter-Berg and Kronsberg sites.

BENCHMARK WINES

Casteller Kugelspiel Rieslaner Auslese
Fürstlich Castell-sches Domänenamt, Castell
Vineyard site: Casteller Kugelspiel
Site area: 15 hectares, wholly owned by Castell
Exposure: northwest
Inclination: steeply sloping
Soil: gypsum marl
Description: Not Franken's most honeyed or massive Rieslaners, these are still big wines packed with dried pear- and apricot-like fruit. Sweet floral, almond and spice notes emerge as the wines mature. Even when young the sweetness does not obtrude and pointed acidity leaves a cool, tart impression in the mouth.
Best vintages: '94, '93, '92, '90
Best drunk: Particularly when mature, these are marvellous wines with all kinds of rich fatty foods. With bottle-age they can accompany roast goose as well as liver pâté or fruit desserts.

Iphofer Julius-Echter-Berg Riesling Silvaner
Spätlese Trocken
Weingut Hans Wirsching, Iphofen
Vineyard site: Iphofer Julius-Echter-Berg
Site area: 70 hectares, 15 hectares Hans Wirsching
Exposure: southwest
Inclination: steeply sloping
Soil: gypsum marl
Description: Silvaner cannot be more concentrated or opulent than this, yet there is nothing exaggerated or over-blown about these magnificent wines. The rich yellow plum- and pineapple-like fruit gives the impression of sweetness but the wines are completely dry. Layer after layer of fruit, spice and earth flavours pour over the palate.
Best vintages: '94, '93, '92, '90, '88
Best drunk: With so much richness these wines demand strongly flavoured, rich dishes such as roast pheasant or wild mushrooms.

Hans Wirsching produces Franken's most elegant dry Rieslings and Silvaners.

support the fruit and the resulting wines taste dilute. In years such as 1985, however, frost can cut the crop to as little as one tenth of the average. Both these extremes give unsatisfactory results for the region's vintners, making it difficult to build up international interest in their wines. Paradoxically, one of the biggest prejudices faced internationally by German wines is the idea that they cannot be drunk with food. It is sad that Germany's most natural 'food wines' should remain so little known.

On the other hand, Franken enjoys the highest domestic standing of all 13 regions and its vintners have succeeded in marketing large volumes of wine from Müller-Thurgau (which covers 47 percent of the vineyard area), Bacchus (ten percent) and other unfashionable modern grapes without apparently damaging their image. Certainly Müller-Thurgau gives more substantial and characterful wines here than in most other areas, but while Bacchus can yield appealingly spicy light wines, it is difficult to find anything complementary to say about grapes like Perle and Würzer. Without great care Franken may be heading for the image and marketing problems that wines from such *Neuzuchtung* have caused in Rheinhessen and the Pfalz, for example. If Franken is to maintain its domestic position and improve its international standing, it must concentrate more upon its traditional strengths.

Randersackerer Pfülben Riesling Spätlese
Weingut Schmitt's Kinder, Randersacker

Vineyard site: Randersacker Pfülben
Site area: 15 hectares, 1 hectare Schmitt's Kinder
Exposure: south to southeast
Inclination: steeply sloping
Soil: weathered limestone, stony top-soil
Description: Few vintners in Franken take sweet wines as seriously as Karl Martin Schmitt or make such successful examples. Only moderately sweet, their rich exotic and peach-like fruit is illuminated by a vibrant acidity. Crystal clear and beautifully balanced, they are a unique expression of Franken Riesling.
Best vintages: '94, '93, '92, '90, '88
Best drunk: Unlike most Franken wines, Schmitt's Kinder Rieslings are best drunk by themselves although mild blue cheese or smoked ham complement them well.

Weissburgunder Spätlese Trocken
Weingut Fürst, Bürgstadt

Vineyard site: Bürgstädter Centgrafenberg
Site area: 55 hectares, 9.5 hectares Weingut Fürst
Exposure: south
Inclination: sloping
Soil: very stony weathered sandstone
Description: Having been fermented and matured in new-oak *barriques* these wines have a character different from most Franken Weissburgunders: hazelnut, melted butter and vanilla are the dominant notes rather than fruit. With a creamy texture and elegant harmony these are some of the best oak-aged whites in the country.
Best vintages: '94, '93, '92, '90
Best drunk: Lobster goes well with these unusual Franken wines, as do pork, veal or pasta in cream sauces.

Würzburger Stein Riesling Spätlese Trocken
Weingut Bürgerspital, Würzburg

Vineyard site: Würzburger Stein
Site area: 85 hectares, 22.75 hectares Bürgerspital
Exposure: south
Inclination: steeply sloping
Soil: weathered limestone, stony top-soil
Description: Sleek and racy, these prove that not all Franken wines are broad-shouldered and pungently earthy. Peach, citrus and smoky aromas are discreet and fine, the interplay of fruit and acidity refreshing and animating. Perhaps not the region's most powerful wines, but certainly among the most elegant.
Best vintages: '94, '93, '90, '88, '86
Best drunk: With their crisp acidity and hint of earthiness these are ideally suited to drinking with river fish. They also complement a range of creamy cheeses.

Würzburger Stein Silvaner Spätlese Trocken
Weingut Juliusspital, Würzburg

Vineyard site: Würzburger Stein
Site area: 85 hectares, 28 hectares Juliusspital
Exposure: south
Inclination: steeply sloping
Soil: limestone, stony top-soil
Description: Power and elegance combine in these full yet beautifully balanced dry wines. The ripe pear, almond and vanilla character is subtle but intense on the nose and palate. Rich flavours and fresh acidity mask the high alcoholic content, which leaves a persistent aftertaste.

Best vintages: '94, '93, '92, '90, '88
Best drunk: There could hardly be better 'food wines' than these. Their combination of richness, freshness and roundness enables them to match a wide range of fish, meat, vegetable and cheese dishes. At their best between one and five years of age, they will also keep a good decade.

BEST PRODUCERS

Weingut Rudolf Fürst

Hohenlindenweg 46,
63927 Bürgstadt
Owner: Paul Fürst
Vineyard area: 10.6 hectares
Grape varieties: 42% Spätburgunder, 15% Riesling, 8% Müller-Thurgau, 7% Frühburgunder, 7% Weissburgunder, 5% Silvaner, 5% Domina, 11% other varieties
Top site: Bürgstädter Centgrafenberg

Paul Fürst produces a diverse range of wines, many among the finest in Franken, from his vines in the first-class Centgrafenberg vineyard. Unusually for Franken, Spätburgunder is the leading variety here. All the better red Pinot Noirs are matured in new-oak casks in a beautiful modern barrel cellar that could be part of a Californian winery. The results are perhaps the most elegant and subtle in Germany. The same cellar houses new-oak-aged Weissburgunder which could easily be mistaken for high-class New World Chardonnay.

Although the Fürst Spätburgunder and Weissburgunder wines have been well received, Rieslings have often been ignored or misunderstood because they are so different from the Franken norm. Their peach-like fruit, often accompanied by floral notes, is the product of the sandstone soil. Particularly as dry or off-dry wines of Spätlese quality, they can marry richness and power with elegance. Wines from the Riesling crosses Scheurebe and Rieslaner are built on a bigger scale but can be equally impressive. Only Silvaner fails to give exciting wines here.

Weingut Juliusspital

Klinikstrasse 5,
97070 Würzburg
Owner: Juliusspital Charitable Foundation
Vineyard area: 115 hectares
Grape varieties: 35% Silvaner, 22% Müller-Thurgau, 18% Riesling, 5% Kerner, 5% Scheurebe, 5% Spätburgunder, 10% other varieties
Top sites: Escherndorfer Lump, Iphofer Julius-Echter-Berg, Randersackerer Pfülben, Würzburger Abtsleite, Würzburger Innere Leiste, Würzburger Stein

Since becoming director in 1986, Horst Kolesch has reversed the fortunes of this enormous estate and

Horst Kolesch sets high standards at Weingut Juliusspital.

pushed it to the forefront of quality-wine production in Franken. Considering that total output exceeds a million bottles per year, the high standard maintained is extraordinary. Among Germany's large wine estates only Reichsgraf von Kesselstatt of Trier in the Mosel-Saar-Ruwer can match the Juliusspital's achievements.

What makes Juliusspital wines stand out is their vibrant fruit and racy brilliance. The region's typical earthy character is woven into the background rather than dominating the fruit. Cellar-masters Friedrich Franz and Benedikt Then set an exemplary standard of winemaking, but the estate's excellent vineyards, almost all of which are located in good or first-class sites, play a vital role. The estate is lucky enough to have holdings in all four of the region's top sites: Escherndorfer Lump, Iphofer Julius-Echter-Berg, Randersackerer Pfülben and Würzburger Stein. Their dry Riesling Spätlesen are rich and concentrated and have distinct individual personalities. More powerful and opulent, the estate's dry Spätlesen from Silvaner are perfect 'food' wines. Massive dry and dessert Rieslaners are an important speciality.

Weingut Johann Ruck
Marktplatz 19,
97346 Iphofen
Owner: Johann Ruck
Vineyard area: 11.25 hectares
Grape varieties: 38% Silvaner,
25% Müller-Thurgau, 10% Riesling,
6% Scheurebe, 5% Grauburgunder,
5% Kerner, 3% Spätburgunder,
2% Traminer, 2% Weissburgunder,
4% other varieties
Top site: Iphofer Julius-Echter-Berg
Since the late 1980s this has been one of the best estates in the Steigerwald. In a gleaming modern winery Johann Ruck makes excellent dry Silvaner, Riesling, Rieslaner and Grauburgunder wines. Although the

Johann Ruck, leading one of the best estates in the Steigerwald.

Riesling vines in the great Julius-Echter-Berg vineyard are too young to give optimum-quality fruit, the wines have plenty of body and are full of earthy and herbal character. The opulent, concentrated Grauburgunders from old vines in nearby Rödelsee are truly exceptional. The Huxelrebe dessert wines, packed to the brim with grapefruit, pineapple and honey flavours, are dazzling.

Weinbau Egon Schäffer
Astheimer Strasse 17,
97332 Escherndorf
Owner: Egon Schäffer
Vineyard area: 3.5 hectares
Grape varieties: 43% Silvaner,
33% Müller-Thurgau,
15% Riesling, 9% Bacchus
Top site: Escherndorfer Lump
This tiny 'no frills' estate makes the best dry Riesling and Silvaner from the excellent Escherndorfer Lump vineyard. Egon Schäffer makes no concessions to fashion and nothing here is done for show. The simple cellars are unlikely to impress but the dry Rieslings and Silvaners that come out of them are uniformly excellent. A conservative, almost old-fashioned wine style is maintained, the wines maturing in barrel until the September following the harvest. Full-bodied and with ample fruit, smoke and earth flavours plus an elegant acidity, the Rieslings have excellent ageing potential. The Silvaners, rich, succulent and buttery, have a strong mineral character from the limestone soil. Although Egon Schäffer concentrates on dry wines, when one or another retains some natural sweetness this is accepted as part of its character. The estate's Müller-Thurgau and Bacchus wines are among the best in the region from these second-class grapes.

Weingut Robert Schmitt
Maingasse 13,
97236 Randersacker
Owner: Bruno Schmitt
Vineyard area: 7 hectares
Grape varieties: 26% Müller-Thurgau,

Winches are needed to hoist machinery on the steepest slopes in Franken.

25% Silvaner, 20% Kerner,
15% Riesling,
14% other varieties
Top site: Randersackerer Pfülben
This is one of Franken's great traditional estates. Like his uncle Robert before him, Bruno Schmitt is a firm believer in fermenting his wines as dry as possible and he never chaptalises them (adds sugar to increase the alcoholic content). In lesser vintages this policy results in a large part of the harvest being sold in litre-bottles as Tafelwein: light, tart wines made for purists, not for the faint-hearted. The estate's dry Spätlese wines from the top Randersacker site are a different matter. Rich and powerful without ever being massive or overblown, they are comparable with top-class dry white wines from France. However, their firmness means that they need several years' maturation in the bottle to reach their optimum harmony and for the bouquet to unfold fully. The Silvaners are model examples of this grape, never lacking the acidity necessary to balance their substantial body and full melon-like fruit.

Weingut Schmitt's Kinder
Am Sonnenstuhl,
97236 Randersacker
Owner: Karl Martin Schmitt
Vineyard area: 13.5 hectares
Grape varieties: 26% Silvaner,
25% Müller-Thurgau, 14% Bacchus,
8% Riesling, 5% Kerner,
5% Scheurebe, 3% Rieslaner,
14% other varieties
Top site: Randersackerer Pfülben
Karl Martin Schmitt is an unashamed modernist, making some of the cleanest and most polished wines in a region renowned for its rusticity. No less unusual for Franken is his preference – which he clearly shares with the estate's customers – for wines with a touch of sweetness. This particularly suits the pronounced acidity of the Rieslings from the excellent Pfülben site and the Rieslaners from the Sonnenstuhl. In most vintages these are the estate's best and a unique expression of Franken wine. Having previously made his wines in cramped conditions in an ancient cellar in Randersacker, he built a new house and winery in 1983 just outside the town at the foot of the

Sonnenstuhl. The Schmitt's winery is beautifully designed, fitting well into the contours of the landscape. Many of its rooms, including parts of the winery, are adorned with rows of impressive landscape paintings. These are the work of Karl Martin's brother Andi, who divides his time between the wine estate and his studio.

Weingut Hans Wirsching

Ludwigstrasse 16,
97346 Iphofen
Owner: Dr Heinrich Wirsching
Vineyard area: 58 hectares
Grape varieties: 34% Silvaner,
18% Müller-Thurgau, 16% Riesling,
8% Scheurebe, 5% Kerner,
5% Portugieser, 4% Bacchus,
3% Weissburgunder,
7% other varieties
Top site: Iphofer Julius-Echter-Berg

During the 1980s this highly regarded family-owned estate was the undisputed leader among Franken wine producers. In recent years the quality competition has become more intense but Wirsching is still on top. Almost regardless of grape variety, Wirsching wines have elegance and finesse: the concentrated yet graceful Rieslings from the great Julius-Echter-Berg vineyard could almost be mistaken for first-class Rhine examples. Silvaners from the same slopes are rich and often show a hint of exotic fruit character, yet they are always well balanced. Just as impressive are the estate's dry Scheurebes, packed with blackcurrant- and peach-like fruit. Indeed, even wines from second- and third-class grapes such as Müller-Thurgau, Kerner and Bacchus are remarkable for their clarity, balance and ample fruit. They are a tribute to the skill of cellar-master Werner Probst, whose patient and cautious handling allows the grapes' full intensity to be captured in the bottle. He makes the wines with the assistance of Dr Heinrich Wirsching and advice from sales director Armin Huth. This team holds Weingut Wirsching on a steady course that promises more remarkable Steigerwald wines.

OTHER WELL KNOWN PRODUCERS

Weingut Bürgerspital zum Heiligen Geist

Theaterstrasse 19,
97070 Würzburg
Würzburg's charitable foundation, founded in 1319, rapidly became one of the region's most important vineyard owners. It now cultivates 100 hectares of vineyard including the wholly-owned Würzburger Stein-Harfe (a sub-site of the Stein) and substantial parcels in the other first-

class sites of Würzburg, the Stein, Innere Leiste and Abtsleite. It has one of the region's best equipped cellars. During the 1970s and 1980s the estate was one of Franken's foremost quality-wine producers, its racy dry Rieslings and Silvaners and high-quality Prädikat dessert wines enjoying the best reputations. The present management has set its sights on re-taking this high ground.

Fürstlich Castell-sches Domänenamt

Schlossplatz 5,
97335 Castell
This estate in the Steigerwald area of Franken is renowned for its excellent Rieslaner and Scheurebe dessert wines which are among the region's best. Its 60 hectares of vineyards include eight wholly-owned sites, one of which is the first-class Schlossberg. Dry Müller-Thurgau and Silvaner wines dominate the production and are of a solid standard, having the pronounced earthy character typical of Steigerwald wines.

Weingut Martin Goebel

Friedhofstrasse 9,
97236 Randersacker
Although his production is rather variable, Hubert Goebel's best Riesling, Traminer and Rieslaner wines are full of fruit and character.

Staatlicher Hofkeller

Residenzplatz,
97070 Würzburg
The wines here are as imposing as the cavernous vaulted cellars below the Residenz, where they are made. New director Dr Rowald Hepp, previously director of Staatsweinguter Kloster Eberbach in the Rheingau, is determined to restore the wines' elegance, which has been lacking in recent years. Dry and naturally sweet Rieslaner are important specialities.

Schloss Sommerhausen

Ochsenfurter Strasse 17,
97286 Sommerhausen
In recent vintages there has been a significant improvement in wine quality at this well known estate. The dessert wines are best and the dry wines interesting if not outstanding.

Weingut Josef Störrlein

Schulstrasse 14,
97236 Randersacker
Founded only in 1970, this up-and-coming estate makes fine dry Riesling and Silvaner.

Travel Information

PLACES OF INTEREST

Aschaffenburg Aschaffenburg is dominated by the imposing bulk of the Renaissance palace Schloss Johannisberg (1607–14). It was built as the administrative centre for the eastern territories of Kurmainz, which extended to Miltenberg. It was also used as a summer residence by the Prince-Bishops of Mainz. Among other things it now houses the museum's many collections, including paintings and porcelain. The Schöntal park in the town centre is also worth a detour.

Castell This village is the epitome of a tiny German princedom, perched below oak forests and surrounded by vines. It has several imposing official buildings as it was once the capital of the eponymous independent state. The Castell archives have records going back more than seven centuries and Fürst Castell's 'new' Schloss was built between 1687 and 1691. The town's large church has a baroque exterior and a classical interior.

Dettelbach Dettelbach is worth visiting for its extraordinarily well preserved fortifications – 36 of the watch towers and two of the town gates survive along with most of the town wall. The pilgrimage church 'Maria im Sand' is designed in a strange mixture of late-Gothic and Renaissance architecture; a style known as 'Julius-Stil'.

Ebrach Kloster Ebrach Abbey In the Mittelebrach Valley of the Steigerwald forest (on the B22) is one of Franken's baroque masterpieces.

Escherndorf The answer to the quiz-show question, 'Which German wine village has the most wine festivals each year?' is Escherndorf, which stages one every weekend throughout September and October.

Iphofen Nestling beneath the slopes of some of Franken's finest vineyards, Iphofen is one of the most fascinating and beautiful wine towns in Germany. Its town wall and the massive

A beautiful gatehouse at the entrance to Iphofen, a town steeped in wine culture.

15th- and 16th- century Rödelseer gate are awe-inspiring. The Marktplatz, dominated by the three-storey baroque Rathaus, is full of fine old houses as are the surrounding streets.

Marktbreit The Renaissance Rathaus (1580) is unusual, having been constructed on a bridge over a stream.

Miltenberg This is one of the finest old towns in Franken. The Marktplatz, Hauptstrasse and Schnatterloch are worth lingering over, as is the town museum which exhibits artifacts from as far back as the Roman period. (Marktplatz 171, open Tuesday to Sunday from April until October.)

Ochsenfurt The streets of this small town are lined with impressive half-timbered houses. The 13th- and 14th-century Gothic St Andreas church has a fine statue of St Nicholas by Tilman Riemenschnieder (1510). The magnificent late-Gothic Rathaus was built between 1497 and 1513.

Sommerhausen The towers and gate-houses of Sommerhausen are favoured locations for artists. One of the towers houses the renowned Torturmtheatre which sets this small town apart from all the others in Franken with town walls, towers and half-timbered houses.

Sulzfeld With three gate houses, 21 towers and almost a complete town wall Sulzfeld has extensive fortifications for a town of this modest size. The Renaissance Rathaus is also substantial.

Volkach This small town has a remarkable number of historical monuments for its size including two magnificent gateways from the 13th and 16th centuries and much of the original town wall. The Renaissance Rathaus (1544) on the Marktplatz and the Gothic Pfarrkirche are the finest of many old buildings in the town centre. The late-Gothic pilgrimage church Maria im Weingarten just outside Volkach is full of magnificent paintings and sculptures, the most important of which is the Rosenkranzmadonna statue by Tilman Riemenschnieder (1524).

Würzburg One of the world's great wine cities, Würzburg is an essential destination in any serious wine tour of Germany. The cultural centre of the city (and of Franken) is the Residenz, a masterpiece by Balthasar Neumann, the first architect of German rococo. It is worth allowing plenty of time to take in the contrasts between the various state rooms in this beautifully restored palace. The Tiepolo ceilings alone deserve a lengthy visit and the cellars (see Staatlicher Hofkeller) should not be missed. Across the

Würzburg, the capital of Franken and epicentre of German baroque.

Main on its left bank lies Würzburg's other outstanding historical monument, the massive Marienburg fortress which was the Prince-Bishops' residence in politically less-stable times. It houses the splendid Mainfränkisches Museum.

In the old town is the gem-like late-Gothic Marienkapelle (1377–1481) with Tilman Riemenschnieder's statue of Adam and Eve. Next door stands the rococo Haus zum Falken. The Neumünster is a Romanesque basilica which gained a dome and was transformed in to a baroque extravagance during the first half of the 18th century. There is also the imposing residence of the Juliusspital Foundation. Its cellars lie behind and beneath the magnificent Renaissance palace which is now a hospital and old people's home. In its gardens stands the superb baroque Vierflüssenbrunnen fountain (1706). The austere medieval atmosphere of the Bürgerspital estate just around the corner offers a complete contrast.

HOTELS AND RESTAURANTS

Romantik-Hotel Post
Goldbacher Strasse 19,
63739 **Aschaffenburg**
Tel: (06021) 21333,
Fax: (06021) 13483
This is Aschaffenburg's finest hotel. It is close to the main railway station and centre of town and has an indoor swimming pool and sauna.

Restaurant zur Iphofer Kammer
Marktplatz 24,
97346 **Iphofen**
Tel: (09323) 6907
This austerely decorated restaurant offers a modern interpretation of traditional regional cuisine with some concessions to contemporary taste. Good rather than spectacular, it is still the best restaurant in the Steigerwald.

Romantik-Hotel Zehntkeller
Bahnhofstrasse 12,
97346 **Iphofen**
Tel: (09323) 3062, Fax: (09323) 1519
This marvellous country hotel in Iphofen's 400-year-old tithe house is

comfortable and tastefully decorated.

Romantik-Hotel Polisina
Marktbreiter Strasse 265,
97199 **Ochsenfurt**
Tel: (09331) 3081, Fax: (09331) 7603
Situated in a forest 2.5 kilometres to the east of Ochsenfurt, this fine country hotel enjoys marvellous views of the Main Valley.

Restaurant Schweizer Stuben
Gieselbrunnweg 11,
97877 **Wertheim-Bettingen**
Tel: (09342) 3070,
Fax: (09342) 307155
Exceptionally creative but never exaggerated or fussy, the cooking here strives for maximum flavour intensity and usually succeeds. The wine list leaves nothing to be desired in respect of German, French or other wines. Andreas Schmitt's second restaurant Taverna La Vigna (same telephone and fax numbers) concentrates on Italian cooking to the same high standards and offers excellent value for money. As a hotel, Schweizer Stuben is also first class.

Bürgerspital Weinstuben

Theaterstrasse 19,
97070 **Würzburg**
Tel: (0931) 13861,
Fax: (0931) 571512
The grandest wine restaurant in
Würzburg, the Bürgerspital serves
traditional regional food. The wines
are from the eponymous estate.

Weinrestaurant Haus des Frankenweins

Kranenkai 1,
97070 **Würzburg**
Tel: (0931) 57077,
Fax: (0931) 17175
The splendidly restored Balthasar
Neumann custom house on the bank
of the Main in Würzburg houses both
an information centre devoted to the
region's wines and the town's best
restaurant. The modern cooking is of
a solid standard and a wide selection
of Franken wines is available.

*An ancient crane on the Kranenkai in
Würzburg used for loading barrels onto
boats on the river Main.*

Juliusspital Weinstuben

Juliuspromenade 19,
97070 **Würzburg**
Tel: (0931) 54080
Enjoy a great bottle of Franken wine
from this first-class estate in its own
cosy wine restaurant.

Hotel Rebstock

Neubaustrasse 7,
97070 **Würzburg**
Tel: (0931) 30930, Fax: (0931) 18682
With its rococo façade this fine hotel
is the most imposing address in town.
The central location is ideal for a
longer visit.

Weinhaus zum Stachel

Gressengasse 1,
97070 **Würzburg**
Tel: (0931) 52770
A simple wine restaurant serving
regional food. Its attractive courtyard
this is the perfect location for lunch
in fine weather.

Hotel Walfisch

Am Pleidenturm 5
97070 **Würzburg**
Tel: (0931) 50055, Fax: (0931) 51690
This traditional hotel on the bank of
the Main in central Würzburg is
comfortable and moderately priced.
There are fine views of the river and
the Festung on the opposite bank.

USEFUL ADDRESSES

Tourist-Information Aschaffenburg

Dalbergstrasse 6,
63739 **Aschaffenburg**
Tel: (06021) 30426

Tourist-Information Miltenberg

Rathaus, Engelplatz 69,
63897 **Miltenberg**
Tel: (09371) 400119

Verkehrsbüro Ochsenfurt

Hauptstrasse 39,
97199 **Ochsenfurt**
Tel: (09331) 5855

Verkehrsamt Volkach

Rathaus, Marktplatz,
97332 **Volkach**
Tel: (09381) 40112,
Fax: (09381) 40138

Verkehrsamt Würzburg

Pavillon vor dem Hauptbahnhof
97070 **Würzburg**
Tel: (0931) 37436
in Würzburg Palais am Congress
Centrum,
97070 **Würzburg**
Tel: (0931) 37335, Fax: (0931) 37652
Haus zum Falken, Marktplatz
97070 **Würzburg**
Tel: (0931) 37398

Württemberg

Württemberg can claim a special place among Germany's wine-growing regions. Two and three centuries ago red wine featured in virtually all the country's vineyards. But as more and more imported red wines came onto the market demand for the domestic product dwindled. The nation's increasing international success with white wines during the 19th century and the first half of the 20th resulted in a wave of replantings in which red grapes were almost always replaced with white. In northerly regions red wine production survived only in isolated areas such as the Ahr, Assmannshausen in the Rheingau and Ingelheim in the Rheinhessen. The Pfalz and Baden, now important producers of quality red wine, always had significant areas of vineyard planted with red grapes but during the 1960s and 1970s few of their wines would have stood competition with red wines from other European nations. Only Württemberg has a tradition, unbroken since at least the 17th century, of making good red wine.

Outside the region this is a little-known fact, principally because the Swabians are such enthusiastic consumers of their own wines. This is one of the few wine regions in northern Europe where wine is still an essential part of the population's daily diet. The typical wine glass is the Viertel, which contains a generous quarter of a litre. The daily Viertel for most Swabians is a pale-coloured, light-bodied red from the Trollinger grape. From an international perspective these unexceptional rosés are rather expensive for what they are and few Germans outside Württemberg drink them.

But Württemberg also produces deep-coloured, rich red wines with a smoke and vanilla character from new-oak barrels that would surprise many drinkers of French, Italian or New World wines. They are made from Lemberger, or blends of Lemberger with other red grapes, and their firm tannins make them considerably more robust and powerful than other German reds. Winemaking has improved so much during the last decade that increasingly good examples emerge from each successive vintage.

Like Franken, Württemberg enjoys a continental climate with cold winters that sometimes lead to widespread frost-damage and hot, dry summers that ripen red grapes well. Most of the region's vineyards lie between Heilbronn and Stuttgart in the Württembergisch Unterland. To the west lies the northern tip of

Württemberg's vineyards lie scattered along the Neckar's tributary valleys.

the Schwarzwald and to the east the Löwensteiner Berge and Schwäbische Alb. These hills and mountains provide effective protection from both sides, giving the region such low rainfall that some artificially irrigated vineyards exist in the driest corners. (Vineyard irrigation systems are allowed to be implemented only with special permission from European Community authorities.)

Württemberg's vineyards are widely scattered, for the most part covering hillsides with favourable aspects in the valley of the River Neckar and its many tributaries. Although the region specialises in red wine production, many of the best sites are warm enough to ripen Riesling grapes, which account for fully one quarter of Württemberg's vineyard area. Where Riesling is planted on limestone, particularly in terraced vineyards along the Neckar Valley itself, wines with plenty of body and some elegance can result.

Württemberg's heavier marl and clay soils give Rieslings with a character very different from those of the light, stony Mosel-Saar-Ruwer, Nahe and Rhine vineyards. With their strong herbal, angelica and earth notes these distinctive wines provoke strong positive and negative reactions wherever they are found. As they age – and most age rather rapidly – they acquire a melted butter and caramel character that makes them smell more like mature Chardonnays than Rieslings. While the best can possess a lavish apricot, pineapple and coconut character, other examples are only heavy, broad and earthy. Certainly Riesling's current vogue within Germany has persuaded some of the region's vintners to plant Riesling in vineyards that are better suited to red grapes.

Real red wine country begins around Heilbronn. Hillsides on the eastern side of the town and those of nearby Neckarsulm and Weinsberg have marl and gypsum marl soils and a southwesterly or westerly aspect that make them ideally suited to a range of red grapes. Some of the region's most important quality wine producers are here, including the research station and wine school normally referred to as Weinsberg (the town where it is situated).

While the Geisenheim wine school in the Rheingau enjoys a sound international reputation, many of Germany's leading vintners hold Weinsberg in higher regard. This is perhaps because, owning nearly 50 hectares of vineyards, the school is also the largest wine estate in the region. The students cultivate the vineyards and work in the cellar, so there is a closer relationship

Limestone soils and steep terraces, such as here at Lauffen in the Neckar Valley, combine to give the region's most elegant Rieslings.

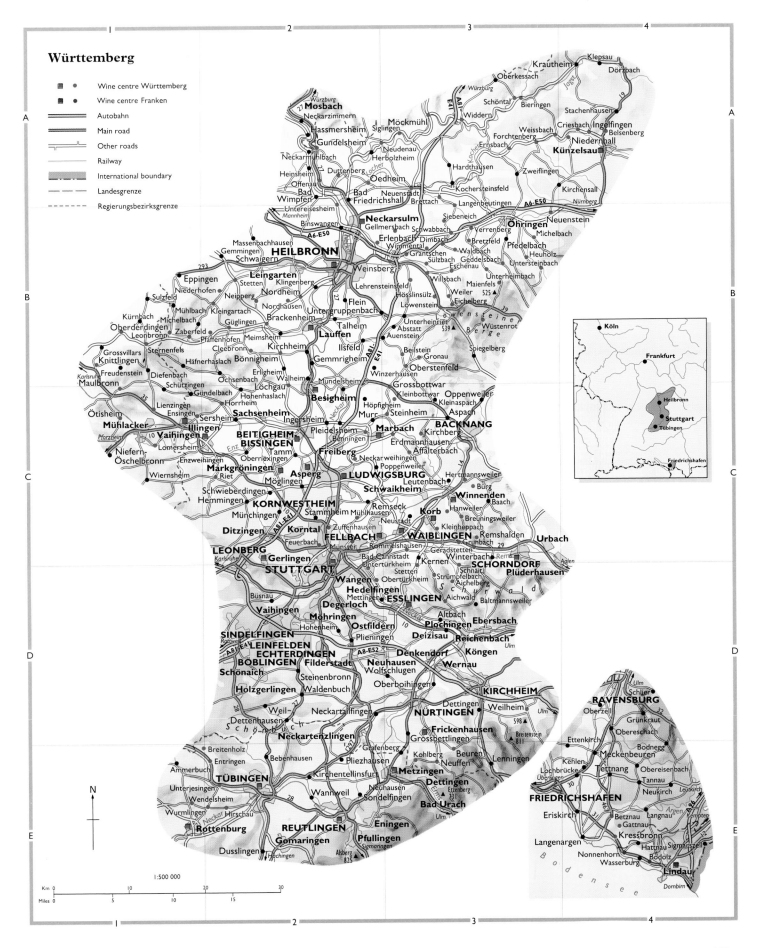

Württemberg

■	●	Wine centre Württemberg
■	●	Wine centre Franken
		Autobahn
		Main road
		Other roads
		Railway
		International boundary
		Landesgrenze
		Regierungsbezirksgrenze

1:500 000

Km 0   10   20   30
Miles 0   5   10   15

N

between theory and practice here than there is at Geisenheim. This is reflected in the consistent quality of the Weinsberg red wines.

As well as educating future vintners and imbuing them with an appreciation of quality, Weinsberg is also carrying out important research into the ageing of wine in new-oak barrels. This is a new development for the region, since in Germany both white and red wines are traditionally matured in large neutral oak casks. The first experiments in Württemberg with new-oak maturation took place in the early 1980s but the results were inconclusive. Since then the region's leading winemakers have learned a great deal about how wine and oak react with one another. As a member of the Association of HADES (an acronym of the names of founder members' estates) Weinsberg is also undertaking practical research in to the influence of new-oak ageing on wines made from the region's more distinctive grape varieties.

More of a working group than a promotional organisation, the Association was founded in 1986 by the Fürst Hohenlohe-Oehringen, Graf Adelmann, Drautz-Able, Ellwanger and Sonnhof estates and the Weinsberg school. Following the lead of Italian winemakers, HADES members sell their new-oak-aged wines as Deutscher Tafelwein, or table wine, to differentiate them from their normal product (although now these wines also often see a touch of new oak). They are bottled in special flute-shaped bottles embossed with the Association's emblem. The HADES wines from the Lemberger grape of the Drautz-Able estate Heilbronn (whose best Lemberger reds are sold under the name 'Jodokus') and from Weinsberg show the area's real potential for red wines. The Lemberger, known as Blaufränkisch in Austria, gives full-bodied wines with plenty of firm tannin and a rich blackberry- or plum-like fruit. After one to two years' ageing in new oak it gains a strong smoky note that perfectly complements its black-fruits character. As long as the yields are kept low, Lemberger reds are rarely short on colour or substance. If they have a weakness it is that they tend to be a little rough and 'chunky'. A spell in French *barriques* seems to smooth them out quite effectively without obscuring the fruit behind a curtain of oak.

To the east of Weinsberg the vineyards become more widely scattered and only those with a southerly exposure are warm enough to ripen noble grapes. The outstanding vineyard is the Verrenberger Verrenberg, owned by the Fürst zu Hohenlohe Oehringen estate. The estate produces some serious red wines from Lemberger and Spätburgunder (Pinot Noir) and, as at many of the region's other top estates, the best reds are made from a blend of Lemberger and grapes of the Pinot family. In theory, Lemberger provides the colour, power and structure while Spätburgunder and/or Clevner (Frühburgunder in Württemberg) contribute

A variety of red and white grapes are cultivated on the gently sloping vineyards around Brackenheim (below), a typical Württemberg wine village near Heilbronn.

perfume, elegance and breed. The Fürst zu Hohenlohe-Oehringen 'Ex Flammis Orior' ('rising from the flames', taken from the Hohenlohe-Oehringen family crest) is a blend of Lemberger and Pinot Noir which seems to prove the theory and has earned considerable praise within Germany.

Other successful examples produced under the auspices of HADES are the 'Cuvée Vignette' from Graf Adelmann, the 'Nicodemus Cuvée' from Jürgen Ellwanger and the 'Julius Cuvée' from Sonnhof, all of which are blended wines. These experiments are less than a decade old but a division has already occurred between vintners who feel that the best Württemberg reds are varietal wines and those who would rather follow the traditions of Bordeaux, the Southern Rhône and Rioja where the greatest red wines are blends of two or more grapes.

The debate concerning the use of new oak was heated during the 1980s but is now over; it is generally acknowledged that the cautious use of new oak can add much to the region's red wines. There are now excellent winemakers actively developing both styles, so even more exciting red wines may be expected from Württemberg in the future.

Some of the most interesting Württemberg Rieslings come from the region's northwestern extremity. The vineyards owned by the Burg Hornberg estate, the Burg Hornberger Wallmauer and

Götzhalde sites, used to belong to neighbouring Baden and were made part of Württemberg only in 1985. They lie along one of the most beautiful stretches of the Neckar Valley, where the river twists and turns between steep forested banks. Terraced vineyards cover only the most sheltered south-facing slopes. The vineyards here benefit not only from the narrowness of the valley, which effectively shuts out cold winds, but also from the protection of the Odenwald to the north. Here Riesling, Traminer and Weissburgunder all give rich, aromatic wines with plenty of fruit.

The vineyards in the valleys of the Neckar's tributaries, the Kocher and Jagst, are also devoted primarily to white grapes, Riesling and a range of other white varieties which give lighter-bodied, rather less aromatic wines.

The isolated vineyards of the Tauber Valley close to Bad Mergentheim are planted primarily with Müller-Thurgau and Silvaner and have more in common with the wines from nearby Franken than with most Württemberg whites.

The slopes of the Verrenberg also yield some remarkable white wines; unmistakable Rieslings with peach-like fruit overlaid by strong earth, fern and herbal notes. As full-bodied dry wines with 12 or more degrees of alcohol – Spätlese or Auslese Trocken – and the typical character from the marl soil, they are among the most expressive wines of the region. Never lush or fat even at this level of richness, Verrenberg Rieslings are more like the firm, 'winey' Rieslings of Alsace than the filigree wines of the Mosel or Rheingau.

Though their character is typical of the region, the ageing potential of Verrenberg Rieslings is not. They can last between five and ten years, depending on the vintage, as opposed to most of the region's whites which need to be drunk young before they lose all their freshness. As they age in the bottle the region's more powerful, richer Rieslings develop butter and caramel notes reminiscent of mature Chardonnays, but in lesser examples this can quickly dominate what little fruit the wines possessed, leaving them flat and flabby after a year or less.

The co-operative of Flein-Talheim, just south of Heilbronn, sets a glowing winemaking example. In Württemberg co-operative wineries, or *Weingärtenergenossenschaften,* account for 85 percent of the region's wines. At Flein, only a short distance away from some of the region's best red wine vineyards, Rieslings with plenty of juicy fruit and an appealingly creamy texture are made. They

187

demonstrate Württemberg's true white wine potential and high-light the mediocre standards of some other co-operatives and estates. Many vintners are still tempted to over-crop their vines with the inevitable result that the wines' character is diluted. The traditional preference within the region for soft white wines has not helped matters, since winemakers are inclined to force their wines into this accepted style rather than let it express its own natural balance.

The most elegant white wines are found further south. One source is the terraced slopes of the Neckar Valley between Heilbronn and Ludwigsburg, although here few vintners are achieving their sites' full potential. One look at the sun-drenched slopes above this tightly winding river shows that it is ideal country for the Riesling grape. In spite of soil differences (limestone predominates here), comparison with the Mosel is irresistible. Perhaps the best wines come from the Dautel estate's vines in the Besigheimer Wurmberg site. However, even here the problems created by extremely dry vineyards are obvious; drought stress can easily rob the wines of fruit and harmony. At present Dautel's best Rieslings come from the less-favoured slopes of the Bönnigheimer Sonnenberg, a site better suited to red grapes.

At Neipperg, west of Heilbronn, there are excellent Riesling vineyards which more frequently achieve impressive results. The von Neipperg family brought the first Lemberger vines to Germany shortly after the Thirty Years' War (1618–48) and the grape variety remained their speciality until after the 1920s. The land is terraced to make cultivation of the steep slopes easier. In a good vintage the Graf Neipperg's Rieslings from the Neipperger Schlossberg and Schwaigerner Ruthe vineyards can have more peach-like charm than any other Württemberg Riesling.

Close to Stuttgart, on the right bank of the Neckar and in the Rems Valley a few kilometres to the east, there are vineyards yielding further excellent Rieslings. The best estate is that of Karl Haidle of Kerner in Remstal, one of the region's leading white wine specialists, whose Rieslings are powerful without being heavy and aromatic without the typical pungent earthiness. Jürgen Ellwanger of nearby Winterbach has also made some good Rieslings, successfully maturing some in new oak (normally a recipe for fruitless wines with about as much flavour as a well-chewed pencil). In the Stuttgart suburb of Untertürkheim, newcomer Hans-Peter Wöhrwag has made some good Rieslings and Gewürztraminers recently from the estate's wholly-owned Herzogenberg vineyard. These should signal an intensification of the quality competition at the southern end of the region, but while good, typical

Above: Rolling hills dominate the landscape at Haberschlacht while steep terraces drop down to the twisting Neckar river at Hessigheim (right and far right). Drought stress here can rob the wines of fruit and balance.

Württemberg reds can be produced here, they rarely compete with the best examples from further north.

There is little Riesling to be found in the isolated vineyards around Metzingen, Rothenburg and Tübingen at the region's southern tip. Silvaner and Müller-Thurgau dominate, but they rarely give anything special in Württemberg. On the other hand Kerner, which elsewhere in Germany is dependable but generally unexciting, yields wines here that can compete even with the Rieslings. The grape usually has plenty of fruit of the tinned pineapple variety but is weak on the balancing acidity. In Württemberg Kerner's wines have not only more forthright fruit, but also a more satisfying balance. Particularly if vinified with a touch of natural sweetness, they can be juicy and zesty, more than justifying the nine percent of Württemberg's vineyard area covered by the vine.

In addition to this range of fairly conventional grape varieties Württemberg is also home to a small number of indigenous grapes that are not cultivated anywhere outside its borders. All these are old, if not ancient, red grape varieties. The most important commercially is Samtrot, literally 'velvet-red', which is a very apt description of its wines. It is almost certainly a mutation of Pinot Noir, which is prone to degeneration of this kind.

There were 123 hectares of Samtrot in Germany in 1992. The grape gives medium- to full-bodied reds full of blackberry fruit which are soft and supple even when drunk young. It is relatively easy to make good wines from this appealing grape, but rather difficult to coax anything more exciting from it. In recent years the Amalienhof estate of Heilbronn, Schlossgut Hohenbeilstein and the Fürst zu Hohenlohe-Oehringen estate have made the best Samtrot wines. However, this variety seems tailor-made for refining powerful, strapping Lembergers. As yet few such blends have been produced, although the Heuchelberg Kellerei of Schwaigern's top red wine, Briolet, is a good example of this marriage.

Muskattrollinger seems be a close relative of the Trollinger, which it resembles in being pale in colour, light in body and quite tart. As its name suggests it adds a pronounced spicy muscat note to Trollinger's typical characteristics. Given a good vintage, this fickle grape can yield remarkably aromatic red wines with more fruit and a better harmony than comparable Trollingers. Graf Adelmann, Amalienhof, Jürgen Ellwanger, Schlossgut Hohenbeilstein and Sonnhof are the only sources of this rarity.

The ultimate in Württemberg's gallery of specialities is the ancient Urban grape, cultivated only by Graf Adelmann and rarely vinified as a varietal wine.

Red wine country at Grosskarlbach between Heilbronn and Ludwigsburg, where Lemberger and Trollinger dominate.

With competition on the domestic market intensifying and Swabian wine drinkers themselves becoming more eclectic, most of Württemberg's vintners will face an increasingly difficult task selling their simple Trollinger 'red' wines. Württemberg's acreage under vine has shrunk from 45,000 hectares at the end of the 16th century to just over 10,000 hectares. It seems inevitable that it will diminish further as the region concentrates on the specialities that make its range of wines so distinctive.

At the top end of the quality scale, consumers are becoming increasingly discerning as the range of high-quality red wines within Germany grows. Until the end of the 1980s it was comparatively easy for the region's top estates to sell red Spätlese and Auslese Trocken for high prices. German wine drinkers have already begun to assess such wines more critically, aware that good wine can also be obtained in Baden and the Pfalz. With luck, the region's vintners will rise to the challenge.

BENCHMARK WINES

Brüssele Cuvée Vignette Tafelwein Trocken
Weingut Graf Adelmann, Kleinbottwar
Vineyard site: Kleinbottwarer Süssmund and Oberer Berg
Site area: Süssmund 5 hectares, Oberer Berg 8 hectares, both wholly owned by Graf Adelmann
Exposure: south-southwest
Inclination: sloping and steeply sloping
Soil: gypsum marl
Description: This wine has such a deep purple ruby colour it could almost come from the Rhône Valley. The bouquet of blackberry jam, cocoa powder and herbs, however, is unlikely to be found in

Michael Graf Adelmann outside the towering Burg Schaubeck.

any other fine red wine. Full-bodied and rich, the many layers of flavour are perfectly integrated with abundant soft tannins to give a satisfying harmony. The herbal aftertaste is fine and persistent.
Best vintages: '94, '93, '90, '89
Best drunk: Remarkably subtle and plush for a German red, this calls for a special meat dish such as beef Wellington with glazed vegetables.

Lemberger 'Jodokus' Tafelwein Trocken
Weingut Drautz-Able, Heilbronn
Vineyard site: Neckarsulmer Scheuerberg
Site area: 100 hectares, 2.75 hectares Drautz-Able
Exposure: south
Inclination: steeply sloping
Soil: gypsum marl
Description: Opaque shading to deep ruby at the rim, this is 'real' red wine. Remarkably full-bodied, it has more than enough rich blackberry, plum and smoke character to balance its firm core of tannins. The long spicy aftertaste is clear evidence of two years spent in new oak.
Best vintages: '94, '93, '92, '90, '88
Best drunk: Red meat or hard cheeses are the best choices for reds with this much muscle and grip. Grouse or mature Gouda would pose no problem.

Verrenberger Verrenberg Riesling Spätlese Trocken
Fürst zu Hohenlohe-Oehringen, Oehringen
Vineyard site: Verrenberger Verrenberg
Site area: 19.5 hectares, wholly owned by Hohenlohe-Oehringen
Exposure: south
Inclination: steeply sloping
Soil: gypsum marl
Description: This is uncompromisingly traditional Württemberg Riesling. The peach-like fruit typical of the grape is almost lost in the angelica, herbal and earth character. Full-bodied but without any trace of opulence, these tightly wound wines need time in the bottle and glass for their concentrated flavours to unfold.
Best vintages: '94, '93, '92, '90, '88
Best drunk: These wines beg for food. They are ideal for oily fish such as eel or salmon and strongly flavoured poultry such as guinea hen or pheasant. They are best drunk from two or three years of age but will keep for a decade and more.

An ancient cask in the cellars of Fürst zu Hohenlohe-Öhringen.

BEST PRODUCERS

Weingut Ernst Dautel
Lauerweg 55,
74357 Bönnigheim
Owner: Ernst Dautel
Vineyard area: 8.5 hectares
Grape varieties: 20% Riesling, 16% Trollinger, 13% Lemberger, 13% Schwarzriesling, 10% Spätburgunder, 8% Kerner, 7% Müller-Thurgau, 13% other varieties
Top site: Besigheimer Wurmberg
   Founded only in 1978 after Ernst Dautel graduated from the Geisenheim wine school, this small estate has enjoyed a meteoric rise to fame and the wine quality improved in leaps and bounds during recent years. Dautel now makes some of the best white and red wines in Württemberg, achieving excellent results with a range of grape varieties. Spätburgunder is one of his first loves, and his 'sweet' fleshy Pinot Noirs are the best in Württemberg made from this fickle grape. His new-oak-aged Lembergers are firm, intense and more elegant than the grape can usually achieve. Dautel's accomplishments with white wine are if anything even greater. His best Rieslings, from the Bönnigheimer Sonnenberg, are big dry wines with plenty of fruit, flesh and earthy character from the marl soil. Although Chardonnay is cultivated only on a semi-experimental scale, Dautel makes a successful Burgundian-style wine from the grape. He is a talented winemaker who knows how to use his modern equipment to best effect rather than letting it dictate how the wines should be made.

Weingut Drautz-Able
Feissstrasse 23,
74076 Heilbronn
Owner: Christel Able
Vineyard area: 13.5 hectares
Grape varieties: 32% Trollinger, 21% Riesling, 9% Lemberger, 8% Spätburgunder, 7% Kerner, 7% Schwarzriesling, 16% other varieties
Top site: Neckarsulmer Scheuerberg
   Brother-and-sister team Christel Able and Richard Drautz run one of Württemberg's best family-owned wine estates. Their Lemberger and Dornfelder reds are deeply coloured, big and powerful, with pronounced smoke and vanilla notes from new oak. Their top wines, among the best reds in Germany, spend fully two years in wood and are marketed as Deutscher Tafelwein under the brand name 'Jodokus'. While most of winemaker Richard Drautz's colleagues in Württemberg are attempting to make more complex and elegant reds by blending varieties, he is pursuing the same goal by using *barrique* casks made from oak from different forests and coopers.
   The estate's reds have attracted a great deal of interest but the white wines are hardly known outside the region. Here too a high standard is maintained and new oak is used for the best examples with considerable success. Drautz-Able is one of very few German estates cultivating Sauvignon Blanc, making from it an oak-aged wine somewhat in the style of a good white Graves. Even better is the rich and opulent new-oak-aged Grauburgunder. Riesling is not Drautz-Able's strongest suit.

Weingut Fürst zu Hohenlohe-Öhringen
Im Schloss,
74613 Öhringen
Owner: Fürst Kraft zu Hohenlohe-Oehringen
Vineyard area: 19 hectares
Grape varieties: 49% Riesling, 16% Lemberger, 12% Spätburgunder, 7% Schwarzriesling, 4% Weissburgunder, 3% Chardonnay, 3% Trollinger, 6% other varieties
Top site: Verrenberger Verrenberg (wholly owned)
   The high proportion of Riesling in this noble estate's vineyards is unusual for Württemberg, as is the consistent excellence of its Riesling wines. Dry and firm in their youth, the herbal, angelica- and peach-like flavours tightly wound, the wines need some bottle-age to show their best but are also long living. The Spätlese and Auslese Trocken wines can last for a decade and more. The earthiness typical of the region's white wines is matched with rich fruit, the crisp acidity exactly balancing the ample body. After a long cool fermentation almost all the estate's Rieslings spend several months in oak, an unusual practice in a region where stainless steel dominates most cellars.
   The estate's red wines are also among Württemberg's best, particularly 'Ex Flammis Orior' (from the family motto) a new-oak-aged blend of Lemberger and Spätburgunder that has plenty of power, rich plum and smoke flavours and exemplary balance. The other red wines are substantial, with plenty of colour, fruit and tannin. Their high standard, along with that of the Rieslings, is a tribute to Siegfried Röll, the talented director who has made the wines here since 1976.

Schlossgut Graf von Neipperg
Im Schloss,
74190 Schwaigern
Owner: Karl Eugen Erbgraf zu Neipperg

191

Vineyard area: 28 hectares
Grape varieties: 26% Riesling,
25% Lemberger, 18% Schwarzriesling,
8% Trollinger, 5% Müller-Thurgau,
4% Gewürztraminer, 4% Muskateller,
4% Spätburgunder, 6% other varieties
Top sites: Neipperger Schlossberg,
Schwaigerner Ruthe
(both wholly owned)

This fine estate was responsible for the introduction of the Lemberger grape to Germany during the late-17th century and is one of the most traditional wine producers in Württemberg. Only during the last couple of years has the estate experimented with some new-oak casks for maturing its best reds. In general, both the red and white wines mature in large casks of neutral German oak as they did centuries ago. Though wine quality here is a little patchy, the estate's best Riesling, Traminer and Muskateller white wines are excellent. When successful they have fine fruit and an elegance remarkable for the region. Among the red wines the Lembergers stand out with their spicy blackberry fruit, full body and supple tannins. It will be interesting to see how the introduction of new oak at the estate affects these wines. There is good reason to hope that the change in style will be successful since the owners are drawing on the considerable experience of Stephan Graf von Neipperg, the owner of Château Canon-la-Gaffelière in St Emilion. For German-speakers the estate's wittily written price list offers considerable amusement.

OTHER WELL KNOWN PRODUCERS

Weingut Graf Adelmann
Burg Schaubeck,
71711 Kleinbottwar
Württemberg's most famous estate is housed in a fairy-tale castle dating back to the 13th century. All the wines from the estate's 16 hectares are sold under the 'Brüssele' name. The best of these, particularly the dry Riesling and Lemberger red wines, can be among the finest in Württemberg. However, in recent years quality has been variable.

Weingut und Schlosskellerei Burg Hornberg
Burg Hornberg,
74865 Neckarzimmern
This important white-wine producer makes good dry Riesling, Traminer and Weissburgunder but the reds are simple and rustic.

Weingut Jürgen Ellwanger
Bachstrasse 21,
73650 Winterbach

From vineyards at the region's northeastern limit, Jürgen Ellwanger produces reliable new-oak-aged reds.

Good new-oak-aged reds can be found here and solid quality across the board, but exciting wines are rare.

Winzergenossenschaft Flein-Talheim
Römerstrasse 14,
74223 Flein
This is clearly Württemberg's best co-operative winery and a good source of dry and sweet Riesling and Kerner, but the reds are dreary.

Weingut Karl Haidle
Hindenburgstrasse 21,
71394 Kernen im Remstal
Hans Haidle has made some very good dry and sweet Rieslings in recent years but his reds are no more than solid and well made.

Schlossgut Hohenbeilstein
Im Schloss,
71717 Beilstein
Hartmann Dippon makes a wide range of well crafted red wines but the Rieslings are unexceptional.

Staatliche Lehr- und Versuchsanstalt Weinsberg
Traubenplatz 5,
74189 Weinsberg
The Weinsberg wine school maintains an impressive standard with its red wines, which are often very good. Some of the white wines however are rather soft and amorphous.

Weingut Wöhrwag
Grunbacherstrasse 5,
70327 Untertürkheim
Although Hans-Peter and Christin Wöhrwag still have some work to do on their red wines, their dry and sweet Rieslings and Gewürztraminers are already impressive. This is an estate to watch.

Travel Information

PLACES OF INTEREST

Bebenhausen Just to the north of Tübingen in the Schönbuch forest lies the former Cistercian monastery of Bebenhausen. Although not the largest or grandest example in Germany, this is certainly one of the nation's most beautiful Gothic buildings. The painted vaulted ceiling of the Sommerrefektorium is spectacular.

Besigheim Situated between the valleys of the Neckar and the Enz, this is one of the most attractive old towns in Württemberg. Plenty of buildings remain as evidence of its importance during the Middle Ages, not least the beautiful Rathaus.

Bietigheim Another well preserved walled town, Bietigheim possesses a dozen or so important buildings. The Renaissance Hornmoldhaus and the 14th-century Unteres Tor gate-house are perhaps the most magnificent.

Esslingen Just to the southeast of Stuttgart on the River Neckar, Esslingen is best known for its 13th-century Stadtkirche St Dionys with its medieval stained-glass windows and the 16th-century Burg, within whose towered walls stands the eponymous vineyard. The half-timbered medieval Rathaus from the first half of the 15th century is equally remarkable. This beautiful old town is an essential stop in any tour of Württemberg.

Heilbronn The outskirts of Heilbronn are dominated by unexceptional suburbs and light industry but the old town boasts a handful of interesting old buildings. The most important of these is the 16th-century Kilianskirche. Its western tower, decorated with sculptures of Bosch-like figures and monk-apes is reason enough to visit the town.

Ludwigsburg This town grew around the baroque Schloss Ludwigsburg which was the seat of the Herzogen von Württemberg. Construction of the Schloss took almost a century (1704–97), developing from a modest hunting lodge into a vast palace. Days could be spent exploring the numerous chambers. The surrounding park, the

Geraniums spill from the window boxes of a classic 17th-century house in Nordheim.

Märchengarten or fairy-tale garden, fully deserves its name. By contrast the classical Schloss Monrepos (1760–65) remained modest in scale. It is now the home of Carl Herzog von Württemberg's wine estate, the Württembergische Hofkammer-Kellerei.

Markgröningen Among dozens of beautifully preserved old buildings in this magical town, the monumental half-timbered Rathaus (part-Renaissance, part-17th-century) is perhaps the finest.

Maulbronn The former Cistercian monastery of Kloster Maulbronn was made famous by Hermann Hesse's Novel *Unterm Rad* (The Prodigy). His description is precise and realistic and those familiar with the book will easily recognise it. Maulbronn was founded in 1115 but most of what remains is high-Gothic, dating from the 15th century.

Öhringen The origins of this small town lie in the Stone Age. The remains of two Roman castles built here can still be seen. The Renaissance Schloss of the Fürsten Hohenlohe-Öhringen now serves as the Town Hall and the town church (1554) belongs to the same period.

Schöntal The former Cistercian Abbey of Kloster Schöntal is one of the most important Renaissance and baroque buildings in Württemberg. The drive up the narrow winding Jagst Valley is worth undertaking for its own sake.

Stuttgart This city has everything: great historic monuments, fine modern architecture, industry, art – and wine. In the centre of town is the 16th-century Renaissance Altes Schloss with its three massive towers and three-storey arcades around the central courtyard. It now houses the Württembergische Landesmuseum (open Tuesday to Sunday, 10am to 5pm) with its fine collection of Roman artifacts, medieval altars and Art Nouveau. Next door is the French-style baroque Neues Schloss which stands in the beautiful Schlossgarten park. A short distance to the west of the city lies the rococo palace of Schloss Solitude (1763–67) which has recently been carefully restored. It mimics the style of the Würzburg's Residenz, but on a less bombastic scale. In complete contrast to these buildings the Neue Staatsgallerie, designed by James Sterling and opened in 1984, stands on sloping ground between Konrad-Adenauer-Strasse and the Urbanstrasse with ramps connecting its various levels. The main collection and the regular special exhibitions here are reason enough to travel to Stuttgart.

Tübingen Situated just to the south of the Schönbuch National Park,

perched on hills directly above the River Neckar, Tübingen is one of the best preserved medieval and Renaissance towns in Germany. Its architectural riches are too numerous to describe here in detail. The mighty Renaissance Schloss Hohentübingen, with its stunning grounds including the famous Platanenallee on an island in the Neckar, should not be missed; neither should the old town itself.

HOTELS AND RESTAURANTS

Insel-Hotel
Friedrich-Ebert-Brücke,
74072 **Heilbronn**
Tel: (07131) 6300,
Fax: (07131) 626060
This fine hotel is perfectly situated on a small island in the Neckar between the main railway station and the old town.

Schlosshotel Monrepos
Schloss Monrepos
71634 **Ludwigsburg**
Tel: (07141) 3020,
Fax: (07141) 302200
This luxurious hotel lives up to the grandeur implied by its name.

Restaurant Delice
Hauptstätterstrasse 61,
70178 **Stuttgart**
Tel: (0711) 6403222
Chef Friedrich Gutscher's one-man show in this miniature restaurant (12–15 covers) is dazzling. Stuttgart's best restaurant offers creative modern cuisine at moderate prices. Reservation is essential. Sommelier Frank Kämmer's cellar offers over 500 wines and a wide range is served by the glass.

Restaurant Herzog Carl Eugen
Schloss Solitude (Kavaliersbau Nr 2),
70597 **Stuttgart**
Tel: (0711) 6990745,
Fax: (0711) 6990771
This restaurant's astonishingly comprehensive wine list and its magnificent situation give it plenty of

appeal. The cooking is good but the prices are high.

Weinhaus Stetter
Rosenstrasse 32,
70182 **Stuttgart**
Tel: 0711 240163
Of the many wine restaurants in Stuttgart this offers the best selection of the region's produce.

Restaurant Wielandshöhe
Alte Weinsteige,
70597 **Stuttgart-Degerloch**
Tel: (0711) 6408848,
Fax: (0711) 6409408
Just to the south of Stuttgart, Vincent Klink runs a luxurious and stylish restaurant where the cooking is as good as the ambience. The style is modern and cosmopolitan but local ingredients are used where possible. Sommelier Bernd Kreis is one of Germany's best.

Wald- & Schlosshotel Friedrichsruhe (also Restaurant)
74639 Friedrichsruhe
(near **Öhringen**)
Tel: (07941) 60870,
Fax: (07941) 61468
Six kilometres to the north of Öhringen in park-like gardens lies one of Germany's most luxurious country hotels, though Schloss Friedrichsruhe is more famous for its superb restaurant. Lothar Eiermann is a top chef and whether he serves a classic or an innovative dish the same high standard applies. In spite of its distance from the nearest salt-water source, the sea food is excellent. The wine list offers everything from local Riesling to California's best. By no stretch of the imagination could the menu be described as cheap, but it is not overpriced.

Hotel Krone
Uhlandstrasse 1,
72072 **Tübingen**
Tel: (07071) 31036,
Fax: (07071) 38718
The imposing but comfortable Renaissance-style Krone enjoys a

The small town of Erlenbach, at the heart of Württemberg's wine region, seems far removed from the industrial centre of nearby Heilbronn.

perfect location between the main railway station and the Neckar.

Restaurant Waldhorn
Schönbuchstrasse 49,
72074 **Tübingen**
Tel: (07071) 61270,
Fax: (07071) 610581
Ulrich Schilling's creative modern cuisine is complemented by a superb, moderately priced wine list.

USEFUL ADDRESSES

Kultur- und Freizeitamt Esslingen
Marktplatz 16,
73728 **Esslingen am Neckar**
Tel: (0711) 3512441

Städtisches Verkehrsamt Heilbronn
Rathaus, Marktplatz,
74072 **Heilbronn**
Tel: (07131) 562270

Fremdenverkehrsamt Ludwigsburg
Wilhelmstrasse 12,
71638 **Ludwigsburg**
Tel: (07141) 910252

Tourist-Information Stuttgart
Königstrasse 1a,
70173 **Stuttgart**
Tel: (0711) 2228240,
Fax: (0711) 2228251

Verkehrsverein Tübingen
An der Eberhardsbrücke,
72074 **Tübingen**
Tel: (07071) 35011,
Fax: (07071) 35070

Baden

While many of Germany's wine regions have had difficulty finding markets in recent years, Baden's leading producers have enjoyed notable commercial success. The region's clever promotional campaigns have undoubtedly helped to raise domestic interest in its wines but there are other good reasons. One is the fact that, of all 13 regions, Baden is best able to produce dry white wines which appeal to international tastes, to lovers of French, Italian and New World white wines.

In spite of this they have a style that is entirely their own. Although Alsace is just across the Rhine in France and many of the same grapes are cultivated in both regions, little expertise is needed to tell their wines apart. Baden's are fruitier, crisper, less weighty and 'winey' than their counterparts from the opposite bank. Wine-drinkers outside Germany are only just beginning to discover the remarkable qualities of the region's best products.

This style is a result of German winemaking traditions combined with a climate similar to that of Alsace. Most of Baden's vineyards are situated on the foothills of the Black Forest where it descends in to the Rhine Rift Valley. The peaks of the Black Forest behind provide not only a breathtaking natural backdrop but also extremely effective protection against cold easterly winds. The Vosges Mountains in France catch much of the rain from the wet westerly air streams. This makes the Upper Rhine Valley between Karlsruhe and Basel an agricultural paradise: all manner of fruit trees, asparagus and vines benefit from the warm dry climate. As a result, Baden is the only German wine-growing region to be classed by the EU as within Viticultural Zone B. Germany's 12 other regions are classed as Zone A, the coolest category, which they share only with Luxembourg's vineyards.

Baden however is a large sprawling region which, though uniformly classed as Zone B, is subject to a variety of climates. Between Karlsruhe and Heidelberg lies the Kraichgau, which has some isolated vineyards in the Neckar Valley to the East. From Heidelberg north lies the Badische Bergstrasse, separated from the Hessiche Bergstrasse only by political anomaly (Badische and Hessiche used jointly to form the Bergstrasse wine region). These vineyards in the north have much in common with the main body of the region to the south, but the vines in Badisches Frankenland

Baden wines owe their full-bodied dry style to the region's warm, sunny climate.

195

Even where vineyards are not organically cultivated, alternatives to chemical treatments are preferred. Here at Neuweier, weeds are mown rather than being sprayed with herbicides.

on the River Tauber grow under conditions virtually identical to those of nearby Franken. The high-altitude vineyards at Singen and around the Bodensee (Lake Constance) in the far south have a completely different climate again.

Throughout the region vineyards tend to be planted on hillsides with westerly or southerly exposure and the very best slopes are just as steep as the top sites of the Mosel Valley. Soil types are varied, ranging from stony volcanic tephrite and weathered granite to chalk and loess. This, together with the microclimatic variation, creates conditions in which many different grape varieties can flourish. The various members of the Pinot family, Riesling, Traminer and Gewürztraminer, Muskateller and Scheurebe can all give first-class wines.

Perhaps the most important of these varieties is the Pinot family of grapes from Burgundy, which together account for nearly half of Baden's 16,425 hectares of vineyard. The region is best-known for its dry Ruländer (Grauburgunder) and Weissburgunder. More full-bodied and supple than dry German Riesling can ever be, these varieties have felt the fullest benefit of the fashion for dry wines which has prevailed in Germany for the last two decades. Predestined for the dinner table yet harmonious enough to drink by themselves, they are the foundation of Baden's success during the 1980s and 1990s.

As in Alsace, Weissburgunder's commercial importance is a relatively new phenomenon. In both regions, though Chasselas or Gutedel and Silvaner are the traditional grapes for everyday drinking, the acreage of Weissburgunder is expanding mainly at Silvaner's expense. Ruländer (Grauburgunder) however has been an important grape in Baden for centuries. In the southern half of of the region it gives the country's most impressive results. Baden Ruländer usually has between 12 and 14 degrees of alcohol, a full degree more than comparable dry Weissburgunder, but it can have even more. The best examples share melted butter and nutty aromas but have quite a different fruit character. Good Weissburgunders tend to develop apricot- and pineapple-like aromas while the typical aromas of fine Grauburgunder are melon and exotic fruits. At the highest levels of richness and alcoholic content, Grauburgunder can smell and taste like honey, even when it is bone dry.

During the last 20 years the style of the region's white wines has shifted towards clean and crisp but the change in style of Pinot Gris wines has been more dramatic. As Ruländer it was often like a caricature of the Tokay d'Alsace wines from across the Rhine: deep gold in colour, heavy, bitter and cloyingly sweet. The best examples had a rich honey and toast character and were dry enough to drink with food, but such wines were few and far between. Around the end of the 1970s, as heavy old Ruländer was becoming less popular (especially with the younger generation of German wine drinkers), some of the region's leading vintners began to experiment with a new style. In order to differentiate this pale, fresh, fruity wine from the old-style Ruländer, it was labelled Grauburgunder. Both the new name, which gave the wines the image of lightness in the minds of German consumers, and the new style were a great success: a fashionable wine was created from an unfashionable grape.

Unfortunately, nothing in the Wine Law prevents vintners from selling Ruländer-style wines as Grauburgunder and vice versa, so neither name is an infallible guarantee of a particular style of wine. In practice, confusion between the wines is not too common and this unofficial classification of wine styles works rather well.

Baden

		Wine centre
		Autobahn
		Main road
		Other roads
		Railway
		International boundary
		Landersgrenze
		Regierungsbezirksgrenze

1 Grosssachsen
2 Dossenheim
3 Impfingen
4 Dittigheim
5 Gerlachsheim
6 Beckstein
7 Dainbach
8 Klepsau
9 Dielheim
10 Malsch
11 Eichtersheim
12 Königschaffhausen
13 Oberbergen
14 Merdingen
15 Efringen-Kirchen
16 Grenzach

1:1000 000

197

New fermentation techniques result in richly spiced, fruity Spätburgunder reds.

A similarly important transformation is currently taking place with the region's Spätburgunder reds. These used to be either pale, brown and sweet-sour or to taste of rather jammy fruit. They lacked the perfume or silkiness of the grapes' best wines. Since the beginning of the 1980s vintners have been experimenting with fermenting their red wines on the skins and maturing them in new or newish oak barrels similar to those used in Burgundy. While only a few vintners have so far mastered this deliberately Burgundian style, the best results from recent vintages have been impressive.

Because this change in style demands considerable investment in fermentation tank capacity and oak barrels, it is taking longer to effect than the development of the new Pinot Gris style, which required no extra technology. However, every year more vintners and co-operatives are making these investments for at least part of their production. Given Baden's 4,250 hectares of Spätburgunder, the region's potential for quality red-wine production is enormous.

Spätburgunder would never have achieved this importance were it not for the fact that Baden has a great tradition for rosé wines. These vary from pale, fruity wines with around 11.5 degrees of alcohol to rich powerful wines with 13–14 degrees. In the past they were usually sweet, but a good proportion (including all the best examples) are now vinified dry. Rosé used to be one of the region's strengths, but determined efforts to improve red-wine quality have all too often been at the expense of the rosés. In order to produce first-class red wines, any grapes affected by botrytis must be excluded, since their presence would affect the wines' colour and fruit. Some vintners use all the best clean grapes for red wine, leaving the botrytized grapes for their rosés which, as a result, have an amber colour and a crude caramel-raisin character. Top-class examples, such as those made by Salwey in Oberrotweil (Kaiserstuhl) or Wolff Metternich in Durbach (Ortenau), have the typical appealing pink hue and vibrant cherry-like fruit.

Covering just over eight percent of the country's vineyard area, Riesling became an important grape variety during the 1980s. Previously it was hardly found outside the slopes of the Ortenau between Baden-Baden and Offenburg, but some Riesling is now grown in all Baden's sub-areas. Many of these vineyards are small and to some extent experimental, having been planted to test the grape's potential in places where it had no track record. Strangely the most northerly parts of the region have so far produced few successful examples, the best made by the Seeger estate of Leimen close to Heidelberg and Reichsgraf und Marquis zu Hoensbroech of Michelfeld in the Kraichgau.

Baden's finest dry and naturally sweet Rieslings, as well as powerful Gewürztraminers, are grown on the steep, stony granite slopes of Durbach.

Real Riesling country begins just south of Baden-Baden in the Ortenau. The stony weathered granite soils of the vineyards here are ideally suited to the vine. They give wines with body and richness comparable with those of the Pfalz but with entirely different aromas and an elegance reminiscent of the best Rheingau and Rheinhessen Rieslings.

The recent fashion for dry Weissburgunder and Grauburgunder wines, the best of which come from Kaiserstuhl to the south, has tended to focus popular and critical attention elsewhere and these remarkable wines remain under-appreciated. The German wine-drinker looking for good dry Riesling will normally think of the Rheingau, Pfalz or Franken first, while wine-lovers in the English-speaking world think of the Mosel-Saar-Ruwer when looking for top-quality sweet Rieslings. Neither group seem to be aware that the Ortenau can compete at the highest level in both styles and is blessed with a string of estates and co-operatives making good- to excellent-quality Rieslings.

The heart of the Ortenau is the wine town of Durbach, situated in the valley of the eponymous stream which flows from east to

west from the forested mass of the Mooswald (part of the Black Forest) down to the Rhine. It is a charming wine town without pretension or kitsch. The population as a whole takes wine seriously even though for most it does not represent their principal source of income. Unusually for Baden, there are three aristocratic estates based here – the Markgraf von Baden (Schloss Staufenberg), Freiherr von Neveu and Graf Wolff Metternich – and a general awareness that the town's vineyards are something special.

The undulating vine-clad hills on the northern side of the valley, crowned with pine forest, enjoy a generally southerly exposure and are almost perfectly sheltered from cold winds by the surrounding hills. Most of these vineyards belong to the Plauelrain site, the best parts of which can match the high-quality potential of other small sites such as Schloss Grohl and Schlossberg. Taken together these constitute the most southerly top-class Riesling vineyard in Germany. Wines from here can possess explosive peach- and apricot-like fruit, often complemented by pineapple, citrus and almond notes. Their racy acidity makes them sleek and elegant rather than lush or extravagant and they are the most refined white wines in Baden.

Durbach has a tradition of quality-wine production stretching back more than 200 years. The first Riesling vineyard was planted at the Markgraf von Baden's Schloss Staufenberg estate in 1776. In 1782 the Markgraf planted another Riesling vineyard on the Klingelberg, from which the Ortenau synonym for Riesling, Klingelberger, originates. Gewürztraminer, known locally as Clevner, has been here several centuries longer and has proved itself no less suited to these vineyards. With its fine rose-water bouquet and vibrant interplay of rich fruit and clean acidity it could hardly be more different from the often massive and opulent Gewurztraminers of Alsace. Andreas Laible, Heinrich Männle and Graf Wolff Metternich are the leading producers, although both Schloss Staufenberg and the village co-operative maintain good standards. Metternich, Männle and Laible also make remarkable Scheurebe wines that bear some resemblance to Durbach's Rieslings but have an added blackcurrant note.

Established in 1950 as a wine research centre, Schloss Ortenberg, with excellent vineyards and a modern cellar, sets exemplary winemaking standards.

Ortenau

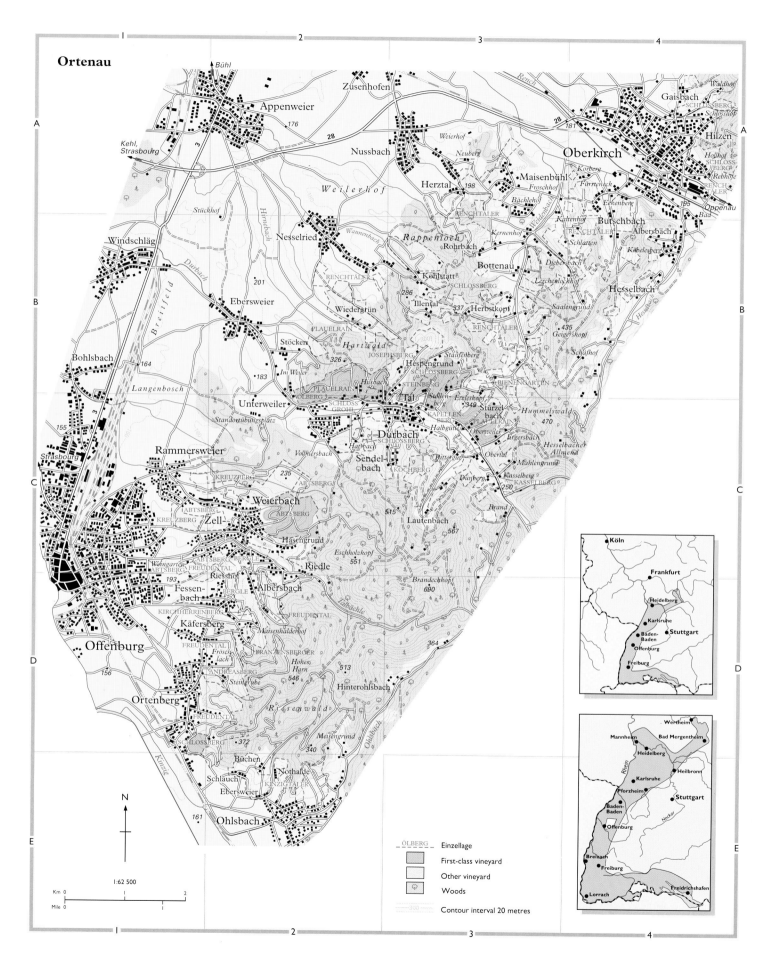

Bühl
Zusenhofen
Appenweier
176
Kehl,
Strasbourg
28
Nussbach
Weierhof
Gaisbach
SCHLOSSBERG
Schlosshof
28
181
Hilzen
Oberkirch
Weilerhof
Neuberg
Maisenbühl
Korberg
Hollhof
SCHLOSSBERG
Rebhofe
RENCHTÄLER
Herztal
198
Froschhof
Fürsteneck
Windschläg
Stückhof
Wannenbach
RENCHTÄLER
Bächlehof
Kaltenhof
Eckenberg
Butschbach
195
Oppenau
Bad
Nesselried
201
Rappenloch
Rohrbach
Kernenhof
Schlatten
Albersbach
Dieberbach
Kobelesberg
Hesselbach
Ebersweier
RENCHTÄLER
Kohlstatt
SCHLOSSBERG
Lerchenlolfhof
Wiedergrün
286
Illental
337
Herbstkopf
Saalengrund
435
Bohlsbach
164
PLAUELRAIN
Hartwald
326
JOSEPHSBERG
Staufenberg
Hespengrund
SCHLOSSBERG
STEINBERG
Geigerskopf
Schafhof
Langenbosch
183
Im Weiler
Hilsbach
BIENENGARTEN
Unterweiler
KOLBERG
PLAUELRAIN
SCHLOSS
GROHL
Tal
Süllen-
berg
Erzleskopf
349
Stürzel-
bach
PLAUELRAIN
Oberweiler
Hummelswald
470
155
Standortübungsplatz
KAPELLEN-
BERG
Halbgütel
Durmh
Ergersbach
Hesselbacher
Allmend
Strasbourg
Durbach
SCHLOSSBERG
Rittersau
Obertal
Mahlengrund
Rammersweier
Vollmersbach
Hatschbach
KOCHBERG
Dinpberg
Kasselberg
KASSELBERG
KREUZBERG
Sendel-
bach
Oberial
250
235
ABTSBERG
Kasselberg
KASSELBERG
Weierbach
KREUZBERG
ABTSBERG
ABTSBERG
Brand
515
Lautenbach
567
Zell-
Hasengrund
Eschholzkopf
551
Weingarten
ABTSBERG BERGLE
FREUDENTAL
Riedle
Brandeckkopf
690
193
Riesshof
Albersbach
Tälbächle
Fessen-
bach
BERGLE
FREUDENTAL
KIRCHHERRENBERG
Käfersberg
Maisenhälderhof
364
Offenburg
FREUDENTAL
Fröschlach
ANDREASBERG
Hohes
Horn
513
156
Steingrube
546
Hinterohlsbach
Ortenberg
FREUDENTAL
Riesenwald
SCHLOSSBERG
372
Meisengrund
340
Kinzig
Büchen
Schlauch
Nothalde
KINZIGTÄLER
Ebersweier
KINZIGTÄLER
161
Ohlsbach

N
1:62 500
Km 0   2
Mile 0   1

ÖLBERG — Einzellage
First-class vineyard
Other vineyard
Woods
Contour interval 20 metres

Köln
Frankfurt
Heidelberg
Karlsruhe
Baden-
Baden
Stuttgart
Offenburg
Freiburg

Wertheim
Mannheim
Bad Mergentheim
Heidelberg
Rhein
Heilbronn
Karlsruhe
Pforzheim
Stuttgart
Baden-
Baden
Neckar
Offenburg
Breisach
Freiburg
Lorrach
Freidrichshafen

The best vineyards of Zell-Weierbach and Ortenberg just to the south have a similar potential for Riesling. The soil is deeper and less stony than in Durbach, resulting in wines that are rather more powerful and less filigree. The wines of the Freiherr von Franckenstein estate (whose name was used by Mary Shelley in her famous novel) offer strong competition even to the best Durbachers. The steep terraced vineyards of Ortenberg's Schlossberg vineyard have a similar potential, which the Schloss Ortenberg wine research estate is determined to realise.

The only other vineyards in the Ortenau capable of yielding white wines to match these lie further north between the towns of Bühl and Baden-Baden. Here there are several vineyards with fine reputations for Riesling, most notably the Mauerberg and Schlossberg of Neuweier. Their reputations were made by the Schloss Neuweier estate whose enthusiastic new owner, Gisela Joos, has restored it to its leading position among producers in this part of the Ortenau. Good wines are also made by the Steinbach-Varnhalt, the Neuweier co-operatives and the large Affenthaler co-operative of Eisental, whose best dry Rieslings from the Bühler Wolfhag can almost compete with those of Schloss Neuweier.

The Ortenau also has a strong tradition for Spätburgunder red wines. While these cannot match the power of the Spätburgunders from the Kaiserstuhl, they can possess a vibrant cherry- and blackberry-like fruit. The problem with Pinot Noir here is that it is easy to capture the fruity charm of the grape but far harder to produce 'serious' red wines with the depth and structure that enable

Above: A Sasbachwalden harvest in full swing. The co-operative's Spätburgunder reds are light but packed with fruit.

Left: Red wine plays an important role at Durbach in the Ortenau.

The warmest vineyards lie on the south face of the flat-topped Kaiserstuhl. The village of Ihringen, overlooked by its vines, takes pride in the red wines it produces from the iron-rich volcanic slopes.

them to age. The Heinrich Männle and Wolff Metternich estates in Durbach and the co-operative of Fessenbach just to the south-east of Offenburg make the best examples of this style. The Kappelrodeck, Sasbachwalden and Affenthal co-operatives also make solid Spätburgunder wines for everyday drinking. Strangely, although the area is successful with the Spätburgunder, the grape's close relatives Weissburgunder and Grauburgunder rarely impress. Perhaps the soils here are just too poor and stony. Whatever the reason, they cannot begin to compete with the Weissburgunder and Grauburgunder wines from the Kaiserstuhl further south.

The Kaiserstuhl, or Emperor's Throne, is the massive stump of an ancient volcano which rises majestically out of the plain of the Rhine Rift Valley. Its landscape is at once beautiful and bizarre. Many of the Kaiserstuhl's best vineyards are precipitously steep and cut in to a jumble of small terraces which hug the twisting contours of these hills. Below them stretch orchards and fields, above them rise forested slopes and finally the green peaks of the Katharinenberg and the Totenkopf. The bizarre elements in this picture are the huge terraces which have replaced many of the original vineyards. Looking like giant steps leading to the throne of the Kaiserstuhl, they were constructed as part of the *Fluerbereinigung* (vineyard reorganisation) during the 1970s and 1980s. They enable vines which previously had to be tended by hand to be cultivated entirely mechanically. The effects of such massive reorganisation on microclimates – and on the local land-scape – are clearly far-reaching.

Climatic conditions are so propitious here that vines cover almost all the land that is not already forested or developed. This is one of the warmest and driest corners of Germany and it is a poor vintage when noble grapes from good sites do not give wines with 13 or more degrees of natural alcohol. Body and weight are Kaiserstuhl wines' strong suit. However the range of grape varieties, in which the traditional Silvaner and work-horse Müller-Thurgau play a significant role, indicates that even in this favoured corner of Germany there are considerable differences between the wines from the best vineyards and the rest.

However warm and southerly the vineyard, noble grapes give remarkable wines only when planted on the best-exposed slopes. The soil type also plays an important role, since in many places the original volcanic tephrite rock has been covered with a thick layer of yellowish loess. Loess is a compacted powdery material, originally carried by the wind from Central Asia many thousands of years ago, and in the Kaiserstuhl loess deposits can be many metres deep. Unlike Riesling, Weissburgunder and Grauburgunder can give good wines when grown on it, but when planted on tephrite they are far more expressive and harmonious. They gain not only a distinctive mineral 'spice' from the soil, but are richer in texture and more succulent. A Grauburgunder from loess with 14 degrees of alcohol is massive and assertive, while a wine of the same alcoholic content from a top site with volcanic soil is rich, succulent and supple.

The very best Weissburgunder and Grauburgunder vineyards are situated at the southwestern tip of the Kaiserstuhl. The Achkarrer Schlossberg and the Ihringer Winklerberg are the most outstanding of these. The Winklerberg is the warmest site in Germany, its terraced slopes rising directly and precipitously from the Rhine plain. Its southwesterly aspect allows the vines to

Kaiserstuhl and Tuniberg

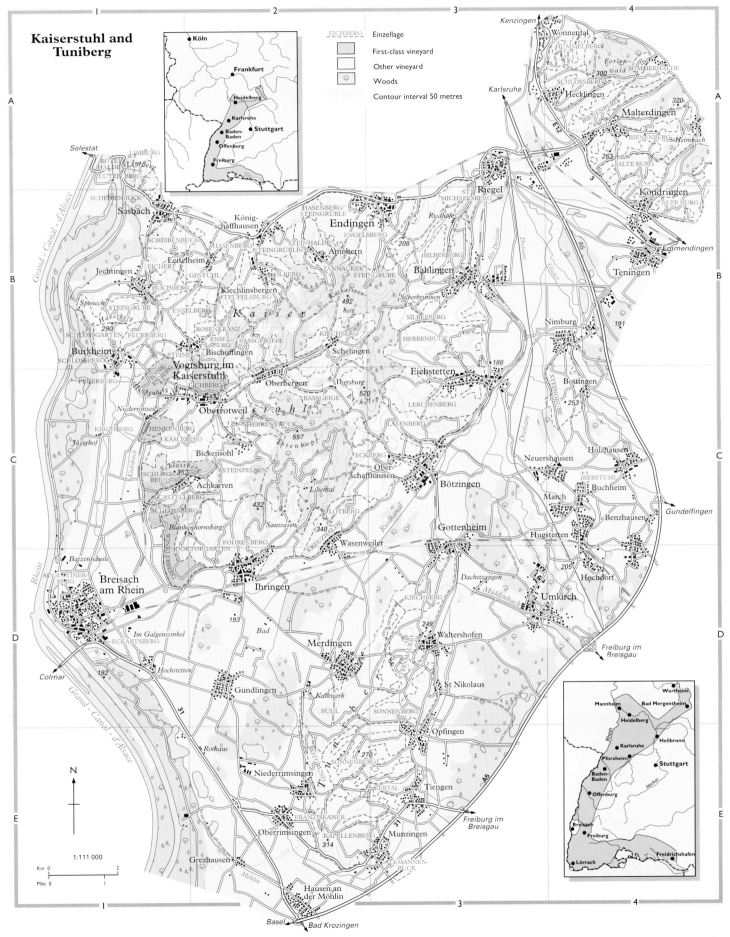

EICHBERG Einzellage

First-class vineyard

Other vineyard

Woods

Contour interval 50 metres

Köln

Frankfurt

Heidelberg

Karlsruhe

Baden-Baden

Offenburg

Stuttgart

Freiburg

Selestat

ROTE HALDE
LUTZELBERG
Limburg

SCHELINGENBUCK

Sasbach

Königschaffhausen

HASENBERG
STEINGRÜBLE

Endingen

Riedhöfe

Riegel

MICHAELSBERG

Kenzingen

Wonnental
HIMMELBERG

Forlenwald
SOMMERHALDE

300

SCHLOSSBERG

Karlsruhe

Hecklingen

BIENENBERG

Malterdingen

320

BIENENBERG
Heimbach

263

ALTE BURG

Köndringen

ALTE BURG

Emmendingen

Teningen

SCHEIBENBUCK

HASENBERG
STEINGRÜBLE

Eichstetten

SCHEIBENBUCK

Leiselheim

Jechtingen

EICHERT

GESTÜHL

Amoltern

Bahlingen

SILBERBERG

Nimburg

191

HOCHBERG

STEINHALDE
STEINGRÜBLE

TANNACKER
STEINGRUBE

Katharinenberg

492

Silberbrünnen

SILBERBERG

HERRENBUCK

STEINGRUBE

253

Bottingen

KIECHLINSBERGEN
TEUFELSBURG

ENSELBERG

ROSENKRANZ
FEUERBERG

ENSELBERG

BASSGEIGE

KIRCHBERG

Schelingen

188

Eichstetten

LERCHENBERG

Burkheim

SCHLOSSGARTEN
FEUERBERG

STEIN

Bischoffingen

Vogtsburg im Kaiserstuhl

EICHBERG

Oberbergen

Vogtsburg

520

BASSGEIGE

LASENBERG

Neuershausen

Holzhausen

FEUERBERG

Niederrotweil

Oberrotweil

HERRENSTUCK

Eichelspitze

557

KIRCHBERG

HENKENBERG
KÄSLEBERG

Jägerhof

Bickensohl

Eidkopf

ECKBERG

Oberschaffhausen

KREBSTUHL

Buchheim

Schlossberg
SCHLOSSBERG

352

STEINFELSEN

Bötzingen

March

Achkarren

CASTELLBERG

SCHLOSSBERG

Lilienthal

432

Benzhausen

Blankenhornsberg

WINKLERBERG

Sauwasen

340

Gottenheim

Hugstetten

205

FOHRENBERG

DOKTORGARTEN

KREUZHALDE

Wasenweiler

Hochdorf

Batzenhäusle

Rhein

ALTE
BURKHEINER
BERG

Breisach am Rhein

DREIBETTENEN

Ihringen

Dachswangen

Mühlenbach

Umkirch

193

Bad

KIRCHBERG

249

Freiburg im Breisgau

Im Galgenwinkel

ECKARTSBERG

Merdingen

Waltershofen

Colmar

192

Hochstetten

St Nikolaus

31

Gündlingen

Kalkwerk

SONNENBERG

Opfingen

BÜHL

Rothaus

270

SONNENBERG

Wertheim

Mannheim

Bad Mergentheim

Heidelberg

Heilbronn

Rhein

Karlsruhe

Pforzheim

Stuttgart

Neckar

Baden-Baden

Offenburg

Breisach

Freiburg

Lörrach

Freidrichshafen

Niederrimsingen

REBTAL

Tiengen

FRANZISKANER

KAPELLENBERG

Oberrimsingen

Munzingen

Freiburg im Breisgau

ALEMANNEN-BUCK

314

Grezhausen

Möhlin

Hausen an der Möhlin

N

1:111 000

Km 0 — 2

Mile 0 — 1

Basel Bad Krozingen

203

bask in the sun until late evening in summer. Paradoxically, the cultivation of such steep sites is a relatively new phenomenon in the Kaiserstuhl, vineyard plantings in the area having been limited until the beginning of the 19th century to flat or gently sloping ground with loess soils. The first vines in the Winklerberg (which was once a quarry) were planted in 1814 and those in the Achkarrer Schlossberg in 1851. The success of the Winklerberg wines, which immediately commanded prices many times those of the area's standard wines, proved the superiority of the volcanic soils and steeply sloping sites. Such prices were more than enough to compensate for the physical difficulty and expense involved in cultivating such vineyards.

Here more than anywhere else in Baden, drought stress is a greater danger than lack of ripeness. The best vintages are characterised by the right combination of sun and rain, rather than simply being those with the hottest summers. A cool, wet summer causes leading vintners of the Kaiserstuhl few worries, because the area's best sites rarely give wines with any hint of greenness or unripe fruit flavours. Even in lesser vintages such as 1987 and 1984, good wines of Kabinett quality and some Spätlese could be made from the noble grapes.

The best part of the Winklerberg is divided among the Dr Heger, Gebrüder Müller and Stigler estates, while most of the Schlossberg is cultivated by Achkarrer's fine co-operative.

Slightly to the north, Bickensohl, Oberrotweil, Bischoffingen, Burkheim, Sasbach and Königschaffhausen also produce plenty of good Weissburgunder and Grauburgunder. Among these, Oberrotweil in the Eichberg, a steep south-facing terraced slope overlooking the town, has the best vineyards, the Henkenberg and Kirchberg.

Both the Freiherr von Gleichenstein and Salwey estates produce good wines from here although they seldom match the best from the Winklerberg. A more remarkable achievement is the quality of wines produced by the Bercher estate from a range of varieties in the rather unremarkable vineyards of Burkheim. Karl Heinz Johner's success in Bischoffingen is similarly striking. He founded his estate in 1985 to pioneer the vinification of German wine in new French oak *barriques* and became one of the Kaiserstuhl's star winemakers almost immediately. While the Bercher brothers and Joachim Heger have also mastered this style of winemaking in recent years, Johner remains Germany's most consistent producer of oak-aged white and red wines.

The production of 'serious' Spätburgunder reds in the Kaiserstuhl is a recent phenomenon, dating only from the late 1980s. A large proportion of the Spätburgunder crop used to be used for rosé or made into unremarkable red wines. This makes it difficult to gauge how close the best examples – wines such as Karl Heinz Johner's 1990 'SJ', Dr Heger's 1990 Auslese Trocken

Three Star and the Berchers' 1992 Spätlese Trocken 'SE' – come to realising the optimum possible here. Most experts seem to feel there is potential for even better wines. If this is correct, then it may be that in 20 or 30 years' time the Kaiserstuhl will be better known for its Pinot Noirs, already the biggest and richest red wines in Germany, than its Weissburgunders and Grauburgunders.

Just to the northeast of the Kaiserstuhl in Malterdingen in the Breisgau, Bernhard Huber has made some remarkably powerful fleshy Spätburgunder reds since 1990. The limestone soil here is arguably even better suited to Pinot Noir than the Kaiserstuhl's volcanic rock. Malterdingen may not be well known now, but two and three centuries ago its wines were widely exported to neighbouring countries. At present the Breisgau is also the source of the best Spätburgunder rosés in southern Baden. The Salwey estate produces elegant, filigree wines from its vineyards in the Glottertal to the northwest of the city of Freiburg.

Between Freiburg and the Kaiserstuhl lie the vineyards of the Tuniberg. This small range of low chalk hills has a loess soil similar to much of the Kaiserstuhl. Good but unspectacular medium-bodied Weissburgunder and Grauburgunder are produced here alongside simple Müller-Thurgau and Silvaner wines. Perhaps the best wines from the Tuniberg are the Spätburgunder reds from the steep terraces of the Munzinger Kappellenberg site at its southern tip. The Dr Heger estate makes the best of these from bought-in grapes, and sells them under the Weinhaus Heger label. For white wines, the often neglected eastern flank of the Kaiserstuhl, traditionally regarded as inferior to the western side, is more interesting. The co-operative winery of Bötzingen has become a reliable source of richly fruity dry Weissburgunder in recent years.

No description of the Kaiserstuhl and surrounding area would be complete without mentioning the Badische Winzerkeller, the regional wine co-operative and Europe's largest winery. Situated just to the east of Breisach, this huge complex makes wines from roughly 4,500 hectares of vineyards scattered throughout Baden. The problem facing this massive organisation is that it has to take the grapes it is given and market a range of wines covering almost the entire quality spectrum.

From Freiburg southward to Basel, vineyards are more widely scattered, the rolling hills as frequently covered with fruit trees or forest as with vineyards. There are few remarkable vineyard sites here and light dry white wines from the Gutedel grape make up the bulk of production. In spite of its name, literally 'good-noble', Gutedel is no more than the humble Chasselas. This ancient grape used to be responsible for the everyday drinking wines of Alsace, but it has been almost completely replaced by Silvaner and Pinot Blanc. In Switzerland it is responsible for Fendant, a rather characterless dry white made appealing only by a spritz of carbon dioxide and views of Alpine peaks. While the grape can yield rather

Top: Gutedel reigns in the Staufen vineyards of the Markgräflerland.
Above: 'Old-fashioned' narrow terraces near Burkheim.
Left: The silhouette of the Kaiserstuhl, massive stump of an extinct volcano.

The rolling hills of the Markgräflerland, best known for its light Gutedel whites.

better wines in the Markgräflerland, they are never more than pleasant thirst-quenchers in warm weather; attempts to make richer more complex wines from the grape have come to nothing. The Nobling vine cross is no better, producing at best light, reasonably crisp white wines with a slightly nutty character. Both the wines are best enjoyed locally with simple food or by themselves as refreshing thirst-quenchers.

The best white wines from this part of Baden are undoubtedly dry Weissburgunders. The chalky soils are well suited to this vine, giving wines which combine body with some elegance. There is also a significant red wine potential which has yet to be fully realised. Spätburgunders from Schlossgut Istein and the Ehrenstetten co-operative have shown that the grape can yield wines with rich fruit and a supple tannin structure, but the winemaking falls far short of that in the best Kaiserstuhl estates. Perhaps a prominent success for one producer would provide the impetus needed to encourage others, just as Karl Heinz Johner's Pinot Noir was the catalyst among Kaiserstuhl winemakers. At present, half-hearted experiments with new-oak ageing are producing rather disappointing results.

The small vineyard area around the Bodensee has arguably even more potential than the Markgräflerland to produce distinctive wines. Among the most picturesque in the region, they produce light, crisp, fruity wines largely as a result of the cool climate. The vineyards are between 400 and 560 metres above sea level. Spring arrives here rather later than in the main body of Baden's vineyards, which means the growing season is shorter than in the Upper Rhine Valley. Many of the best sites lie on slopes that rise directly from the northern bank of the lake. Mist that often hangs over the water also reduces the amount of sun they receive.

Here as in the Mittelrhein, some places on the Mosel, Rüdesheim and the Rheingau, the success of the Bodensee itself as a tourist location threatens the development of quality winemaking. A great deal of wine is made with undemanding consumers in mind. There is no denying that a panorama of snow-capped mountains across shimmering waters helps mediocre wines to taste better than they actually are.

When they are good however they are perfect summer wines, lighter in body than the norm in Baden with fresh fruit aromas and refreshing acidity. The high humidity makes red wine a difficult proposition (since it encourages rot) but marvellous Spätburgunder rosé can be made. The Markgraf von Baden's estate based at his Schloss Salem residence, Aufricht and Schloss Rheinburg make the best examples.

No less successful are the Müller-Thurgau and Bacchus wines, particularly those vinified with a touch of sweetness to accentuate

their abundant fruit. Müller-Thurgau is the most widely planted vine in Baden, accounting for a third of the vineyard area. Much of it has been planted in vineyards created during the vineyard reorganisation projects of the 1970s and 1980s. During this period the area under vine in Baden doubled and production quadrupled. Most of the region's everyday drinking wines are now produced from this normally unremarkable grape. However, there are at least a few places where it can give more than simple quaffing wine. Bodensee Müller-Thurgaus can have an almost Riesling-like crispness and elegance. Good examples almost entirely lack the spurious spiciness that afflicts inferior wines from this grape. And Bacchus gives more aromatic wines here, with a healthy acidity that keeps them clean and refreshing.

Few attempts to make more serious dry white wines from Weissburgunder or Grauburgunder have yielded competitive results. One exception is the Weissburgunder from the Staatsweingut Meersburg's wholly-owned Hohentwieler Olgaberg vineyard close to the town of Singen. The Olgaberg used to be called Himmelreich ('Kingdom of Heaven'), a more appropriate name for Germany's highest-altitude vineyard. The volcanic soils of its steep slopes give Weissburgunders with an opulent, almost exotic, fruit and a fascinating spiciness from the soil. The Staatsweingut Meersburg has also made excellent dessert wines from Grauburgunder grapes grown in the top sites of Meersburg, directly on the lake's northern shore. Autumn fogs encourage the

The Meersburg vineyards on the banks of the Bodensee (Lake Constance) can produce dry white and unctuous dessert wines.

development of noble rot and selective harvesting results in Auslese wines with richness and elegance.

The few vineyards scattered at the other end of the Bodensee belong to other regions. Those of Betznau and Gattnau are part of Württemberg and those from Nonnenhorn to Zech belong to Franken. Vines here feel the climatic influence of the mountains just across the border in Austria and only simple wines for everyday drinking can be produced. Müller-Thurgau, Bacchus and Kerner dominate.

In the valley of the Tauber, the northernmost part of the region, conditions are as cool but not as humid as those around the Bodensee. The 800 hectares of vineyards have a continental climate and limestone soils resembling those of nearby Franken. The wines are sold in the Bocksbeutel bottles typical of that region. Müller-Thurgau is again the dominant grape and can give superior wines whose strength is power and richness rather than crispness. The largest producer here, the Beckstein co-operative, is also the best.

If Baden has a problem it is may be in over-ambition. It sometimes seems that vintners and co-operative winery directors plan a new series of premium wines, then try to make the contents of the bottles live up to their stylish packaging, rather than starting with the nuts and bolts of vineyard cultivation and cellar work. Certainly the region produces a large quantity and remarkable variety of fine wines, but perhaps the recent crop of designer wines should be treated with some scepticism.

BENCHMARK WINES

Burkheimer Feuerberg Weissburgunder Spätlese Trocken
Weingut Bercher, Burkheim

Vineyard site: Burkheimer Feuerberg
Site area: 10 hectares, 7 hectares Bercher
Exposure: south
Inclination: sloping
Soil: weathered tephrite (volcanic)
Description: These rich dry Pinot Blancs are made in a full-throttle oak-aged style that makes them excellent and distinctive alternatives to high-class Chardonnays. Their rich, full-bodied texture is ideal for the dinner table and their complex smoke, butter, pineapple and spice character as fascinating as any German Riesling.
Best vintages: '93, '92, '90, '89
Best drunk: Rich fish dishes, lobster, crab and roast veal are all well suited to these Kaiserstuhl bombshells.

Durbacher Plauelrain Riesling Spätlese
Weingut Andreas Laible, Durbach

Vineyard site: Durbacher Plauelrain
Site area: 187.5 hectares, 4 hectares Andreas Laible
Exposure: south
Inclination: steeply sloping
Soil: weathered granite
Description: Baden is perhaps the last place most wine-drinkers would look for top-class sweet Rieslings. However, Durbach's granite soils give wines with enough fruit and mineral character to balance a touch of natural sweetness. This juicy and refreshing wine gives an explosion of peach, melon and almond on the tongue.
Best vintages: '94, '93, '92, '90, '89
Best drunk: Like the naturally sweet Riesling Spätlese of the Mosel and Rhine regions, these wines are best drunk by themselves. For the adventurous however there are some combinations that are worth a try – such as fish and chips.

The buttressed terraces of the first-class Ihringer Winklerberg in the Kaiserstuhl, Germany's warmest vineyard. Its rich, fruity wines have a fascinating mineral acidity.

Durbacher Schlossberg Riesling Spätlese Trocken
Gräflich Wolff Metternich'sches Weingut, Durbach

Vineyard site: Durbacher Schlossberg
Site area: 17.5 hectares, wholly owned by Wolff Metternich
Exposure: south
Inclination: steeply sloping
Soil: weathered granite
Description: There are certainly more powerful dry Rieslings made in Germany, but none more sophisticated. Although they possess at least 12 degrees of natural alcohol, the abundant apricot-like fruit and racy acidity completely mask it, giving them a deceptive delicacy. The finish is long and crisp.
Best vintages: '94, '93, '92, '90, '89
Best drunk: Failing langoustines or scampi, a simple salad or quiche makes a marvellous foil for these wines.

Ihringer Winklerberg Grauburgunder Spätlese Trocken
Weingut Dr Heger, Ihringen

Vineyard site: Ihringer Winklerberg
Site area: 150 hectares, 7 hectares Dr Heger
Exposure: southwest
Inclination: very steep, terraced
Soil: weathered tephrite, stony top-soil
Description: These are typical modern Kaiserstuhl wines that marry opulent richness with remarkable elegance. The full rich melon, honey and spice aromas and flavours are balanced by the mineral acidity that underpins their considerable substance and power. In spite of between 12.5 and 14 degrees' alcohol, the finish is clean and fresh.
Best vintages: '93, '92, '90, '89, '88, '86
Best drunk: Almost any dish with a rich cream sauce or plenty of fat, such as roast goose, suits these unique wines.

Michelfelder Himmelberg Weissburgunder Spätlese Trocken
Weingut Reichsgraf und Marquis zu Hoensbroech, Michelfeld

Vineyard site: Michelfelder Himmelberg
Site area: 19 hectares, 15 hectares Reichsgraf zu Hoensbroech
Exposure: south to southwest
Inclination: sloping

Soil: deep chalky loess
Description: The Pinot Blanc grape cannot give more elegant wines than these. With their perfect balance of peach-like fruit, moderate alcohol and crisp acidity they are a complete contrast to the big, rich wines it yields further south. The subtle mineral notes at the long finish add the final touch to one of Germany's least well known top-class dry wines.
Best vintages: '94, '93, '92, '90, '89, '88
Best drunk: Treat this wine as a Chablis. In particular it begs for sophisticated fish dishes with sole, turbot or sea bass.

Spätburgunder 'SJ' Deutscher Tafelwein
Weingut Karl Heinz Johner, Bischoffingen

Unlike other benchmark wines in this atlas the 'Selektion Johner' Spätburgunder is a blend of the best barrels of Pinot Noir from a single vintage, regardless of their original vineyard. The heart of the 'SJ' cuvée is usually wine from old vines on the volcanic soil of the Bischoffinger Steinbuck site.
Description: Arguably the best red wines in Germany, these serious Pinot Noirs can compete with fine red Burgundy. Their rich black cherry- and bramble-like fruit is interwoven with strong spicy and smoky oak aromas. Rich in tannin but with no rough edges, they have a 'sweetness' from super-ripe grapes that is rare among German reds.
Best vintages: '93, '92, '90, '89
Best drunk: Smooth enough to enjoy without food, Johner's 'Reserve' Spätburgunder needs roast beef or game to show its best. Truffles or wild mushrooms add the final touch to this magical combination.

BEST PRODUCERS

Weingut Bercher

Mittelstadt 13,
79235 Burkheim
Owners: Eckhardt and Rainer Bercher
Vineyard area: 18 hectares
Grape varieties: 41% Spätburgunder,
12% Grauburgunder,
12% Riesling, 12% Müller-Thurgau,
11% Weissburgunder,
5% Chardonnay, 7% other varieties

Brothers Eckhardt and Rainer
Bercher concentrate their energy on
the making rather than the marketing
of their wines and it is therefore not
widely known that their estate is the
quality leader in the Kaiserstuhl. Every
wine from the simplest to the
grandest is extremely well made and
there is not a single grape variety in
the Berchers' vineyards from which
they do not make first-class wines.

Perhaps because of their Kaiserstuhl
location, their wines from the Pinot
grapes attract the most attention.
Their dry Weissburgunder,
Chardonnay and Grauburgunder
whites are rich and powerful but
always retain perfect balance. During
recent years the estate's red wines
have improved in leaps and bounds:
no German Spätburgunder is silkier or
more concentrated. For the
maturation of the best wines from all
these grapes new oak is used with
confident restraint.

The Berchers also make some of
the best dry Riesling, Gewürztraminer
and Muskateller in Baden; wines that
are far superior to anything else from
these grapes in the Kaiserstuhl. Their
achievement is all the more
remarkable considering that some of

*Rainer and Eckhardt Bercher make
classic Kaiserstuhl dry whites and reds.*

the other top Kaiserstuhl estates have
better vineyard holdings.

Weingut Dr Heger

Bachenstrasse 19,
79241 Ihringen
Owner: Joachim Heger
Vineyard area: 14.25 hectares
Grape varieties: 23% Spätburgunder,
21% Riesling, 19% Grauburgunder,
17% Weissburgunder,
9% Silvaner, 11% other varieties
Top sites: Achkarrer Schlossberg,
Ihringer Winklerberg

Founded by Dr Max Heger in 1935
this important Kaiserstuhl estate is
owned and directed by Joachim
Heger. Since he began making the
wines at the beginning of the 1980s
the estate has shot to prominence
and it is now with good reason the
region's most renowned estate. The
superb dry Grauburgunders from the
great Ihringer Winklerberg vineyard
combine the richness and opulence of
so many top-class wines from this
grape with a pronounced mineral
character and a unique elegance. The
sleek, dry Weissburgunders lack
neither depth nor harmony but
seldom reach the same standard.

These wines made the estate's
name but more recently the reds have
been hitting headlines. Joachim
Heger's old vines in the Winklerberg
enable him to produce Spätburgunder
with a Burgundian richness and
concentration. While he has not yet
perfected this style, his reds are
already among the best in Germany. A
high standard is also maintained with
the fresh and elegant Pinot Noir
rosés. The estate's Scheurebe and
Muskateller wines attract little
attention but they strike an excellent
balance between aromatic
extravagance and racy elegance.

*Joachim Heger produces rich, opulent
dry Grauburgunders.*

Weingut Reichsgraf und Marquis
von und zu Hoensbroech

Hermannsberg,
74918 Angelbachtal-Michelfeld
Owner: Rüdiger Reichsgraf und
Marquis von und zu Hoensbroech
Vineyard area: 17 hectares
Grape varieties: 40% Weissburgunder,
15% Riesling,
15% Grauburgunder,
8% Silvaner, 7% Spätburgunder,
15% other varieties
Top site: Michelfelder Himmelberg

Rudiger Reichsgraf und Marquis von
und zu Hoensbroech runs the
Kraichgau's best wine estate with the
help of his son Graf Adrian. Theirs
was one of the first German wine
estates to produce high-quality dry
white Weissburgunders and the wines
are still among the most elegant and
refined examples in the country.

During the late 1980s, vines in the
Eichelberger Kapellenberg site were
acquired specifically to improve the
quality of the estate's dry Rieslings.
During the early 1990s improvements
were also made to the dry
Grauburgunders. The range of wines
proves that this often-ignored part of
Baden possesses considerable
potential for fine wine production and
that Baden wines need not always be
big and alcoholic at the expense of
delicacy and freshness. The only
disappointments here are the rather
plain reds.

Weingut Bernhard Huber

Heimbacher Weg 19,
79364 Malterdingen
Owner: Bernhard Huber
Vineyard area: 11.75 hectares
Grape varieties: 46% Spätburgunder,

*Rudiger Graf zu Hoensbroech crafts
elegant dry white Weissburgunders.*

11% Chardonnay, 10% Riesling,
8% Müller-Thurgau,
7% Weissburgunder,
6% Grauburgunder, 5% Freisamer,
7% other varieties

Since leaving the co-operative and striking out alone in 1987, Bernhard Huber has established his estate in Malterdingen as the top quality-wine producer in the Breisgau. In particular his deeply coloured, rich, fleshy Spätburgunder reds have attracted high praise from many sides. With their firm tannins they need several years' ageing before they reach their peak and have the potential to age for ten years and more.

Bernhard Huber also makes a range of distinctive white wines: even his dry Müller-Thurgau is full of fruit and spicy flavours. His dry Rieslings are among the best south of the Ortenau. No less impressive are his fragrant, grapey dry Muskatellers. However, his greatest ambitions in the white wine field are focused on his new-oak-aged Chardonnay, Weissburgunder and 'Malterer' (a blend of various grapes). Good as these are, the style's potential is certainly greater. This estate has a promising future.

Weingut Karl Heinz Johner

Gartenstrasse 20,
79235 Bischoffingen
Owner: Karl Heinz and Irene Johner
Vineyard area: 8 hectares
Grape varieties: 36% Spätburgunder,
23% Müller-Thurgau,
15% Grauburgunder,
12% Weissburgunder,
10% Chardonnay,
4% other varieties

With the Weissburgunder and Spätburgunder wines from the '86 (only his second) vintage, Karl Heinz Johner became an overnight sensation in German winemaking circles. With these wines he proved that high-quality new-oak-aged examples can be produced in Germany and that he is one of the nation's most sophisticated winemakers. Since then he has gradually expanded his range of wines while maintaining the highest standards. He has also built a stunning new California-style winery at the edge of the village of Bischoffingen to house the new-oak *barriques* through which all his wines pass. Karl Heinz Johner is unique among Germany's vintners not just for this but also for marketing his entire production – excepting a few dessert wines – as 'Deutscher Tafelwein'. The estate's best dry Chardonnays, Grauburgunders and Spätburgunders are sold with the additional designation 'SJ' (Selektion Johner). These are stunning, the 1990 Spätburgunder 'SJ' being perhaps the

Winemaker Karl Heinz Johner, master of barrel fermentation and new-oak-ageing.

best German red wine made in modern times. However, the standard-quality wines are also of dependable excellence. Wood is used with unmatched precision and flair.

Weingut Andreas Laible

Am Bühl 6,
77770 Durbach
Owner: Andreas Laible
Vineyard area: 4 hectares
Grape varieties: 31% Riesling,
25% Spätburgunder, 11% Traminer,
9% Gewürztraminer, 9% Scheurebe,
5% Weissburgunder,
10% other varieties
Top site: Durbacher Plauelrain

Andreas Laible is unique among Baden's many talented winemakers. His Riesling, Gewürztraminer, Muskateller and Scheurebe wines are unlike any others in the region, but among Baden's best wines. Whether dry or sweet they are bursting with fresh fruit and are beautifully balanced. Indeed, many of them have an elegance like that of top-class Mosel wines. The acidity is fresh and racy, giving the wines a cleanness and delicacy that is remarkable considering their southerly origin. The finest of the dry wines are the Rieslings, which have a rich apricot, almond and floral character and a silky texture. However, these are overshadowed by the naturally sweet Traminers and Gewürztraminers which are astonishingly elegant, especially since these closely related grapes both tend to heaviness. Laible's possess a rose-water bouquet and flavour that could hardly be finer. The estate's Scheurebe wines manage to marry an explosive, vibrant grapefruit character with a dazzling delicacy. All these wines are the product of hard work as much as

they are the result of a remarkable talent, since the estate's precipitous vineyards in the Durbacher Plauelrain have to be cultivated entirely by hand.

Weingut Heinrich Männle

Sendelbach 16,
77770 Durbach
Owner: Heinrich Stefan Männle
Vineyard area: 5 hectares
Grape varieties: 46% Spätburgunder,
12% Riesling, 10% Weissburgunder,
8% Scheurebe, 8% Müller-Thurgau,
6% Traminer, 6% Grauburgunder,
4% Cabernet Sauvignon

Heinrich Männle enjoys a good reputation for his red wines but his white wines are even better. Whether dry or naturally sweet they are full of fruit and possess a racy elegance. There is never anything loud about them, they are understated compared with many of Durbach's other examples. This has much to do with the conservative winemaking style but is also a product of the vineyards' position. The Männles' vineyards all lie in the Kochberg site to the south of Durbach. Here there are few south-facing slopes, the hillsides generally facing east, west or even north, which results in rather less dramatic and aromatic wines. The Kochberg is traditionally regarded as a red-wine site and logically enough Spätburgunder reds make up almost half the estate's production. They are made in a rather traditional style and are dependably good rather than exciting.

Weingut Schloss Neuweier

Mauerbergstrasse 21,
76534 Baden-Baden
Owner: Gisela Joos
Vineyard area: 7.5 hectares
Grape varieties: 84% Riesling,

12% Spätburgunder,
2% Weissburgunder,
2% Gewürztraminer
Top sites: Neuweier Mauerberg,
Neuweier Schlossberg

Since Gisela Joos bought this once-renowned estate and appointed Alexander Spinner as winemaker in 1992, it has shot back to prominence almost overnight. There is now no better source of dry Riesling in Baden and few estates in Germany making better examples. This would not have been possible without the estate's substantial holdings in the first-class Mauerberg and Schlossberg sites of Neuweier, which are comparable with the best sites in Durbach and have a similar weathered granite soil. They give complex, fascinating Rieslings with an intense peach-like fruit and a pronounced mineral character. The estate's conscientious low-yield policy means that with 11–12 degrees of alcohol the wines are packed with aroma and flavour. Neither the owner nor the winemaker is interested in producing high-alcohol wines, aiming instead for Rieslings with the best possible concentration and harmony. They are already close to realising their goal.

Weingut Salwey

Hauptstrasse 2,
79235 Oberrotweil
Owner: Wolf-Dietrich Salwey
Vineyard area: 19.5 hectares
Grape varieties: 47% Spätburgunder,
15% Grauburgunder,
8% Riesling, 8% Silvaner,
8% Weissburgunder,
7% Müller-Thurgau,
7% other varieties
Top site: Oberrotweiler Eichberg

Wolf-Dietrich Salwey combines a real love of wine with a stringent approach to wine quality. He makes a wide range of white, rosé and red

Wolff Dietrich Salwey's range includes reds, dessert wines and fruit brandies as well as dry white wines.

wines from vineyard holdings around Oberrotweil and in Glottertal in the Breisgau. Even from humble grapes such as Silvaner and Müller-Thurgau he manages to make appealingly fruity dry white wines year after year. At the other extreme Salwey is also one of the few vintners in this part of Baden who takes the making of dessert wines seriously, regularly producing excellent Auslese and BA wines. His Spätburgunder rosés are always crisp and elegant and his red wines from the same grape full and rich with well judged oak character. If there are slight weaknesses in this impressive palate of wines they are the dry Weissburgunder and Grauburgunder which are always good but have seldom been exceptional in recent vintages.

Gräflich Wolff Metternich'sches Weingut

Grohl 2–6,
7770 Durbach
Owners: heirs of Graf Wolff Metternich
Vineyard area: 33 hectares
Grape varieties: 32% Riesling, 30% Spätburgunder, 10% Weissburgunder, 8% Traminer, 7% Müller-Thurgau, 6% Grauburgunder, 5% Chardonnay, 2% other varieties
Top sites: Durbacher Schloss Grohl, Durbacher Schlossberg (both wholly owned)

With good reason, the Wolff Metternich estate has traditionally been regarded as Durbach's top estate. Here director-winemaker Ottmar Schilli has made some of the best dry Riesling ever produced in Baden. They combine a wealth of peach- and apricot-like fruit with such racy elegance that even examples with 13 degrees of natural alcohol do not show the slightest hint of heaviness. The Riesling dessert wines are magnificent, always full of honeyed character from botrytis.

The estate's achievements are far from being limited to the Riesling grape, however. It makes the best dry Weissburgunder and Grauburgunder in the Ortenau, along with magnificent dry and sweet Traminer and Sauvignon Blanc (for which grape it is the only commercial producer in Baden). While the Spätburgunder red wines are deeply coloured and intense, the style is often found too Germanic by those used to good red Burgundy. The rosés from the same grape are exceptionally fine.

OTHER WELL KNOWN PRODUCERS

Winzergenossenschaft Beckstein

Weinstrasse 30,
97922 Lauda-Königshofen
This co-operative makes the best wines in the Badisches Frankenland. The excellent dry Weissburgunders are worth hunting down.

Winzergenossenschaft Bickensohl

Neulindenstrasse 25,
79235 Bickensohl
This is perhaps the most dependable co-operative in the Kaiserstuhl. Dry Grauburgunders are particularly good.

Winzergenossenschaft Bötzingen

79268 Bötzingen
The dry Weissburgunders of this Kaiserstuhl co-operative stand out from a solid range of well made white wines.

Weingut Hermann Dörflinger

Mühlenstrasse 7,
79379 Mülheim
Quality is rather variable here but when on form this is one of the best estates in the Markgräflerland.

Winzergenossenschaft Durbach

Nachweide 2,
77770 Durbach
The Riesling wines of this co-operative offer the leading wine estates of Durbach some serious competition. The Spätburgunder reds are also of dependable quality.

Winzergenossenschaft Fessenbach

77654 Fessenbach
The almost supernaturally fruity Spätburgunder reds at this small co-operative are outstanding.

Weingut Freiherr von Frankenstein

Weingartenstrasse 66,
77654 Offenburg
Although the wines are rather variable in quality, the best dry and sweet Rieslings are similar to superior examples from Durbach.

Weingut Freiherr von Gleichenstein

Bahnhofstrasse 12,
79233 Oberrotweil
Although wine quality has improved here during the last few years this well known Kaiserstuhl estate could do still better.

Schlossgut Istein

Im Schloss,
79588 Istein

Harvesting Grauburgunder for quality dry whites at Achkarren.

Albert Soder's bone-dry white wines often tend to be rather neutral but are all well made. The red wines are unexceptional.

Weingut Franz Keller

Badbergstrasse 23,
79235 Oberbergen
The Keller family, as famous for their Schwarzer Adler restaurant as for their wines, are part of the Kaiserstuhl landscape. Their new-oak-aged Grauburgunder and Spätburgunder are serious wines.

Winzergenossenschaft Königschaffhausen

Kiechlinsberger Strasse 2,
79346 Königschaffhausen
The consistently good wines of this small co-operative are dominated by its deeply coloured, powerful Spätburgunder reds. With a little fine-tuning of the oak character they would be first class.

Weingut Lämmlin-Schindler

Mülheimer Strasse 4,
79418 Mauchen
Always fresh, clean and fruity, the dry white wines of this estate are among the best in the Markgräflerland.

Markgräflich Badisches Weingut Schloss Staufenberg

Schloss Staufenberg,
77770 Durbach
In good vintages this important estate can make excellent dry Riesling and Spätburgunder rosé, but the quality has been inconsistent.

Winzergenossenschaft Sasbach

Jechtinger Strasse 26,
79361 Sasbach
This Kaiserstuhl co-operative is best known for its powerful dry red Weissburgunders and Spätburgunders.

Weinbauversuchsgut Schloss Ortenberg
Burgweg 19a,
77799 Ortenberg
Since Winfried Köninger became director here in 1991 there has been a considerable improvement in the quality of the wines. This important estate is worth watching.

Weingut Reinhold und Cornelia Schneider
Königschaffhauser Strasse 2,
79346 Endingen
Founded in 1981 this small estate has rapidly made a name for itself with its fine dry Ruländer and Weissburgunder.

Weingut Seeger
Rohrbacher Strasse 101,
69181 Leimen
Thomas Seeger's slightly inconsistent but often impressive red wines already make him the Badische Bergstrasse's leading winemaker. His ambition promises yet more.

Weingut Stigler
Bachenstrasse 29,
79241 Ihringen
This estate makes perhaps the best traditional-style white wines in the Kaiserstuhl and produces the most stylish price lists and publicity material in Germany. Sadly, the reds are too 'old fashioned' to appeal to contemporary cosmopolitan tastes.

Travel Information

PLACES OF INTEREST

Bad Mergentheim With the rediscovery of its spring in 1826, Bad Mergentheim became an important spa town. Many of its finest buildings, however, date from earlier centuries. The Deutschordenschloss castle (1565–74) in the centre of town and the neighbouring baroque Schlosskirche (completed in 1736) give the town an imposing aspect. Many well preserved half-timbered houses date from between the 16th and 18th centuries.

Baden-Baden The Romans discovered the hot springs that gave the town its name, building baths here in 117AD and making the town their regional centre. During the 19th century Baden became a popular holiday destination for affluent Europeans, and so it remains today. The Stiftskirche is built on Roman remains, though much of what is visible dates from the latter half of the 15th century. Little else in the town remains from the 17th century or earlier owing to the fire of 1689 which razed almost the entire town to the ground. The Rathaus, previously a Jesuit college, was rebuilt soon after the fire but many buildings such as the Neuen Schloss were not restored until much later (in this case 1843–47). The Kurhaus (1821–22) was designed by Friedrich Weinbrenner, the architect who gave Karlsruhe its classical face. From the summit of the Hohenbaden and the Merkur there are magnificent views.

Birnau A short drive northwest from Meersburg on the bank of the Bodensee lies the baroque Abbey of Birnau, overlooking vine-clad slopes above the lake. Next door is one of the many wine estates belonging to the Markgraf von Baden, where visitors can taste wines and enjoy a light lunch or dinner.

Ettlingen The history of Ettlingen's Schloss goes back to 1412. The present baroque building stands on the site of the Renaissance Schloss which was destroyed by the French in 1689. It is now used for concerts and houses the town's central library, the Albgau (regional) Museum and a collection of Karl Albiker paintings. Most of the houses in the old town date from the 18th century. The baroque sandstone Rathaus is most impressive.

Freiburg One of the most beautiful cities in Baden, Freiburg is set beneath the hills of the Breisgau, its wooded and vine-clad Schlossberg visible from the town centre. The city's magnificent cathedral and its elegant streets lined with imposing old houses give it great character and charm. Many excellent hotels and restaurants make it an ideal centre for a wine tour of southern Baden. If there is time for only one stop in Baden then it must be Freiburg, where the fullest expression of the region's character can be found— and a little magic too.

The majestic peaks of the the Swiss Alps, from the wine village of Birnau on the banks of the Bodensee.

An ornate rococo shop sign in old Freiburg and (right) the bustling Markt from atop the Münster.

This has something to do with the architecture, with its inhabitants and with the lively university which exerts a strong influence on town life. Large numbers of tourists seem to be absorbed effortlessly here, without dominating the town as they can elsewhere. The great Münster of Freiburg, with its soaring tower crowned with a filigree spire of carved sandstone, was completed around 1320. This and the busy market around it have been the centre of town since the 14th century. The market is at its best before 10am when some of the town's top chefs can been seen making last-minute purchases. (Many of the tourist restaurants around the marketplace are best avoided.) The cathedral interior deserves as much time as the magnificent exterior. Wandering around the streets it is difficult to believe that the old town was almost completely destroyed in 1944. Its restoration, which took 30 years, was

effected with painstaking attention to detail. There is a magnificent view of the town from the Schlossberg, the top of which can be reached by foot or cable car. Its sloping vineyards yield some of the Breisgau's best Rieslings. The Augustinermuseum, in a former Augustinian abbey on Augustinerplatz, has a collection of Gothic and Renaissance paintings and sculptures as well as more modern works.

Heidelberg Heidelberg makes a good base from which to tour northern Baden, or indeed the Pfalz (a short hop across the Rhine on the A656, then the A650). This university town, nestling in the lower Neckar Valley where it emerges into the Rhine Valley, has been painted and photographed too frequently to need much introduction. Its castle, a complex of towers and walls, was built between the 15th and 17th centuries before being partially destroyed by Louis XIVth's troops. The Friedrichsbau within its courtyard

is one of the finest Renaissance buildings in Germany. The 220,000-litre barrel in the castle's cellars is one of its many attractions. A walk along the Philosophenweg on the opposite bank of the Neckar offers the best view of the castle. Most of the old town is baroque, having been built after the great fire of 1693. The Rathaus, Jesuitenkirche and Alte Universität are the finest buildings from this period. One of the few impressive pieces of architecture to have survived the fire is the Hotel 'zum Ritter'. The streets of the old town are well worth exploring, as is the Kurpfälzisches Museum (just off the Universitätsplatz) which houses a marvellous collection of German Romantic art.

Karlsruhe Many of Karlsruhe's classical buildings were lost or partially destroyed during World War II but the magnificent Schloss and the classical buildings around the Marktplatz on the main axis of the

town south of the Schloss have been lovingly restored. The city's foundation in 1715 was followed by a period of frantic construction. Work on the Schloss (a residence of the Markgrafen von Baden) began in 1725. However, it was the architect Friedrich Weinbrenner who gave the town its classical face during the early years of the 19th century. As the city grew, its classical symmetry became less severe. It is now an important centre for light industry and the seat of Germany's supreme court.

Lindau im Bodensee The old town of Lindau remains unusually well preserved because it is situated on an island in the Bodensee (hence its full name). It is worth exploring at leisure.

Meersburg It is hard to imagine a more picturesque wine town than Meersburg. Its two castles perch on a plateau above vine-clad slopes commanding breathtaking views across the Bodensee to the Alps beyond. The primitively constructed

Schloss Meersburg, formerly the Prince-Bishops' estate, became Germany's first State Domaine in 1802.

Altes Schloss is the oldest castle in Germany, its recorded history stretching back to 630. The baroque Neues Schloss dates from 1740 and now houses a school as well as the Staatsweingut Meersburg. (The wines here should be treated with some scepticism.) When there is no fog the boat trip to Konstanz offers marvellous views of the lake. A boat to the botanic garden on the Mainau island is another popular day-trip.

Neuweier Schloss Neuweier has considerable architectural merit. The largely Renaissance castle of 1548–49 is well preserved.

Offenburg The baroque Rathaus (1741) is the most impressive of the few older buildings left in the centre of Offenburg.

Rastatt Rastatt gained considerable importance when Markgraf Ludwig Wilhelm von Baden moved his court here during the last years of the 17th century. The massive baroque Schloss in the town centre was completed in 1721 and in size and grandeur is second only to that of Mannheim among buildings of this period.

Reichenau This is the largest island in the Bodensee and has a few vineyards producing pleasant light wines. Quiet and secluded, it has three churches as well as renowned vegetable gardens.

Singen (Hohentwiel) Although Singen has developed into an industrial centre, the old town, with its late Romanesque church and imposing Town Hall, are well worth seeing. The medieval fortress with its 16th-century Schloss is spectacular and gives magnificent views of the Bodensee and Switzerland. The Staatsweingut Meersburg's best wines, powerful spicy dry Weissburgunders, come from the volcanic soil of the hillsides below the fortress.

Stuppach This village lies six kilometres south of Bad Mergentheim on the B19. In the Pfarrkirche is Grünewald's magnificent 'Marientafel Madonna' (1519).

Tauberbischofsheim The façade of the Kurmainzischen Schloss of Tauberbischofsheim dates from the 16th century, but has frequently been rebuilt and re-styled. The Schloss now houses the regional museum for the Badisches Frankenland (open every afternoon except Monday). The town's back streets are worth exploring for their many old houses.

Weinheim This old town at the northern edge of Baden has three medieval watch towers. Its Schlossgarten is an essential stop for gardeners.

HOTELS AND RESTAURANTS

Maritim Parkhotel
Lothar-Daiker-Strasse 6,
97980 **Bad Mergentheim**
Tel: (07931) 5390,
Fax: (07931) 539100
This modern hotel in the Kurpark is the town's most comfortable and best equipped, with an indoor swimming pool and sauna. But such luxury is not without its price.

Bad-Hotel zum Hirsch
Hirschstrasse 1,
76530 **Baden-Baden**
Tel: (07221) 23896,
Fax: (07221) 38148
This moderately priced hotel has a nostalgic feel in both the decor and restaurant.

Brenner's Parkhotel
An der Lichtentaler Allee,
76530 **Baden-Baden**
Tel: (07221) 9000,
Fax: (07221) 38772
Set between great old trees in a park on the bank of the Oosbach stands one of Europe's great hotels. The ultimate in style, comfort and luxury is reflected in its prices.

Hotel-Restaurant Bareiss
Gärtenbühlweg 14,
72270 **Baiersbronn-Mitteltal**
Tel: (07442) 470, Fax: (07442) 47320
Baiersbronn is a picturesque Black Forest town with 15,000 inhabitants

and more top hotels and restaurants than many of Germany's larger cities. Kurhotel Mitteltal is one of the finest modern hotels in Germany, offering an extraordinary range of facilities. The food in the first-class restaurant is excellent and its international wine list superb. Booking is essential.

Wald- und Sporthotel Traube Tonbach/Restaurant Schwarzwaldstube
Tonbachstrasse,
72270 **Baiersbronn-Tonbach**
Tel: (07442) 4920,
Fax: (07442) 492692
Harald Wohlfahrt, one of Europe's top chefs, has made Schwarzwaldstube one of Germany's premier restaurants. The creative modern cuisine is of the highest calibre and the wine cellar leaves little to be desired. The slightly less extravagant second restaurant Köhlerstube (same telephone and fax numbers) also offers excellent value for money. As a traditional-style hotel the Traube Tonbach (same numbers again) is excellent.

Schlosshotel Bühlerhöhe/ Restaurant Imperial
Schwarzwaldhochstrasse 1,
77652 **Bühl**
Tel: (07226) 55100,
Fax: (07226 55444)
The DM150 million invested by Max Gründig in Schlosshotel Bühlerhöhe

certainly show in this ultra-luxurious hotel. The comfortable restaurant offers very good cooking, but everything is expensive.

Hotel-Restaurant zum Ritter
Badische Weinstrasse 1,
77770 **Durbach**
Tel: (0781) 31031
This beautifully restored 400-year-old house is now one of the best hotels to be found in Baden's wine towns and villages. While the restaurant is not quite up to the standard of former years, the mostly classical cuisine is good.

Hotel-Restaurant Colombi
Am Colombi-Park,
79098 **Freiburg**
Tel: (0761) 21060, Fax: (0761) 31410
The best hotel in Freiburg has everything expected of a first-class hotel including indoor pool, gymnasium and elegant, modern rooms. The restaurant is also first class, the refined international cuisine beautifully prepared and served. The wine list offers a wide selection of Baden wines as well as the famous names of France and Italy, all at reasonable prices.

Hotel-Restaurant Markgräfler Hof
Gerberau 22,
79098 **Freiburg**
Tel: (0761) 32540, Fax: (0761) 37947
Hans-Leo Kempchen's restaurant is an essential stop on any wine-lover's tour. The cooking is organised around the best seasonal ingredients and the wines include an amazing range from Baden as well as red Bordeaux. Ask the advice of chef and sommelier and allow plenty of time. The moderately priced hotel rooms are simple but comfortable.

Hotel 'Der Europaische Hof'
Friedrich-Ebert-Anlage 1,
69117 **Heidelberg**
Tel: (06221) 5150,
Fax: (06221) 515555
This famous hotel is Heidelberg's best and has prices to match its reputation.

Oberländer Weinstube
Akadamiestrasse 7,
76133 **Karlsruhe**
Tel: (0721) 25066
This is exactly what one expects of a Weinstube in Baden – and more. The cooking is perhaps a touch fussy but the wine list is superb, with many older Baden wines plus a small but well selected range of French reds. In fine weather it is worth reserving a table in the small courtyard.

Seehotel Siber (also restaurant)
Seestrasse 25,
78464 **Konstanz**
Tel: (07531) 63044,
Fax: (07531) 64813
Chef Bertold Siber is the established gastronomic star of the Bodensee. It is hard to imagine a better location for a

romantic dinner than the restaurant terrace on the bank of the lake in Konstanz. This is not the most innovative cooking in Baden, but Siber's refined modern dishes are perfectly executed. The stylish, elegant hotel is comfortable without excessive luxury – but everything is expensive.

Weinstube Weingut Seeger
Rohrbacher Strasse 101,
69181 **Leimen**
Tel: (06224) 72181,
Fax: (06224) 78363
A five-minute drive south of Heidelberg on the B3, Seeger is one of the finest Weinstuben in Baden. The austere modern interior belies the clichéd image of such establishments. The traditional regional cooking is always tasty, the local wines match the best from the Ortenau or Kaiserstuhl and the prices are moderate. Not surprisingly this makes it very popular and booking is recommended.

Hotel und Restaurant Drei Stuben
Kirchstrasse 7,
88709 **Meersburg**
Tel: (07532) 80090 (hotel);
(07532) 6019 (restaurant)
Stefan Marquardt is one of southern Baden's most talented young chefs. His sophisticated modern cooking has

a distinctive Italian influence. The rooms in this restored half-timbered house are elegant and cosy.

Restaurant Schloss Neuweier
Schloss, Mauerbergstrasse 21,
76534 **Neuweier**
Tel: (07223) 57944,
Fax: (07223) 58933
Restaurant Schloss Neuweier, whose wine estate is one of the finest in Baden, offers a refined version of the region's traditional cooking. The wine list includes French and Italian wines as well as the best local examples.

USEFUL ADDRESSES

Kultur- und Verkehrsamt Bad Mergentheim
Marktplatz 3,
97980 **Bad Mergentheim**
Tel: (07931) 57135

Kurdirektion Baden-Baden (Abteilung Information)
Augustplatz 8,
76530 **Baden-Baden**
Tel: (07221) 275200

Freiburg-Information
Rotteckring 14,
79098 **Freiburg**
Tel: (0761) 3689090,
Fax: (0761) 37003

Tourist-Information Heidelberg
Pavillon am Bahnhof, Kurfürstenanlage,
69115 **Heidelberg**
Tel: (06221) 21341,
Fax: (06221) 15108

Stadt-Information Karlsruhe
Karl-Friedrich-Strasse 22,
76133 **Karlsruhe**
Tel: (0721) 1333455

Verkehrsamt Lindau
Am Hauptbahnhof,
88131 **Lindau im Bodensee**
Tel: (08382) 26000

Kur- und Verkehrsamt Meersburg
Kirchstrasse 4,
88709 **Meersburg**
Tel: (07532) 82383,
Fax: (07532) 7881

The inviting entrance to Zum Becher, one of many Weinstuben in the beautiful old walled town of Meersburg.

215

Saale-Unstrut
and Sachsen

With the reunification of Germany in 1989, the wine world's attention was suddenly focused upon the small wine-growing regions in what used to be East Germany. It should hardly be surprising that, having been held back by decades of centralised direction, their wines were found lacking when judged against those produced under more favourable circumstances in western regions. However, their novelty and scarcity value on the open market guaranteed healthy sales for the wines from the moment they were made widely available.

The vintners of Saale-Unstrut and Sachsen were immediately faced with fundamental changes in almost every aspect of their work, including the arrival of the complex bureaucratic restraints which already weighed heavily upon German vintners in other regions. After several difficult years some good wines are now being produced, and the point has been reached where at least the regions' true potential can be objectively assessed.

The most northerly vineyards on the Rhine lie close to Bonn at the 51st degree of latitude, which is where the most southerly vineyards of Saale-Unstrut and Sachsen begin. In spite of being so far north and having distinctly continental climates, both regions enjoy climatic conditions as favourable for viticulture as those in the more easterly vineyards of Franken.

SAALE-UNSTRUT

Most of the Saale-Unstrut vineyards are situated to the south of Halle and to the west of Leipzig in the valleys of the Saale and Unstrut rivers. There are a few further vineyards just under 50 kilometres north close to Süsser See (Sweet Lake) directly to the west of Halle. All lie within the state of Sachsen-Anhalt.

In spite of their proximity to major industrial centres, the valleys of the River Saale and its tributary the Unstrut offer vineyard landscapes as picturesque and charming as any in Germany. Vines cling to the better exposed south- and west-facing slopes between orchards and verdant woodland and the valley floors are used for agriculture. The vineyards are dotted with fine houses built during the 18th and 19th centuries by the wealthy citizens of nearby towns. Several magnificent castles and the former Cistercian

Verdent rural landscape around Freyburg in the Unstrut Valley.

monastery of Kloster Pforta punctuate the landscape, adding to the impression that little has changed in centuries.

The precise origins of viticulture in the region are unclear but the first written evidence dates from 1066. It records that the Pfalzgraf von Sachsen ceded a vineyard to Kloster Goseck, implying that viticulture was already well established. Just under a century later, Kloster Pforta planted the Pfortensa Köppelberg vineyard, which (now known as Pforter Köppelberg) is still being cultivated. During the 16th century the vineyard area was far larger than it is now, extending up the valley to Jena, whose citizens owned fully 700 hectares of vineyard. Most of this fell out of cultivation during the Thirty Years' War (1618–48). Subsequent attempts to rebuild the region's vineyards and wine culture were interrupted by the arrival of the Phylloxera epidemic which first appeared in Germany in 1887.

Recovery from the devastation wrought by this destructive aphid has been slow and erratic, but since the beginning of the century the region's area under vine has grown from a mere 75 hectares to around 390. The relatively short growing season limits the range of grape varieties that will ripen regularly, and late-ripening noble grapes such as Riesling and Traminer can be successfully cultivated only in the most favoured locations, such as the Freyburger Schweigenberg and the Pforter Köppelberg. Most of the vineyards are planted with Müller-Thurgau (37 percent) or Silvaner (28 percent). Bacchus, Gutedel and Weissburgunder, well suited to the weathered sandstone and limestone soils which predominate, also play important roles. It is unlikely that new grape varieties will be introduced to any significant degree.

The Winzergenossenschaft Freyburg makes and markets wines from 250 hectares of vineyard. A further 60 hectares are cultivated by the Landesweingut Naumburg/Kloster Pforta, which was founded as the Staatliche Weinbauverwaltung by the Prussian State in 1899, leaving just 20 percent of the vineyard area in the hands of independent vintners. Many improvements still have to be made before the wines will meet international standards, but at least the progress at estates such as that of Udo Lützkendorf (former director of the Landesweingut) in Bad Kösen is positive. Traditionally, the region's white varietal wines have been vinified dry, but a few vintners are now experimenting with wines that retain a touch of natural sweetness. This is particularly successful in Saale-Unstrut Riesling and Traminer.

The Rotkäppchen Sektkellerei in Freyburg, which makes sparkling wines using base wines from outside the region, is an important feature of the region's industry. Rotkäppchen was founded in 1856 and, like many other companies in former East Germany, came close to bankruptcy immediately after the fall of the Berlin Wall. It has now successfully rebuilt its reputation and its flourishing sales should secure its future.

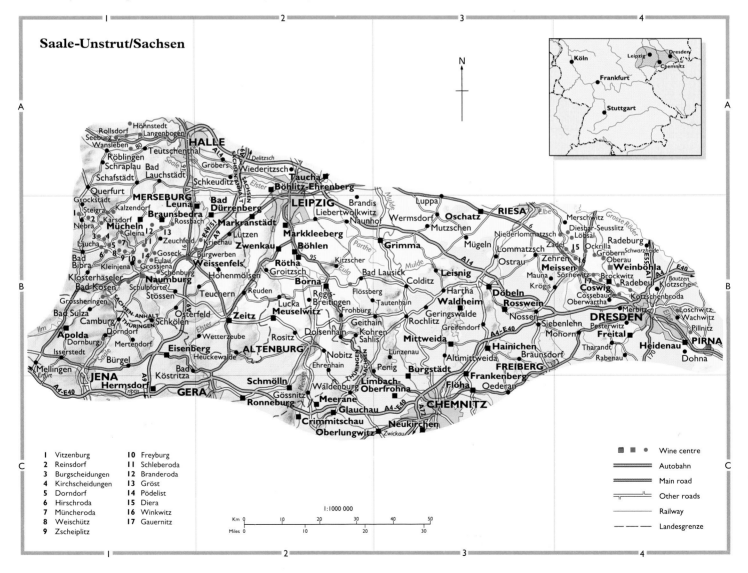

Saale-Unstrut/Sachsen

1	Vitzenburg	10	Freyburg
2	Reinsdorf	11	Schleberoda
3	Burgscheidungen	12	Branderoda
4	Kirchscheidungen	13	Gröst
5	Dorndorf	14	Pödelist
6	Hirschroda	15	Diera
7	Müncheroda	16	Winkwitz
8	Weischütz	17	Gauernitz
9	Zscheiplitz		

Wine centre
Autobahn
Main road
Other roads
Railway
Landesgrenze

1:1 000 000

Both Saale-Unstrut and Sachsen have a major practical problem in their vineyards that needs to be resolved as swiftly as possible. During the 1970s and 1980s large areas were replanted with unusually wide row spacings between the vines. Compared to the 1–1.6 metres between rows usual in western regions, these new vineyards were planted with gaps of 3–3.5 metres which enabled them to be cultivated using normal tractors, allowing considerable savings to be made in labour costs. However, the arrangement is far from ideal for the vines or for the quality of their fruit. Although the yield figures for the Saale-Unstrut and Sachsen look low, the yield of grapes per vine is actually higher than in other regions owing to the unusually low density of vines. The more grapes a vine has to support, the less intense and characterful the resulting wine. Also, widely spaced vines grow more vigorously since their roots have proportionally more soil from which to draw nitrogen. Prolific vegetative growth is usually at the expense of the grapes' development, since the plant's energy is divided between the two growth functions.

While old-style densely planted terraced vineyards yield better quality fruit than the 'modern' plantings, however, their steepness

Right: Vines adorn a winemaker's home in Saale-Unstrut.
Below: Schloss Neuenburg and the Gothic Marienkirche dominate the ancient town of Freyburg.

and the narrow spaces between rows mean that they have to be cultivated almost entirely by hand. Vintners with steep vineyards in the Mosel-Saar-Ruwer, Nahe, and Rheingau are already finding it difficult to recruit vineyard workers. While many of the Saale-Unstrut's vineyards are tended by their owners in their spare time, those tended by paid workers will surely, sooner or later, present their owners with a difficult dilemma.

SACHSEN

For reasons that are not entirely clear, the wines of Sachsen have enjoyed a more dramatic renaissance since 1989 than those of Saale-Unstrut. It is the most easterly and, with a mere 319 hectares of vines, the smallest of Germany's 13 wine-growing regions. All its vineyards lie within the valley of the Elbe which stretches from the Dresden suburb of Pillnitz to Diesbar-Seusslitz just north of Meissen. Here the climate is if anything more continental than in Saale-Unstrut, the summers hot and dry and the winters sometimes bitterly cold. Spring comes early, as early as in the Hessische Bergstrasse, but this brings with it the danger of late frosts. On average, three harvests per decade are destroyed or dramatically reduced in size by frost in late April or early May, as was the case in 1991. Early winter frosts often cut short the growing season, since once the vines have lost their leaves the grapes cannot ripen further. A severe winter can also kill the vines, necessitating expensive replanting programmes. In an effort to minimise the risk of such disasters, vines are cultivated on south- and southwest-facing slopes in the more sheltered parts of the Elbe Valley.

Baroque Schloss Wackerbath, with its formal gardens and (right) extensive vineyards, is one of Sachsen's outstanding landmarks.

Viticulture began here as far back as the 12th century, and by 1250 many craftsmen in Dresden and Meissen found they could earn more from their wine than they could from plying their trade. Following the Napoleonic secularisation in the early 19th century, the first wine school in Europe was opened in Meissen in 1811. This was the region's golden age, when 1,636 hectares of vines covered every available slope. By 1945 only 67 hectares remained. The regeneration of the region since then has been a long process. The Königlicher Weinberg of Pillnitz, once the property of the King of Sachsen, was been replanted as recently as the early 1980s.

The earlier arrival of spring and the warmer summers here make it possible to cultivate noble grapes more widely than in the Saale-Unstrut. Weissburgunder accounts for 15 percent of the vineyard plantings, Grauburgunder and Traminer 11 percent each and Riesling 13 percent. The stony granite and gneiss soils suit Riesling well, and the variety's frost-hardiness gives it a further advantage in Sachsen. Some promising wines were produced from the '93 and '92 vintages and Riesling undoubtedly has a good future here. The best results so far have been achieved with Weissburgunder and Grauburgunder, which give harmonious medium-bodied dry wines, and with the *Neuzuchtungen* Kerner and Bacchus. The latter gives aromatic, fruity wines with enough acidity to be crisp and refreshing. However, considerable research and replanting will be necessary before inferior varieties such as Goldriesling and Gutedel can be replaced with noble grapes and

the right microclimates found to achieve the optimum results.

There are 2,000 members of the regional co-operative, the Sächsische Winzergenossenschaft in Meissen, which processes the harvests from 195 hectares of vineyard. This is by far the largest producer in Sachsen and it maintains a solid standard. With 93 hectares, the Staatsweingut Schloss Wackerbarth accounts for almost all the rest. Previously known as Weingut Radebeul, the estate's origins go back to 1250. In 1836 it made its first sparkling wines and this style now accounts for a large part of its product.

Such dominant forces leave few vineyards for the region's dozen or so independent vintners. Schloss Proschwitz is the largest and most prominent of these estates. Dr George Prinz zur Lippe was 34 years old when he gave up his business consultancy in Munich, bought back the 12 hectares of vineyards which had been confiscated from his family and began to rebuild the estate. His first vintage was vinified at the Fürst zu Castell estate in Franken, so the grapes had to be transported halfway across Germany. Happily there are other examples of such determined and optimistic spirit among the regions' vintners: Jan Ulrich of Seusslitz and Klaus Zimmerling of Dresden have already demonstrated their confidence that Sachsen's vineyards can produce wines of a style and quality similar to those of their western counterparts.

Imposing churches and monuments in central Dresden, which was painstakingly rebuilt after 1945, and the historic town of Meissen with its medieval cathedral and castles, offer more than enough reason to visit Sachsen. The vintners of Sachsen and Saale-Unstrut have a lively and growing incentive to realise the considerable potential of their small but important regions.

BENCHMARK WINES

SAALE-UNSTRUT

Freyburger Schweigenberg Traminer Spätlese Trocken
Weingut U Lützkendorf, Bad Kösen
Vineyard site: Freyburger Schweigenberg
Site area: 10 hectares, 7 hectares U Lützkendorf
Exposure: south
Inclination: steeply sloping
Soil: limestone
Description: Successful wines from this grape with as little as 11.5 degrees of alcohol are few and far between. In spite of their atypical lightness and crisp acidity, these Traminers have the rose-petal character and ripe fruit flavours expected of the grape.
*Best vintages: '94, '93
Best drunk: Regardless of the style, Traminer is usually a difficult wine to match with food. The acidity of this example however makes it well suited to full-fat cheeses.

SACHSEN

Pillnitzer Königlicher Weinberg Bacchus Kabinett Trocken
Weingut Klaus-Zimmerling, Dresden
Vineyard site: Pillnitzer Königlicher Weinberg
Site area: 10 hectares, 3 hectares Klaus Zimmerling
Exposure: southwest
Inclination: steeply sloping
Soil: weathered gneiss
Description: This wine smells and tastes almost like a glass of kir – but with less alcohol. Pleasant as Bacchus can be, it is usually a superficial wine but here it has blackcurrant-like fruit, a unique raciness and mineral character.
*Best vintages: '94, '93
Best drunk: Bone dry but fruity, these wines are ideally suited to drinking with cheese, cold cuts or salad.

Schloss Proschwitz Grauburgunder Spätlese Trocken
Weingut Schloss Proschwitz (Prinz zur Lippe), Meissen
Vineyard site: Schloss Proschwitz
Site area: 12 hectares, wholly owned by Prinz zur Lippe
Exposure: southwest
Inclination: sloping
Soil: loess-loam over granite sub-soil
Description: These sophisticated dry Sachsen wines need not fear comparison with their counterparts from regions further west. Clean apple and melon-like fruit and an excellent balance of fruit, alcohol and supple acidity make them extremely appealing.
*Best vintages: '94, '93
Best drunk: These medium-bodied dry wines can be drunk with all manner of lighter foods. The best combinations are with prawns, scampi or elegant fish dishes.

**Older vintages cannot be recommended because most Sachsen and Saale-Unstrut producers have existed in their present form only since the early 1990s.

BEST PRODUCERS

SAALE-UNSTRUT
Weingut U Lützkendorf
Saalberge 31,
06628 Bad Kösen
Owner: U Lützkendorf
Vineyard area: 6.5 hectares
Grape varieties: 40% Silvaner,
20% Riesling, 10% Weissburgunder,
30% other varieties
Top sites: Freyburger Schweigenberg,
Pfortener Köppelberg

Udo and Uwe Lützkendorf already make the region's best wines. Their dry Rieslings and Traminers are good, their dry Weissburgunders and Silvaners solid and clean. The rapidity with which this standard was achieved promises further improvements.

SACHSEN
Weingut Schloss Proschwitz
01665 Proschwitz über Meissen
Owner: Georg Prinz zur Lippe
Vineyard area: 12 hectares
Grape varieties: 35% Müller Thurgau,
19% Grauburgunder,
10% Weissburgunder, 10% Scheurebe,
10% Morio-Muskat,
16% other varieties
Top site: Schloss Proschwitz

Since the family regained control of this estate in 1991, tremendous progress has been made. The dry Grauburgunders are already comparable with good examples from northern Baden; the other wines are not far behind. All are clean and fresh and with a little more depth and individuality would be first class. This is the owner's goal, and his energy and determination suggest that it is only matter of time before he achieves it.

Weingut Jan Ulrich
Meissener Strasse 4,
01612 Diesbar
Owner: Jan Ulrich
Vineyard area: 10 hectares
Grape varieties: 50% Kerner,

15% Riesling, 15% Goldriesling,
20% other varieties

At 10 hectares, this is one of the largest privately owned vineyards in Sachsen. Jan Ulrich's first wines showed exceptional promise. Brimming with fruit and crisp acidity, the well crafted dry Rieslings and Kerners are already among the region's best.

Weingut Klaus Zimmerling
Pillnitzer Landstrasse 1412,
01326 Dresden
Owner: Klaus Zimmerling
Vineyard area: 3 hectares
Grape varieties: Riesling, Traminer,
Bacchus, other varieties
Top site: Pillnitzer Königlicher
Weinberg

Klaus Zimmerling's may not be the most polished wines but they have more character than anything else in Sachsen. They are firm and have a mineral note but possess more than enough fruit to balance their pronounced acidity. This is the only estate in the region that vinifies a substantial proportion of its crop in wood.

Travel Information

PLACES OF INTEREST

SAALE-UNSTRUT
Bad Kösen This attractive small town in the valley of the Saale is in the process of rebuilding its traditional function as a spa. Nearby stands Kloster Pforta, home of the Landesweingut Naumburg whose recorded history goes back to the 12th century.
Freyburg This attractive small town in the Unstrut Valley is best known as home to the Rotkäppchen sparking wine company. Founded in 1856, this was the most important wine company in former East Germany. In its imposing vaulted Domkeller stands a massive 160,000-litre cuvée barrel made in 1897. The town is dominated by the 13th-century early Gothic Marienkirche and, above the town, the Neuenburg castle whose construction was begun in the 11th century.
Grossjena In the Unstrut Valley just upstream from Naumburg, the most remarkable monuments are to be found in the Markgrafenweinberg

vineyard. In the early 18th century an unknown artist carved into the rock intricate reliefs of biblical scenes and wine motifs.
Naumburg Founded in 1010 at the junction of two important trading routes, Naumburg is the Saale-Unstrut's most important town and an essential stop in any tour of the region. Naumburg's skyline is dominated by the 13th-century cathedral's four towers; the Gothic sculptures and reliefs within are equally spectacular. The Rathaus in the magnificent Marktplatz consists of three late-Gothic buildings which were given a Renaissance façade in 1611. It is worth allowing plenty of time to explore the main streets and narrow back streets.
Schönburg Only a few kilometres downstream from Naumburg on the Saale lies the village of Schönburg and the castle after which it was named. Built in the 12th century, it stands on a plateau 70 metres above the river, giving it commanding views of the Saale Valley.

SACHSEN
Diesbar-Seusslitz This attractive wine village is at the northern limit of Sachsen vineyards. The Gothic abbey was drastically remodelled in the baroque style of the modest Schloss (1726) which stands next to it. The Schlosspark is beautiful.
Dresden Dresden is one of the least well known of the world's great wine cities. This may be because of the city's virtual destruction in 1945. However the care and dedication with which so many of its great monuments have been restored is reason enough to spend time there. The Zwinger baroque palace (1709–32) is one of the 18th century's greatest architectural achievements. It now houses the 'Alte Meister' art museum (open daily except Mondays) which exhibits

Udo Lützkendorf (left) and his son Uwe, setting exemplary standards.

Georg Prinz zur Lippe, rebuilding the family estate at Schloss Proschwitz.

Left: The glorious Schloss Pillnitz, in whose cellars Klaus Zimmerling makes the area's best wines.
Above: A sculpted Bacchus adorns the Wallpavillon of the Zwinger palace in Dresden.

important works by Raphael, Titian and Rembrandt, and the Grünes Gewölbe museum (open daily except Thursdays). The latter exhibits an extraordinary collection of gold and jewellery. Hardly less impressive than the palace is the neighbouring Semperoper, or Opera House. The Catholic Hofkirche, with its 85-metre tower, completes the complex. The restoration of the Stadtschloss on the other side of the Zwinger, and the Frauenkirche, are to be completed in 2006 for the town's 800th anniversary. Until recently the latter remained a pile of rubble as a memorial to the destruction of 1945. Ten kilometres southeast of the town centre in the suburb of Pillnitz (which can also be reached by boat along the Elbe) is the baroque Schloss Pillnitz in extensive grounds. Klaus Zimmerling now makes wines in the Schloss cellars. Close by are the slopes of the Pillnitzer Königlicher Weinberg which produce Dresden's best wines.

Meissen This beautiful town's awe-inspiring monuments stand on the triangular hill of the Bersporn above the River Elbe. The Albrechtsburg castle is the most important secular late-Gothic building in Germany. Its complex vaulting is a masterpiece of medieval engineering. From 1710 until 1864 the castle housed the famous Meissen porcelain factory, the Königlicher Porzellan Manufaktur. Alongside it stands the Gothic Dom whose construction spanned the 13th, 14th and 15th centuries. In the Marktplatz of the old town below is the late-Gothic Rathaus (1472), the Frauenkirche from around 1500 and

the Renaissance Brauhaus (1569). The Franziskanerkirche on Heinrichsplatz houses the town museum (including a wine museum, open daily except Fridays). The Meissener Porzellan Manufaktur (Talstrasse 9, open daily except Mondays) has its own impressive museum.

Schloss Moritzburg The massive baroque Schloss Moritzburg palace was built between 1723 and 1736 by Herzog August der Starke on the site of a hunting lodge 14 kilometres northwest of Dresden. A tree-lined avenue leading directly to Dresden was constructed and an artificial lake sunk next to it. The Schloss houses a baroque museum with important collections of furniture and porcelain as well as hunting trophies and coaches.

Pirna This small town, a short drive southeast of Dresden on the left bank of the Elbe, was an important trading centre during the Middle Ages. The 15th–17th century fortress of Sonnenstein stands on a rocky plateau above the town and was a vital stronghold until the early 18th century. The late-Gothic and Renaissance houses around the Marktplatz indicate how affluent the town once was.

Radebeul Just to the northwest of Dresden lies the wine village of Radebeul and the baroque mansion of Schloss Wackerbarth. The Museum Haus Hoflössnitz, housed in the eponymous Renaissance Schloss, includes displays relating to the region's winemaking history.

HOTELS AND RESTAURANTS

SAALE-UNSTRUT
Hotel Altdeutsche Weinstuben zum Künstlerkeller
Breite 14,
06632 **Freyburg**
Tel: (034464) 27292,
Fax: (034464) 27307
The cellar of this small, modestly priced hotel houses a wine restaurant decorated by local artists.

Hotel und Restaurant Rebschule - Haus des Saale-Unstrut Weins
Ehranberge 33,
06632 **Freyburg**
Tel (and Fax): (034464) 27647
An ideal spot, in vineyards above the town, to sample the region's wines.

Hotel und Restaurant 'Zur Alten Schmiede'
Lindenring 36–7
06618 **Naumberg**
Tel: (03445) 8616, Fax: (03445) 8161
The region's best restaurant, in a restored ancient forge, offers a range of local wines and traditional cooking.

Gasthaus am Neumarkt
Neumarkt 15
06712 **Zeitz**
Tel: (03441) 712677,
Fax: (03441) 714033
A small, comfortable, family-run hotel close to Freyburg and Naumberg.

SACHSEN
Maritim Hotel Bellevue
Grosser Meissener Strasse 15,
01097 **Dresden**
Tel: (0351) 56620, Fax: (0351) 55997
One of the finest new hotels in Germany. The stylish baroque building is furnished with elegant antiques.

Restaurant Rossini (in Hotel Dresden Hilton)
An der Frauenkirche 5,
01067 **Dresden**
Tel: (0351) 4841741,
Fax: (0351) 4841700
This innovative Italian restaurant is among Dresden's best. Sachsen and Italian wines are moderately priced.

Weinstube Vincenz Richter
An der Frauenkirche 12,
01665 **Meissen**
Tel: (03521) 3285
A beautiful Renaissance house built in 1523, with a pleasant courtyard.

USEFUL ADDRESSES

SAALE-UNSTRUT
Fremdenverkehrsverein Freyburg
Markt 12, 06632 **Freyburg**
Tel: (034464) 260, Fax: (034464) 222

Rotkäppchen Sektkellerei
Sektkellereistrasse 5, 06632 **Freyburg**
Tel: (034464) 233

Tourist-Information Naumburg
Am Markt 6, 06618 **Naumburg**
Tel: (03445) 2514

SACHSEN
Dresden-Information
Prager Strasse 10,
01069 **Dresden**
Tel: (0351) 4955025,
Fax: (0351) 4951276

Meissen-Information
An der Frauenkirche 3,
01665 **Meissen**
Tel: (03521) 4470

Index and Gazetteer

This index and gazetteer includes references to vineyard sites, producers, grape varieties and places of interest. Map references follow page numbers.

Acknowledgements

The author and series editor owe a debt of gratitude to a great number of wine-growers, merchants, writers and friends of wine who have contributed in various ways to the making of this atlas.

Those to whom special thanks are due include Gerhard Benz, Theo Haart, Alfons Hausen, Ursula Heinzelmann, Horst Kolesch, Peter Jost, Dr Alex Michalsky and Bernhard Prass; Hilke Nagel and the Verband Deutscher Prädikatsweingüter, the Charta Association, Willi Haag, Bernhard Breuer, Gary Grosvenor; Dr Hans Beat Koelliker, Sylvie Hofmann and colleagues at Hallwag AG, Ruth Cunney and, especially, Hanne Evans.

The making of this atlas would simply not have been possible without the professional talents and meticulous care lavished upon text, design and cartography by Diane Pengelly, Paul Drayson and Zoë Goodwin.

Picture Credits:
All photographs reproduced in this book are by Faber & Partner Fotografie with the exception of the following:
AKG London 222–3, 223; Robert Dieth 216–7, 220, 221, 222 (bottom right), 222 (bottom left).